The Rest is History

BUCHTEL BOOKS

Miss Harriet Angel, editor, *Recipes by Ladies of St. Paul's Church: A New Edition with a Photo Insert and an Introduction by Jon Miller*

Glenna Snow, editor, *Glenna Snow's Cook Books: A New Edition with a Photo Insert and an Introduction by Kevin Kern*

Mark J. Price, *The Rest is History: True Tales from Akron's Vibrant Past*

The Rest is History
True Tales from Akron's Vibrant Past

MARK J. PRICE

BUCHTEL BOOKS • AKRON, OHIO

Originally published by The Akron Beacon Journal Company

New Material Copyright © 2012 by the University of Akron Press

All rights reserved • First Edition 2012 • Manufactured in the United States of America. • All inquiries and permission requests should be addressed to the Publisher, The University of Akron Press, Akron, Ohio 44325-1703.

16 15 14 13 12   5 4 3

LIBRARY OF CONGRESS CATALOGING-IN-PUBLICATION DATA
Price, Mark J., 1963–
The rest is history : true tales from Akron's vibrant past / Mark J. Price.
    p. cm.
Summary: "Award-winning journalist, Mark J. Price, whose popular weekly column "This Place, This Time" has appeared in the Akron Beacon Journal since 1998, explores the history of Akron, Ohio and Summit County through compelling vignettes"—Publisher summary.
ISBN 978-1-935603-67-2 (pbk. : alk. paper)
1. Akron (Ohio)—History—Anecdotes. 2. Akron (Ohio)—Biography—Anecdotes. 3. Akron (Ohio)—Social life and customs—Anecdotes. 4. Summit County (Ohio)—History—Anecdotes. 5. Summit County (Ohio)—Biography—Anecdotes. 6. Summit County (Ohio)—Social life and customs—Anecdotes. I. Title.

F499.A3P75 2012
977.1'36—dc23

2011050866

The paper used in this publication meets the minimum requirements of American National Standard for Information Sciences—Permanence of Paper for Printed Library Materials, ansi z39.48–1984. ∞

Cover: Photograph of Main Street in Akron, 1941. Courtesy of Special Collections, Michael Schwartz Library, Cleveland State University. Design: Amy Freels. *The Rest is History* was designed and typeset by Amy Freels in Adobe Caslon, printed on sixty-pound white, and bound by BookMasters of Ashland, Ohio.

To my beautiful wife, Susan Gapinski Price, who makes every day a happy day, and my devoted parents, Angela Bollas Price and Joel Edwin Price, who taught me how to read and write.

Contents

Acknowledgments

This book is a group effort. Thousands of people have helped me put it together over the past 15 years. I am grateful to every person who ever contributed to its creation, including librarians, archivists, historians, reporters, photographers, editors, artists, authors, researchers, secretaries, clerks, genealogists, friends, relatives and, of course, Akron Beacon Journal readers.

I am forever indebted to Akron-Summit County Public Library's Special Collections Division: Manager Judy James, Iris Bolar, Cheri Goldner, Jane Gramlich, Joanne O'Dell, Mary Plazo, Kit Zerbe, marketing director Carla Davis and local history expert Michael Elliott. Again and again, this diligent staff has helped me retrieve the most obscure, weird (and sometimes silly) information that I would not have found any other way.

Similarly, the University of Akron's Archival Services staff has bailed me out countless times on difficult research. My thanks to head archivist S. Victor Fleischer, Craig Holbert, Mark Bloom, retired director John V. Miller, and former associate Stephen H. Paschen, now the archivist at Kent State.

Obviously, this book would not be possible without the University of Akron Press. I am extremely grateful for the advice and guidance of director Thomas Bacher, Carol Slatter, Amy Freels and Julia Gammon. If it weren't for them, you wouldn't be reading this!

Several local experts have provided invaluable assistance over the years. Among them are Dr. George W. Knepper, University of Akron distinguished professor emeritus of history; Leianne Neff Heppner, Summit County Historical Society executive director; David Bersnak, Kenmore Historical Society president; Liz Cross, Cuyahoga Falls Historical Society curator; David A. Lieberth, deputy mayor of Akron; David Giffels, University of Akron assistant professor; Steve Keller, Barberton Historical Society president; Bernie Gnap, Barberton Historical Society guru; and Lt. James Buie, Capt. John Cunningham and Sgt. Tom Dye, Akron police historians. When I have questions, they always have answers.

Sincere thanks to Beacon Journal Editor Bruce Winges, Managing Editor Doug Oplinger, Features Editor Lynne Sherwin, Copy Desk Chief Kathy Fraze, and Executive News Editor Mark Turner; my former editors Debbie Van Tassel, Stuart Warner and Jim Kavanagh; editors Scott Babbo, Kerry Clawson, Kim Drezdzon, Jamie Hogan, Bill Lilley, Elissa Murray, Mary Kay Quinn, Olga Reswow, Joe Thomas, Monica Thomas, Deanna Stevens Ulrich and Darrin Werbeck, reporters Katie Byard, Jim Carney and Dave Scott; photojournalists Kim Barth, Mike Cardew, Michael Chritton, Bob DeMay, Phil Masturzo, Karen Schiely, Ed Suba Jr. and Paul Tople, designers and graphic artists Alan Ashworth, Dennis Gordon, Kathy Hagedorn, Edna Jakubowski, Deborah Kauffman, Brian Shellito, Rick Steinhauser and Rich Stallsmith; and Beacon Journal librarian Norma Hill.

I am so fortunate to have a loyal following of dedicated readers who routinely offer insights, share memories and supply ideas. Among them are Barb Baker, Drina Beeman, Robert Creswell, Craig Erskine, Georgia Gay, C.T. Halfhill, Steve Hammond, Jeff Iula, Mark Jeney, Robert M. Kraus Sr., Pat Marks, Kevin Murphy, Randy Norris, Dan Rinaldo, Julie Sabbagh, Sam Salem, Andre Sams, Rick Schneider, Jim Skeese, Ron Syroid, LeRoy Teeple, David Weyrick and Larry Zvara.

I also am lucky to have the support and counsel of a coterie of friends and relatives, including Al and Bootsie Bollas, Nick and Lindsey Bollas, Jon Bollas, Paul Brodsky, Steve Brunot, Joe and Kelley Cali, David de la Fuente, Joe Del Medico, Mark and Diane Ferenchik, Jeff

Gallatin, Susan Glaser, Chuck Klosterman, Steve Neff, Debby Stock Kiefer, Joe Kiefer, Laura Meckler, Alex and Susie Menassa, Lou Poplos, Edd and Monica Pritchard, Tim and Sharon Ricks, Rick Senften, M.L. Schultze, Rene and Pete Stamatis, Glenn Stephenson, and Lawrene and Darryl Trump. They rock!

Special thanks to my mother, Angela Bollas Price, for providing me with detailed, vivid recollections of what Akron was like in "the good old days."

Finally, thank you to my wife (and co-worker) Susan Gapinski Price for her constant support, advice and encouragement. Without her, I'd be history.

—Mark J. Price

Foreword

One of the great things about working in a newsroom is that we get to write history as it unfolds. As journalists who share a common trait—insatiable curiosity—we often are the first to see it happen and the first to share it with the world. We then generally move on to the next story. That is the nature of what we do.

The Akron Beacon Journal's Mark J. Price is different. He looks back. Unlike the reporters who work the phones or traverse the city during the day, it is not unusual to find Mark late at night, long after others have gone, on the floor with old newspaper clippings and photographs spread before him, framed by dark file cabinets and a lonesome fluorescent light. Mark digs through drawers, history books and microfilm to find great stories that define Akron's history, then brings them back to life to share with today's readers.

Mark came to the Akron Beacon Journal as a copy editor in February 1997. (For those of you who may not know, copy editors write some of the most important words in the newspaper—the headlines.) Shortly thereafter, he came up with the idea of a weekly history feature about Akron and environs. One of my predecessors had the good sense to listen and take him up on the proposal. So Mark's weekly "This Place, This Time" local history feature began in 1998 and continues to this day.

He has established himself as one of our finest researchers and most entertaining writers. His readers remind us constantly that they enjoy reliving Akron's past through his words. Longtime residents say the articles bring back fond memories. Those who are newer to Akron are captivated by his narratives.

So, from the pages of the Akron Beacon Journal (which dates to 1839, making it Summit County's oldest continually operating business) and Ohio.com, we offer this collection of colorful characters and memorable events that shaped the Akron of today—thanks to the hard work of Mark J. Price.

Bruce Winges
Editor, Akron Beacon Journal

Introduction

Is it possible to be in two places at once? I'm pretty sure it is.

When I visit communities in Northeast Ohio, I don't just see what's there now. I look beyond the fast-food restaurants, big-box retailers and drugstore chains to glimpse the distant past.

I try to picture the landmark buildings that stood for generations at major intersections before falling to demolition crews. I reconstruct old neighborhoods on streets that no longer exist, imagining what life must have been like in bygone times.

For nearly 15 years, I've been writing about local history and nostalgia for the Akron Beacon Journal. In 1998, I suggested to an editor that the newspaper should start publishing a weekly feature about local history. We were headed toward a new century, and it seemed like the perfect time to look back.

My editor liked the concept and named the series "This Place, This Time," a title that I still have trouble remembering! Is it "This Place, This Time" or "This Time, This Place"? It's appeared both ways in the newspaper.

My first article—about the Flatiron Building in downtown Akron—was published May 10, 1998. At last count, I've written nearly 800 stories.

I'm always stitching together information from a variety of resources: microfilm, interviews, historical societies, local experts, libraries, vintage books, city directories, maps, Internet sites. I'm a regular visitor at Akron-Summit County Public Library's Special Collections Division and the University of Akron's Archival Services.

I don't consider myself an historian, but I really do like learning about the past. Dr. George Knepper's 1981 book, *Akron: City at the Summit*, was a major influence. I remember picking it up in a bookstore in the 1980s and being amazed by the historic pictures. It made me look at my hometown in a different way.

People often ask how I find ideas for articles. My desk is a complete mess. I have legal pads, manila folders and cabinet drawers filled with ideas.

Every time I run across a story possibility, I jot it down or save it in a file. There is a steady flow of tips from readers, editors, co-workers and others in the community. I am also fortunate to have built-in knowledge from anecdotes that have been handed down in my family for nearly a century.

Truthfully, I can never catch up. We make local history every day.

For years, Akron Beacon Journal and Ohio.com readers have requested a compilation book of my articles. It was extremely difficult sifting through nearly 15 years of work, but I think this is a good representation of reader favorites.

The real-life stories range from quirky to poignant, from humorous to tragic, and all points in between. Read about the U.S. president who strolled through the countryside, the Akron stagehand who became a Hollywood icon, the beloved beagle that attended elementary school, the natural landmark that slid underground, the pop concert that made girls faint, the lost cemetery that turned into a city park, and the world-famous gadget that caught on in Northeast Ohio.

As they say, the rest is history.

Thank you for reading.

—Mark J. Price

Mark J. Price

A Tale of Two Akrons

RIVAL COMMUNITIES COULD NOT GET ALONG UNTIL THEY FOUND MIDDLE GROUND

(Originally published Sept. 26, 2005)

When traveling downtown, Akron motorists will find a jog in the road. Three major streets—Main, High and Broadway—veer off at an unexpected angle just south of Mill Street.

What is this? Couldn't city planners draw a straight line?

Actually, they couldn't. This is what happens when you wedge two villages together.

Long before the Civil War, Akron residents fought a battle between North and South. Two rival communities duked it out for supremacy.

One was called Akron. The other was called Akron, too.

They remained bitter enemies until residents finally discovered the middle ground.

As many local history buffs know, Gen. Simon Perkins of Warren founded the original Akron in 1825. The square-shaped village was centered on Main and Exchange streets.

Dr. Eliakim Crosby of Middlebury platted the second Akron in 1833. The rectangular village, originally called Cascade, was centered at Market and Howard streets.

The towns seemed to have a lot in common. Both had populations of about 400. Both had thriving business districts. Both had a stake in the 1832 opening of the Ohio & Erie Canal.

And both had a profound dislike for the other.

A lawless wasteland known as The Gore separated the feuding villages. According to definition, a gore is a triangular piece of land. Neither village owned the wedge, but young ruffians sometimes ventured into the neutral zone to engage in brawls.

"It was called the 'gore,' whether because of its shape, or the amount of blood it caused to be spilled, is not known," William B. Doyle quipped in his 1908 history of Akron.

Only two roads connected the towns, and residents were not too keen on using them. Locust and Bowery streets in the south linked with Oak and Wooster streets in the north. Main, High and Broadway hit dead ends just below The Gore.

As if things weren't dysfunctional enough, both communities had roads to Middlebury, the jealous neighbor to the east. The village—at East Market, South Arlington Street and Case Avenue—was further along in development because it was nearly two decades older. Its peak population of 500 plunged, though, when the canal bypassed Middlebury in favor of Akron.

Dr. Crosby defected from Middlebury to pursue a scheme that many thought was crazy. He wanted to build a mill race from the Little Cuyahoga River to the Ohio & Erie Canal. Water would provide power for several factories, including Crosby's proposed Stone Mill near Lock 5.

He enlisted the aid of Gen. Perkins, who gave his blessing to the project, a decision that South Enders later regretted.

Middlebury leaders scoffed at the plan and vowed to build their own mill race. Crosby could not resist taunting them.

"Gentlemen, your scheme won't work, but mine will," he said. "And what's more, it will cause the grass to grow in your streets, and make a goose pasture of your town."

Crosby's mill race traveled down the middle of Water Avenue (later renamed Main Street) and curved west along the northern edge of Mill Street. It helped turn the village of Cascade into a sturdy little center of industry.

Among the factories it powered were Howard & Fenn, Allens & McMillan, Hart & Associates, Hiram Payne's distillery and the Aetna and Portage blast furnaces. Several local landmarks were built during this time, as well, including the Cascade House, Ohio Exchange, Stone Mill and Stone Block.

The heart of the community, though, was Philander D. Hall's general store in the Cascade Building on the southwest corner of Market and Howard streets. The intersection was known as Hall's Corners for decades after the store opened.

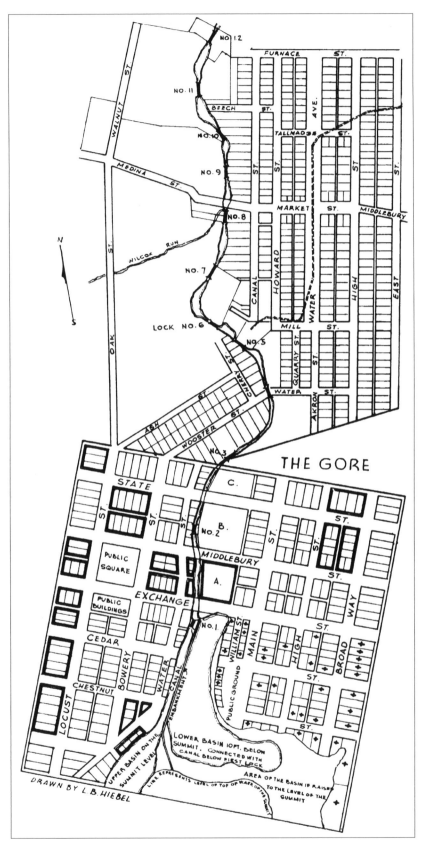

A plat map shows the off-kilter relationship between North Akron and South Akron in the 1830s. The Gore was the wedge-shaped wasteland between the rival villages.

Further south, the citizens of Akron were getting a little worried about Cascade's sudden rise. They had landmarks, too, such as Henry Clark's Tavern on the northeast corner of Main and Exchange, May's Block on the northwest corner and Moses Hall's Mammoth Store on the southwest corner.

They had blacksmiths and cobblers and tinsmiths and carpenters. Canal engineer Richard Howe had moved to the village in 1828 and built a fine brick house at Exchange and High streets.

But the North Enders were getting too big for their britches. When the new village began to call itself Akron, too, it was the final straw for South Enders.

A major battle was fought over a simple sign on Middlebury Road, now known as Buchtel Avenue. It read "AKRON, ONE MILE" and pointed toward the southern village.

The northern villagers were outraged. They traveled to Middlebury, dug up the sign and pointed it down Market Street. This, in turn, infuriated the southern villagers, who reclaimed the sign and pointed it back down Middlebury Road.

"Back and forth the sign was changed several times," Karl H. Grismer wrote in his 1952 history of Akron. "Guards were posted. Fists flew—and so did rocks. Several men were injured in the scuffles."

Finally, the villagers agreed on a solution. Two signs were made: "NORTH AKRON, ONE MILE" and "SOUTH AKRON, ONE MILE." They were posted along the appropriate routes.

At times, the intense rivalry was almost comical. Churches were built on the neutral ground of The Gore because some worshippers refused to set foot in the opposing village.

The Methodists and Congregationalists constructed their churches facing west, and worshippers temporarily found peace, at least on Sundays. The Baptist Church of Akron suffered a bitter divide, though, when leaders built the church facing south.

The bickering was almost nonstop. So what did the villages decide to do? Merge!

Residents didn't like each other, but they knew they needed each other. They would have more clout if they joined forces. North Akron and South Akron jointly petitioned the Ohio legislature in late 1835. The state granted a town charter on March 12, 1836.

Of course, that didn't end the squabbles. The first mayoral election was held June 14, 1836, in Clark's Tavern at Main and Exchange. Dr. Crosby, a Democrat, ran against Seth Iredell, a Whig.

The South Enders exacted their revenge on Crosby, founder of the rival town, by voting overwhelmingly for his opponent. Iredell was elected Akron's first mayor.

It took several years, but Akron residents patched up their differences. They celebrated together when Summit County was formed in February 1840 from sections of Portage, Stark and Medina counties. They cheered again in May when Akron was selected over Cuyahoga Falls as the county seat. Officials agreed that The Gore was the best place to build the new courthouse, sheriff's department, jail and county offices. The central location would be convenient for all citizens.

In 1881, Akron historian William Henry Perrin recalled that "local jealousies were for the time being subordinated to the common weal." He said the former foes found themselves cordially "shaking hands across the gore-y chasm."

Today, a jog in the road at Main, High and Broadway reveals where two rival communities were spliced together. The mismatched streets of old enemies didn't quite line up.

Summit Beacon Editor Hiram Bowen, founder of the newspaper that became the Akron Beacon Journal, may have summarized it best when he called for a public truce in 1840.

He saw the new development as a new beginning, and his words proved to be prophetic.

"The 'Gore' is situated midway between North and South Akron, and a more beautiful and commanding site cannot be found for public buildings in the state," Bowen wrote. "It is said that almost every township in the county can be seen from the buildings on this spot.

"Its location, as regards Akron, is auspicious—and our citizens will henceforth unite their common energies in developing the great natural resources for which Akron has become so justly celebrated."

Today, the Summit County Courthouse stands on The Gore, a former lawless wasteland. It's just south of the jog in the road.

Farewell to a Farm

MONTROSE COMMERCIAL DISTRICT SWALLOWS UP FORMER RURAL PARADISE

(Originally published Feb. 14, 1999)

The 103-acre Rothrock farm seemed to stretch forever in Copley Township. Its fields were ripe with crops. Its orchards were laden with fruit. Its barns were filled with animals.

How strange it is today to see the Montrose commercial district where prime farmland used to be.

Helen Foord, 88, was a young girl when she lived and worked on Rothrock farm from 1917 to 1920. Days were long back then. Work was difficult. Chores were many. But she loved the farm.

And she despairs when she visits the old neighborhood and sees the concrete-and-glass Montrose area swallow everything in its path. "It's like going to a funeral place and seeing someone who's very dear to you, and you know you'll never see them again," she said. "It puts a knot right in my stomach."

When Foord visits Montrose, she looks beyond the one-mile strip of stores and restaurants on Route 18. She looks into the past and sees a dirt road with horse-drawn buggies.

"A man named Crosier had a farm right by where that Chi-Chi's is now," she said.

And the Super Kmart? "A woman named Switter had that place."

Acme Supermarket? "There was a farm there, too."

What about Restaurant Hill, that mountain of plush hotels and chain restaurants overlooking Interstate 77? "You mean Stony Hill," Foord corrected.

Nearly everything has changed since Foord lived on Rothrock farm nearly 80 years ago. The few things that do remain from those days are about to change, too.

Rothrock Road, a fishhook-shaped street that parallels I-77, connects Route 18 with Cleveland-Massillon Road, dividing Copley Township on the west from Fairlawn on the east.

Motorists use it as a shortcut to the Super Kmart, Best Buy, Toys R Us, Cracker Barrel and other businesses in Montrose.

"The traffic is just horrendous," said Anne Halamay, who has lived with her husband, Eugene, for 13 years at

506 Rothrock Road, part of the Rothrock property that Foord once called home. "You have to wait to cross the street to get to the mail."

Last vestiges of farmland are sandwiched between Interstate 77 and Rothrock Road. "We have a horse," Halamay said. "Can you imagine a horse in the middle of Montrose?"

Signs of change, more accurately "For Sale" signs, rise above the Copley side of Rothrock Road. Mogen Real Estate, Bentley Realty Services and Spalding Associates Realty are advertising 10 properties in a half-mile stretch of the road. The Halamays are among those who are selling.

Jim Pickard, vice president of Mogen Real Estate, said the price for the Halamays' house and property at 506 Rothrock Road is $896,000—that's $160,000 an acre for the 5.6-acre property. The land cost $75,000 in 1986.

The land is zoned retail, which means its farming days are over. "Everyone on that strip is facing the same decision," Pickard said.

There are few places left to develop in Montrose except for Rothrock Road and Cleveland-Massillon Road, Pickard said.

"When the highway went through, that's when it started to change its complexion," Pickard said. "I can't imagine a neighborhood with a six-lane highway in your backyard."

Of course, Montrose is not the only place in Summit County where farmland is disappearing. In 1959, Summit County contained 50,149 acres of farmland, according to Travis Smith of the Ohio Agricultural Statistics Service in Reynoldsburg. That number plummeted to 19,088 acres by 1992, the most recent census available.

Rothrock Road residents watched the Montrose development creep toward their homes in the 1980s and 1990s.

"It's like a chain reaction. I wish it would've stayed the other way," Anne Halamay said. "I feel real sad that it went crazy—and they didn't plan. That's progress, I guess."

Helen Foord, 88, visits with Kirby, an 18-year-old retired racehorse owned by Anne and Eugene Halamay, on one of the last vestiges of the Rothrock property in 1999.

THE WAY IT WAS

Helen Foord, the former Helen Luckl, was born in Hencse, Hungary, in 1910 and moved to Akron in November 1912 with her grandmother, Magdalena Luckl. They lived with Foord's uncle and aunt, Andrew and Anna Sanyo, on a small farm on Hawkins Avenue in Akron. The Luckls moved with the Sanyos to an 80-acre farm on Sourek Road and then to the 103-acre Rothrock farm, which the Sanyos bought from Samuel S. Rothrock for $13,000 on Oct. 30, 1917.

The Rothrock family had owned the property since 1871. Samuel S. Rothrock was "a typical Ohioan" who "was reared to agricultural pursuits," according to the 1898 book *A Portrait and Biographical Record of Portage and Summit Counties, Ohio.*

"He commenced life for himself empty-handed as regards money, his first earnings being $20 per month, given by his father. He is a man of industrious and frugal habits, and his competency places him and his family in easy circumstances."

The Rothrocks raised five daughters in their farmhouse, which the 1898 book describes as "the abode of hospitality" where "the friends as well as the strangers receive a cordial welcome."

GOOD PLACE TO LIVE

Helen Foord enjoyed living with her Uncle Andrew and Aunt Anna on the farm where Hungarian and German were the languages of choice.

But the workload was tremendous for a young child.

"I had to gather eggs, feed the chickens, give them water, and things of that nature," Foord said. "I could harness and hitch a horse to a buggy. I was driving a hay wagon. I was milking two cows at morning and two at night."

She helped with the planting and harvesting, the hoeing, weeding and picking.

The fields were filled with corn, wheat, potatoes, onions, beans, tomatoes, strawberries, sugar beets and other produce. The orchard's trees bore apples, pears, cherries and damson plums.

Helen Luckl Foord (left), about 9 years old, stands with her aunt and uncle Anna and Andrew Sanyo, cousin Theresa Sanyo and Jack the dog in this photo taken about 1919 at the Rothrock farm in Copley Township.

There were horses, cows, pigs, chickens, ducks, geese, a buggy horse named Sparky, a bull named Roger and a pet dog named Jack. "I remember threshing day and butchering day and the day they filled the silo," Foord said.

She also remembers vines of Concord grapes that attracted the Smucker Co. in Orrville. "Before the dew was off the grass, they were there with trucks and everything," she said. "The old man was standing there with a check for $500 in his hand."

The farm's amenities included a house, horse barn, cow barn, chicken coop, pig sty, corn crib and outhouse. The outhouse "was as different as anything you can imagine," Foord said.

Her Uncle Andrew built a rain gutter that ran from the house, through the summer kitchen, a small building where food was cooked during warmer months. The gutter then ran underground to the outhouse, out to the pasture and into a cesspool. It might not be considered a modern convenience today, but it did the job

nicely in the early 1900s. Besides, plumbing was something the farm did not have.

"We had three good wells. One at the house, one at the horse barn and one at the cow barn," Foord said. "We also had two brooklets, plus mineral springs."

HELPING HANDS

Neighbors helped each other in those days, Foord said. The Sanyos could count on assistance from the Prentis, Miklos, Deeks, Sommers and Yoey families.

The rule was: "We're helping you today; tomorrow's our turn," Foord said. On threshing day, the neighbors used a steam-powered thresher to beat grain from the husk. They filled burlap bags with grain and tied the bags with twine.

"We would ring the dinner bell. Everyone would stop and come tromping down to the house," Foord said. "They'd wash their hands and faces and eat."

The farmers' wives served a feast of fried chicken, fresh vegetables, "enough biscuits to feed a restaurant" and homemade pie.

"After eating, the men would lie down under the pine trees for a while, then get back to work," Foord said.

The women collected the dirty dishes, washed them and then served themselves. There weren't enough plates to go around.

Farm kids always had to do chores before catching a horse-drawn wagon to Copley School, Foord said. In the winter, they kept warm on the wagon by carrying burlap bags filled with four heated bricks.

There wasn't much time for children to play, she said, but she does recall soaring on a rope swing in the summer and running barefoot next to Jack the dog.

She also toyed with the kittens that watched thirstily as she milked cows in the barn. Every once in a while, Foord shot a stream of milk their way. "They'd lick it like a kid drinking water out of a water fountain," she said.

Despite the many chores, there was a sense of freedom on the farm that was exhilarating. "If I moved my arms fast enough, I felt like I could fly," Foord said.

It was a good place to grow up, she said. "Oh, my lands, yes."

"I liked it over there. I liked animals. I liked to see things grow. I was very unhappy when I had to leave."

LEAVING THE FARM

Helen Luckl Foord was 10 when she moved from the Rothrock farm in 1920 to work as a live-in domestic helper in Akron.

In 1927, she married George Henry Foord, a man she had met at Summit Beach Park, and the couple had three children: Rosemarie Foord, George Henry Foord Jr. and Helen Helton.

Helen Foord continued to visit her relatives at the farm until 1943, when the Sanyos sold the property and moved to Norton.

Robert and Helen Juve bought the land at 444 Rothrock Road in 1946, lived there for 50 years and raised three kids.

Little by little, the 103-acre property was whittled away. A 1947 tornado destroyed the horse barn and knocked over 125 trees.

The Juves, who sharecropped the land while raising cattle and horses, lost about 36 acres when Route 21 was rebuilt as a highway in the early 1950s. They lost another 4 acres when the last link of Interstate 77 was built in the early 1970s. They divided up the rest and sold it, including 5.6 acres to the Halamays in 1986.

The cow barn is the only building still standing from the original Rothrock farm property.

There were only 15½ acres left when the Juves sold the property in 1997 for $825,000. "It's not a good place to live anymore," Robert Juve said.

It's certainly not the place that Helen Foord remembers. The dirt roads are paved. The fields are parking lots. The night sky is obliterated by mercury-vapor lights.

Store after store, condominium after condominium, development after development.

Montrose will soon engulf what's left of Rothrock farm. "It makes me want to cry," Foord said. "When I see that good farmland made a mess of like that, it makes me want to fall on the floor and have a 2-year-old tantrum."

Trail to the Chief

PRESIDENTIAL VISIT SURPRISED TALLMADGE FARMERS 100 YEARS AGO

(Originally published May 28, 2007)

Two well-dressed gentlemen made an unexpected visit as Tallmadge farmer Frank Thomas stacked straw on a quiet spring evening.

Thomas was laboring atop a small mountain of grain when he glanced down and noticed a tall stranger peering up. "Good evening," the lanky fellow said. "Would you like to meet the president of the United States?"

The farmer slid down the stack to investigate. Surely someone was pulling his leg.

There stood a short, stocky man in formal attire—definitely out of place for cow country. He had a thick mustache, wide grin and pince-nez glasses.

"Delighted," President Theodore Roosevelt said as he shook the farmer's hand.

Vice President Charles W. Fairbanks, the tall companion, introduced himself. The men had been enjoying a brisk hike and needed to take a breather.

Their unannounced visit May 29, 1907, was a pleasant surprise in local history. Farmers couldn't believe their eyes 100 years ago as the U.S. leaders strolled down a country lane with a Secret Service agent lagging behind at a respectful distance.

Earlier that afternoon, Roosevelt and Fairbanks had attended the Canton funeral of former first lady Ida Saxton McKinley. Roosevelt (1858–1919), a former vice president, rose to office after President William McKinley was assassinated in 1901.

Fairbanks (1852–1918), a former Indiana senator who was born in Union County, Ohio, is probably better known today for inspiring the name of an Alaskan city than being vice president. The post-funeral hike was Roosevelt's idea.

On the return trip from Canton, the president's private railroad car stopped for a couple of hours at Akron Junction near the Old Forge intersection of North Arlington Street, Home Avenue and East North Street. The car—sidetracked somewhere near Eastwood Avenue and Evans Avenue—had to wait to attach to a Baltimore & Ohio train that would take Roosevelt to Indianapolis for a speech the next day.

Roosevelt looked out the window around 5:30 p.m., saw the beautiful countryside and decided to end the sad day on a positive note. He was a fitness enthusiast who loved the outdoors.

"Fairbanks, if you are going to walk with me on this hike, you will have to move along at a lively gait," Roosevelt said. "I want to get a mouthful of fresh air, and here's the place to get it."

The men stepped outside with a solitary bodyguard. Crab apple blossoms and flowering dogwoods beckoned them east.

Although Akron newspapers reported that the men walked on "the Tallmadge road," an early name for Eastwood, old Summit County atlases indicate the actual route was Evans Avenue. The names of eyewitnesses match the names of Evans property owners in the early 1900s.

David E. Thomas and his wife, Fannie, who lived on a 48-acre farm in Tallmadge Township, saw the strangers pass and wondered whether they might be from the Cuyahoga Falls sanitarium.

"They walked up the road as if they were walking for a wager," Fannie Thomas told the Beacon Journal in 1907. "When they came back, they were not going so fast."

Roosevelt, 48, stood 5-foot-8 and weighed 200 pounds, but still outpaced Fairbanks, 55, who had longer strides at 6-foot-4. They were sweating by the time they crossed Brittain Road into southwest Tallmadge. That is when they spotted Frank Thomas on his straw stack.

"I won't forget the visit," Thomas told the Akron Press. "No, sir. Never."

After shaking off his initial surprise, the farmer offered some country hospitality. "Don't you want a drink of fresh milk?" he asked the men.

"Yes, I do," Roosevelt replied.

Thomas excused himself and came back with a cool glass from the farmhouse cellar. His family followed him outside to meet the distinguished guests.

"I will never forget the expression made by the president when he finished the milk," Thomas said.

"By gosh," Roosevelt told him. "That's good milk!"

The Thomas children tossed a ball around with the president until the hikers bid farewell.

Roosevelt and Fairbanks trudged within a mile of Tallmadge Circle before turning back. By then, news had spread throughout the community. Families came out to greet them.

Roosevelt was in good spirits and talked to everybody as he passed, witnesses said. He stopped to chat with David and Fannie Thomas and four sons in front of their farm.

"Mrs. Thomas, how many children have you?" he asked.

"Eight," she replied. "Six sons and two daughters."

"Good," Roosevelt said. "Just as soon as I go home, I am going to tell Mrs. Roosevelt that I found one woman who has one more child than she has."

Wearing down after a three-mile hike, Roosevelt and Fairbanks made a final stop at the home of Wallace Wuchter and his wife, Sarah, who lived near the tracks. "You have some beautiful scenery about here," Roosevelt said.

Sarah Wuchter told the guests she would have cooked spring chicken if she had known they were planning to visit.

"The spring chickens are powerful nice, Mr. President," Wallace Wuchter said.

"You could not have cooked enough spring chicken to satisfy me now," Roosevelt joked.

About 40 people were waiting at the private car when the U.S. officials returned. "Hurrah for Roosevelt and Fairbanks!" they cheered. Roosevelt told the group that the men had a happy time wandering the beautiful country.

"I have only one regret as I leave here, and that is that Mrs. Wuchter did not have an opportunity to cook that spring chicken," he said.

Roosevelt and Fairbanks boarded the train and it chugged off to Indianapolis. The next day, the president spoke to a crowd of 150,000 people.

In Tallmadge, the excitement of the presidential visit subsided—until a large flat package arrived at the

President Theodore Roosevelt (left) and Vice President Charles W. Fairbanks, shown relaxing in 1904 in Oyster Bay, N.Y., were in the mood to exercise 100 years ago on the outskirts of Akron. *Courtesy of the Library of Congress*

Wuchter home. Inside was a White House letter dated June 1, 1907. Enclosed were autographed portraits of Teddy Roosevelt.

"My Dear Mr. Wuchter: I send you three photographs—one for yourself and the other two I will ask you to give to the two Mr. Thomases (Frank and David) at whose farms I stopt," Roosevelt wrote.

"One of them gave me a glass of milk and the other had four such nice sons. Give my regards to your wife and all the Mr. and Mrs. Thomases and the other friends I met. Sincerely yours, Theodore Roosevelt."

Teacher's Pet

AKRON BEAGLE NEVER MADE IT PAST SECOND GRADE

(Originally published April 22, 2002)

He slept through most of his classes, never learned to read or write and had to be held back six times in the second grade. Even so, Duke was one of the most remarkable classmates ever to tread the halls at Akron's Betty Jane Elementary School.

The neighborhood dog walked to school every morning, reported to homeroom and attended classes until the final bell. It was a strange thing to see. The beagle seemed to think he was a student.

Even stranger, the school seemed to accept him as one. Pupils, teachers and principals welcomed Duke with open arms in the 1960s and 1970s. Everybody knew him.

"He would follow the kids to school," said former Betty Jane Principal Meryl Boxler, 74. "He was in a second-grade classroom in the basement, and he would stay in the classroom and go home in the evening."

It was a five-block waddle from Duke's Moody Street home to the Darrow Road school. "Yeah, that was my dog . . . He stayed in the second grade for six years," said George Adolphson, 69, of Springfield Township.

Adolphson's four children—Edward, Earlene, Greg and Eric—all went to Betty Jane. One day in 1965 or 1966, Duke tailed Edward, the oldest son, to school.

Instead of turning back for home, the dog entered the building, scampered down the stairs and tracked his young master to the second-grade classroom.

Duke caused a sensation, of course. Dogs aren't supposed to go to school.

The floppy-eared visitor amused the pupils and their teacher. Instead of expelling Duke, the instructor let him stay. So the gentle dog plopped into a corner and drifted off to sleep.

The next day, Duke returned to class. And the day after that. After a few weeks, it no longer seemed strange to have a dog in class. Everyone got used to it.

"He went with my oldest son in second grade," Adolphson said. "Then my daughter was in second grade the following year. He just stayed in the second grade through all six years."

Duke always returned to teacher Barbara Howell's class—even after the Adolphson kids were promoted to higher grades.

"He would walk to school with us," said Greg Adolphson, 40, now a Columbus resident. "He had his own place to go. He never stayed with me. He went to the second-grade room down in the basement."

Duke even went to class when the Adolphson kids didn't go. "If they were sick, my wife would go out to the door and say, 'Duke, they're sick. They're not going today,'" George Adolphson said. "And off he'd go. He'd go to school by himself."

At the end of the day, the dog was just as self-sufficient. "He never walked home with me," Greg Adolphson said. "He just came home by himself."

The biggest challenge to Duke's education was the arrival of Boxler as principal in 1969.

"My first experience with him was the first day I was there," Boxler said. "When the kids come, here comes the dog. So, of course, I was ready to take him out."

Not so fast, Mr. Principal. Teachers and pupils rushed to the defense of Duke.

"I think they were ready to say, 'If the dog goes, you go,'" Boxler said with a laugh. "I was told I did not have priority . . . The dog had more seniority, and if the dog left, I left."

To tell the truth, it wasn't a difficult decision to keep Duke in the classroom. Boxler loved pets.

Plus, the dog kept quiet, stayed out of trouble and never made a mess. "He was no bother, no bother," Boxler said.

The retired principal is still amazed at how well the dog blended in with the classroom.

"It was an odd thing because it was a natural thing," he said. "The children just petted him, but it wasn't like—oh, you know how they fuss around an animal that comes to school—it was just like one of the kids coming. He'd just come in and take his place."

Duke's gentle disposition had a way of winning over everyone. "He was a good dog," Greg Adolphson said.

Duke the beagle rests his posterior on the floor of Barbara Howell's second-grade classroom at Akron's Betty Jane Elementary School in April 1973. He's pictured between the desks of students Karen Holcomb, 8, and Eric Adolphson, 7.

"He was a fat dog. He just liked to play, and he was real friendly toward people . . . The kids at school, they just loved him. He would just lay down in class and sleep the whole day."

The only complaints were minor. Duke sometimes snored a bit too loudly and his fur sometimes smelled a bit too earthy. "You'd give him a bath, and the first thing he'd do is run outside and find some mudhole and roll around in it," Greg Adolphson said.

Duke truly was happiest when he was around children. "I took him hunting one time and he heard kids playing in the school ground," George Adolphson said. "I had to go get him."

The plump, graying beagle eventually began to slow down. It was inevitable. "Everybody loved him so they fed him all the time, and he kept on getting fatter and fatter and fatter," Greg Adolphson said. "The janitor up at the school just loved him, too, and he'd share his lunch with him."

In the summer of 1973, the basement at Betty Jane was remodeled for the third grade. There was some speculation on whether Duke would return to his old room or follow his second-grade teacher upstairs.

But just as classes were about to begin in September, 10-year-old Duke suffered a heatstroke. "It caught up to him," Greg Adolphson said. "All that weight, and he had a bad heart."

"He actually died on the first day of school," George Adolphson said.

Duke's passing saddened all at Betty Jane. The Adolphsons sent a thank-you note to the pupils: "He died very quietly with many wonderful memories of attending your wonderful school and its people. Thank you for caring and doing so much to make him (and us) happy to have been the owners of a dog so loved and cared for by all."

Nearly 30 years later, Duke still brings back fond memories. "He was just a unique dog, and I just didn't realize how different he was," Greg Adolphson said.

"All I knew was that he belonged," Boxler said. "And that's all there was to it."

Risque Business

DANCER'S ACT STARTLED AKRON IN 1908

(Originally published May 7, 2001)

It could have been the bump. It could have been the grind. Whatever it was, Myrtle Clark did it a little too often and a little too well. The burlesque performer's hoochie-coochie dance at the Grand Opera House offended Akron's refined sensibilities in May 1908.

The bawdy act was so shocking, so indecent, that Akron residents began to lament the moral decay of society, but not before selling out every show and giving standing ovations.

Clark was merely one performer in the Monte Carlo Girls, a troupe of dancers, comedians and musicians that traveled from city to city. The company returned every spring to the theater at 38–44 N. Main St., promising "funny men, pretty girls and high-class vaudeville."

When the curtain went up on Thursday, May 7, 1908, every seat was filled from the lower floor to the balcony. Nearly all patrons were men.

"And what was there for all these anxious men to see and hear?" the Akron Beacon Journal asked the next day. "Just what there is in any burlesque show: Indecent jokes, vulgar songs and girls dressed with an art that seeks to show what should be hidden."

It was a public parade of pulchritude that the anonymous reviewer found repulsive. "In some scenes, waists were cut so decollete that they could have been dispensed with and nothing more revealed. In others, girls of much avoirdupois stretched daring fleshings."

The audience of "depraved men" clapped and whistled during the suggestive song-and-dance numbers. Clark took the spotlight in the second act. As one witness would recall later: "Myrtle shed garments like a maple tree shedding leaves in autumn."

With serpentine movements of the hip, the hoochie-coochie dancer brought down the house. Tame by today's standards, Clark's act didn't actually involve nudity. She did, however, bare her torso, where it was revealed that a single red rose had been placed for decoration. With that grand finale, the dancer scampered offstage to a round of rollicking applause.

Akron Detective Bert Eckerman, who was in the audience "to see that the show didn't get too vulgar," immediately went backstage and arrested Clark and Monte Carlo Girls manager Timothy O. Sullivan on charges of "giving an unbecoming performance."

"Why, I didn't do anything to be arrested for!" Clark protested. "You ought to see it when we put the whole thing on. That was mild."

The dancer and her manager appeared in court the next day before Mayor William Sawyer. "The courtroom and lobby were packed by a motley throng of men, and when the girl entered the room to enter her plea, there was a craning of necks and much subdued whispering," the Beacon Journal reported.

The two out-of-towners posted a $100 bond Friday, and the case was continued to Monday. That meant the hoochie-coochie dancer was free to perform her act that weekend.

Although the Grand was packed both nights, Clark's performance must have lacked the intensity of Thursday night's show. There were no more arrests.

On Monday, the dancer and her manager pleaded guilty to putting on an immoral show. They paid a $10 fine and skedaddled out of Akron, presumably to other communities where Clark's talent could be more fully appreciated. The show must go on . . . no matter what comes off.

Nearly 35 years later, veteran Akron newsman H.B. "Doc" Kerr reminisced about Myrtle Clark's scandalous performance. His recollection, however, differed in one major respect from original accounts: He said Clark attempted to prove in court that there was nothing wrong with her act.

The mayor "ruled that a mere description of the dance was inadequate," Kerr recalled in 1943. "He had to have a demonstration to be convinced. The audience—goggle-eyed and breathless—silently voted its approval."

The dancer put on her costume, including the rose, and danced the hoochie-coochie before the mayor,

Akron's Grand Opera House, which operated from 1907 to 1934 at 38–44 N. Main St., was famous (and infamous) for its burlesque shows. The theater was built on the site of the original Grand Opera House, which opened in 1897 and burned down in 1905.

Kerr wrote. When she was done, the court erupted in applause, he said.

Strangely, Akron's 1908 newspapers didn't mention this unscheduled performance. Perhaps they were trying to preserve decorum in an increasingly corrupt world.

Or maybe Kerr's memory was playing tricks on him after all those years.

If it didn't happen that way, it probably should have. After all, there's a famous saying in show business: Always leave them wanting more.

Friend or Foe

WORLD WAR I ENEMIES BECAME UNLIKELY PALS

(Originally published Nov. 12, 2001)

Walter B. Wanamaker smiled when he saw the man who had tried to kill him. Then he shook his hand.

"Hello, Ernst," he said. "Have you ever put on weight!"

It had been 13 years since German war ace Ernst Udet shot Wanamaker's plane from the sky over Bezu-St. Germain, France. The Akron man was lucky to survive the World War I dogfight. His defeat came at the gloved hands of a living legend.

Udet shot down 62 enemy planes for Germany during the war and was second only to Manfred von Richtofen, "The Red Baron," who recorded 80 victories. Wanamaker had the distinction of being Udet's only American victim.

That was on July 2, 1918. Army Lt. Wanamaker, a member of the 27th Pursuit Squadron, was piloting a blue, French-built fighter plane: a Nieuport 28. He and eight other Allied pilots were flying a mission behind German lines when they spotted enemy planes at 16,000 feet.

"There were 11 planes in the German squadron," Wanamaker later told a reporter. "But we went after them. It was the most thrilling fight I had ever been in, and the second-longest air fight in the war. It lasted 32 minutes."

Machine-gun fire cut through the air as the planes veered, rolled, lunged and dodged. Wanamaker had a German plane in his sights when Lt. Udet surprised him from behind.

"I don't know how Udet came at me," Wanamaker recalled. "I suddenly discovered a red Fokker was pouring lead into my plane. I tried to evade him by going into a tailspin.

"Down I went to 4,500 feet, figuring he'd leave me if I played possum. But it didn't fool him. A bullet struck my gas tank. Another hit the prop. Gas rushed into my face."

The engine stalled. Wanamaker tried to glide to safety, but Udet attacked his prey again. The bullet-riddled plane hit the ground with a sickening crunch, turning end over end, cracking in half at the cockpit.

Udet quickly landed to take a better look at his conquest. By the time he got to the wreckage, German infantrymen had surrounded the plane. Udet was surprised to find the pilot alive.

Shot in the thigh, suffering a broken leg and drifting in and out of consciousness, Wanamaker looked up at Udet and asked for a cigarette.

The German had assumed his adversary was French, and was surprised to hear English.

"I gave him one and then I asked him how it happened that an Englishman was flying in a French plane," Udet later wrote. "He said: 'Guess again. I'm not English. I'm American. Straight from Akron, Ohio.'"

BACK HOME

As Udet waited for medics to arrive, he cut a piece of fabric from the rudder of Wanamaker's plane. The section contained the plane's serial number: N6347.

Udet had the Akron man sign the war trophy, and apologized for shooting down his plane.

"Don't feel badly," he told Wanamaker. "I've got 38 already. You're the 39th."

Wanamaker was hospitalized for four months until the war's end on Nov. 11, 1918. When he returned to Akron, he became a lawyer. He was named assistant county prosecutor in 1921 and special prosecutor in 1925. In 1930, he was elected Summit County common pleas judge, a post he held until 1958.

But Wanamaker found himself locked in a bureaucratic struggle over his military record. The U.S. government still listed him as missing in action and refused to acknowledge that he had been injured in battle and was entitled to medical benefits.

UNLIKELY FRIENDSHIP

That's when an old enemy flew to the rescue. Through a 1930 magazine article, the judge discovered that Udet was working as a stunt flier for German movies. Wanamaker wrote to the war ace to see if he wouldn't mind vouching for injuries he caused.

Udet's reply was immediate.

"To my certain knowledge, you were seriously injured in the fall and could be extricated from the machine only with difficulty," he wrote. "You were carried to the rear of our lines on a stretcher and later visited by me and photographed, although you knew nothing about it."

Wanamaker presented the letter to the government and proved his case. His records were straightened out.

Udet and Wanamaker began an unlikely friendship, writing notes and exchanging photos. The German reported he would visit Cleveland in September 1931 for the National Air Races, and asked Wanamaker to attend.

As told in Udet's autobiography, *Ace of the Iron Cross*, the Cleveland crowd was dazzled by his stunt flying. He demonstrated pinpoint accuracy, piloting his Flamingo airplane upside-down and low to the ground.

FACE TO FACE

The high point, though, came when the pilot landed. Wanamaker was introduced over the loudspeakers. The former adversaries stood face to face. Smiling.

"I am glad that I have the pleasure to meet today my old enemy," Udet told the crowd. "But now he is no enemy of mine. I am the very best friend he has today. From now on, everything is forgotten which happened before. And I give him now what I took away."

The German handed Wanamaker a framed piece of old linen with the serial number N6347. It was the section of rudder he had cut away from the Akron man's plane in 1918.

"That's real nice, really nice, that you would think of this," Wanamaker said.

That night, Udet joined Wanamaker and his wife, Isobel, for dinner at their home at 880 N. Portage Path. The host bought German wine for the occasion. Udet stayed the night.

"Had he died, I would have never come to this comfortable town," Udet later wrote. "Then the woman with the blonde hair would have hated me. Me, the one who killed her husband."

Two very different fates awaited the two men.

Judge Walter B. Wanamaker lived to be 71 years old. He died of cancer on May 26, 1965.

World War I veteran Walter B. Wanamaker served as Summit County common pleas judge from 1930 to 1958.

Ernst Udet was 45 when he shot himself to death on Nov. 17, 1941. He was weary of feuding with Nazi Field Marshal Hermann Goering, and was stuck in a desk job with the German Luftwaffe when he wanted to fly.

If you ever visit the U.S. Air Force Museum in Dayton, be sure to look for a certain display. It's a piece of fabric cut from the rudder of a World War I plane.

The serial number is N6347.

Great Myths of Akron

NOT EVERYTHING YOU'VE LEARNED ABOUT SUMMIT COUNTY IS TRUE

(Originally published Jan. 17, 2005)

If you hear something enough times, you start to believe it. If you hear something all your life, you accept it as fact. That doesn't necessarily make it true, though.

Colorful legends abound in Akron and Summit County. They pass from generation to generation, growing larger with each telling. Some tales are true, some tales are false. The hard part is telling one from the other.

Today we present some of the Great Myths of Akron. How many of these have you heard? How many do you believe?

Claim: Akron is the highest place in Ohio.

Reality: Akron isn't even the highest place in Summit County. Yes, the name is derived from the Greek word "akros," which means "high place," but it was selected because the town was the highest point on the Ohio & Erie Canal. A spot near Goodyear Heights Reservoir is Akron's highest point at 1,206 feet above sea level. The highest elevation in Summit County—1,320 feet above sea level—is near Broadview and Brush roads in Richfield. If you really want to visit the highest place in Ohio, climb Campbell Hill in Logan County's Bellefontaine. It's 1,549 feet above sea level.

Claim: Akron's founder built Perkins Stone Mansion.

Reality: Gen. Simon Perkins of Warren laid out Akron in 1825, but he never lived here. His name often is confused with that of his son, Col. Simon Perkins Jr., a leading Akron citizen whose fabulous Greek Revival home on Copley Road was completed in 1837 and serves today as the home of the Summit County Historical Society.

Claim: Portage Path once served as the western boundary of the United States.

Reality: Technically, Ohio wasn't a state at the time. The Indian portage between the Cuyahoga and Tuscarawas rivers was an ancient boundary between Indian nations. The Treaty of Fort McIntosh, signed in 1785, established the trail for nearly 20 years as a general boundary line between Indians and white settlers. Ohio didn't become a state until 1803.

Claim: Cuyahoga means "crooked river."

Reality: It depends on the accent. Ohio historians believe Mohawk Indians called it "Cayagaga," which translates to "crooked river." However, Seneca Indians referred to it as "Cuyohaga," which means "place of the jawbone," an apparent reference to a dinosaur fossil. The funny thing is that Summit County residents still disagree on how to pronounce it.

Claim: The John Brown House was a stop on the Underground Railroad.

Reality: The famous abolitionist lived in the Diagonal Road home from 1844 to 1846, but there is no proof that it ever was used to harbor escaped slaves. Brown made history in 1859 by raiding a federal arsenal at Harpers Ferry, Va., to start a slave uprising. He was captured and executed. If Brown had lived in Akron a little longer, you can bet there would be more stories about the Diagonal Road home.

Claim: Akron doesn't have a town square.

Reality: It does have one. It's just in the wrong place. Gen. Simon Perkins mapped out Perkins Square at the present site of Bowery and West Exchange streets, but merchants ignored it. The business district sprouted a few blocks away at South Main and Exchange streets. Today, the old square is the park in front of Akron Children's Hospital.

Claim: Charles Goodyear was an Akron resident.

Reality: He never set foot in Akron. In early 1839, Goodyear discovered vulcanization—the process of treating crude rubber with sulfur and heat to make it stronger—at his home in Woburn, Mass. He died in debt in 1860. Goodyear Tire & Rubber Co. co-founders Frank and Charles Seiberling named their company for him in 1898.

Claim: Stan Hywet Hall was brought stone by stone from England.

Reality: Can you imagine the shipping charge? Frank Seiberling's 65-room mansion, built in 1912, was designed by Cleveland architect Charles Schneider. The myth of a piecemeal delivery and reassembly may have originated with the Seiberling family's visit to England to tour old manors for design tips. The Seiberlings did import some paneling from an English mansion that was going to be razed. Otherwise, the family gathered ideas, not building materials.

Claim: On a clear day, you can see the masts of Lake Erie ships from Highland Square.
Reality: The real myth is believing that we have clear days in Northeast Ohio. Just kidding, convention bureau. This rumor was long associated with The Frontier, a 30-room mansion where Clara Ritchie lived on the southwest corner of Portage Path and West Market Street. The mansion stood from 1905 to 1961. Supposedly, a person could peer through a telescope on the roof and see ships to the north. This legend fell apart in 1962 after the eight-story Highland Tower was built and no masts were visible. Anyone needing proof can visit the 14-story Tower Eighty a block away. Lake Erie is nowhere in sight.

Claim: A meteorite marks a prominent grave in Glendale Cemetery.
Reality: The UFO has been identified, and it's of terrestrial origin. Samuel Lane, former Akron mayor, Summit County sheriff, Akron Daily Beacon editor and local historian, died June 14, 1905. His grave marker at Glendale is a 6-foot rock with red and black stripes. Rumors have persisted for decades that the strange rock fell to earth from the heavens. In the 1980s, though, a geologist identified it as carboniferous conglomerate. Basically, it's iron ore. It appears to have come from Painesville, not outer space.

Claim: The Soap Box Derby originated in Akron.
Reality: We took a good thing and made it better. The first national race was in Dayton in 1934. Journalist Myron E. Scott came up with the idea in 1933 after photographing boys riding down a Dayton hill in makeshift cars. The city lost interest, though, so the race moved to Akron in 1935. We've had it since.

Claim: The Akron Airdock is so large that it rains inside.
Reality: This depends on your definition of rain. Dr. Karl Arnstein, the airship designer and vice president of Goodyear-Zeppelin Corp., noted in 1930 that the claim was "somewhat exaggerated." On foggy mornings, when relative humidity was high inside the dock, a sudden temperature drop caused condensation, he said, and the moisture fell to the floor in a mist. Arnstein doubted it was rain. Others who've worked at the hangar insist they know rain when they see it. Let's call this one a wash.

Wouldn't Cadillac Hill's slope be a good place to test the brakes of new firetrucks in Akron? Here's how the South Bates Street hill looked in September 1976.

Claim: The Akron Fire Department tests its new firetrucks on Cadillac Hill.
Reality: Boy, that would be a tough one to explain to taxpayers. Bates Hill, the original name of the steep slope between West Market Street and Glendale Avenue, has a grade of 25 percent. If the city really wanted to test the brakes of a $300,000 vehicle, wouldn't it choose a safer place? Like the Swiss Alps.

Claim: The group Devo is from Akron.
Reality: Oh, no, it's not Devo. Actually, most of the quirky band grew up in Cuyahoga Falls and Kent, although Akron's mutato influence cannot be denied. Devo formed at Kent State and held its first gig there.

Claim: Norka is Akron spelled backward.
Reality: OK. That one is true. Just testing you.

Claim: Barberton's Lake Anna is bottomless.
Reality: Did you hear about the swimmer who got caught

in a vortex at Lake Anna and was whisked underground to the Portage Lakes? Some people think that tale is real. It's not. The lake is about 35 feet deep. It has a bottom. For safety's sake, take our word for it.

Claim: A railroad car lies at the bottom of Blue Pond.

Reality: Not anymore. For decades, East Akron residents have circulated a tale about a freight car submerged in the pond. The story is based on fact. A small car fell into the pond around 1919 during construction along Goodyear Boulevard. Laborers eventually lifted it out. Either that, or it was whisked underground to the Portage Lakes.

Claim: An airplane lies at the bottom of Nimisila Reservoir.

Reality: Not anymore. A Corsair built by Goodyear Aircraft Corp. crashed into the reservoir around 1943 after a test pilot ran into mechanical trouble. The pilot parachuted to safety, but the airplane slammed into the water about 300 feet offshore. The military wreckage was removed a few days later, but rumors continued for years that a ghost plane lurked beneath the surface.

Claim: Akron cereal king Ferdinand Schumacher buried a treasure in Akron.

Reality: Hmmmm. According to legend, the U.S. government paid Schumacher a fortune in gold coins to supply the Union Army with oatmeal during the Civil War. He died in 1908 after suffering a series of financial setbacks. The gold wasn't found. Did he bury it? Clearly, this tale is absurd. It's ridiculous. It's unbelievable. And if anyone should happen to find those coins, don't forget to give us a cut.

Lights, Camera, Akron!

CLARK GABLE GOT HIS ACT TOGETHER IN RUBBER CITY
BEFORE HE HIT ROAD TO HOLLYWOOD

(Originally published Sept. 20, 2004)

We'd like to take credit for discovering one of Hollywood's biggest stars, but, honestly, we barely noticed the kid when he was here. Clark Gable was just another small-town boy trying to make good in the city. He was tall, muscle-bound, friendly, polite. Akron's rubber factories were filled with thousands of earnest young men just like him, and thousands more were on the way in search of work.

No one in town had any reason to believe that Gable would ever be famous—not even Gable. Yet, there definitely was something memorable about him, and it wasn't just those lips, those eyes and those ears. Gable lived in Akron for only a few years, but the experience changed his life. This is where he got his start in show business.

William Clark Gable was born Feb. 1, 1901, in Cadiz, Ohio. His father, William Henry Gable, was a farmer and oil driller. His mother, Adeline, died when he was 7 months old. Gable spent most of his childhood in Hopedale, a coal-mining village in Harrison County, but moved with his father and stepmother, Jennie, to Portage County in 1916. The family settled on a farm in Palmyra Township.

"I fed the hogs, the rest of the stock, plowed in the spring until every muscle ached, forked hay in the hot sun until I was sweating crops of calluses," Gable later recalled. "I did what I was expected to do on the farm, but it takes a certain knack for farming in the old-fashioned way. I just didn't have what it takes."

Nor was he too happy with his education. Gable was an ox of a teenager who towered over classmates at Edinburg High. He dropped out of school in 1917. "I'm not going to ride on that bus every day with a lot of kids half my size," he told his father.

Andy Means, a childhood pal from Hopedale, pulled Gable out of the doldrums. Means was moving to Akron to find a job. Gable decided to do the same. "Akron was the biggest place I'd ever seen . . . Andy Means and I arrived with our straw suitcases and the big boxes of food my mother had made up for us," Gable recalled.

Levi Williamson, another friend from Hopedale, had moved to Akron but was away on military duty. His mother, Mrs. J. Williamson, offered Gable lodging in their home at 1163 Getz St. in South Akron.

"Little did we think when we were kids and young men together that we were training one of the gang to be America's No. 1 movie idol," Williamson noted.

By 1919, Gable landed a $95-a-week job as a clerk at the Firestone Steel Products rim plant at Miller and Sweitzer avenues. He stayed there about a year before leaving for bigger bucks at the Miller Rubber Co. on South High Street.

Irene Fess, who worked at Firestone, told an Akron reporter in 1934 that Gable was charming and fun to be around. "He was just a big, overgrown boy, very fond of playing his ukulele whenever we got together," she said. "He was a great 'kidder.'"

Recently married, Fess was quick to point out that she never was one of Gable's girlfriends. "In fact, Clark didn't single out any particular girl, but he always went around with our crowd on parties," she said.

Who had time for girls? Besides working six days a week, Gable took night classes at the University of Akron because his dad wanted him to be a doctor.

"I never had any full-fledged romances in my youth because I never had time for them," Gable once said. "I was always trying to stay one jump ahead of the bread line in the early days—and in some of the later ones."

After Williamson returned from the service, Gable moved to a duplex on Steiner Avenue. He lodged with Lewis J. Grether's family at 24 Steiner while Andy Means stayed with Walton Taylor's family at 22 Steiner.

The next-door neighbor left an impression on Grace Taylor Hockenberry and her stories would be the envy of many fans. "I could hear him taking his bath in the mornings," she later said. "He always ran downstairs two at a time. He never wore a hat. He was always in a hurry."

All of South Akron was Gable's stomping grounds. He liked to hang out at Haun Drug Co. on the south-

William Henry Gable visits his son in Akron about 1919. He wanted the boy to study medicine, but Clark had other ideas.

west corner of Main and Miller streets. His landlord, a pharmacist, allowed the youth to volunteer as a soda jerk.

Gable also helped out at Gates & Kittles, a men's clothing store across South Main. He worked part time as a salesman, peddling suits for $18 to $25, and wore snazzy new clothes as a fringe benefit. "He danced around while he worked," tailor George Radoichin recalled with amusement.

The turning point in Gable's life came around 1920 when Andy Means talked him into going to a play. *The Bird of Paradise* was at Akron's Music Hall, a 2,000-seat auditorium at 44 E. Exchange St., the present-day site of the Beacon Journal. When the lights dimmed, a new world opened for Gable. The reluctant theatergoer suddenly found himself enjoying the romantic drama. He wanted to see more.

Gable began skipping his night classes to attend more plays. He started hanging out at the Why Not Eat? restaurant, a local stage hangout, and struck up conversations with actors. They encouraged him to apply for a job at Music Hall.

Gable accepted a volunteer position as a callboy. His job was to notify actors when it was time to go onstage. "I got the people out in time for the curtain whether they liked it or not," he explained. Soon the director allowed him to appear as an extra. Sometimes he even had a line or two. "I decided I would rather be an actor than a doctor or anything else," Gable said.

One night, he invited his father to see him at Music Hall. William Henry Gable was sure his son had gone mad. Acting was not a career!

In a bit of revisionist history, the Akron Times-Press reported in 1931 that Gable had been wildly popular among fans. "His parts grew in size and importance," the paper reported. "His stage appearance 'clicked.' Akron liked to watch the husky hill lad more. Audiences heartily approved of his looks."

In truth, not even his director, Ed Clark Lilley, remembered much about him. "He was one of hundreds who came to me looking for jobs," he said. "He was hired at the Music Hall as atmosphere."

Gable's fledgling theater career was cut short in Akron when his stepmother Jennie grew ill with tuberculosis and died on the Palmyra farm. Gable's grief-stricken father decided to move away to Oklahoma and begged his son to follow. The good son listened.

Mars A. "Doc" Parkhill, an old friend, ran into Gable at a shoeshine parlor on South Main. "I'm going to Tulsa, Okla.," Gable told him. "My father is out there. He has a garage and an oil lease to tend. He needs help."

Gable had the acting bug, though. He joined a theatrical troupe, toured the West and ended up in Hollywood by 1924. Akron didn't hear about Gable for a few years. He worked as a movie extra and played bit roles—basically the same work he did at Music Hall. The parts grew bigger and by 1931, he was stealing scenes in such movies as *Dance, Fools, Dance*, *The Painted Desert*, *The Secret Six* and *A Free Soul*.

Akron residents began to line up for his movies and racked their brains trying to recall the amiable rubber worker. Gable won an Oscar in 1934 for *It Happened One Night* and achieved screen immortality in 1939 in *Gone With the Wind*. He earned the nickname "The King" of Hollywood during his 75-movie career.

He never returned to Akron. Beacon Journal reporter Art Cullison interviewed Gable in 1958 with his fifth wife, Kay, during an appearance in Cleveland. "I flew over Akron on the way in today and pointed out to Kay where I used to work," Gable said. "But I don't know when I'll ever get back there."

Clark Gable died of a heart attack in November 1960 after completing *The Misfits* with Marilyn Monroe. He was 59.

Most of his Akron haunts—including Music Hall, Haun's, Gates & Kittles, Miller Rubber, Firestone Steel Products and Why Not Eat?—disappeared over the last 85 years. Even the lodging houses are gone.

No, we can't take credit for discovering a star, but we can claim a supporting role. Akron gave Clark Gable his first applause.

Little Boy Lost

ORRVILLE BOY'S DISAPPEARANCE IN 1928 STILL MYSTERY TODAY

(Originally published Dec. 17, 2001)

This is a story without a happy ending. In fact, there is no ending. And there may never be one.

Nearly 75 years later, we still don't know what happened to little Melvin Horst.

The 4-year-old boy vanished without a trace on Dec. 27, 1928, while playing near his home in Orrville. The disappearance, which horrified Wayne County and startled the nation, remains one of Ohio's greatest mysteries.

Zola Horst last saw her son through a kitchen window as she prepared dinner. Melvin was scampering around their yard at Vine and Paradise streets, bundled up in a hat and coat, carrying a red toy truck he had just received as a Christmas gift.

An hour or two later, when Zola called for her son to come inside for supper at 4:30 p.m., there was no response.

Melvin's father, Raymond Horst, brother, Ralph, 8, and sister, Elgie, 2, arrived at the table as Zola looked outside. Darkness was closing in on the quiet town. She called for Melvin again. And again.

Something was wrong. She and her husband telephoned neighbors and the parents of Melvin's playmates. No one knew where he was.

"We were genuinely frightened when it was 6:30," Zola Horst would recall days later. "At 7 we had notified the constable and at 8:30 the alarm was sent out."

Melvin's young friends told the Horsts that their son had gone to play that afternoon in a vacant lot off Chestnut Street near the railroad tracks—about a block away from home.

He and four neighbor boys had horsed around in the field until he realized it was late. "Goodbye, Bobby," Melvin told an 8-year-old chum. "I got to go home now."

Only a block from home, little Melvin Horst walked away into oblivion.

Orrville declared an emergency that night. A fire alarm called the village's 4,500 residents to attention, and hundreds rushed to see what was wrong.

Village Marshal Roy Horst, Raymond's brother, explained that his blue-eyed, dark-haired nephew was missing. About 400 volunteers quickly fanned out, going door to door, searching every neighborhood.

As temperatures dipped into the low 30s, searchers began to fear the worst. Night turned into day, but there still was no sign.

News of Melvin's disappearance spread across Ohio and beyond as newspapers and radio carried the urgent story. Hundreds of tips poured in to police.

Melvin was spotted in a car at an Akron gas station. Melvin was spotted with an elderly couple on a Columbus streetcar. Melvin was spotted on a Mansfield train.

It was widely believed that the boy was abducted while taking a shortcut through an alley near his home. Police rounded up vagrants and interrogated them, but learned nothing.

"I have always warned him against strangers and told him repeatedly never to speak to people whom he did not know and never to get into their automobiles," his distraught mother told the Akron Beacon Journal.

Everyone had a theory. The boy may have been kidnapped to be raised as someone else's child. Hoboes may have pulled him into a train car and killed him. A motorist may have accidentally run him over, panicked and disposed of the body in a car trunk.

Police thought there had to be a motive. There was no ransom note, though, and Raymond Horst, a roofer, had little money.

Officers believed Melvin had fallen victim to an enemy of his uncle. Or he may have stumbled across some illegal activity. The boy was known to say "I'll tell my Uncle Roy on you" when he witnessed improper behavior.

Villagers thought the case was cracked on Jan. 2, 1929, with the arrest of a 62-year-old bootlegger and his 17-year-old son. The two lived around the corner from the Horsts and had many run-ins with the marshal.

One of Melvin's pals told police he saw the suspects lure the boy into their home. On that evidence, the man and his son were indicted, tried and sentenced to 20 years for child stealing.

(Left) Melvin Horst, 4, was playing near his Orrville home in December 1928 when he vanished without a trace. Where did he go?

(Above) In 1953, former Orrville residents Raymond and Zola Horst observe the 25th anniversary of their son Melvin's 1928 disappearance. They still hadn't given up hope that he would be found alive.

The only problem was it wasn't true. The boy had been lying through his teeth. The two spent three months in prison in 1929 before being acquitted in a second trial.

The case took a bizarre turn in 1930 when the fibbing boy's father and a friend were arrested. The men confessed that Melvin was killed in a garage after finding them sipping whiskey.

Neither man admitted being the killer, though. As it turned out, their so-called confessions were given under duress in a police grilling. The prosecutor dropped charges. There was no evidence and no body.

And no more arrests.

The Horst family kept their Christmas tree up for nearly two years, but Melvin never came home to see it. Eventually, they put his toys away in a drawer.

Every year around Christmas, reporters would visit the family to renew interest in the case.

"My little boy may be alive. Maybe he's dead. But it is the uncertainty that is so hard to bear," Zola Horst said in 1935.

"I don't know any more than I did on Dec. 27, 1928, when Melvin didn't come in from play," Raymond Horst said in 1939.

"We will never give up hope until we have definite proof that Melvin is dead," Zola Horst said in 1953.

The Horsts moved to Marshallville in the 1930s then to Eustis, Fla., in the 1940s. They pursued many tips over the years and endured countless crank letters and bogus confessions.

It was all to no avail.

Raymond Horst died in 1961 at age 60. Zola Horst died in 1986 at age 87.

Their old house still stands at Vine and Paradise. The story of Melvin's disappearance has been handed down from generation to generation in the community.

"I don't know that we ever close a case, but it's not active by any means," says Orrville Police Capt. Jay Lax, a 24-year veteran with the department.

There is always the hope that a discovery might be made in an Orrville attic, cellar or garage.

"If a body's found, we would try to identify the remains," Lax says. "Although, after all this time, I don't know how we'd ever identify. I mean, they didn't keep really good dental records back in those days."

Melvin's older brother, Ralph, passed away nearly 10 years ago. He had heard so many conflicting theories about the 1928 disappearance, but the leads never went anywhere.

Melvin Horst would be 77 years old this year. Maybe he is dead. Maybe he is alive. "You don't know," says Ralph's widow, Irene Horst. "That's the sad part. You never have a conclusion to it.

"And never will."

The Pedestrian

AKRON MAN ENJOYED LIFE'S TREK AT A SLOWER PACE

(Originally published Dec. 9, 2002)

There was a time in Akron when everyone seemed to know Orlando Nelson Potter. He was one of those colorful characters who stood out in the gray city, a free-spirited individual with a flair for eccentricity.

Eloquent yet irascible.

Charming yet crusty.

Potter was a poet, a philosopher and, most famously, a pedestrian. He didn't have much use for automobiles. Walking was his preferred mode of travel.

Potter made a living by selling advertisements to small newspapers in Northeast Ohio. He was a roadside attraction in the 1930s, trudging along in an oversized coat and derby hat.

Motorists often stopped to offer the elderly fellow a ride, but he shooed them away. It was routine for him to hike 13 miles to Wadsworth, 19 miles to Ravenna or 20 miles to Medina.

He averaged 18 miles a day in the 1930s—rain, sun or snow. "I've walked about 300,000 miles or more in my life and I'm going to add to that aplenty," Potter told the Akron Times-Press in 1932.

And then, as if to prove it, he walked all the way to Pittsburgh for his 75th birthday. It took him three days.

The 115-mile journey garnered a great deal of press coverage, and Potter used the public spotlight to call for the immediate repeal of Prohibition.

"Many prohibitionists are too cantankerous," he said. "They are as dangerous as religious fanatics and they will cause trouble if we don't obtain repeal soon."

The funny thing was, Potter never drank a drop in his life. He was a teetotaler. He didn't smoke, either.

And being a lifelong bachelor, Potter probably abstained from a few other vices as well.

What Potter found intoxicating was the exchange of ideas. He enjoyed philosophizing about life, a practice that earned him such nicknames in the press as "The Socrates of Akron" and "The Peripatetic Poet."

In his earlier days, he had been a teacher of English and Latin at an academy in Iowa. He was fond of reciting Shakespeare, Milton and Kipling, and enjoyed discussing politics.

Inside his overcoat, he carried 16 pounds of newspaper clippings, documents and other scraps of paper for easy retrieval should he ever need to prove a point during a discussion. He also carried unfinished poems that he had been composing for years and sometimes decades.

For long walks, he stuffed his pockets with pumpernickel sandwiches and bottles of milk. He always kept a pouch of small rocks in case any ferocious dogs should give chase.

"Nothing is more effective than a barrage of stones when trying to get past snarling dogs on a dark highway," he said.

Potter did his best thinking on walks. He crafted poetry in his head and devised great inventions that never would be built.

One such contraption was the Potter Pedestrianator, mechanical shoes that would allow a man to travel 80 miles a day without working up a sweat.

Another idea came to him as he hoofed it from Orrville to Wadsworth in December 1936. "When the wind was against my back it was all right, but when it blew in my face, I had to hold my nose to keep it from freezing," Potter said. Eureka! The Nose Muff was just what the world needed.

Akron reporters loved Potter. They found all kinds of ways to write about him. When he shaved off his beard in exchange for a free chicken dinner at a local restaurant, it was a story. When he feasted on hazelnuts after finding a shrub in the Gorge between Akron and Cuyahoga Falls, it was a story.

Newsmen were fascinated that a man of such advanced years could stay so fit and healthy. "I'm sort of like a horse," he said. "A horse doesn't rightly get old. He just lives along and then all of a sudden he drops over."

And even though he was in his mid-70s, that didn't mean he was old, he insisted. "There's no such thing as age when you get up where I am," he said. "Age is just a psychological phantasmagoria then, I guess."

Radio listeners got an earful when Potter was interviewed one evening for a live program on WADC.

With his derby hat and newspaper-stuffed overcoat, Orlando Nelson Potter was a familiar sight in Akron during the 1930s.

"To what do you attribute your amazing health and vitality?" the host asked innocently.

"To a magnificent set of bowels," Potter responded.

The philosopher was a bit obsessive about his eating. Before a big walk, he dined on oatmeal. "I figure that a man is just a human horse, and if oats is good for horses, it ought to be good for man," he maintained.

During walks, he liked to nibble on rye bread because it gave him "the best mileage."

About the only false step Potter ever made was when he tried to enter politics instead of staying on the sidelines. He ran for state legislator in 1936.

"There's only one thing that worries me," he said. "And that, strangely enough for a man who is practically 80 years old, is the feminine contingent. Confound it, women don't like me because I'm a bachelor."

Potter did indeed lose at the polls, although a female conspiracy never could be proved. "I'd rather walk than run, anyway," he joked after the loss.

When Potter turned 80 in 1937, he decided to celebrate the occasion by—what else?—hiking up to Cleveland to see the opera.

An Akron Times-Press reporter agreed to join him on the 32-mile journey, but got only as far as Ghent. It was raining and the journalist was cold, so he hitched a ride back home.

Potter, however, slogged onward and arrived at Cleveland Public Hall in time to see *Aida*. It was a 12-hour trip by foot. The next day, he walked to Akron.

In the twilight of his years, the aging pedestrian bemoaned the rising number of automobiles on Ohio's roads. He had been knocked down three times by inconsiderate motorists who had ventured too close. "It's getting increasingly hard to be a walker in these days," he said with a sigh.

Potter kept his regimen going until he could walk no longer. In December 1938, he caught a bad cold. At least, that's what he guessed it was. He wasn't sure because he rarely got sick and had suffered only two minor colds in the past 60 years.

But this illness wouldn't go away. It got worse. Potter finally was admitted to Akron City Hospital, where doctors diagnosed pneumonia.

It was too late. Nothing could save him. Not even oatmeal. Potter was 81 years old when he died on Dec. 23, 1938.

Mourners, young and old, packed the Eckard funeral home on East Market Street for the memorial service. Six local journalists served as pallbearers.

Then the Akron philosopher's casket was loaded into a hearse for the short trip to Hillside Memorial Park in Ellet. After all that walking, Orlando Nelson Potter was finally traveling by automobile.

That'll Be the Day

MUSIC LEGENDS PACKED AKRON ARENA IN 1950S

(Originally published Oct. 8, 2001)

Rock 'n' roll shook the walls and rattled the rafters at the Akron Armory. During the 1950s, the cavernous building on High Street was home to some of the greatest concert bills in rock history.

It's where Buddy Holly courted Peggy Sue, Fats Domino climbed Blueberry Hill, Chuck Berry saluted Johnny B. Goode and Jerry Lee Lewis felt a whole lot of shakin' going on.

Goodness gracious, what a great place to see a show. Former Akron disc jockey Alan Freed and rock promoter Irvin Feld brought star-studded revues to the downtown arena. The concert bills were packed with musicians destined for the Rock and Roll Hall of Fame.

One unforgettable show was on Oct. 14, 1958, when Buddy Holly and the Crickets headlined. It was the group's third show at the armory in 13 months, and the only time Holly received top billing in Akron. Four months later, the 22-year-old singer was killed in an Iowa plane crash.

"As I think back, it was probably the most exciting concert I've ever attended," says Tom Woodliff, 62, of Akron's Ellet neighborhood. "Probably, I suppose, because it was my first."

Also on the bill were Clyde McPhatter, Frankie Avalon, the Elegants, Bobby Darin, the Olympics, Jack Scott, Dion and the Belmonts, Jimmy Clanton, Bobby Freeman, the Danleers and Little Anthony & the Imperials. The Coasters and Duane Eddy were last-minute additions.

Yes, they all performed on the same night. In fact, they performed twice: at 7:30 and 10 p.m. And tickets cost only $3. "Concerts were much different then as opposed to now," Woodliff says. "The performers simply went on stage and sang. There were no sideshows, no fireworks, nothing but the music itself."

Everything ran like clockwork. The entertainers hit the stage, played their hit songs, then exited the spotlight, only to be replaced by the next act.

The armory stood from 1918 to 1983 on a site now occupied by the Ocasek office building. It had seating for 3,000 and needed every bit for the Holly concert. The historic event received little notice in the Akron Beacon Journal, though. The paper thought rock 'n' roll was merely a fad.

"Boy, I sure remember that concert," says Becki Besozzi of Copley. "I was three weeks shy of my 13th birthday and my friends Margie and Lorna McDavitt and I saved our allowances for those tickets.

"It was our first concert and probably the latest we were ever allowed to stay out without adult supervision."

Former Akron resident Bob Keller, 53, of Calhoun, Ga., remembers begging his parents to let him see the concert when he was 10½ years old. "My stepfather knew people at WAKR radio and he got tickets," Keller says. "One drawback: My mother was going to accompany me. So with my new white bucks on and my mom in tow, off we went."

Irma Keller was from the swing era, but she liked rock 'n' roll, enjoyed buying 45s and was a fan of Elvis Presley. "I don't know who had the better time," Bob Keller says. "She bragged till Christmas about what a great time she had, and my friends thought I had the coolest mom in Akron."

Karen Houlahan, 58, of Aurora, still has her program and third-row ticket stub. "When I think of all the concerts I've been to since then, there's no comparison," she says.

Although it has been more than 40 years, memories of the armory show are still vivid. "Frankie Avalon sang *DeDeDinah*, Bobby Darin did *Splish Splash*, Jimmy Clanton crooned *Just a Dream*," Besozzi says.

Woodliff was amazed by a talented guitarist who wasn't even advertised on the bill. "Duane Eddy brought the house down with his music," he says. "The walls were shaking and everyone was caught up in it."

The crowd cheered as Buddy Holly belted out such tunes as *That'll Be the Day*, *Peggy Sue* and *Oh, Boy!* "It made you speechless," Houlahan says. "It was just wonderful."

Woodliff recalled several girls getting up on stage with Holly and dancing while he performed. "It looked for a while as though the concert might get out of hand, but fortunately the authorities stepped in and everything turned out all right," he says.

Joyce Evans, 58, of Suffield Township, was fortunate to meet some of the stars that night. She and her sister Barbara got to go backstage because their father, Akron police officer Paul Morgan, was helping with security.

The musicians were milling around, chatting with one another and waiting to perform. The sisters were surprised at how personable the celebrities were.

"They took time to talk to you," Evans says. "Even though my sister and I were just teenagers, they were nice. I guess the best way to explain it was they were normal."

Evans recalls approaching Avalon and asking him to sign her autograph book.

"The big thing was Frankie Avalon wished me luck and kissed me on the cheek," she says. "I told all my friends I wasn't going to wash my face forever. That was a big deal when you're 13 or 14 years old."

Avalon impressed more than one girl that night. After the concert, Besozzi and her friends went behind the armory to the celebrity buses and collected autographs. "Frankie Avalon held my hand from the bus window while we talked about heaven only knows what," she says.

When the crowd broke up, Officer Morgan took his daughters for a bite to eat at the Western Drive-In. Diners got an unexpected thrill when Eddy, Clanton and some of the others arrived. "They came walking in, sat in the booths and ordered, and acted like everybody else did," Evans says.

All heads turned when a lanky Texan entered the room. "I remember Buddy Holly coming because he

Buddy Holly and the Crickets headlined a memorable concert at the Akron Armory on October 14, 1958.

had those big, thick glasses and kind of a floppy hairdo," Evans says. "I remember when he came in, some of the girls calling out his name."

Sadly, Akron never got to see Buddy Holly again.

The young star was killed Feb. 3, 1959, in a plane crash that also claimed the lives of Ritchie Valens and the Big Bopper. "It was sad that Buddy and the others were killed," Woodliff says. "I think his innovative style would have influenced rock 'n' roll even more had he lived.

"I am grateful that I did get to see him, though. It's not often a person can say they watched a legend in action."

Driving Around With Buddy Holly

(Originally published Oct. 8, 2001)

William C. Mallardi didn't get to see Buddy Holly's concert, but he was in attendance for a most unusual encore. "I actually picked up Buddy Holly and the Crickets in my car and took them out to supper," the 64-year-old Barberton resident says.

The chance encounter took place in April 1958, before Holly became the headliner at the Akron Armory. Mallardi, then 21, and his cousin Jerry Morrison wanted to go to the show but didn't have tickets. So they drove around the block in Mallardi's 1953 Plymouth while the concert was in progress.

"I saw four dark figures struggling down the sidewalk," Mallardi says. "Three of them were carrying guitars and the poor drummer was actually carrying his own drum kit. It was all banded together."

Mallardi recognized the quartet. He pulled his car over on Broadway, had his cousin roll down the window and shouted: "Hey, Buddy Holly, is that you?"

Yes, it was. The musicians explained that they were trying to find the Anthony Wayne Hotel on Main Street, Mallardi says.

"Would you like a lift?" Mallardi asked. The band accepted. "They were nice, polite young men," he says. The drum kit fit in the trunk but the guitars did not.

"Buddy stood on the curb and he handed in the guitar cases to the Crickets (Jerry Ivan Allison, Niki Sullivan and Joe B. Mauldin). They're all three of them in the back seat and they're piling the guitars on their knees."

Holly got in the front seat with Mallardi and his cousin. "I was on such a natural high that I had Buddy Holly and the Crickets in my car that I couldn't feel the seat," Mallardi says.

As they drove, Holly asked: "Do you know anyplace this time of night where we could get something to eat?"

He suggested the Capri restaurant on North Main, famous for spaghetti and meatballs.

"So Buddy says, 'Bill, if you'll take us, I'll buy your and your cousin's meal,'" Mallardi says.

The musicians dropped off their instruments at the hotel and Mallardi took advantage of the once-in-a-lifetime situation. He told Holly about a song he wrote at age 14 titled *I Want a Girl*, then proceeded to croon a few bars to the band.

Mallardi says the reaction was: "That's not too bad." The musicians gave him their manager's business card and later autographed the back of it.

Soon the men were feasting on $1.89 spaghetti at the North Hill restaurant. "We sat down at a great big round table that held all six of us," Mallardi says. "About 10 feet away, there was a jukebox. I went over and played *That'll Be the Day*."

No other customers were in the restaurant, but a waitress was excited to meet the musicians and had them sign a menu.

After dinner, Holly picked up the tab, Mallardi says. "So we all got back in the car, drove across the viaduct, got back to the hotel, got out and shook hands all around," he says. "They went up to their rooms and we left."

The tale has one postscript. Mallardi mailed sheet music for his song to Norman Petty, Holly's manager, in Clovis, N.M. Weeks later, Petty's office sent a rejection note, saying the tune wasn't commercial enough.

Mallardi's dream of being a rock singer was shattered, but his brief career was memorable. Not many local residents can claim to have sung to Buddy Holly.

A Way With Words

AKRON SPELLING CHAMP LEARNS COLD REALITIES AT NATIONAL BEE IN 1936

(Originally published May 21, 2000)

MacNolia Cox thought it was fun to read the dictionary. Yes, fun.

She started with "A" and worked her way to "Z," learning words, definitions and spelling. Especially spelling. It was her favorite hobby—along with reading and studying, she said.

Shy, soft-spoken and sweet, MacNolia was a typical 13-year-old in most regards. Typical, that is, except for those frequent comparisons to boxer Joe Louis, track star Jesse Owens and singer Ethel Waters.

After MacNolia won the Akron district spelling bee in 1936, Summit County residents held her in the same regard as other famous black Americans.

MacNolia, an eighth-grader at Colonial School in Kenmore, was the first black to win the Akron contest and the first to go to the National Spelling Bee in Washington, D.C.

Her Akron triumph was a stunning achievement, particularly when weighed against the times. Only a decade earlier, four members of the Ku Klux Klan had been elected to the city's school board.

More than 3,000 people filled the Akron Armory for the district bee on April 22, 1936. The 2½-hour contest featured 51 children from across Summit.

Tension filled the air as the spellers took the stage and dissected word after word. One by one, the contestants fell. Some youths cracked under the strain, breaking into tears after being eliminated by a misspelling.

With relative ease, MacNolia spelled daft, writ, pretentious, brusque, abstemious, gradate, felicitate and apoplexy. Finally, there were only two contestants left on the stage: MacNolia and St. Vincent student John Huddleston, 14.

The two dueled back and forth, but John finally tripped up on sciatic and MacNolia got it right. The Armory crowd roared with approval when she spelled voluble to win the bee.

MacNolia would represent Akron at the national bee on May 26, 1936. "I'm glad I won, and I hope I win in Washington," the shy girl, smiling broadly, told the Beacon Journal.

The teen won $25 and a trip to the nation's capital. Before the journey, she received one more reward: She was the honored guest of composer Fats Waller and dancer Bill "Bojangles" Robinson for a concert at the RKO Palace Theatre in Cleveland.

When it came time to leave for D.C., MacNolia was surprised to find thousands of well-wishers gathered at Union Depot. The crowd cheered and clapped while a military band played tunes in the girl's honor.

Accompanying MacNolia on the trip were her mother, Mrs. Alberta Keys, her teacher, Miss Cornelia Greve, and Beacon Journal reporter Mabel Norris.

"This is the most fun I've ever had in my life," MacNolia said as she boarded the train for D.C. Unfortunately, the teenager was about to learn some cold realities about life in the 1930s.

When the train arrived at the Maryland state line, MacNolia and her mother were forced to move to the black-only car. Because Washington was a segregated city, she and her mother had to stay with Dr. T. Edward Jones, a black surgeon, while other district spelling champs stayed in a hotel.

MacNolia and her mother weren't allowed to use the main elevator when they arrived at the spelling bee banquet. They had to climb a back stairwell. Then when they got to the banquet hall, they were relegated to a table at the side of the room—apart from other spellers.

Despite all of the distractions, MacNolia kept her poise when the competition began and stood tall while other spellers fell by the wayside. She exuded confidence onstage and it appeared that a victory was ahead.

But the dream exploded. It can never be proved whether the judges, mostly white Southerners, set out to knock MacNolia from the bee. But the fact remains that she was blindsided by a word that wasn't on the approved list.

Although MacNolia had memorized 100,000 words, Nemesis wasn't one of them. Nemesis, the Greek goddess of vengeance, was a proper noun in MacNolia's dictionary, and capitalized words weren't supposed to be in the bee.

She gave it her best attempt, but fell short with "Nemasis." Although Norris raised a fiery protest, the judges ruled that Nemesis, through popular usage, was an acceptable word that meant "fate."

It was over. Akron's spelling champ finished fifth in the nation and won a $75 prize.

Upon returning to Akron, MacNolia was delighted to find a parade in her honor. Hundreds of autos joined in the procession from Union Depot to Colonial School, where dignitaries made speeches and bestowed congratulations on the young celebrity.

"This is just the beginning for her," said Arlena Bauford, president of the Akron chapter of the National Council of Negro Women. "She has demonstrated what she can do, and what we, as a race, can do."

The future looked bright, but MacNolia never made it to college as many had hoped for her. "My grandmother, though she would've loved to have sent my Aunt Mac to college, unfortunately was unable to do so," said MacNolia's niece Georgia Gay. "And back during those times, they were not too willing to give out grants and scholarships to those of us of color."

MacNolia grew up, got married, raised a son. She had the brains to be a doctor but settled for being a domestic employee of an Akron physician.

"She had the potential, but it was never realized. . . . It is sad. It is very sad," Gay said.

MacNolia Cox Montiere died of cancer on Sept. 12, 1976. Her obituary proudly mentioned the 1936 Akron spelling bee victory.

Akron spelling champ MacNolia Cox, 13, meets composer Fats Waller (left) and dancer Bill "Bojangles" Robinson on May 4, 1936, at the RKO Palace Theatre in Cleveland.

Over the years, Akron has produced five national spelling champs: Dean Lucas (1927), Alma Roach (1933), Clara Mohler (1935), Jean Chappelear (1948) and William Kerek (1964). MacNolia Cox isn't on the official list, but she's still considered a champion in Akron.

That First Hill

ORIGINAL RACERS RECALL 1934 SOAP BOX DERBY ON TALLMADGE AVENUE

(Originally published July 20, 2009)

That first hill was a real doozy. Just ask the guys who raced down it 75 years ago.

In the summer of 1934, nearly 300 boys competed in the inaugural Akron Soap Box Derby on Tallmadge Hill. More than 30,000 spectators packed the red-brick slope on East Tallmadge Avenue (now West Avenue) just east of Brittain Road.

The Aug. 3 race was open to boys age 6 to 15 in homemade cars. The crowd surged and cheered as daring kids zoomed by in the strangest-looking vehicles ever cobbled together.

Children built rickety cars from orange crates, toy wagons, baby carriages and other parts salvaged from attics and cellars. "They were made out of anything we could get our hands on," recalled retired toolmaker Mike Politz, 89, of Cuyahoga Falls. "Wagon wheels. Scraps of wood. We tried to make them look as closely as a racing car as we could."

Politz, who grew up on Tyler Street off Wooster Avenue, was 14 when he entered the derby. In his father's garage, he sawed a wood frame, stretched canvas across it and painted it blue. "In those days, I called my race car a 'chug,'" he said.

He designed a primitive brake that dragged a pad on the ground when he stomped on a pedal. It took a while, but the wagon wheels eventually slowed.

When the chug was complete, Politz took a white-knuckle test drive down old Tallmadge Parkway near Portage Country Club. "My dad followed me down the hill in his car, and when I rolled to a stop, he said that I reached 60 miles an hour," Politz said.

A carnival atmosphere prevailed on race day. At the top of the hill, vendors sold hot dogs and hamburgers for a nickel apiece. Spectators brought chairs, climbed trees and scaled billboards. The crowd stretched as far as the eye could see.

Goodyear athletic director Ed "Chief" Conner served as the official starter, while Chevrolet district manager Fred Wieland waved a checkered flag at a blue-chalk finish line.

Races were held from 2 to 8 p.m. Friday. WTAM radio announcer Tom Manning provided live coverage of each heat.

Unfortunately, the chug didn't live up to expectations. "There were three cars in the race, and I came in last," Politz said. "I don't know what was wrong with it. It just didn't go fast enough, that's all."

As a consolation prize, Politz's father treated his son to a Coca-Cola at Leon's restaurant at Brittain and Tallmadge. "Even though I didn't win a trophy, my memories are worth far more than a trophy," he said. "I enjoyed myself very much."

West Akron stockbroker John Trecaso, 86, is another racing pioneer. He remembers when he and his older brother Joseph built cars at their home on Oakland Avenue on North Hill. "My father had a grocery store right near Temple Square," Trecaso said. "My brother and I went down in the basement and we saw this plank that my father used to take outside to put his vegetables on. Unknown to him, we took it, cut it in half and made two Soap Box Derbies."

For auto bodies, the boys took thick fabric and painted it white. John, 11, attached cart wheels to his racer while Joseph, 12, used buggy wheels.

Some drivers wore leather helmets borrowed from the Red Peppers football team. After Trecaso won his first heat, someone handed him a cloth helmet that looked like an aviator cap. "It couldn't help you," he said. "It just made you look good."

Tallmadge Hill was steep. The race didn't start at the top because organizers feared the kids would roll too quickly. Some boys, like Trecaso's brother, still lost control.

"He crashed into the crowd," Trecaso said. He recalled watching worriedly from the slope as Joseph drove off the road below. Fortunately, no one was hurt.

The 1934 race was the Trecaso brothers' only derby run. "We built another one, but we didn't race it," he said.

Springfield Township resident Leroy Quinn, 83, a former machinist and truck driver who grew up on Old Home Road, was only 8 when he first raced.

His uncle, a Goodrich supervisor, helped him build a car with a wood frame and aluminum body. The white vehicle had rubber tires, a hand brake and a picture of Popeye. "You just squeezed in, and that was it," he said. "If you turned over or anything, you couldn't get out."

Quinn remembered wearing a helmet and sitting in his car at the starting line when a sudden downpour drenched him. "We were soaked," he said.

The little boy was a big competitor. He won several heats on Tallmadge Hill, but he regrets not capturing a title. "I should have won it, but what happened, I done a stupid thing," Quinn said. "When I got down close to the finish line, I turned around to see where the other cars was. They were behind me. When I turned around to look, I started weaving. That's how I lost it."

New Franklin resident Jim Hendrickson, 85, a former body shop worker, painter, truck driver and pattern maker, is Quinn's cousin. He grew up in East Akron and was 10 years old when he built his 1934 derby car.

He fashioned a frame out of a 6-foot plank, attached a sheet-metal body and painted it red. "I had baby buggy wheels on it," he said. "I put the little ones on the front and the big ones on the back so I'd be going downhill all the time."

There was a 250-pound limit, so he drilled holes in the back of his car and filled it with sand to bring it up to weight and make it go faster.

He was one of the few boys to test the course before the race. It was a family effort, really. "We went out to Tallmadge Avenue," he said. "My grandfather and my uncle stopped all the traffic . . . and I went down Tallmadge Hill and tried that car out before we ever raced."

On the big day, Hendrickson won heat after heat. Although it was fun to race, he enjoyed going up the slope, too. "The greatest thrill of all in the first year was to come back up the hill after you won a heat," he said. "A motorcycle cop towed you up. He gave you a rope and you held on in the car."

Young racers wait their turn near the top of Tallmadge Hill during the first Akron Soap Box Derby on Aug. 3, 1934. Located east of Brittain Road on East Tallmadge Avenue, the red-brick hill served the derby for two years until Derby Downs opened near Akron Municipal Airport.

Hendrickson made it to the finals and finished in fourth place. He still owns the silver loving cup that he won that day.

Charles Baer, 11, won the 1934 race. Rubber executive Charles W. Seiberling presented a $50 check and trophy to the boy. "I'm going to spend the $50 to get my mother some false teeth," Baer announced. The crowd roared.

Baer won a trip to Dayton, the 1933 birthplace of the derby, to compete in the All-American Soap Box Derby. The following year, the national derby moved to Akron's Tallmadge Hill.

In the 1935 Akron race, Hendrickson finished second while Quinn was third. Winner Loney Kline advanced to the All-American, where he placed third.

The derby abandoned Tallmadge Hill after Derby Downs opened in July 1936. Many of the Tallmadge racers competed for several years at the new track. "It was nice. It was better," Quinn said.

Still, the racers look back fondly at the red-brick hill where they got their start. "It was a great time in my life," Hendrickson said. "I'll never forget it."

Poor Lost Souls

HISTORY OF SUMMIT COUNTY INFIRMARY BURIED DEEP IN PAST, BUT CLOSE TO HOME

(Originally published May 18, 2009)

Grass grows in unusual patterns at Schneider Park in West Akron. In certain areas, the earth has settled into a curious grid of ridges and hollows. Some secrets are buried forever in Akron's past, but others lie just beneath the surface.

The 15-acre park off Mull Avenue is one of the last vestiges of a 230-acre farm where the Summit County Infirmary operated for 70 years. Today, the quiet neighborhood has tree-lined streets, upscale homes and well-kept lawns. In the 19th century, it was a shelter of last resort for the homeless, helpless and hopeless.

Originally known as the county poorhouse, the infirmary was a grim institution for destitute, elderly or disabled people who had no place else to live. Its residents, who were called inmates, were required to work on the farm if they were physically able. Mentally ill individuals were locked away in squalid quarters. Hundreds died there.

"Are you talking about the Graveyard Path?" asked Ralph Witt, 84, of Akron, who grew up on Delia Avenue. "That's the Graveyard Path. It cut through from Sunset View, across Schneider Park and came out on Crestview there."

When Witt was a boy, the park didn't exist. The land was a wild, muddy swamp, and some neighborhood children were afraid to go near it. "That's where they buried the people," he said. "I used to see some bones every once in a while. They were sticking out of the ground."

His childhood chum James Giffels, 84, of Fairlawn, who grew up on Avalon Avenue, remembers taking the shortcut to St. Sebastian in the late 1930s. "We used to walk through there and we'd see all this stuff," he said. "Somebody—I suppose kids—had dug up some of those graves. Everything was thrown all around."

In 1849, Summit County commissioners paid $3,953 for Joseph McCune's 150-acre farm at the southwest corner of West Market Street and Portage Path. The farmhouse and barns were remodeled to accommodate about 50 paupers. Over the decades, the county added buildings while buying more land.

In 1865, construction began on a $20,000 infirmary on the farm. Built from bricks made by pauper labor, the two-story edifice stood south of West Exchange Street near the present site of Westminster Presbyterian Church between Rose Boulevard and Mull Avenue.

The Gothic-style infirmary faced north and had wings to the east and west. Interior features included a front parlor, sitting rooms, bedrooms, dining areas, kitchens, pantries, closets and washrooms. Behind the building was an "insane department" with grated doors and cells.

At the opening ceremony in 1866, commissioners praised the building "as an ornament and an honor to the county and a mark on the exalted humanity and liberality of her people."

Two years later, inspector A.G. Byers begged to differ. In an 1868 report to the Ohio Board of State Charities, he described a hellish tour of the facility. "There were quite a number of filthy insane, idiotic and epileptic inmates," he wrote. A terrible stench permeated the entire building, he noted, and some inmates were kept outside in "rude board pens."

"In one, there was an insane man whose hip and knee joints were entirely anchylosed," Byers wrote. "He was entirely naked and performed locomotion by sliding about on his posterior with the aid of his hands. . . .

"In the other pen were four females, one a miserable driveling idiot, eating its own filth, and the other three insane. They were also all of them entirely naked, and their condition was indescribably pitiable." A director pledged to clothe the inmates after Byers left.

Conditions improved gradually at the infirmary. The county built additions to the main building in 1875, 1880 and 1887. Laborers built livestock barns, stables, butcher shop, blacksmith shop, greenhouse, icehouse, dairy and laundry. The farm was self-sufficient with grain from the field, fruit from the orchard and meat from the slaughterhouse.

Following a visit in 1890, the Akron Daily Beacon reported that everything was in order: "The grounds about the buildings are kept clean and neat and free from rubbish of every kind and the buildings are kept in excellent condition."

The infirmary's population fluctuated from a low of around 40 to a high near 215. Residents included widows, widowers, immigrants, alcoholics, amputees, social outcasts, disease sufferers, lonely hearts and lost souls.

When inmates died at the infirmary, they were buried in a potter's field. The size of the graveyard is unknown, but it must have held hundreds. At some point, the county expanded the burials to paupers who didn't live at the infirmary.

Akron's rapid growth led to the infirmary's demise. The city needed more land for housing. In 1915, voters agreed to sell the farm and build the Summit County Home in Munroe Falls.

Philip H. Schneider, director of the Central Associated Realty Co., submitted the winning bid of $301,879 to develop the "Sunset View subdivision."

The Akron Evening Times interviewed infirmary residents in May 1919 as they prepared to move to the new facility. Johnnie Pepples, 63, had lived at the infirmary since age 20 when he maimed a foot in an industrial accident.

"When I first came here, the days seemed like months and the months like years, and it seemed ages between springs, but now the time goes so fast that I can't keep track of it," he said.

John W. Leonard, 86, gave a wistful reaction: "I'll kind of hate to leave this old place. Must seem kind of funny, I know, but this has been the only home I've had for the last six years and I've grown sort of attached to it."

The $69,655 Summit County Home opened that month on 440 acres in Munroe Falls. Schneider tore down the old infirmary, mapped out roads and built fancy homes. Nearly every block was developed except for a swampy area where the infirmary had buried its destitute.

Some remains were to be exhumed and reburied in Munroe Falls. However, the later discovery of bones proved that the effort was far from exhaustive.

When Schneider died in 1935, he deeded the land to the city, which built a park in his honor.

In 1942, West Akron boys Lawrence Sues, Charles Menches, James Hamlin and Jack Jost look at a Schneider Park boulder dedicated to the memory of Philip Schneider, donor of the park.

Akron resident Charles Billow, 81, who grew up on Delia Avenue, remembers how he used to ride his sled down Mineola Avenue. "My dad always said: 'Be careful. Don't go down that hill too far,'" he said.

His great-grandfather, George Billow, founded the family business, Billow Funeral Home, which handled some of the burials at the infirmary.

Michael Elliott, reference assistant at Akron-Summit County Public Library, has pored over Billow's records, sorted probate documents and scanned death certificates in an ambitious effort to unearth infirmary history.

Over the years, several genealogists have contacted Elliott while trying to trace relatives who lived at the poorhouse. "That got me going and interested in the history of the infirmary," he said.

Elliott decided to reconstruct the infirmary cemetery. So far, he has documented 300 infirmary burials from 1908 to 1916, plus 156 deaths from 1867 to 1908.

"I think it will be a great resource for library patrons searching their family history," he said. "Although, to be accurate, it will never be 'done' due to the lack of complete records."

The Graveyard Path is reluctant to reveal its secrets. "Who knows how many deaths never got recorded," Elliott said.

Get the Drift?

AKRON PLOWED A LOT OF CASH INTO 1930 STREET CLEANER, BUT IT DIDN'T QUITE WORK OUT

(Originally published Dec. 12, 2005)

Akron officials hailed the machine as a white knight of the road. Critics called it a white elephant in the garage. Either way, it didn't quite work out.

In 1930, the city plowed more than $12,000 into the purchase of Snogo, a revolutionary vehicle that was guaranteed to clear Akron's streets after a winter storm.

The Snogo—pronounced "snow go," get it?—had more gadgets than a Swiss army knife. It was the finest two-auger, rotary, blower, plow, snorkel, chute, conveyor system ever bolted onto the cab of a truck.

Rube Goldberg couldn't have envisioned a stranger-looking apparatus, but Akron just had to have one.

You see, the previous winter had been rough. One bad storm dumped 6 inches of snow, burying Mayor G. Lloyd Weil in a mountain of complaints.

Although 50 men and 12 trucks worked virtually nonstop to clear drifts, downtown streets were still impassable 48 hours later. Something had to be done.

Service Director Fred R. Swineford called in heavy equipment the following year. The Akron Board of Control ordered the Snogo machine from Klauer Manufacturing Co. of Dubuque, Iowa. The vehicle cost $12,123 in taxpayer money—a whopping price during the Depression when every penny mattered. In today's dollars, the bill would amount to $134,000.

Swineford called the machine a good investment for the city, and said it "should pay the same rate of return to the public" as a piece of fire equipment.

The blower could throw snow a couple of hundred feet. The loader could fill a large truck in 45 seconds. Swineford predicted that overnight crews would have downtown streets cleaned before morning traffic.

City mechanics rolled the plow into a corner of the Johnston Street garage. The metal beast would slumber in its lair until a heavy snowfall lured it outside to feed.

It's sad to say, but Snogo starved that winter. Ohio was locked in a strange weather pattern. The scattered snow was seldom deep enough for the giant plow.

Mayor Weil's critics howled when a 3-inch snowfall snarled traffic for 24 hours. "Citizens learned, for one thing, that the snow cleaner is so highly efficient that it cannot function unless the snowfall measures 4 inches or more in depth," the Beacon Journal jeered Dec. 27, 1930.

"They learned further that the purchase of the snow cleaner drained the street cleaning department fund to such an extent that Henry Dreyer, superintendent, when faced with the task of swiftly cleaning the streets without the snow cleaner, did not have enough money in his department fund to hire extra men to do the work with shovels."

The mayor just couldn't win. Citizens weren't happy with the streets before the snowplow. Now they weren't happy with the snowplow.

Only a handful of taxpayers actually got to see their money at work. The weather was just too mild for "the white elephant." Over the next two years, Snogo emerged from the city garage exactly two times.

TWO TIMES?!?!?!

Former postmaster C. Nelson Sparks made the plow a campaign issue while running for mayor in 1931.

Coincidentally, Weil chose not to seek re-election for a third term. He spent the next year digging for gold in Arizona. There's probably an analogy there somewhere.

After Mayor Sparks took office in January 1932, he began to clean house. Snogo had to go.

"By and by, we shall have all the ancient and worthless things around city hall and the city departments wiped off the books," Sparks announced. "Then the people should keep a closer check on what's going on, so no more $11,000 pieces of equipment are bought."

The Akron City Council authorized purchasing agent Burt J. Hill to find a buyer for the barely used plow. The city of St. Catherines, Ontario, offered $1,000, but Akron considered that amount to be a little too low.

Akron auto mechanic Homer L. Binkley hops aboard the Snogo plow, the city's $12,123 weapon against drift-covered streets, in 1932. The well-oiled machine left the Johnston Street garage only twice over three winters. Mother Nature was quite the prankster. Akron Mayor G. Lloyd Weil took a little heat for buying a plow during the Depression.

So Hill approached Klauer, the Iowa manufacturer of Snogo. The company happily bought back its machine for a mere $2,500.

Another city would surely want the thing. These machines worked wonders in mountain communities. Akron lost $9,623 on the deal, but local officials were pleased to salvage some money from "obsolete equipment."

Sparks said the city street crews would operate just fine without the snowplow. Plenty of people were searching for work. "We will use hand labor if there is snow enough this winter to require clearing of the streets," he insisted.

Akron learned a valuable lesson about accountability that year. It also may have gleaned a little something about patience.

Mother Nature is quite a prankster. On the weekend that Snogo was shipped to Iowa, a big snowstorm hit

Akron. The city scrambled to hire hundreds of men to shovel Dec. 10, 1932, as the snowplow crept quietly out of town.

Workers toiled downtown as the mercury plunged to 16 degrees. It took a lot longer than 45 seconds to fill a truck with snow.

Street Superintendent Henry Dreyer was not too pleased. The drifts proved to be deep.

He filed a formal protest, saying the Sparks administration never should have sold Snogo because it provided "a very valuable service."

Alas, it was too late. Snogo was Snogone.

"Maybe you only used a piece of equipment like this once in several years, but when you need it, you really need it," Dreyer lamented.

It snowed all winter. And the next, too.

The Wolf Ledge

ONCE A SPOT OF NATURAL BEAUTY, AKRON LANDMARK IS BURIED IN THE PAST

(Originally published Jun. 9, 2006)

One of the most beautiful places in Akron's history is hidden deep in the crevices of a residential neighborhood. The Wolf Ledge, a natural ravine with 30-foot cliffs and a shallow cave, took centuries for nature to create and years for man to destroy.

Located south of East Exchange Street until the early 1900s, the giant rock formation was a marvel of erosion. A tiny stream—Wolf Run—had gnawed away at its sandstone base, carving out a rocky gulch that raced east to west.

The ravine began near present-day Spicer Street and extended all the way toward the Ohio & Erie Canal near Main and Cedar streets. The exposed ledge rose near Kling Street and cut across Allyn, Sumner and Sherman streets before descending near Grant Street.

Its jagged line followed a rough course between Power Street to the north and Cross Street to the south. In the 1880s, a wooden bridge was built over the chasm at Sumner Street.

"This ravine was a landmark of old Akron," local historian Cloyd R. Quine (1881–1967) remarked in a 1950 study titled *The Old Wolf Ledge*. "With its high, overhanging cliffs and cave, and the rippling brook, it was one of the town's most famous beauty spots."

The ledge and stream derived their name from the wolves that early settlers used to hunt in the vicinity.

One of the featured attractions of the ravine was a 20-by-8-foot recess at the base of a large outcropping. Area residents referred to it by several names, including Indian Cave, Under the Rocks and Old Maid's Kitchen (a name also bestowed upon Mary Campbell Cave in the Gorge Metro Park).

"Always the neighborhood children used it as their favorite playground and many were the Indian arrowheads turned up there by diligent searchers," Beacon Journal reporter Ken Nichols reminisced in 1957.

Kids liked to build bonfires outside the cave and scratch their initials into the soot-blackened walls. In the wintertime, they sledded on southern hills leading to the ledge and skated on Brown's Pond, a small lagoon formed by Wolf Run. In the summer, they enjoyed picnics.

Young adults visited the cave, too. They brought small kegs of beer purchased at the Wolf Ledge Brewery on Grant Street—better known as the Burkhardt Brewing Co. (and now the site of the Akron Board of Education Maintenance Building). The brewery was at the western end of the ledge, which, come to think of it, may not have been an ideal situation for safety.

It wasn't all fun and games, though. Four quarries operated along the ledge. The ravine's sandstone was used in the construction of downtown landmarks, including the Everett Building at Main and Market.

The rapidly growing neighborhood, primarily populated by German immigrants, was nicknamed the Wolf Ledge for the ravine that ran through it. Its general boundaries were East Exchange, Spicer Street, South Street and Washington Street (now Wolf Ledges Parkway).

"The district in recent times has often been called 'Goosetown,' but most Wolf Ledgers resent this term," Quine noted. "At most it should be applied to the district south of South Street which was settled by Platt Deutsch and Slavs, with a business center at South and Grant streets."

As Akron's population surged in the 20th century, the neighborhood began to diversify and lost its distinct flavor. A mixture of nationalities followed the streetcar line down Grant Street. More housing was needed to meet local needs. City officials began to murmur about all that available land along the ravine.

In 1915, Akron officials pointed out Wolf Run's "tendency to choke up with refuse and overflow onto adjoining properties" during heavy rains.

In 1916, the City Council proposed building a reinforced concrete bed for the stream.

No, that wouldn't suffice. In 1917, the city embarked on a $130,000 project to encase Wolf Run in a storm sewer.

Workers funneled the ancient stream into an underground pipe. After all those centuries, erosion would no longer be a factor at The Wolf Ledge.

As local development moved closer, more and more debris was tossed into the gully. Small sections were partially filled.

In January 1921, Akron officials proposed filling in the rest of the ravine to make "public playgrounds, athletic fields and recreation spots." The council voted unanimously to buy the land on both sides of the ledge.

Trucks began dumping fill dirt and other materials that summer. The cave disappeared, the quarries disappeared, the cliffs disappeared. Eventually, the ground was raised to an acceptable level.

Akron extended its streets and built new homes along four blocks in the neighborhood. Boss Park is among the landmarks situated over the site.

Today, there's a noticeable dip in the road on Sumner, Sherman and Allyn. That's about all that's left of the famous ravine. "Its course can be traced by the lowest ground to which the land slopes north and south between Power and Cross streets," Quine noted in 1950.

The Wolf Ledge is buried and forgotten. Here's the ultimate insult, though: Hardly anyone calls it by the correct name.

During an urban renewal project in the early 1960s, Washington Street was renamed Wolf Ledges Parkway.

Ledges? Wait a minute. It should be ledge! Too late. All the signs had been made.

In the early 1900s, icicles dangle from Akron's Wolf Ledge, a natural ravine that rose near Kling Street and cut across Allyn, Sumner and Sherman streets before descending near Grant Street.

"Someone apparently made an error," City Planning Department librarian Louise Morris explained in 1970. "That's the only explanation we have as to why the 'S' was added to the name."

Regardless of wrong or right, Akron residents have called it Wolf Ledges ever since.

This year, another big change is coming to the neighborhood. Spicer Village, a $32 million residential and retail development, is scheduled to break ground south of East Exchange and east of Brown Street.

That's pretty close to Akron's former beauty spot. If construction crews should stray a few blocks over, they just might hit something hard when they begin to dig.

Akron at the Movies

IN THE RUBBER CITY, CELLULOID HAS ALWAYS RULED

(Originally published May 3, 1999)

The Majestic Theatre doesn't look so majestic anymore. Its ticket booth and front entrance have been boarded up for years. Its movie marquee has been ripped away, leaving a patch of splintered wood. Its white tile facade is chipped and yellowed.

The weather-beaten exterior only hints at the chaos inside the red brick building on South Main Street in Akron. Debris is strewn everywhere. The roof's collapse was more than a decade ago, judging by the 20-foot trees that grow from the floor.

The theater's old stage is a moldering heap. The projection booth is long gone. It's an unseemly end to a theater that sparkled with Hollywood glitter from 1914 to 1953. After all, The Majestic is the theater credited with introducing the silver screen to the world.

Projectionist Harry C. Williams, in 1925, coated the South Akron theater's white-cloth screen with silver paint in an effort to better reflect the light of motion pictures. He also applied a silver paintbrush to the movie screen at the Norka Theatre on East Market Street.

The results were so satisfactory that other movie theaters adopted the technique. According to local history, the trend spread from Akron to the rest of the nation until the phrase "silver screen" came to symbolize Hollywood movies.

Summit County residents still remember The Majestic, although it was only a small, neighborhood theater that closed 46 years ago. In its day, The Majestic was a hallowed building, a place where factory-town reality evaporated into Hollywood fantasy.

It was not alone. The Palace. Loew's. The Colonial. The Strand. The Forum. The Allen. The Orpheum. The Liberty. The Ritz. The Rialto. The Ideal.

All were popular hangouts where children attended matinees on Saturday afternoons and young lovers had dates on Saturday nights. For 50 cents, a moviegoer could see a double feature, newsreel, cartoons and coming attractions—and still have change for popcorn, candy and a soft drink.

Most of yesterday's theaters are gone, but they still flicker in the minds of those who spent their youth there. Bob Taylor, 76, a Goodyear retiree, said the movies meant everything to him as a child. "Me and a buddy, Bob Hardy, wanted to say we sneaked into every theater in Akron—and we did," Taylor says. "There was an art to doing it downtown. We got in Loew's, The Palace, The Colonial. . . . At The Colonial, you had to climb the spouting and get on the marquee and then climb into the men's room and then go downstairs.

"The hardest one was Loew's. There was no way to get in except for the exit doors. When you opened the doors, the light would blind everyone inside and the ushers would come get you. They'd catch us and take us out."

Taylor remembers going with his friend to Loew's in 1933 to see *The Eagle and the Hawk*, a war movie starring Cary Grant and Fredric March. The boys arrived at 8:30 a.m. and didn't leave the theater until 9 that night. "We saw it five or six times," he says.

Taylor can trace motion picture history simply by recalling his visits to local theaters. "I saw the first talkie at The Strand: *The Jazz Singer* (1927) with Al Jolson," he says. "The first Technicolor I ever saw was at The Spicer Theatre—called *Becky Sharp* (1935) with Miriam Hopkins."

Summit County's introduction to movies occurred in the late 19th century. Inventor Thomas Edison's kinetoscope, a forerunner to the motion picture projector, made its Akron debut at the Palace Drugstore on Jan. 13, 1894.

Viewers cranked a handle on the peep-show machine and watched a short loop of film. The moving pictures featured such novelty acts as acrobats performing, couples dancing and, most famously, a man sneezing.

The flickering images were viewed as an idle amusement—no serious threat to the live entertainment offered at Akron's Grand Opera House, the Academy of Music and, later, the German-American Music Hall.

The first significant movie to be shown in Akron was an 1896 boxing match between "Gentleman Jim" Corbett and "Ruby Bob" Fitzsimmons in Carson City, Nev. The motion picture debuted in Akron on Aug. 3–4, 1897, at Columbia Hall on Main Street.

Former circus performer Achille Philion, who made Akron history by owning the area's first "horseless car-

Akron moviegoers flock to the Strand Theater on South Main Street in July 1947 to attend the world premiere of a 28-minute Warner Bros. feature about the All-American Soap Box Derby.

riage," opened The Unique vaudeville theater in 1905 at 115 S. Main St. On weekends, he began to show motion pictures, including *The Great Train Robbery*, the first film with a plot. That's why The Unique is generally credited to be the first motion picture theater in Akron. Philion closed the theater after two years, but it whetted public appetite for the new form of entertainment.

Soon thereafter, nickelodeon theaters began to crop up in downtown Akron storefronts. The word "nickelodeon" derived from the 5-cent cost of admission and the Greek word for "music hall." A pianist usually provided live accompaniment for the silent films.

Two of Akron's great theaters—The Colonial (1902) on East Mill Street and The Grand (1907) on North Main Street—started out as playhouses. They dabbled in vaudeville, but The Colonial evolved into a movie theater while The Grand turned into a burlesque house.

The Colonial at 48–50 E. Mill St. was a baroque theater with a gallery, lower floor and two balconies. The L-shaped building, which was decorated in gold leaf and ivory, had 1,600 seats. It provided 67 years of entertainment before closing in 1969. It was razed in 1970 to make room for Zion Lutheran Church's parking deck.

The Grand was a brick-and-marble theater built at 38–44 N. Main St. on the site of the Grand Opera House, which had been destroyed by fire in 1905. It never achieved the popularity or the longevity of The Colonial. By the time The Grand closed in 1930, it was primarily a strip club. The building was razed in 1934. Today, the site is a parking lot across the street from the Summit County Department of Human Services.

Movie theaters sprouted along downtown Akron's streetcar routes. Among the earliest were The National (1907), The Dreamland (1910) and The Waldorf (1912), all on South Main Street, and The Luna (1909) on South Howard Street. The Orpheum (1914) and The Strand (1915) soon joined crowded South Main.

In these film houses Akron residents first viewed silent-film stars such as Charlie Chaplin, Harold Lloyd, Mary Pickford, Douglas Fairbanks, Theda Bara, Buster Keaton, Lillian Gish, Rudolph Valentino, and Laurel and Hardy.

Akron Beacon Journal writer Ken Nichols (1911–1987), a famed chronicler of local history, was passionate about the city's old theaters. His 1968 master's thesis for the University of Akron is called "In Order of Appearance: Akron's Theaters 1840–1940." It features a prophetic quote from Maurice C. Winter, whose theater empire included The Norka (1910), The Bank (1911) and The Winter (1912).

"I believe it will not be long until every residence whose owner can afford it will have a room to show films for the benefit of the family," Winter told The Akron Times in 1913. It was an uncanny prediction of television, which decades later doomed many theaters.

When older Akron residents think of the golden age of Hollywood, their minds race back to downtown movie palaces, the theaters where *Gone With the Wind* and *The Wizard of Oz* were viewed for the first time in 1939.

"My favorite theater? I had fun at the Palace, but I went to Loew's a lot," said Romola Snook, 88, a former Akron piano teacher. "We'd also go to The Liberty and Orpheum. . . . The Colonial had plays on Saturday afternoons. . . . The Strand Theatre had a lot of movies from Europe. Some of them were operas. You could see an opera in a movie."

The Keith-Albee Palace, though, is of particular significance to Snook. "I took lessons from Kathryn Bernower, the organist for the silent pictures at the Keith-Albee," she said.

The Palace, which opened in 1926, was a beautiful 2,200-seat theater with an arcade entrance at 41 S. Main St. Its domed ceiling was decorated in ivory and gold. The spacious theater started out as a vaudeville house but was transformed into a movie theater. It closed in 1966 and was demolished four years later. Akron-Summit County Public Library's parking lot was built on the site.

Loew's Theatre, which opened in 1929 at 182 S. Main St., was—and still is—the most lavishly decorated theater in Akron. Now known as the Akron Civic Theatre, the castlelike interior boasts a ceiling with twinkling stars and floating clouds. The 3,400-seat Moorish theater also is adorned with statues, an ornate lobby grand staircase, balcony and the mighty Wurlitzer pipe organ that rises from the stage.

At Loew's and The Palace, Akron moviegoers were introduced to Humphrey Bogart, Judy Garland, Clark Gable, Betty Grable, Errol Flynn and Bette Davis.

Downtown Akron's theaters are fondly remembered, but local residents are just as nostalgic for the movie houses that were closest to home, the ones they walked to as children and gained a sense of independence from their parents. Most city neighborhoods had at least one movie theater. The smaller theaters often showed second-run features or B-movies, but that didn't seem to matter to popcorn-munching children at matinees.

Bernie Gnap, 50, a Barberton Historical Society member, will never forget his first trip to The Boulevard Theatre in Kenmore, where he grew up. He was only 2 years old in 1951 when he went to the Kenmore theater with his mother and sister to see the movie *The Blue Veil*, a film starring Jane Wyman.

Although he was young, he recalls the day vividly. "I was entranced by the movie—it was the first one I had ever seen," Gnap says. "I wanted to get into the movie. I saw these larger-than-life characters and I thought it was a dimension of reality that you could walk into. . . . I went running down the aisle toward the screen and my mother came running after me. The usher told my mother: 'Lady, PLEASE, control your son.'"

The Boulevard, which had been open for more than 40 years, closed in 1957. "I felt bad for it sitting here unused. It was neglected," Gnap says. "For years and years, it was boarded up. It was torn down and gutted in the '60s. I wish it were still here. At least we have the memories and can think back."

Gnap returned recently to the former site of the old theater on Kenmore Boulevard. A neatly landscaped park and gazebo stand on the lot between brick buildings.

He pointed out where the main entrance used to be, where the light bulbs blinked on the old marquee. He looked at the green grass and remembered the red, florid carpet that once covered the floor. He scanned the bricks of next-door buildings and looked for traces of pastel wallpaper that decorated the theater's walls.

And for the briefest of moments, Gnap was a 2-year-old boy again, running up the aisle and trying to climb into the fantasy world on a movie screen. "It wasn't just beloved by me," Gnap said of The Boulevard Theatre. "It was beloved by everybody who used to come here for entertainment. This was the place to come before television. This was the VCR of its day."

Many of Summit County's old movie theaters blinked out of existence in the 1950s and 1960s. Competition from television proved to be too much for some theaters. Many residents preferred to stay home to watch the free entertainment on their TV sets instead of going out to the movies.

Promoting larger screens and color technology, the movie industry responded with a variety of gimmicks to draw audiences. Moviegoers donned blue-and-red glasses to watch 3-D movies like *Bwana Devil* (1952) and *House of Wax* (1953) pop off Akron screens.

Carloads of families—and a few couples who didn't much care to see a movie—pulled into drive-in theaters such as The Gala, The East, The Ascot, The Summit, The Starlight, The Skyline and The Montrose.

Wide-screen formats such as CinemaScope, VistaVision and Panavision were used to showcase epic films such as *The Ten Commandments* (1956) and *Ben-Hur* (1959). Cinerama, an unusual format that used three movie projectors on a wide, curved screen, was also a brief craze.

Vincent Lauter, 93, the former owner of Barberton's West Theatre and Magic City Drive-In, has seen the novelties come and go. He built The West in 1947 and learned quickly that good service and a quality product are what kept customers coming back.

Of Slovenian ancestry, Lauter immigrated from Austria to the United States when he was nearly 8 years old. He grew up in Barberton and worked for 30 years in Akron's Western-Union office before getting the idea to build a 700-seat movie theater.

"I got 300 Slovenian families to buy stock in the West Theatre—most of them were naturalized citizens," he says. "I bought the land . . . it was just a swamp on the edge of Wooster Road there."

Lauter also received backing from a Slovenian-owned insurance company in Cleveland. "People helped me along," he says. "People were very nice.

"The whole thing cost $670,000—everything from the seats in the building, we got the very best of everything. We had a really up-to-date theater with all-marble entrances and marble in the restrooms."

Television took a bite out of business in the early 1950s, but Lauter stayed the course by offering a wide range of movies. "We were a second-run house," he says. "We had youngsters waiting for Disney pictures. We had movies for schools. In fact, I had Slovenian movies there. We'd have six or seven buses from Cleveland to see the Slovenian movies."

Lauter proudly paid off the theater's debt in 1978. He sold the movie house in 1994—and it's still in operation. "When I gave it up, I had spent 50 years at the theater," Lauter says.

The movie business has changed greatly since 1947—and not necessarily for the better, according to Lauter.

"The theaters today are mostly chains," he said. "They don't look after their customers. I used to greet everyone. I used to meet the people leaving to make sure everything was OK."

Multiplexes—corporate theater complexes that feature several movie screens and stadium seating—now rule the film world in Summit County and elsewhere.

Of the more than 80 indoor theaters built in the first half of the century in the county, only six are still operating as theaters: The Civic, The Highland, The Linda, The Lake, The West and The Park.

In the 1960s and 1970s, many old theaters were demolished, reduced to parking lots, forgotten. Other theaters found new uses.

The Ohio Theatre is now Hilarities comedy club in Cuyahoga Falls. The Nixon Theatre in North Akron was remodeled as a showroom for Liberty Harley-Davidson. The Alhambra Theatre in East Akron became Buckeye Surplus store. The State Theatre is now the bar section of trendy Treva restaurant in downtown Akron.

Yet the movie industry prospers, with the large multiscreen theaters built this past decade in Montrose, North Akron, Cuyahoga Falls, Green and Macedonia.

The movie industry took in a record box office of $7 billion last year in North America, a 9 percent increase over 1997. The accomplishment was achieved despite heavy competition from cable television, videocassette recorders, satellite dishes, DVD players and Internet technology.

After enough time passes—a few more decades, perhaps—lost theaters like The Palace, The Colonial, The Strand, The Majestic and The Boulevard will be forgotten by most.

By then, as difficult as it is to fathom now, Summit County residents will probably be nostalgic for the good old days of the 1990s, the golden age of multiplexes.

Under the Bridge

IT WAS A SHOCKING CRIME IN 1922. THE SEARCH DRAGGED ON AND THEN AN OUTRAGEOUS TWIST

(Originally published Sept. 30, 2002)

Anyone could tell that something dreadful had happened. The automobile had skidded across the road and smashed into the side of the iron bridge over the Cuyahoga River.

In the darkness, someone had hurled a 9-pound brick through the windshield onto the driver's side. The abandoned vehicle's engine was running; its headlamps were still on.

There were signs of a terrible struggle inside the car. Russell Palmer's ripped overcoat, crumpled hat and empty billfold were strewn about the front seat.

Outside, Palmer's car keys and other personal effects were found near the edge of the Gorge Bridge. On a support beam below, a blanket dangled like a shroud over the river.

It didn't take a vivid imagination to realize the horrible fate that Palmer had met. He had been robbed, killed and dumped in the river.

The infamous 1922 crime shocked the citizens of Akron and Cuyahoga Falls and baffled authorities in both communities. Who killed Russell Palmer?

Palmer, 30, secretary-treasurer of the Meadowbrook Country Club near Stow, was a World War I veteran and a member of a prominent family in Summit County. His father, Thomas J. Palmer, had served as state senator and county dog warden.

He and his wife, Helen, had been married for four years and lived on Yale Street in Akron with their 17-month-old daughter. Life was normal.

But it changed overnight. A charity dance on Feb. 4, 1922, kept Palmer working late at the country club. He telephoned his wife, Helen, about 2:45 a.m. "I'll be home soon," he said. He never got there.

Palmer was carrying $60 in dance proceeds when he left the club. A few hours later, a milkman spotted Palmer's crashed vehicle on the Gorge Bridge and called police.

Investigating officers quickly sized up the crime scene and peered over the edge of the bridge. A man-sized hole was visible in the thin ice below.

They used grappling hooks to drag the river. They exploded dynamite in the water. They called in professional divers from Cleveland.

Hundreds of spectators gathered over the next few days to watch the grim search. "You can say for me that I think the body of Russell Palmer is in the river and it will be found if it is there," Akron Chief Detective Harry Welch told reporters. "When it is found, then I'll make up my mind how it got there."

Summit Sheriff Pat Hutchison, though, developed a theory about the violent crime and reconstructed it for reporters. "Some hobo was standing at the north end of the bridge with the rock ready," Hutchison said. "He was going to smash it through the first car that came along, and that just happened to be Palmer's ...

"It went through the windshield and struck Palmer on the head. That sort of knocked him out and he zigzagged across the bridge and then scraped into the side of it.

"The hobo ran up to the car and Palmer put up a fight. He finally got pitched over the railing and went down through the ice."

A grappling hook pulled up a shred of cloth, but nothing more. Divers searched the cold water for weeks, but could not find Palmer's body, prolonging the agony for his grieving wife. Finally, the hunt was called off.

Surely the body would surface eventually. But months passed. And then years. Summit County courts officially declared Russell Palmer dead in 1929. His widow, Helen, collected $8,500 in life insurance. She raised their daughter alone until she met a gentleman who fell in love with her and proposed marriage.

Life got back to normal.

Until 1936. That's when a businessman in Tacoma, Wash., admitted being responsible for Russell Palmer's unfortunate demise 14 years earlier.

His name was Ross T. Cartier. He was a pharmacy owner who had been a respected member of Tacoma society until authorities caught him embezzling $1,500 from a post office in his store.

Cartier had fled to Arizona and was hiding under the assumed name of Ross Smith when police tracked him down.

He was a cocaine addict. He had tuberculosis. He had brought shame to his wife and two children.

As Cartier awaited trial in Tacoma, authorities realized that he didn't seem to have any record before 1923. They pressed further about his past, and that's when they discovered that sometimes dead men do tell tales.

"I am Russell Palmer," Cartier finally confessed.

The news went off like a bombshell in Akron, and with wrenching results.

"I would have to be convinced beyond all doubt," said Palmer's stunned former wife. "Russell is dead. I'm positive of that."

Thomas Palmer refused to believe as well. "The authorities will have to produce the man they say is my son or submit other absolute proof, before I will take stock in any identification," he said.

Photographs of Cartier did resemble Palmer, although the Tacoma man's hair had turned white. Fingerprints from Palmer's military records would confirm the match.

But Thomas Palmer was dead before the proof arrived. The despondent father shot himself in the head at his Akron office.

In October 1936, Palmer-Cartier-Smith was sentenced to two years in a federal penitentiary in Washington. As he headed to prison, he told reporters why he left Akron in 1922, but his rambling explanation didn't ring true then, nor does it now.

"I was held up and robbed on the Cuyahoga River bridge and thought I would leave town to avoid embarrassment, as people wouldn't believe the holdup story," he said.

It seemed Palmer had staged his crime scene so well that he accepted the fantasy as reality. He said he walked to the train depot that night, bought a ticket and rode out West.

He couldn't explain how a man who had just been "robbed" of all his money could afford a ticket. "Well, that's all in the past," he said with a shrug.

Police found evidence of robbery and murder in a wrecked automobile that was abandoned atop the Gorge Bridge between Akron and Cuyahoga Falls in 1922. Authorities searched this area of the Cuyahoga River for weeks to find the motorist's body. Meadowbrook Country Club official Russell Palmer called his wife to tell her he would be right home. He never got there.

On that, his ex-wife agreed. "So far as I'm concerned, Russell Palmer is dead and we're living a new life," she said. "Why don't you let me alone?"

The Beacon Journal has no further record of Palmer after his 1936 sentencing. In February 2003, he would be 112 years old.

It's a safe bet that he's dead. This time.

Edison: A Love Story

FAMOUS INVENTOR FOUND HIS MATCH IN AKRON

(Originally published Feb. 13, 2000)

Thomas Alva Edison toiled for years in his New Jersey laboratories, inventing electrical devices that changed the world and made him wealthy and famous. From a personal standpoint, however, he made his greatest discovery in Akron.

It wasn't the incandescent lamp. It wasn't the phonograph. It wasn't the motion picture camera. It was a love that lasted the rest of his life.

Mina Miller, the daughter of Akron industrialist Lewis Miller, was studying piano in Boston when she met Edison in July 1885. The 20-year-old student was introduced to the 38-year-old widower at a party held by their mutual friends Ezra and Lillian Gilliland.

Clearly smitten with the dark-haired woman, Edison journeyed a month later to see Mina at the Chautauqua Institution, which her father had co-founded a decade earlier in southwest New York.

Courtship blossomed into love along the tranquil shores of Lake Chautauqua. The inventor of the incandescent lamp melted like a wax candle in Mina's company. And she found his scientific genius to be most charming.

They met again in Boston and took a September trip to the White Mountains of New Hampshire. Edison, a former telegraph operator, taught Mina how to read Morse code during their journey.

Once she was proficient, he tapped out a message on her hand: "Will you marry me?"

She accepted—under one condition. Edison, one of the world's most famous men, still had to ask Lewis Miller for permission to marry his daughter.

In a letter dated Sept. 30, 1885, he wrote to the Akron millionaire: "Some months since, as you are aware, I was introduced to your daughter Miss Mina. The friendship which ensued became admiration as I began to appreciate her gentleness and grace of manner, and her beauty and strength of mind. That admiration has on my part ripened into love, and I have asked her to become my wife. She has referred me to you, and our engagement needs but for its confirmation your consent."

Not only did Lewis Miller approve of the wedding, he provided the setting.

Thomas Edison and Mina Miller were married Feb. 24, 1886, in Oak Place, the Miller family mansion that stands today on the hill overlooking Akron's Innerbelt.

More than 80 guests attended the ceremony, which the Akron Daily Beacon called "the most notable nuptials" in local history.

"The decorator's hand had wrought beautifully in every corner of the ample residence," the newspaper reported. "A floral ball was suspended over the foot of the staircase, and wreathed smilax on the brightly burning chandeliers, and bloom and potted plants gracefully placed lent beauty and fragrance to the scene."

The bride wore a white silk dress and a necklace of pearls and diamonds. The groom wore a black suit and tie. The Rev. E.K. Young, pastor of the First Methodist Episcopal Church, performed the ceremony at an altar in the mansion's parlor.

Afterward, well-wishers congratulated the newlywed couple as they stood under a giant wishbone of flowers in the house's library.

The couple honeymooned at Edison's winter home in Fort Myers, Fla., and then moved to Glenmont, a 23-room mansion in Llewellyn Park, N.J.

Edison had three children from his first marriage to Mary Stilwell, who died in 1884 of typhoid fever. He and Mina would have three more children.

Being married to the world's greatest inventor must have been a challenge. Edison was consumed with his inventions—for which he had 1,093 patents.

Needing little sleep, he sometimes worked more than 24 hours without a break. Mina Edison made sandwiches and coffee at 2 a.m. and delivered them to her husband and his lab assistants.

Edison was brilliant, eccentric, stubborn and occasionally irascible, but according to his wife, he "always remained the same genial, lovely man."

"There were no trials, there were no tribulations in being the wife of such a man," Mina Edison told the

Associated Press a few months before her death in 1947. "I can look back on those wonderful years and see nothing in them but compensation."

During their 45-year marriage, the Edisons regularly visited her family in Akron and his hometown of Milan, Ohio. "The Wizard of Menlo Park" became "Akron's favorite son-in-law."

The inventor worked until his final days, taking out a final patent only months before his death.

"He never gave a thought to whether his work would bring him fame or give his name a lasting place in history," Mina Edison said in 1947. "He was like other great men of genius who did what they did because there was in them some strange urge to do it."

Thomas Edison died at Glenmont on Oct. 18, 1931, at age 84. Three days later, electric lights across the nation were dimmed for 1 minute in his memory.

Edison bequeathed $40 million to his widow. She lived to be 83, dying on Aug. 24, 1947. They are buried behind their New Jersey estate, which is now a National Park Service museum.

In 1973, Edison was the first person inducted into the National Inventors Hall of Fame, then housed at the U.S. Patent and Trademark Office in Arlington, Va. In July 1995, the hall of fame debuted at Akron's Inventure Place—only a mile from the house where the world's greatest inventor discovered the power of love.

Mina and Thomas Edison visit his laboratory in 1906.

The Lizard Lady

YOUNG WOMAN'S DEATH IN 1910 WAS STRANGE NEWS INDEED, TOUGH TO STOMACH

(Originally published Dec. 8, 2003)

The strange case of Lovie Herman puzzled doctors for more than a decade. Many physicians examined the Akron native during her short, troubled life, but each diagnosis seemed to conflict with the previous one, and the treatments did little to comfort her.

The 20-year-old woman weighed less than 90 pounds even though she stood 5 feet 6 and had a hearty appetite. She suffered stomach pains, hemorrhages and occasional blackouts, and had great difficulty breathing. Her skin grew splotchy and her lips turned purple.

At one time or another, health experts suggested that the mystery illness might be tuberculosis or typhoid fever or heart trouble or a respiratory problem.

Or maybe it was something else entirely.

When Herman lost her struggle shortly after midnight on Dec. 9, 1910, the reported cause of death jolted the medical community and sent a shock wave through Northeast Ohio.

It was the stuff of nightmares.

Dr. Alex J. McIntosh, Herman's attending physician, certified that his patient had succumbed "due to stomach trouble caused by lizards in the stomach poisoning the entire system."

Newspaper reporters snapped to attention. Did he say lizards? "There is absolutely no question about the lizards being found in the girl's stomach, for I have the two largest ones preserved in a bottle in my office," McIntosh said. He also reported finding a batch of eggs in a tiny ball.

The green reptiles had been in her system a long time, he said. Herman's family told him that she had taken a dip in a "cool, refreshing spring" near Millersburg a dozen years earlier, and it must have been there that the girl accidentally swallowed tiny lizards or possibly their eggs, he said.

A few days before Herman's death, McIntosh said he had given the woman a strong dose of medicine under the assumption that she was suffering from a tapeworm. That's when, he said, she could feel the reptiles "crawl up her throat."

"They are each 3½ inches in length," he said. "One lizard is as well formed as any I have ever seen. I also extracted several smaller lizards from Miss Herman's stomach, but I have kept only the two largest ones. The head, mouth and tail on both are to be plainly seen."

The weird tale sent the local media into a feeding frenzy. Bold headlines screamed out from the front pages. "Two Lizards In Stomach Cause Death," the Akron Beacon Journal reported.

"Live Lizards, For 13 Years In Girl's Stomach, Slowly Poison To Death," the Akron Press countered.

Lova J. Herman, known as "Lovie" to her family, had been sick since she was a child. She was treated at a Chicago sanitarium for suspected tuberculosis, but she wasn't cured. She then moved to Cleveland with her mother, Ellen, to be treated at Lakeside Hospital for suspected heart troubles.

McIntosh, a Cleveland physician, deduced that Herman was suffering from a parasite because of her abnormal appetite. After making the shocking discovery of the lizards, he said, he withheld food from his patient for a few days in an attempt to starve any remaining reptiles. Then he gave her another dose of medicine.

" . . . Miss Herman was thought to be improving, but at midnight Thursday she died in her mother's arms just after remarking that she thought she was going to recover," the Akron Press reported. Her body was transported to Akron for a funeral service at her brother Harvey Herman's home at 896 St. Clair St.

Seventeen doctors attended a postmortem exam at the house, including McIntosh, Summit County Coroner Harry S. Davidson, Dr. Clinton J. Hays of Akron, Dr. Edgar S. Menough of Cleveland and Dr. William S. Chase of Akron.

"The postmortem proved the previous diagnosis correct," McIntosh announced. "The lizards had eaten almost through the walls of the stomach and a few small ones as thick as a broom straw remained."

But he was quite alone in that professional assessment. Other doctors harrumphed loudly at his assertions.

Lizards can't live inside the human body, can they? In 1910, an Akron woman's strange death sent the local media into a feeding frenzy.

Davidson, who had grown up on a Jefferson County farm, had been skeptical from the start. "We found nothing in the stomach," he said. "The organ was in a congested condition, and the girl's heart was twice its normal size. The condition of her heart, I believe, was the cause of death."

An air-breathing reptile would suffocate in the stomach and couldn't escape the gastric acids, Davidson told reporters. "Dr. McIntosh at the postmortem failed to enlighten 16 other physicians present, except when we questioned him closely," he said. "The only thing I could see was that the stomach was inflamed and congested. That could be caused by the action of the heart."

Cuyahoga County Coroner Max A. Boesger agreed that lizards couldn't survive in a stomach for any length of time. "Tapeworms live inside the human body because that is their natural habitat," he said. "Lizards do not like being there."

Cleveland Health Officer Clyde E. Ford flatly refused the death certificate that McIntosh had written.

"I will not accept such a certificate because I do not believe that her death was caused by poisoning produced by lizards in the stomach," Ford said. "It is too absurd to discuss. It is simply impossible."

Eli and Ellen Herman trusted their daughter's doctor, though, and voiced support for him.

"Dr. McIntosh was too interested in Lovie's recovery and showed too much kind attention during her illness to invent any mythical story," Ellen Herman said. "We believe Dr. McIntosh in spite of Dr. Ford, Coroner Davidson or anyone else."

The family may have been on the doctor's side, but medical science was not.

Confronted with allegations that his claims were false, McIntosh held a closed-door meeting at Ford's Cleveland office on Dec. 13, 1910, and completely retracted his lizard story.

The Beacon Journal buried the headline "Lizard Story Fake" deep inside the paper.

Today, the lizard story is regarded as an urban legend, along with similar folk tales about snakes, frogs and other frightful creatures invading the human body and wreaking havoc.

Lovie Herman's 1910 death certificate can be found on file at the Ohio Historical Society in Columbus. The cause of death has been scribbled out.

NFL Revisits Akron

HOME TEAM'S STAY IS JUST ONE GAME AS HAPLESS, HOMELESS DALLAS TEXANS WANDER THROUGH IN 1952

(Originally published Nov. 25, 2002)

The Dallas Texans were a really bad football team. OK, that's not exactly true.

They weren't bad.

They were terrible.

Bumbling. Incompetent.

But for one day, and one day only, they were ours . . . ALL OURS!

Fifty years ago, one of the strangest games in NFL history took place in Akron.

Ohio, as you may have noticed, is not Texas. Nonetheless, through unusual circumstances, the Akron Rubber Bowl served as the home of a Dallas team on a bitterly cold afternoon.

It was Nov. 27, 1952.

Thanksgiving Day.

The bruising Chicago Bears faced the winless Texans. It was the NFL equivalent of the sand-kicking bully harassing the skinny kid at the beach in those old Charles Atlas ads.

The Texans had been homeless since the new franchise tanked a few weeks earlier in Dallas. Owner Giles Miller, a Texas millionaire, nearly lost his shirt when the Lone Star State turned its back on the team. He had expected fans to fill the Cotton Bowl to see his Texans play, but there was little interest from the beginning, and the constant losing didn't help.

Although the Texans had some good players, the team routinely lost games by 20 points. The Texans seldom scored touchdowns, rarely made field goals and often missed extra points.

After seven straight losses, Miller bailed out, and the NFL took over the foundering team, moving its base to Hershey, Pa. Remaining "home games" would be played in other cities. And that's how Akron landed its first NFL game since the Akron Pros had quit the league in 1926.

It was announced that the game would follow the City Series championship at the Rubber Bowl on Thanksgiving Day.

The Texans practiced Tuesday and Wednesday at Buchtel Field before a handful of spectators. There wasn't a lot to see.

"Those who came expecting to see a rock 'em, sock 'em scrimmage such as Akron U's Zips stage were disappointed," Akron Beacon Journal sportswriter Don Plath noted in 1952.

"Over near the goal post on the south side of the field, a group of about 20 players were involved in a volleyball game using the crossbar instead of a net."

Texans coach Jimmy Phelan put on a brave face for the press about his team's chances against the Chicago Bears. "If we don't make the silly mistakes we have been making all season, we'll give 'em a good rassle," Phelan said.

"We have been donating all season, and it's about time we started to believe in the old saying: 'Charity begins at home.'"

Of course, Phelan's team didn't have a home, but that was beside the point.

Legendary Bears coach George Halas said his team was ready for the challenge. "Our defensive unit looked real good last Sunday, and if our offense can show as well, we'll give Akron a top show," he said.

"Just forget the records of the last two teams and remember that both are hungry for a victory, and you can see why everybody connected with this game is expecting a rough battle."

An enthusiastic crowd of 14,284 fans turned out that chilly Thursday morning to watch as East beat South 26–19 in the City Series championship game.

Then, much to the NFL's chagrin, the crowd went home. It was Thanksgiving, after all. The turkey was waiting.

When the NFL game kicked off at 2:45 p.m., only 2,208 spectators were in the 35,000-seat Rubber Bowl. They sat shivering in the 20-degree cold.

Looking around at the empty seats, Phelan joked that there was no need to introduce the players over the loudspeakers: Athletes could go into the stands to shake hands with each fan.

When the Bears took the field, Akron sports fans got a pretty good preview of the Pro Football Hall of Fame—a full decade before it was founded.

Coach Halas, a future hall of famer, trotted out quarterback George Blanda, a future hall of famer. Teammates included linebacker George Connor and tackles Clyde "Bulldog" Turner and Bill George, all future hall of famers.

To top it off, former Bears great Harold "Red" Grange, a future hall of famer, was announcing the game, which aired on national television and radio.

The Texans' roster wasn't as stellar, but it did have bright spots. Frank Tripucka, the father of future NBA star Kelly Tripucka, was a capable quarterback. Defensive tackle Art Donovan and rookie defensive end Gino Marchetti were bound for the hall of fame, although the Texans had little to do with that.

The Nov. 27 game began, as expected, with the Texans falling behind. Bears player Don Kindt tackled halfback Buddy Young in his end zone for a safety: Bears 2, Texans 0.

But then things began to get interesting.

Tripucka marched the Texans down the field, and fullback Zollie Toth scored on a 3-yard run. Just before halftime, the Texans scored again on a pass to Dick Wilkins. After an extra point—yes, they made an extra point—the Texans led 13–2.

In the third quarter, the Texans found themselves in the totally unfamiliar position of being ahead 20–2.

That's when the Bears woke up. Blanda caught fire, throwing lightning bolts to his receivers. Chicago's vaunted running game began to find traction.

The Bears narrowed the gap to 20–9. Then 20–16. Late in the fourth quarter, the Bears finally leaped ahead 23–20.

On any other day, the Texans would have been cooked. But this was Thanksgiving, darn it, and this was Akron.

There was time for one last drive. Keeping his wits about him, Tripucka threw a series of precision passes, left and right, as if he were the future hall of famer. His supposedly hapless team tramped 73 yards to the Bears' 1-yard line.

Then, with 34 seconds left, Tripucka kept the football, vaulted over the Chicago defense and fell across the goal line.

If there had been more than 2,208 fans on hand, there might have been pandemonium, but the goal posts were safe this day.

Even so, the Texans did beat the Bears 27–23. For one glorious day in Ohio, the Texans weren't so bad.

The euphoria evaporated, of course. The Akron thriller was the only game the Texans ever won. The team ended the season with two embarrassing losses and a pitiful record of 1–11.

One week after the Akron game, the NFL announced that it had found a permanent home for the football franchise.

And guess where?

The team would move to Baltimore and be renamed the Colts. A football dynasty was in the making. By the end of the 1950s, the Baltimore Colts were champions of the NFL.

And Colts stars Art Donovan and Gino Marchetti, who had watched their team go from worst to first, got the last laugh.

Dining at Kippy's

TASTY MEMORIES OF A DOWNTOWN LANDMARK

(Originally published March 2, 2000)

You know the food is good when people are willing to stand in line to eat it.

Kippy's was a popular restaurant for more than 40 years in downtown Akron. It was open 24 hours a day, seven days a week, and packed in customers around the clock. If you were hungry, Kippy's was always there to serve.

Bob Heath was 19 years old in 1938 when he and his mother, Gail Heath, opened the restaurant at 103 S. Main St. The original Kippy's was below street level at the southeast corner of Main and Mill, across from the First National Tower. It was housed in the former Ptomaine Tommie's, a 1930s hamburg joint with a decidedly unappetizing name.

So who was Kippy? After all these years, the truth can be told: There was no Kippy. "It was just a name we made up," said Heath, 81.

He and his mother liked the sound of the word after getting the idea from Skippy, a newspaper comic strip in the 1930s. "We just dropped the 'S' and made it Kippy," Heath said.

The original menu was pretty simple: "Hamburgs, coffee, pie, chili, bottled pop, milk—that was pretty much it," Heath said. In the early days, Heath had to work 16-hour shifts. The restaurant was always open, but it only had three employees.

"I worked the grill, worked the counter," Heath said. "I did whatever had to be done: washed dishes, mopped the floor."

Kippy's had seating for 25—when you could find seating. "You'd have to stand and wait," said Clara Anderson, 79, of Cuyahoga Falls. "It was a treat to go to Kippy's to get a hamburg and french fries."

Anderson's husband, Bernard, worked at Kippy's as a cook in the early 1940s, earning $18 a week, she said. "That was big bucks for us," she said. "$4.50 paid the rent."

Heath expanded Kippy's menu—adding steaks, chicken and a complete breakfast line—and expanded his family, too.

He was managing the Spotless Spot restaurant on Arlington Street when he met his future wife, Ginger, a waitress he had hired. "He couldn't fire me, so he married me," she said with a laugh. The couple have been married 61 years and are the parents of Robert Jr. and Sandy.

In 1947, Heath moved Kippy's to more spacious quarters at 45 S. Main St., the former home of the Continental Grove lounge. That restaurant had seating for about 100, including a curved counter with room for about 50.

The huge counter snaked through the restaurant. "It's a good way to utilize a narrow building," Heath explained.

For decades, customers gulped down Kippy Burgers, Biggy Burgers and Finger Lickin' Chicken, washing the meals down with milkshakes and soda.

"Have a flirtation with a Kippy creation," one advertisement read. "Freeze your teeth and give your tongue a sleigh ride," a milkshake slogan suggested.

The new Kippy's was a good place to do some star-gazing. Big-name performers—from Dick Haymes to Patti Page to the Ames Brothers—could be spotted in the restaurant, grabbing a bite to eat before or after their shows at the Palace Theatre.

Heath, who also was a professional boxing promoter, brought many famous fighters to town, including Sugar Ray Robinson, for bouts at the Akron Armory.

Another side business was Heathco Adjustable Awning, which the Heaths operated from 1950 until its closing this year.

If all of that wasn't enough to keep the Heaths busy, Kippy's turned into a restaurant chain.

In 1940, Kippy's opened a restaurant at 2100 Front St. in Cuyahoga Falls. It moved across the street in 1946 and remained there another 38 years.

Kippy's opened at Arlington Plaza in 1966 and Norton Center in 1972. Each restaurant proved to be an instant success.

"The minute we opened, they just packed the place," Ginger Heath said.

"Every location we opened," Bob Heath agreed.

Kippy's had peak employment of about 130 workers at its four restaurants, all of which were open 24 hours. "We were always able to get excellent, excellent employees," Heath said. "You can't do it on your own."

"They were just like part of the family," Ginger Heath said.

Rita Ventrone, 72, of Akron, worked at the downtown Kippy's from 1950 to 1969—first as a waitress, then as a manager. "It was just a nice place," she said. "I waited on people who would come in with their children and, years later, those children would come in with their children."

The service industry was different back then, she said. "You knew everybody," she said. "You knew all the customers . . . Service is nothing today. It's tips, tips, tips today."

She remembers huge crowds of teens after high-school football games at the Rubber Bowl. "We had them lined up clear past Bear's Furniture, those kids," she said. Ventrone enjoyed the work no matter how busy it was. "I liked meeting people," she said. "I still do."

A 1956 Beacon Journal advertisement for Kippy's promises "a pleasant, comfortable respite" at the restaurant's locations in downtown Akron and Cuyahoga Falls.

The strain of running the restaurants was getting to be too much in the 1970s, Heath said. "The glamour was wearing off," he admitted.

The Main Street neighborhood was deteriorating. Competition from other restaurants was increasing. The building leases were running out. "It was a good time to call it quits," he said.

The downtown Kippy's closed in 1979 after its lease expired. Arlington Plaza and Norton Center followed suit in 1980. The Cuyahoga Falls restaurant, the last link in the Kippy's chain, closed in 1984.

Once open 24 hours, Kippy's restaurants were closed forever. "We've got a lot of good memories there," Heath said.

So do the people who dined there.

Rescue at Sea

BRAVE LITTLE GIRL BECAME GOODYEAR AIRCRAFT MASCOT
AFTER SURVIVING WWII TORPEDO ATTACK

(Originally published June 14, 2004)

Mary Ann Mayers was as cute as a button, an all-American girl with blue eyes, blond pigtails and a friendly smile. She wore dainty outfits and pretty ribbons, and liked to play with dolls and draw pictures with crayons. Don't be fooled by calico and lace, though. Mary Ann was plenty tough. She had nerves of steel.

The 8-year-old girl displayed great courage in World War II when a Japanese submarine sank her family's ship in the Java Sea. She and her parents plunged into the shark-infested waters and managed to stay afloat on a wooden oar. Although Mary Ann was wounded, she refused to cry.

Akron's Goodyear Aircraft Corp. couldn't have chosen a better mascot in 1942 than "the bravest girl in the Pacific."

The Massillon native, an only child, had moved with her parents, Ruth and W.M. "Mike" Mayers, to the Far East when she was 3½ years old. Mary Ann's father was manager of the Goodyear Orient Co. and supervised crude rubber purchases on Sumatra in the Dutch East Indies (now Indonesia). The family lived on Goodyear's Dolok Merangir plantation before moving to the Wingfoot Estate.

Now 71, Mary Ann Mayers Byrne, a resident of Mequon, Wis., has vivid memories of her early years on the island. "I learned the language a lot faster than my parents did, which is true of any child, I guess," Byrne said. "So I was jabbering in Javanese long before they knew what in the world was going on. I was the interpreter for a long time."

Other Goodyear executives and their families lived at the compound, an international community. "I had Dutch friends and Belgian friends and Swiss friends and English friends," Byrne recalled.

In the fall of 1941, her father was transferred to Singapore, but the family didn't live there long. When Japan attacked Pearl Harbor on Dec. 7, it simultaneously bombed Singapore. "Apparently there had been rumors around Singapore," Byrne said. "I remember my dad saying that his Japanese barber had been very, very nervous a week before that."

Sirens blared. Bombs exploded. The Mayers family scrambled into a bomb shelter. "I vividly remember that night and the planes going over," Byrne said. "It could have been scary, but my parents made it a very secure situation."

For at least six weeks, the bombings continued, Byrne said. When it became clear that Japan would seize Singapore, Mayers fled with his family to Java.

In the town of Surabaja, they booked passage on a Dutch ship named the Van Cloon. Built in 1912, it was an old rust bucket, a 4,519-ton vessel that creaked. "It was a very disheartening thing," she said. "I remember my parents saying that it was horrendous to think you'd be crossing an ocean in something like that, but then we got onboard."

The ship was launched at midnight Feb. 6, 1942, with 120 passengers and crew members. It traveled west toward Ceylon (Sri Lanka), but didn't even get close. Before breakfast, the crew held a safety drill. Mike Mayers was handed a rotting life vest.

"One of the Dutch officers jokingly said, 'Well, I certainly hope you know how to swim,'" Byrne said. Hours later, as passengers relaxed on the sunny deck, a dull thud was heard. The ship's siren shrieked. A Japanese sub had surfaced and was firing shells over the ship.

"The captain told everyone to stay low and sheltered and said that he had signaled to the submarine that we were unarmed and didn't have any cargo," Byrne recalled. "He was hopeful that they would just leave us alone. But they didn't."

As the shelling intensified, the Van Cloon's captain made a decision to abandon ship. The passengers rushed to the lifeboats.

The Mayers family climbed into a boat on the starboard side, but it tilted crazily when a sailor got tangled in a rope. The crew cut the cord, and the boat fell hard and swamped.

"Everyone was bailing," Byrne said. "My mother was using her purse to bail. I remember I was just frantic because my crayons and my little trucks that I liked to play with were in her purse. And those, of course, went to the bottom of the sea."

The gray submarine began to fire torpedoes. The Van Cloon exploded in flames. "The sub was firing at close range and we could see the crew," Byrne said. "My parents knew that we were going to be sucked down with the Van Cloon if we didn't swim away."

They eventually found refuge on a wooden oar with a Sikh Indian, Byrne said. Jagged debris showered the oily water around them.

"As we were swimming, I suddenly felt something on my hand," Byrne said. "My first impulse was to say that my hand was broken. I took it out of the water and there was this gash of flesh out of it. I had been struck by shrapnel from the torpedo."

A second piece of shrapnel struck her father in the head and gashed his temple. He faded in and out of consciousness as blood poured down his face. "Don't cry, honey," he told his daughter. And she didn't.

The other lifeboats had floated away on the port side of the sinking ship, leaving the Mayers family and the Sikh to drift by themselves for nearly an hour. The Japanese vessel submerged. Fortunately, a Van Cloon officer sent a lifeboat back after realizing that people were missing.

Mary Ann and her mother were pulled to safety but the officer said the boat was too crowded. The men would have to stay in the water, he said. "I won't go unless my daddy goes, too," the girl announced. "Can't you see my daddy has been hurt?"

She started to jump back into the water but was pulled back. The officer relented. They squeezed into the lifeboat until some of the passengers could be transferred to another. For about six hours, the boats drifted—about 80 miles from land. To pass time, Mary Ann chatted in Javanese and dined on cold fried rice and water.

Finally, a friendly airplane, the Catalina Flying Boat, discovered the survivors and looped around to reassure them. Looking through binoculars, the captain announced: "A ship comes. May God be with her."

He didn't tell anyone what else he saw. The Japanese sub's periscope was in the water. The USS Isabel steamed toward the lifeboats, but spotted the enemy sub and attacked it with help from the Catalina. The sub disappeared.

Goodyear Aircraft mascot Mary Ann Mayers, 9, whose bravery was an inspiration for Akron workers, is pictured on a 1942 war poster. The poster used language that was common at the time but is inappropriate today.

When the girl spotted the U.S. flag on the rescue ship, she sang *The Star-Spangled Banner*. "I vividly remember seeing that ship in the distance coming towards us," Byrne said. "That was a very thrilling thing."

The Isabel welcomed the survivors aboard. All were safe. The Mayers family would return to Akron on a circuitous journey from Australia to the Panama Canal to New Orleans.

In April 1942, Goodyear Aircraft held an "Eight Ball Rally" to promote America's goal of producing a warplane every eight minutes. The Mayers family attended, and Mary Ann, now 9, gave a short pep talk. "Hurry and build more planes to send over there," the little girl told the crowd, which roared.

Goodyear Aircraft adopted Mary Ann as a mascot. "Mary Ann War Production Day" was held May 21, and photos of the girl were given to every worker.

Mary Ann appeared in newspaper stories and radio programs and was about to embark on a national press tour when her immune system decided otherwise.

"I ended up getting every childhood disease known to man within the first couple of months when we got back," Byrne said. "Suddenly I had the mumps and the measles and the chickenpox. One thing after another."

The Mayers family settled in Hudson, where Mary Ann grew up. She graduated from Laurel School for Girls in Shaker Heights, majored in art at Kent State University and became a professional artist.

She married Dr. Richard Byrne, a Kent native, in 1956 and the two have lived in the Milwaukee area for 44 years. They have four grown children—Heather, Evan, Bryan and Gwynn—and five grandchildren.

Goodyear Aircraft's mascot won't be able to attend the Corsair Homecoming this weekend at Aero Expo 2004 in Akron, but she wishes Akron well.

She was happy to be a part of Akron's war effort in 1942. "Something like that makes a very large impression on a child's memory," she said.

Osmond Mania

TEENY-BOPPERS SWOONED AT AKRON CONCERT IN 1972

(Originally published July 21, 2003)

Unless you were there, you can't begin to imagine the chaos. A high-pitched, ear-splitting wail rose above the Akron Rubber Bowl as thousands of teary-eyed girls screamed at the top of their lungs. Eeeeeeeeeeee!

The teeny-boppers trembled and cried, surging toward the stage, pledging undying love to five young men in white jumpsuits. And then, one by one, the girls began to pass out.

About 20,000 fans (and a handful of skeptical parents) attended the Osmonds concert July 21, 1972. The Osmond brothers—Alan, Wayne, Merrill, Jay and Donny—had topped the U.S. charts and captured the hearts of America's daughters. Donny, then 14, was especially popular.

The Belkin Productions show didn't start until 8:30 p.m., but the day began early for many. Linda Brinkerhoff, 44, of Stow remembers going to the concert with her best friend. "We got ourselves all dolled up and went there at the crack of dawn," she said. "Our parents dropped us off there, and we're thinking 'Aren't we brilliant?'"

The two infatuated girls had everything planned. "We're thinking we're going to meet them and have lunch and probably come home with an engagement ring," she said. But when the girls arrived, they weren't alone. Other fans had already beat them there.

Kathi Lowery, 42, of Akron was among the early birds. She had staked out a gate with her sisters and cousin, enduring a 12-hour wait and 90-degree heat. "We were out there all day," she said. "We fried out there in the sun. It was such a hot day."

Fans killed time by telling stories, playing games and dreaming about boys from Utah. Excitement rippled through the crowd when the teen idols arrived by bus and pulled inside a gate. Most fans didn't see a second bus arrive or notice a pretty, dark-haired girl step off.

Marie Osmond, 12, still a year away from fame, was traveling with her parents, George and Olive Osmond. Brinkerhoff and a few others got to chat with her.

"She was sewing and ironing on that other bus with her mother," Brinkerhoff said. "She was very nice, slightly shy at first, a little bit reserved. And then I think she kind of enjoyed getting a little bit of attention."

When the bowl opened at 7, there was a mad rush to get inside. Lowery, who had waited since morning, was dismayed. "We were at the wrong gate," she said. "We had to go behind everybody else."

Uniontown resident Don Sabatino, 62, the former director of auxiliary services and programs for the University of Akron, was in charge of security and concessions at the 1972 concert. "We had the stage on about the 30-yard line at the closed end of the bowl," he said. "And we had snowfence all across the front of the stage from side to side so people on the field couldn't go past the stage."

Expecting a pleasant night of wholesome fare, Sabatino invited the Akron City Council and their families to attend the show, and seated them in the press box. "None of us were ready for what happened," he said.

The anticipation built as opening act Bo Donaldson and the Heywoods hit the stage. The crowd was loud, but the set concluded without incident. "We want the Osmonds!" the crowd began to chant.

"We were fairly close to the stage and I remember the announcements that everyone should stay seated," said Sandi Golias, 39, of Uniontown. "But, of course, when the Osmonds came out, everyone stood up."

Eeeeeeeeeeeee! The teen idols took the stage and kicked off a well-choreographed set of hits, including *One Bad Apple, Yo-Yo, Down By the Lazy River, Go Away Little Girl, Crazy Horses* and *He Ain't Heavy, He's My Brother*. Little brother Jimmy, 9, came out to sing *Long Haired Lover From Liverpool*.

"I remember their studded jumpsuits with their colored, trademark neck scarfs," said Joan Gipson, 42, of Akron. "Donny had a purple scarf with matching socks."

Renee Recob, 36, of Springfield Township, was only 5, but still recalls the hot pants she wore. "That was my first concert," she said. "I remember it very clearly. Oh, Donny. I was going to marry him."

Lowery had different taste. "I liked Jay," she said. "Boy, I liked Jay . . . My sister liked Merrill and my cousin liked Alan."

Mary Kay Coss, 40, of Akron, didn't know she was going to the show until her brother Nick Bulgrin sur-

Dig those white jumpsuits! The Osmond brothers (from left) Merrill, Alan, Donny, Jay and Wayne received a wild welcome when they performed July 21, 1972, at the Akron Rubber Bowl. Girls screamed, cried and lost consciousness as they cheered the teen idols.

prised her with tickets. "He put me up on his shoulders so that I was level with the stage, and I remember Donny was singing and he came over and he knelt down right in front of me," Coss said.

He sang *Puppy Love* to her. "All I remember is screaming," she said.

Golias' father, Sam Swesey, escorted four girls to the show. "My poor father had to stand out there and hold two screaming, crying girls on his shoulders while the other two screamed and cried at his side," she said.

Selena K. Wilson, 44, of Akron, said she never saw so many shrieking girls in her life. "When Jay, the drummer, threw his drumsticks into the audience, I thought two girls in front of us were going to tear each other's hair out to get them!" she said.

The concert soon took a bizarre, dangerous turn. "Everybody just sort of rushed the stage and got pretty squished," said Cathy Hoffman, 43, of Stow, who still owns her 1972 ticket stub. "It was very hard to breathe. Once they started, you couldn't even dance around to the music or sway."

Sabatino, whose crew had tried to plan for everything, was confronted with a mob of kids. "Everything was perfect. And then, when the Osmonds got out there, all of a sudden, we started having this hysteria among these young girls.

"There was a little girl standing right behind me, and she just screamed 'Ohhh, Donny!' and she just absolutely passed out." Others quickly followed.

Dixie Hardesty, 46, of Hebron, remembers gazing up at Donny from the front row with her sister and two cousins. "We were screaming and crying 'There he is! There he is!' Next thing I know, my sister is limp.

"I don't know if it was from the heat or because she saw Donny. She passed out and my cousin passed out within 5 minutes." Sabatino's crew began pulling unconscious girls from the surging crowd. The girls were lifted up past the Osmonds and carried backstage to be revived.

Swooning girls packed locker rooms, halls and the backstage field as Mrs. Osmond and Marie assisted the medical staff. Hardesty found her sister, Michaele, recuperating in a cot-filled room that "looked like a dormitory." Their father, who had been waiting in a camper outside, was so upset that he made them leave the show.

Meanwhile, the frenzy continued, even though the show was stopped at one point to get the girls to move back. "I remember we were really close to the stage and all of these screaming girls were pushing and fainting and falling and getting stepped on," said Rhonda Kapper, 42, of Hartville. "It was scary, but, boy, was Donny dreamy!"

After the Osmonds took their final bows, a fireworks display began. Fans tried to push through the fence, not knowing that unconscious girls were sprawled on the other side. "I'm yelling at our people, 'Hold the fence! Hold the fence!' and the fireworks were going off overhead," Sabatino said. "And I thought 'This has got to be what Vietnam is like.'"

At least 18 girls were treated at hospitals that night. Luckily, the most serious injuries were a broken arm and a broken leg.

Despite the craziness, the concert was still pretty great. "It was a good show," Lowery said.

"Oh, it was," Sabatino agreed.

Even the stars remember it. Last November, Brinkerhoff got to meet Donny Osmond after a concert in Cleveland. She mentioned that she had gone to the 1972 show in Akron. "As soon as I said that, he said 'Now that is one concert I will never forget. When you say Akron, I think of that nightmare Rubber Bowl concert.'"

Eeeeeeeeeeeee!

Ripley Contributed to Akron Folklore

DOES IT REALLY RAIN INSIDE THE AIRDOCK? YOU DECIDE

(Originally published Feb. 11, 2002)

Shocking! Strange! Unusual!

Something really weird happened when cartoonist Robert L. Ripley visited Akron in 1930.

The creator of the *Believe It or Not!* comic strip gave a speech, judged a contest and gathered some material for his popular feature. In the process, he turned a third-place prize into a first-rate legend.

It goes something like this: The Akron Airdock is so large that clouds form inside the hangar and it sometimes rains.

Believe it. Or not.

To tell the truth, Ripley wasn't expecting to stir up any controversy when he arrived in the Rubber City on Feb. 14, 1930. It was a standard appearance for the New York artist, who had traveled to 68 countries in search of the world's "strangest and most unusual facts."

Since debuting in 1918, *Believe It or Not!* had become one of the most popular syndicated features in newspapers.

The Akron Beacon Journal, which published the strip daily, promoted Ripley's visit for weeks. The Akron Times-Press, which carried John Hix's rival cartoon *Strange as It Seems*, didn't breathe a word.

Ripley, 37, was one of the featured speakers at the Lincoln Republican Club's annual banquet at the Akron Armory. In conjunction with the talk, Ripley asked the Beacon Journal to sponsor a contest in which Akron readers submitted amazing ideas for his cartoon.

Thousands of entries poured into the newspaper office. Local judges whittled down the list and forwarded hundreds of the best suggestions to Ripley's studio in advance of his visit.

Ripley kept a busy schedule in Akron. He visited the Beacon Journal, Central High School and the Shrine Club. He took a tour of the mammoth new Goodyear-Zeppelin Corp. airdock—for reasons that became apparent later—and enjoyed his first blimp ride aboard the airship Mayflower.

"Ripley is just as likeable as an old shoe," the Beacon Journal reported after the artist's newsroom visit. "There is nothing high hat about him. He gets a kick out of talking with strangers and obtaining their reactions to his cartoons.

"Every time he goes to another community, whether to make a public address or just to loaf, he has pencil and paper handy, that his inherent curiosity won't be lost if he runs across an idea."

Contest winners were announced that night to a crowd of 3,000 at the GOP dinner. Ripley's speech preceded stately lectures by U.S. Rep. Burton L. French of Idaho and former U.S. Rep. James T. Begg of Sandusky.

"It seems strange that I should be here in a Republican gathering of this sort," Ripley told the amused crowd. "I am a Democrat, you know. But then I suppose it is all right. I always did have a hankering to help the underdog."

Fifty prizes were awarded in the *Believe It or Not!* contest with runners-up receiving autographed copies of Ripley's new book or cash awards up to $25.

The grand prize, a check for $250, went to Lewis Lahiff of Akron, who "has held 333 steady jobs in Akron and vicinity, but who is without a job at present."

Charles Sigler of Barberton won $100 for his second-place tale about a man "who perspires on one side of the face only."

Goodyear worker Clyde E. Schetter took $50 for his third-place entry "concerning the Goodyear-Zeppelin hangar."

Only third place!

No explanation was given about what Schetter had suggested, but Beacon Journal readers didn't have to wait long to see.

On March 3, 1930, a drawing of Akron's airdock was plastered across Ripley's cartoon: "IT RAINS INSIDE THIS WATER-PROOF BUILDING!

"Altho it is covered with a water-tight roof and all doors and windows are closed, the Goodyear-Zeppelin dock at Akron, Ohio, is so large (43,000,000 cubic feet) that sudden changes of temperature cause clouds to form inside the hangar—and rain falls."

The Goodyear-Zeppelin airdock was featured in *Ripley's Believe It or Not* in 1930.

The airdock is such a magnificent building that superlatives don't seem to do it justice.

Built in 1929 by Wilbur Watson & Associates of Cleveland, the black, cocoon-shaped hangar is 1,175 feet long, 325 feet wide and 211 feet high.

It's big enough to house two aircraft carriers, seven football fields or 100,000 people. It's as high as a 22-story building.

But does it really rain inside?

Some Goodyear-Zeppelin workers insisted it did. It might be sunny outside, they said, but it could be drizzling inside while airships were being built.

Ripley's cartoon, which was published in several languages from Europe to Asia to South America, elevated Akron's tale to the international level.

It certainly caught the attention of weather experts. Nesbitt Hoyt Bangs, assistant editor of the Bulletin of the American Meteorological Society, wrote to Goodyear-Zeppelin Corp. from Stockbridge, Mass. "Mr. Ripley having called my attention to the fact that condensation is at times sufficient in your new zeppelin hangar to cause precipitation, I am writing to ask if some member of your staff could not send me an account of what actually does take place, including any data as to temperature, etc. that may be available," Bangs wrote.

Dr. Karl Arnstein, world-renowned airship designer and vice president of Goodyear-Zeppelin, promptly replied. Ripley's tale was "somewhat exaggerated," he told Bangs in a letter preserved at the University of Akron Archives.

"The actual facts are as follows," Arnstein wrote. "On a particularly foggy morning the relative humidity inside the dock was very high. A sudden temperature drop caused condensation of some of this moisture which fell to the floor in a mist. Whether the amount of water which fell merits the title 'rain' is somewhat questionable."

It might look like rain and feel like rain, but . . .

Well, let's face it. We're not going to resolve this today. Akron residents have debated the topic for more than 70 years.

Some swear it's true. Others are skeptical.

Regardless of scientific explanations, the rain-in-the-airdock story has become firmly entrenched in local folklore.

It's just one of those things that you either believe—or not. At least Ripley gave us a choice.

A Loop in Time

EAST AKRON BUSINESS DISTRICT REVOLVED AROUND
STREETCAR STOP ON SOUTH ARLINGTON

(Originally published Oct. 11, 2004)

There really was no reason to go anywhere else. Just about anything a person needed could be found along a few bustling blocks of South Arlington Street in East Akron. The business district sprang to life on the city's streetcar line, which raced along Arlington to a reversing loop near Seventh Avenue and returned downtown.

In the 1930s and 1940s, the Seventh Avenue Loop, as the area was known, turned into an east-side Highland Square. The heart of the district was a 2½-block strip from Baird Street to McKinley Avenue, although clusters of storefronts stretched north of Lovers Lane and south of Fourth Avenue.

Shoppers strolled along the wide sidewalks and had their choice of quality stores. Brick and frame buildings, usually one or two stories tall, lined both sides of Arlington. The small-but-mighty district had grocery stores, movie theaters, drugstores, fruit markets, meat markets, clothiers, hardware stores, dry cleaners, cafes, bars, dairy stores, barbershops, specialty shops, doctor's offices and even a funeral home.

"You didn't have to leave the neighborhood," said Joe Galizio, 81, a Kent resident who grew up in East Akron. "We had everything you could think of. We had an A&P, we had a Kroger, we had two independent hardware stores, we had two theaters."

Day or night, the place was jumping, he said. "Arlington Street was like Times Square in New York," Galizio said. "There were people on the sidewalk continuously."

It wasn't always that way. Arlington used to be a dirt road to the boondocks. In 1915, Akron announced a new streetcar line between Lakeside Park at Summit Lake and the South Arlington loop—a quarter-mile outside city limits.

Motorman Edward McPhillen ran the first car, leading an inspection party of 20 Northern Ohio Traction & Light officials, politicians and reporters. The trip around the loop was uneventful because there wasn't much to see.

Galizio's father, Ben Galizio, was among the first to set up shop there in 1917. He must have realized that developers were about to march down Arlington to map out housing allotments.

He opened a general store called Ben's Place on the east side of Arlington between Seventh and McKinley. In the 1920s, he moved across the street to a new brick building and renamed his business the Arlington Provision Co. During the Depression, the name switched to Ben's Market when the store changed addresses on the block.

Joe Galizio recalls the chicken coops in front of the store. In those days, customers always picked their own chicken. "We weighed it live, gave them a price and then we had a chute behind the meat counter," he said. "You'd drop that chicken down the chute. We had four or five guys down there. They'd get the chicken and that's where they would dress it."

The fast-growing neighborhood became a melting pot as the city grew. Among the local ethnicities were Italians, Jews, Poles, Greeks, African-Americans, Germans and Syrians. "My father and mother could talk five languages so they had a good business," said Dorothy McLane, whose father, Frank Birtich, owned the Lovers Lane Department Store.

McLane remembers South Arlington as a shopping mecca with popular stores, heavy traffic and countless pedestrians. "Everybody knew everybody," she said.

Although businesses came and went with each decade, local landmarks seemed endless. There was the Loop Cash Market, Isaly Dairy, Edward Karpel's 5 & 10, Acme No. 57, Tiedeman Brothers Meat Co., A&P Tea Co., Hannan's Coffee Shop, People's Drug, Evans-Talis Dry Goods, Lea Drug, White Castle Lunch, Stump Hardware and People's Paint and Wallpaper.

Farther out were Leo Berg's Used Cars, Arlington Lumber & Supply (later Allied Auto), Speed Queen service station, Eckard funeral home and George Kesselring's Barbershop.

"The only place we ever went was Isaly's because we picked our papers up in front of Isaly's," recalled Akron resident Mel Hynde, 82, a Beacon Journal paperboy in the 1930s on McKinley Avenue and Bittaker Street.

Butcher Leo Dill (left) and store owner Ben Galizio work the counter at Arlington Provision Co. in the 550 block of South Arlington Street in Akron about 1926. The general store was south of the Seventh Avenue Loop, where streetcars turned around and went back downtown.

The loop business district drew customers from several blocks around, he said. "It pulled all the way from the top of what would be Fifth Avenue hill clear out to what is East Archwood Avenue now and then on down to Kelly Avenue and then down around Second Avenue," Hynde said.

Peter Panutsos' candy store was a favorite among kids. "I remember hand-dipped chocolates and it was a confectionery like Mary Coyle's," Galizio said. "You could sit down, enjoy a soda. The whole nine yards."

Staley and Sultana Yogmour's building at 551 S. Arlington St. offered Gus' Shoe Repair, hat cleaning, barbershop, magazine stand and candy counter. They lived in an upstairs apartment.

"There was a shoe repair on one side and hat cleaning on the other," said granddaughter Olga Yogmour, a Cuyahoga Falls resident who remembers the block from the 1940s. "They used to put the hats on the block and brush them with something that smelled like cleaning fluid. It had a shoeshine stand in there."

Samuel Waldman owned People's Variety Store in a white brick building at 573–575 S. Arlington and later renamed it People's Paint and Wallpaper. "He was in the china business before the wallpaper, and it was People's Variety," recalled daughter Ida Waldman, 88, of Akron. "He had everything. Then he slowly changed to wallpaper and paint. It was there for years and years and years."

Perhaps the area's best-known landmarks were the twin movie theaters a block apart: The Regent at 518 S. Arlington and the Cameo at 558 S. Arlington. Both were owned by Max Federhar. "I know when I was a kid, my mother and my grandmother were in the box offices of the two theaters, and they needed a baby sitter," said Federhar's daughter Toby Sholiton, 80, of Copley Township. "So I saw a double feature in one theater and then went to the other one."

Her dad also owned the Norka, Strand and Highland. "I remember going with him to see Al Jolson in the first talking movie, *The Jazz Singer*," she said.

Galizio recalls going to Saturday matinees for a nickel. "They had the serial movies where somebody was tied to the tracks and the train was coming and, just about the time the train got there, that's the end of the movie," he said. "You had to wait until next week."

The city discontinued the Arlington streetcar line in the 1930s and replaced it with buses. Akron's streetcar system was completely gone by 1947.

The Seventh Avenue Loop neighborhood began to suffer when mass transit gave way to automobiles. Acme, Kroger and A&P pulled out of the block to open supermarkets down the street. "The small stores just couldn't make it," Galizio said. "There was just no parking. People like the idea of being able to pull in and park."

When the major anchors pulled out, the district started to drift. Other stores arrived, but old landmarks began to close. Many were gone by the 1950s. "You know what happens when you have a boarded-up storeroom," Galizio said. "You get the decay, and it just got worse and worse."

In the early 1960s, business owners and community leaders pushed for rehabilitation. In the late 1960s, turbulent times caught up with the aging district.

Tensions boiled over in 1968 when a public disturbance on Wooster Avenue spread to South Arlington and escalated into six days of looting, fires and gunshots. Another disturbance in 1969 lasted four days.

McLane still recalls the police tear gas. She was working at People's Paint when she saw teens tossing firebombs. "When it first started, I was at the back door of the store, and I knew these kids," she said. "I said, 'Why are you doing this?' They didn't say nothing."

For several years, South Arlington descended into drugs, prostitution and street crime. But the neighborhood made a comeback in the 1970s.

Old, decaying properties were demolished. Other buildings were cleaned up. A trio of new anchors—cornerstones of revival—stabilized the neighborhood and breathed new life into it.

In 1974, Living Stone Apostolic Church was dedicated at 587 S. Arlington. The Robert Street Church of God was reborn in 1980 as Arlington Church of God at 539 S. Arlington. East Akron Community House moved to 550 S. Arlington in 1985.

A new collection of fond memories is being gathered every day on the block. Still, the old memories linger. The former streetcar loop, or what's left of it, is now a parking lot for trucks. Few buildings from that era remain. "Not only are the stores all gone, but so are all the people," Hynde said.

"I go down there every once in a while, and I can't believe it," McLane said.

"We have a lot of fine memories," Galizio said.

Akron Unzipped

WE DIDN'T INVENT THE SLIDE FASTENER. WE JUST GAVE IT A BIG TUG

(Originally published March 31, 2008)

There was nothing to button, hook, lace or tie. The B.F. Goodrich Co. of Akron introduced a pair of rubber galoshes in 1923 that made a lasting impression on the world. The fancy footwear featured an ingenious slide fastener with interlocking metal teeth. With a quick pull of a tab, the overshoes opened wide or sealed shut.

Unfortunately, salesmen weren't sold on the product's suggested name: the Mystik Boot. It just wasn't snappy enough.

"What we need is an action word," Goodrich President Bertram G. Work (1868–1927) told a group of sales representatives. "Something that will dramatize the way the thing zips."

Wait a second. That was it. "Why not call it the Zipper?" he said. Goodrich trademarked the Zipper Boot, and it became a hot seller for the company. Through common usage, the name eventually transferred to the metal fastener itself and became a generic word.

Akron didn't invent the zipper. We did, however, give it a big tug. Frederick H. Martin, manager of footwear development for Goodrich, stumbled across the slide fastener in 1920 when he attended a leather style show in New York.

He passed a cigarette stand one day and noticed the innovative seals on pouches of tobacco. Martin wondered if Goodrich could apply the technology to rubber overshoes.

Before returning to Akron, he made a trip to the Hookless Fastener Co. in Meadville, Pa.

In 1917, Hookless engineer Gideon Sundback had patented the "Separable Fastener," an interlocking device that historians credit as the modern zipper. It was an improvement over Chicago inventor Whitcomb L. Judson's "Clasp Locker," which used a hook-and-eye system.

Martin toured the plant and brought back a few samples of Hookless Fastener No. 2 with him to Akron.

James W. Schaade, general manager of the Goodrich footwear department, was enthusiastic about Martin's boot idea and put a team to work on it. They enlisted the aid of Hookless engineers, who visited Akron and offered suggestions.

The men developed rubber compounds and tried out different sizes of fasteners. Workers put on overshoes and splashed around to see how the top-secret proto-types performed.

The boots had to be rugged and waterproof, yet snug and cozy. The slide fasteners had to be sturdy and secure, yet simple and smooth. Finally, after two years of experiments, the galoshes won approval.

Goodrich received exclusive rights to apply slide fasteners to rubber overshoes. The Akron company ordered tens of thousands of fasteners, forcing the Pennsylvania plant to add two work shifts.

Thanks to President Work's suggestion, the name changed from Mystik to Zipper just before the galoshes went into production.

"The Zipper Boot is a marvel of comfort and smartness," the company advertised in 1923. "It is worn right over your shoes or slippers. On and off in a jiffy—nothing to button, hook, lace or tie. The Hookless Fastener—exclusive on Zipper footwear—does the trick. A little pull of the tab and ZIP!"

Another early advertisement featured Paramount Pictures actress Bebe Daniels demonstrating the elegance of Goodrich's boots. The Zippers could fit over dainty slippers, street shoes or dancing pumps, providing protection against wet weather.

The footwear provided "a touch of style and individuality that makes every lady and miss want a pair," the ad explained in the Saturday Evening Post.

Public demand was immediate and intense. Goodrich sold nearly 500,000 pairs of Zipper Boots in the first year, prompting the company to offer a variety of styles and sizes "for men, women and the kiddies."

Applied to all sorts of clothing, the zipper's popularity spread around the world. Sales skyrocketed for the Hookless Fastener Co., which became the nation's leading zipper manufacturer and later changed its name to Talon International Inc.

The Goodrich footwear was so popular that it even spawned a sports franchise in Northeast Ohio.

In 1925, the University of Akron held a campus contest to come up with an official name for the school's athletic teams.

Freshman Margaret Hamlin won a $10 prize after students voted for her unique suggestion—the Zippers—inspired by Goodrich's galoshes.

The Akron Zippers played for nearly 25 years before the university decided to shorten the name to the Akron Zips in 1950. The school's kangaroo mascot, Zippy, proudly wore a zippered pouch.

The Zips, Zippy, the Acme-Zip Game, WZIP, the Zip Strip, Zip Cards—they all owe their names to a spiffy pair of rubber galoshes.

No, Akron didn't invent the zipper. You might say, though, that this was the first place where it "stuck."

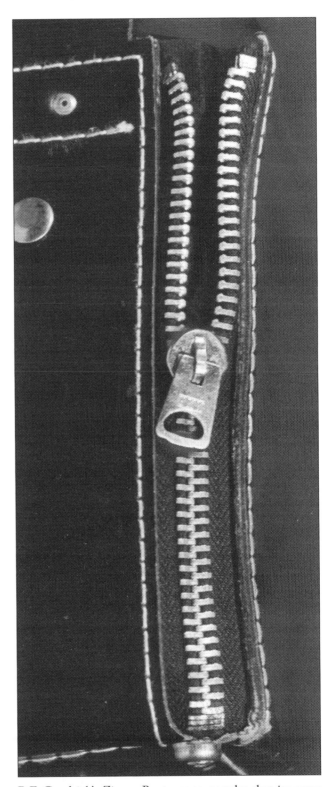

B.F. Goodrich's Zipper Boot was so popular that its name transferred to the slide fastener—and, in turn, the University of Akron.

Memories of Polsky's

AKRON DEPARTMENT STORE CLOSED IN DECEMBER 1978

(Originally published Dec. 22, 2008)

The locks clicked shut on a deserted building with empty cases and barren counters. Five floors of merchandise had been reduced to a single floor of odds and ends.

Although Christmas carols played merrily, there was little joy to be found. Polsky's department store was closed. The Akron retailer met its demise at 5:30 p.m. Dec. 23, 1978, after 93 years in business.

Akron resident Jim Gaffga, 52, who served 30 years ago as Polsky's supervisor in charge of operations, had the bittersweet assignment of locking the doors. "To me, that was an honor," he said.

Gaffga was a University of Akron student who joined the company in 1976 as a part-time security agent. It was like joining a big family. The store treated its employees with dignity, he said.

"That was the thing about Polsky's. They made you feel important," he said. "As a supervisor, I made $155 a week. That's $3.87 and a half cents an hour. That didn't matter."

As the final customers exited Polsky's, Gaffga followed behind with a ring of keys. "We were seeing the end of an era," he said.

The A. Polsky Co. was named for Abram Polsky, a native of Poland who came to New York in 1868 at age 20. He hopped a train to Iowa, where he earned a living as a door-to-door peddler, carrying a backpack and selling wares to the wives of farmers. Eventually, he earned enough money to buy a horse and wagon.

In the mid-1870s, he went into business with his brother-in-law Samuel Myers. They opened a shop in Youngstown, moved it to Orwell in Ashtabula County and then settled in Akron, a canal town of 20,000.

Myers & Polsky dry goods opened in 1885 at 165 S. Howard St. After Myers retired in 1892, the store became A. Polsky Co.

Polsky owed his success to "good judgment in buying, honest methods in selling and courteous treatment to all." He always asked customers: "Did you find what you wanted?"

Helping out in the store were sons Harry Polsky (1875–1958) and Bert Polsky (1881–1970).

One day, a traveling salesman brought in a load of ready-to-wear skirts. It was an unusual product, since most women sewed their own garments.

"I wouldn't know what to do with them if I bought them," Polsky told the salesman.

Son Harry chimed in: "You buy them and I'll sell them." The skirts sold out. Polsky's became a leading retailer in ready-to-wear garments.

Business boomed while the city grew. The Polsky's store added departments and moved to bigger quarters on South Howard Street. In 1913, it opened a four-story annex on South Main Street near Market Street.

Tragedy struck in 1915, when Abram Polsky, 67, died from an allergic reaction to an anesthetic during a routine throat exam.

Dr. Bob Morgenroth, 93, of Chapel Hill, N.C., was born two months after Polsky died. He has fond memories of the early Main Street store because he and his twin brother, Bill, grew up there.

"The Polskys and the Morgenroths were very much interrelated," he said. "My dad was Abraham Morgenroth. He worked for Harry and Bert Polsky. He sold women's coats, dresses and furs. In fact, he was in charge of that department."

Abraham Morgenroth's sister Fannye married Harry Polsky, and his brother Simon Morgenroth married Rose Polsky. Along with Bert and Hazel Polsky, the three families lived in consecutive mansions on Diagonal Road.

The twin boys had the run of the store. They worked as box makers, but spent a good deal of time getting into mischief. "Our patron saints were the Katzenjammer Kids," Morgenroth said.

"When the sales girls bent down to pick up the hangers, we hid behind the counters and hit them with open safety pins flung by rubber bands. We also dropped rubber balloons filled with water from the top of A. Polsky onto the street below."

Motorists drive past the art-deco facade of the A. Polsky Co. at South Main and State streets in 1938. The building opened in 1930 and added a fifth floor in 1941.

MOVE TO NEW LOCATION

When its biggest competitor, the M. O'Neil Co., moved south to Main and State streets in 1928, Polsky's followed suit. The company bought land across from O'Neil's and broke ground Oct. 20, 1929, on a four-story, $2.1 million building. The art-deco store opened Sept. 16 at 225 S. Main St.

Polsky's expanded its departments to include shoes, clothing, millinery, cosmetics, furniture, appliances, home furnishings, chinaware, sporting goods, carpets, books, stationery, a beauty salon and a portrait studio. In 1941, the store added a fifth floor.

Polsky's Tea Room, famous for its chicken pot pie, was a popular restaurant on the mezzanine level. Former customer Ruth Powell, 87, of Akron, recalls meeting her mother, Effie Ross, for lunch.

"When I worked at Hardware & Supply, oftentimes we would walk down there," she said. "I liked their vegetable plate."

In addition to the delicious food, the service was exceptional. Neatly dressed waitresses doted over customers at every table. "It was a little bit more elegant," Powell said. "It wasn't this rush-in-and-rush-out business. You could sit and talk."

Jim Gaffga, supervisor in charge of operations at Polsky's, locks the South Main Street doors Dec. 23, 1978, while security officer John Kohari watches.

She enjoyed visiting the store during the holidays, when downtown Akron was decked out. "Of course, it was always a treat to go to Polsky's and O'Neil's to see the windows at Christmas," Powell said. "It was so much fun to see the different things that they had."

HOLIDAY SALES RUSH

Catherine Decker, 86, of Akron, who worked at Polsky's in the 1950s, remembers the annual crush of holiday shoppers. "One year, the day after Christmas, I went in and worked a full day," she said. "All I did was write up credit slips for shoes that people had bought for Christmas that didn't fit."

Decker started in the boys department, transferred to the gift department and ended up in the authorizing department. She didn't just work at Polsky's. She shopped there, too. "To me, it was a nice store," she said. "They had the expensive stuff and then they had the more reasonable stuff."

Harry and Bert Polsky continued to run the store after selling the business to Hahn Department Stores, a New York company that later changed its name to Allied Stores Corp. Harry died in 1958 at age 82. Bert died in 1970 at age 88. By then, Polsky's was a chain with stores in downtown Canton, Mellett Mall in Canton and Summit Mall in Fairlawn.

After being under the Polsky family's supervision for 85 years, the company went through four presidents in a decade. Still, its employees remained loyal.

During the Blizzard of 1978, when most businesses were closed, Gaffga drove to Polsky's to unlock the doors. "That store was open," he said. "I guarantee you that store was open, and I opened it."

Polsky's drew fewer customers in the 1970s. Spending habits changed as people moved to the suburbs. Allied Stores determined it would take $25 million to make Polsky's competitive. Instead, it jolted Akron with the announcement on Nov. 1, 1978, that all four Polsky's stores would close by year's end. More than 500 jobs would be lost.

Employees received the sad news in a staff meeting. "No one knew," Gaffga said. Customers flooded the aisles over the next month as merchandise was liquidated floor by floor. Some people didn't buy anything. They just wanted to see the store one last time.

Gaffga locked the doors for the final time Dec. 23. His bosses let him keep his Polsky's security badge and key ring as mementos.

The building remained empty while developers tried to figure out what to do. Ideas included turning it into a hotel, a jail and an apartment complex.

After those plans fell through, the Prudential Insurance Co. donated the building to the University of Akron in 1987. Following a $28.5 million renovation, the building reopened in 1994 as UA offices and classrooms.

"I miss it," Decker said. "I wish you could go back maybe for one or two days to a place like that."

"We live in a different era now," Powell said.

"We had a beautiful time of our lives," Morgenroth said.

"Everything changes, but you've still got to keep going," Gaffga said.

Parma Forever

KIDS STAYED UP LATE TO ENJOY JOKES OF TV'S HOOLIHAN, BIG CHUCK IN '70S

(Originally published Oct. 18, 2010)

Parma sounded like a wonderful place. Located somewhere in Northeast Ohio, it was an exotic land of polka music, white socks, pink flamingos, kielbasa and pierogis. And lots and lots of high-pitched laughter.

Everything I knew about Parma I learned from television. When I was growing up in Summit County in the 1970s, the most important part of the weekend began at 11:30 p.m. Friday on WJW-TV 8 in Cleveland.

"From the heart of Playhouse Square in downtown Cleveland! From high atop the Television 8 building! It's *The Hoolihan and Big Chuck Show!*"

Here we gooooo again.

Every Friday night, my friends and I stayed up late to watch the 2½-hour program, a gaudy kaleidoscope of old horror movies, vaudevillian comedy sketches and crazy sound effects.

The co-hosts were the two coolest guys in the world—or so it seemed among the cultural sophisticates in elementary school. Broadcasting veteran Bob Wells, alias "Hoolihan the Weatherman," and Chuck Schodowski, a TV engineer and producer known as "Big Chuck," teamed up in 1966 after Cleveland legend Ernie "Ghoulardi" Anderson left Shock Theater to strike it rich in Hollywood.

A Parma resident of Polish descent, Schodowski was a supporting player on Ghoulardi's show and a big influence on its polka-laden humor.

Smooth, talkative Hoolihan and shy, reserved Big Chuck were an unusual team, but the dynamic worked. Their studio set consisted of two chairs, a coffee table and a colorful backdrop of posters featuring Dracula, the Wolfman, Frankenstein's Monster and Phantom of the Opera.

Neighborhood kids had Friday-night sleepovers, nibbling popcorn and chugging Coca-Cola while feasting on horror movies such as *The Brain That Wouldn't Die*, *Fiend Without a Face*, *The Crawling Eye*, *Attack of the 50 Foot Woman*, *Earth Vs. the Spider* and *The Blob*.

It didn't matter if we had seen the films a dozen times before. We had to keep watching.

Before commercial breaks, Hoolihan and Big Chuck kept us entertained with their studio banter. They cracked jokes, told funny tales, read fan letters and introduced comedy skits. To avoid singling out a group, the show created "Certain Ethnic" humor. Big Chuck often played a bumbling Certain Ethnic man with a bushy mustache, striped sweater and big hat.

The skits ended with a high-pitched laugh that became the show's signature. Much to the annoyance of parents, kids practiced that laugh over and over: "Ahhhh haaaaa haaa. Haha haha. Uh-huh-huh."

Hoolihan and Big Chuck had many recurring segments, including *The Kielbasy Kid*, *Ben Crazy*, *Soul Man*, *Mary Hartski* and *Readings by Robert*. They also made videos for novelty songs, including *Monster Mash* (by Bobby "Boris" Pickett), *The Streak* (by Ray Stevens), *Junk Food Junkie* (by Larry Groce) and *Snoopy Vs. the Red Baron* (by the Royal Guardsmen).

Fans really enjoyed *Pizza Fight of the Century*, a contest featuring champion "Mushmouth" Mariano Pacetti, who wore a cape and a title belt.

Each week, Pacetti battled a challenger to see who could eat the most pizza in 60 seconds. Hilarity ensued when they stuffed their mouths with pizza.

Fans still smile over the time Mushmouth lost to a German shepherd that gulped down an entire pizza. It was disqualified for not being human.

The show always ended with a pajama party in which Hoolihan and Big Chuck wore leg-baring PJs while reading fan jokes. The program faded to black with Peggy Lee's song *Is That All There Is?* with the plug pulled on the words "if that's aaallll."

In the days before videocassette recorders were common, my friends and I dreamed of owning one so that we could stay up all night and watch the program over and over.

Hoolihan and Big Chuck were superstars to me. I will never forget the time that I spied Bob Wells dining with his family at a Perkins restaurant. All I could think was, "Hoolihan eats pancakes! Hoolihan eats pancakes!"

Cleveland horror hosts Chuck Schodowski (left) and Bob Wells, stars of *The Hoolihan and Big Chuck Show* on WJW-TV 8, speak at the University of Akron student center on Feb. 21, 1974.

The TV co-hosts often made personal appearances at Halloween fun houses like the Haunted School House and Hudson Jaycees Haunted House. They also raised money for charities by competing in basketball, softball, football and other sports.

In 1978, the Hoolihan & Big Chuck All-Stars played softball against Summit County Sheriff Anthony J. Cardarelli's team at Akron's Firestone Stadium. My mother piled a bunch of happy kids into her 1972 Chevy Nova to see the zany game.

The score didn't matter to us. We just liked the slapstick humor—like when the All-Stars pitched a grapefruit painted like a softball. It splattered when the batter tried to hit it.

After the game, I took a photo as Hoolihan signed autographs for my pals. I saw Big Chuck climb aboard the team bus, so I followed him with my camera and cornered him in the aisle.

"Can I take your picture?" I asked in awe.

"Sure," he said.

Click. Click. Oops. I had run out of flashbulbs.

When I developed the film, the photo showed a silhouette against a window. That's it. No Big Chuck. I was disappointed, but I had to admit, it was funny.

"Ahhhh haaaaa haaa. Haha haha. Uh-huh-huh."

The next year, shock waves rippled through Ohio when Hoolihan left the show to move to Florida. Schodowski chose supporting player Lil' John Rinaldi to be the new co-host.

The Big Chuck and Lil' John Show carried on the Channel 8 tradition, but I slowly lost interest. It wasn't the program's fault.

In the 1980s, I had a driver's license and no longer stayed home Friday night. Then I went to college. It was like losing touch with an old friend.

Years passed. After Fox acquired Channel 8 in the 1990s, the show switched from horror films to everyday movies, and moved from Friday to Saturday. Even when I didn't see the show, I took comfort in knowing that it was still on television.

My nostalgia grew in 1997 when I attended the first Ghoulardifest convention, which reunited the cast. Watching the show again, it felt just as fun as I remembered from childhood.

It was the end of an era when Schodowski announced his retirement after 47 years. The final program aired June 16, 2007.

A year later, I began to date a nice Polish girl from Parma. I thought it would be fun to give her a souvenir from Ghoulardifest, so I went to Big Chuck's table and asked if he and Hoolihan could autograph a photo "for my girlfriend."

My Parma date was amused to receive the memento, but she inquired about my phraseology. Whoops. I hadn't officially used that word before, had I?

"So I'm your girlfriend?" she asked.

Big Chuck found out I had a girlfriend before my girlfriend found out she had a boyfriend.

"Ahhhh haaaaa haaa. Haha haha. Uh-huh-huh."

I've learned quite a bit about Parma since then. Great place!

It's even more wonderful than it looks on television.

On Saturday, my fiancee and I got married there.

Bliss on the Way up; Terror Going Down

BALLOONIST'S 1875 FLIGHT AT SUMMIT FAIRGROUNDS HAS DEATH-DEFYING FINISH

(Originally published Sept. 27, 2010)

If the ride up was thrilling, the ride down was terrifying. Everything else was sheer entertainment—at least for the spectators gaping far below.

Summit County fairgoers witnessed an exhilarating display of courage in 1875, when an agriculturist became an aerialist.

Northampton Township farmer John C. Johnston, a mechanical genius who enjoyed poring over scientific manuals, volunteered to pilot a gas balloon at the fair. In those fledgling days of flight, balloon ascensions were a major attraction.

Johnston purchased the airship from Professor John Wise, a famous aeronaut from Philadelphia, who pledged to supervise the Sept. 27 flight, but canceled his appearance at the last moment because of illness.

The farmer was on his own.

Johnston, a former county commissioner and township clerk, was considered a bit of an eccentric by his neighbors because he experimented with scientific instruments at his homestead on present-day Chart Road in Cuyahoga Falls.

The Sunday Akron Times once described him as "a person of exceptional learning and shrewdness when it came to things of a technical nature but of rather pitiful ignorance when it came to farm matters."

Johnston's balloon, which he dubbed the Summit, was made of cotton and flax, and sealed with a top-secret varnish. Covered with cotton netting, the bag was 50 feet in diameter and had a capacity of 23,000 cubic feet.

It was attached to a willow basket, 4 feet in diameter and 3 feet deep, which was equipped with a barometer, thermometer, grappling hook, anchor, drag ropes and other gear.

Hundreds of fairgoers waited excitedly Sept. 27 at Akron businessman Philander D. Hall's grounds on the northeast corner of South Maple and South Balch streets, across from Akron Rural Cemetery (now Glendale).

DANGEROUS MIX

That morning, Johnston and a crew of men carted the balloon's envelope to a municipal gas main off North Main Street north of Market Street. They spent more than three hours filling the bag with illuminating gas, a mixture containing hydrogen, methane and other chemical compounds.

After wheeling the balloon to the fairgrounds about 1 p.m., Johnston spent another two hours tinkering with the controls and making sure everything was in working order.

Finally, he was ready. At 3:22 p.m., he nodded to the men holding the tethers. "Let go," Johnston said.

Spectators roared with approval as the Summit began its slow climb. "Though the breeze had gradually been rising, swaying the balloon from side to side as it was raised and lowered, the ascent was beautifully made amid the cheers of the multitude," the Akron Daily Beacon reported. "The course, after rising above the trees, being almost due south. The aeronaut vigorously waved his flag as he sped upward and onward."

COURSE CHANGE

The balloon floated majestically toward Summit Lake and rose to about 4,500 feet. Suddenly, it caught another current, changed course and began drifting northeast. Cows, chickens and other farm animals looked up in fright at the strange bird. Johnston's balloon soared over downtown Akron, North Hill and Cuyahoga Falls.

The Summit was about 6,500 feet high when a loud clap of thunder filled the air. It was a shocking sound because the sky was clear. That wasn't thunder. With a blast like a cannon, the balloon popped.

"When the balloon was at its greatest height—about 6,500 feet—persons who watched its flight were startled to see the airship suddenly change its shape, and at the same time to descend rapidly, so rapidly, in fact, that everybody expected to see the aeronaut dashed to the ground and killed," the Akron Daily Argus reported.

Witnesses saw Johnston frantically tugging on ropes and throwing out ballast as the Summit plummeted near the jagged cliffs of the Gorge between Akron and Cuyahoga Falls.

Northampton Township farmer John C. Johnston took the ride of his life in 1875.

In less than 10 seconds, most of the gas had leaked out of the balloon.

SURPRISE ENDING

What happened next was nothing less than astonishing. The collapsed balloon doubled up on itself and formed a makeshift parachute. It was just enough to slow the descent.

Johnston missed the Gorge and crashed into a freshly plowed field on Frederick Manton's farm close to where present-day Howe Avenue meets state Route 8 in Cuyahoga Falls.

Shaken and dazed, the balloonist miraculously escaped injury except for a minor cut on his arm.

The death-defying flight became front-page news across the country.

Most people would have given up aeronautics at that point, but Johnston vowed to fly again. He carted his ruptured balloon back home to Northampton. His wife, Margaret, spent months mending the envelope with her sewing machine, reportedly using thousands of spools of thread.

The following year, Johnston triumphantly returned to the county fair. It didn't take long for disaster to strike again.

As Johnston's balloon took off, a strong gust of wind blew it into a tree limb, which tore a hole in the fabric.

Gas leaked out of the bag. After a short flight, Johnston crash-landed in Middlebury, dejected but once again unhurt.

That was it. He gave up on his lofty dreams and returned to farming.

TRAGIC ENDING

A decade later, tragedy struck when typhoid fever claimed the lives of Johnston's wife, Margaret, 45, son, John, 28, and daughter, Minerva, 20, over a four-month span in 1884–85.

Johnston joined them three years later in the family plot at Northampton Center Cemetery on West Bath Road. He died before his 55th birthday.

At a sheriff's sale, Cuyahoga Falls hay dealer J.B. Fisher bought an old balloon.

He used it as a tarpaulin to cover his haystacks.

Handled With Care

FORMER O'NEIL'S DELIVERY DRIVERS REMINISCE ABOUT LONG HAUL AT CHRISTMASTIME

(Originally published Dec. 20, 2004)

After you purchased the deluxe refrigerator, the china cabinet and the three-piece sofa, how in the world did you get it home?

You didn't. They did. The hardworking haulers at the M. O'Neil Co. always delivered the goods. Whether it was something as large as a piano or as small as a spool of thread, the O'Neil's delivery department made sure that merchandise arrived safely at a customer's doorstep.

Drivers worked long hours and traveled great distances—through rain, sleet or snow—to brighten the holidays for thousands of shoppers within 200 miles of downtown Akron.

The South Main Street store's fleet of trucks transported furniture and packages to every nook and cranny in Northeast Ohio.

"Thanksgiving till Christmas, you worked from 6 o'clock in the morning till midnight," recalled Goodyear Heights resident John Arnett, 73, who delivered for O'Neil's from 1950 to 1978. "I could never do it today, I'll tell you." The closer it got to Christmas, the heavier the workload.

O'Neil's furniture trucks usually carried two-man crews—a driver and a helper—who spent six-day weeks on the road. Some drivers hauled bulk, though, and traveled alone. Uniforms consisted of brown pants, tan shirts and brown caps with O'Neil's insignias. Originally, the men wore ties, too, but those got in the way.

Each day, workers loaded trucks, delivered goods and then returned to the store to pick up more merchandise.

"We had to really bust our tail," said New Franklin resident Pat Lawler, 77, an O'Neil's delivery employee from 1943 to 1966. "We had to make sure everything was out. I quit (for the day) one morning at 5 o'clock."

Toys, clothes, appliances, furniture, mattresses, televisions, bathtubs, you name it. O'Neil's had everything, and it all went out on the trucks for delivery.

"You'd never see your family from one Sunday to the next Sunday," said Green resident Dick Detwiler, 76, who worked at O'Neil's from 1953 to 1979. "I think most of the drivers will admit that our wives raised our families."

Veteran drivers didn't really need maps. They had the routes memorized and could deliver in the dark without even checking an address. "I was on Goodyear Heights for 11½ years, and I delivered that route constantly without a spotlight," Lawler said. "We knew the houses. We knew the customers."

The drivers never could predict when a routine assignment might turn into an adventure. Arnett recalls trying to deliver a pool table to a customer whose house was too small. "We tried every way there was to get it in his basement," he said. "So he took the blocks out of the side of the basement. We slid it in through the blocks, and then he had a man block it back up. He wanted it bad."

Some customers were more demanding than others. Detwiler and his brother were making a delivery one winter in Medina when the matron of the house insisted they take off their boots. They weren't wearing boots, but they obliged by taking off their shoes.

"She opened the front door and threw them out in the middle of the yard in the snow," Detwiler said. "We had to go out there in our socked feet. And she said 'The next time, you'll listen to what I tell you to do.'"

Sofa beds were the bane of most O'Neil's deliverymen. The furniture was heavy and difficult to grip.

"Sometimes you'd have a Hide-A-Bed and it would go to a third- or fourth-floor apartment and you'd have to go up the stairway with it," Detwiler said. "That was probably the hardest thing to deliver at that time."

Lawler's sore back is a reminder of the time he carried a sofa bed by himself. "I put a Hide-A-Bed over my shoulder one time," he said. "I weighed about 145 pounds. Well, I paid for it later. I'm still paying for it. You strained everything."

GREAT CAMARADERIE

The delivery department typically employed 60 to 70. Retirees recall a great camaraderie among the men. It was like a family.

"There were a lot of brothers and cousins that worked there," Arnett said. "The Kimerer brothers, the Bittner brothers, the Kreitz cousins."

Pat Lawler (left) and his uncle Lloyd Keenan work together in 1958 on a delivery route for the M. O'Neil Co. in Akron. *Courtesy of the Lawler family*

"One of the fellows took grease and laid it on one of his sandwiches like mayonnaise," Detwiler said. "We was with him when he ate that. He bit into that, and grease came out of the corner of his mouth before he'd realized what he had eaten."

Lawler remembers having a little fun while driving his truck down a steep hill on state Route 303. "I was doing 85 miles an hour down there one night," he said. "I had a helper who was no good, and I was trying to scare him to death. I looked over, and one of the other guys was passing me."

As long as the job got done, the bosses didn't mind a little clowning around.

TWO BOSSES REVERED

The retirees speak in reverent tones about two men in particular: Dewey P. McFee, the delivery superintendent, and John Feudner, the store superintendent who later became O'Neil's president and chairman.

"Back in them days, if you needed anything, you'd go see Mr. Feudner and talk to him just like he was your dad," Arnett said.

Feudner was known to award large checks to workers suffering financial distress or other personal calamities, and he'd let them pay it back a little each week if possible. Or sometimes he'd just give it to them outright. "We took care of O'Neil's, but O'Neil's took care of us," Lawler said.

McFee was an efficient, respected supervisor who always looked after his men. "He could've fired any one of us, but he had our job at one time and never forgot," Lawler said.

"He was a wonderful man to work for," Detwiler said.

Arnett recalls how sad the delivery workers were when McFee died in November 1959. "We all went up in front of O'Neil's and stood while the funeral came right down Main Street," he said.

"I've got to say that was the best bunch of guys I ever worked with," Detwiler said. "You knew the parents, you knew the grandparents, you knew the kids, the wives," Lawler said. "You knew everybody."

Employees used to hang out together, go bowling, hit a bar or two, see a ballgame, enjoy a company outing. They were loyal to O'Neil's and each other.

"The guys would do anything for you," Arnett said. "If somebody had to move, we would go out and help them move. If somebody had to put in a cement drive, we would go out. They helped me put in my driveway."

Despite the heavy workload, the drivers maintained a good sense of humor and enjoyed pulling occasional practical jokes on one another.

"They would put Limburger cheese on the engine, put grease on the gearshift lever," Arnett recalled.

One joker liked to grease the handles of furniture dollies, ensuring a slippery grip. His co-workers finally got even with him one day.

O'Neil's delivery drivers (from left) Howard Hatch, Joe LaRocca, Paul Kimerer, Bill Salisbury, Lloyd Keenan and Dick Geul gather around a Cleveland-made White truck, the newest addition to the downtown Akron department store's fleet in 1937. *Courtesy of the Lawler family*

The busiest day of the year was Christmas Eve, and the delivery department always held a party that evening in the garage. Drivers would return from their routes, wolf down a sandwich, socialize a bit and then reload the trucks and head back out.

"Everything that sold on Christmas Eve day up to 5:30 was guaranteed delivery that night," Detwiler said. "No matter where it was at or how big an item. Every item in that delivery department was gone before the night was over."

"On Christmas Eve, we'd work till everything was delivered," Arnett said.

Finally, in the early morning, they could return to their families to enjoy the holiday.

"When you went to go home after the party, you got a ham, you got a week's pay, you got a fifth of whiskey," Lawler said. "A company wouldn't do that anymore."

The drivers said the magic of the job began to fade when the delivery department moved in the early 1970s to a warehouse on Gilchrist Road. It just wasn't the same anymore.

And it got worse. O'Neil's retirees, along with the rest of the community, felt a deep pain when the downtown store closed in January 1989.

"I've never been back down there," Arnett said. "Nope, never been back."

Many of the O'Neil's drivers from the 1940s and '50s have passed away, but you can still find the furniture they delivered in a lot of homes in Ohio.

"It was a good bunch of guys to work with," Detwiler said. "A lot of good memories. A lot of fun."

"I miss it every day," Lawler admitted.

He dreams about the job all the time. The other morning, he woke up and told his wife that he was going to collect his pay.

"From what?" she asked.

"I delivered my route all night last night," he said.

Shattered Crystal

DINER DISASTER A FORGOTTEN TRAGEDY

(Originally published May 13, 2002)

There was barely enough time to scream.

One minute, the Crystal Restaurant was filled with customers. The next minute, the Crystal Restaurant was gone.

The downtown Akron building collapsed like a house of cards, burying its horrified occupants in a jagged mass of bricks, glass and lumber.

The disaster was so sudden that patrons were trapped at their tables and waitresses were entombed beneath the counter. Before the dust could settle, nine were dead and 30 were injured in one of the worst catastrophes in Akron history.

The date was May 15, 1916. Restaurant owners George and Gust Serris were trying to keep up with the dinner rush at 145 S. Main St. Families, downtown workers and out-of-town visitors had packed the eatery.

The brothers always prided their establishment on its "swift service, sensible prices, courteous treatment and high quality."

They had opened the Crystal Restaurant in 1913 at Main and Quarry (now Bowery) in a narrow, brick building that served as the Akron Beacon Journal's home from 1898 to 1911.

On this evening, the dining atmosphere was less than ideal. Customers were jostled by the bone-jarring noise of excavation.

Workers were clearing an adjacent lot for construction of the new Delaware Building, and a crew from the Franklin Bros. Co. was using dynamite to blast away large sections of rock.

An angry Gust Serris stormed out to complain at 6 p.m. He told the crew that the explosions were rattling dishes and ruining dinner. Five minutes later, two more blasts shook the building.

And then the world turned upside down. "I was standing behind the counter near the long mirror, cutting bread," waitress Clara Leonhart, 23, later told the Akron Press. "I saw the glass give and the heavy tile counter tilt toward me. I screamed when I saw the south wall bend outward."

The brick wall collapsed with a thunderous crash, pulling down the roof. The building shuddered violently, the floor caved in and the other walls began to topple.

"I was startled from my meal by the sound of crashing glass," reported Sgt. E.A. Blair of the Ohio National Guard. "I saw the large plate-glass windows in front of the restaurant bent as though with a strong wind."

Beams and bricks rained on diners. It all happened so fast, witnesses said there was little time to react. "The front of the building sank with a deafening, splintering crash, and I saw several people go down with the broken timbers like flotsam in a whirlpool," Blair said.

The kitchen was the only part of the restaurant left standing. Had it fallen, the ensuing fire would have raced through the debris, claiming a higher toll.

Blair and about 15 others escaped harm by rushing into the kitchen and exiting through a back door. Nearly everyone else was trapped in the rubble.

"I remember falling, then waking up in darkness," Leonhart told reporters. "Below me I could hear groans and screams. Sometimes they were louder than others. I could hear things move above and below me. With the movement, the screams seemed to increase."

The collapse could be heard for blocks. A gray cloud of dust rose above the city. Hundreds of worried citizens rushed to help. Safety crews and volunteers combed the rubble for victims. Many of the survivors were buried for up to 15 minutes.

"I could hear men tramping above me and when the tramping grew louder, the weight pressed harder and harder," Leonhart recalled. "Every minute I expected to be crushed as the wreckage was moved to take out bodies."

Bruised and bloodied survivors were rushed by stretcher to City Hospital and Peoples Hospital. The lucky ones suffered only broken bones and cuts. Nine of the victims were beyond help. Some were crushed to death. Others suffocated before rescuers could find them.

Tragic tales emerged from the mountain of debris. Waitress Mary Gallup had been employed at the Crys-

A large crowd gathers at South Main and Quarry streets in downtown Akron as victims are pulled from the rubble of the Crystal Restaurant disaster on May 15, 1916.

tal Restaurant for only two hours. She and her husband, Edward, had moved to Akron six days earlier in search of a better life.

"My wife is in there! My wife is in there!" Gallup cried after pushing through the crowd. "Save her! Save her!" He later had to identify her body at the morgue.

William and Annie Lawson were enjoying a night out with their 5-year-old daughter, Mary. Having finished her meal, Mrs. Lawson decided to step outside for fresh air. "I am through, but I'll stay with Papa," Mary said.

Mrs. Lawson exited onto the sidewalk as the restaurant collapsed behind her. She suffered minor bruises. Her husband and daughter died at their table.

Akron recoiled in horror at the disaster. There were immediate calls for investigation.

State inspectors determined that Franklin Bros. Co. had planted dynamite too close to the restaurant. The building collapsed because its foundation had been undermined.

There would be no criminal charges, however. No state law had been broken. "To bring a charge that could result in no more than a nominal fine for an act that cost the lives of nine would be mockery at the law," Mayor William Laub said.

Franklin Bros. faced 42 lawsuits from victims' families. By 1917, the company had settled every case, paying $75,000 total.

Life went on in Akron. In late 1916, George and Gust Serris opened the New Crystal Restaurant at 6 N. Howard St., where they continued to offer "swift service, sensible prices, courteous treatment and high quality" through the mid-1920s.

The restaurant eventually returned to South Main Street, undergoing a succession of owners, addresses and incarnations. The Crystal name endured for decades in Akron and was still being used as recently as the 1970s.

Today, the 1916 disaster is forgotten. Most who pass the Delaware Building are unaware of its tragic beginning.

That was predicted long ago. A few days after the collapse, an Akron Press reporter went to the ruins and discovered hundreds of people standing in the rain, staring at the "death hole."

Two women were conversing quietly in the crowd. "Do you think people will remember the horror?" one asked. "For a time," the second one said. "But they soon forget."

The Akron Idol

JAMES DEAN LOOK-ALIKE WES BRYAN MADE A NAME FOR HIMSELF IN LATE '50S

(Originally published Sept. 29, 2003)

People often stopped and stared when Bryan Mintz walked into a room. His brooding good looks reminded them of a famous movie star.

He couldn't possibly be that actor, though. James Dean was dead.

This is the strange-but-true story of an Akron construction worker who looked so much like an American idol that he became one himself in the late 1950s. As a consequence, he befriended another icon, Elvis Presley, and launched a successful career as a singer, songwriter and producer.

When Bryan Mintz changed his name to Wes Bryan, his world changed, too. "It's a crazy history, I guess," said Bryan, 66, who now resides in North Hollywood, Calif.

Bryan, a native of Murphy, N.C., remembers being "a young and dumb kid" when he came to Akron in the mid-1950s to work for his father, Noah Mintz, a building contractor. "Boy, that was a nice time," Bryan said. "I have a lot of fond memories of Akron."

He and his father specialized in houses and garages, and Bryan couldn't resist signing his work. He always carved his initials into the studding. "I had a fixation on that," he said.

One fateful day in 1956, Bryan's life took a turn. He was dining at Kippy's Restaurant in Akron when a stranger approached him. Did he know he looked like James Dean? Bryan had heard this before. Many times.

He was a big fan of Dean and had mourned with the rest of his generation when the movie idol was killed at age 24 in a California car crash on Sept. 30, 1955.

"I remember seeing his movies, and people started making comments that I had a similarity to him," he said. "I thought he was a fine actor."

He was flattered by the comparisons, but he didn't quite see the resemblance. "I didn't really pay heed to what they were talking about," he said.

But the stranger at Kippy's was persistent. He was Irving Waitzkin, owner of Portraits by Irving, a studio on South Main Street. Waitzkin took the bemused 20-year-old to the Akron Beacon Journal and intro-

duced him to Sunday Editor Hal Fry, who asked photographer Bill Samaras to take several pictures.

On March 24, 1957, the Beacon Journal published a giant photo of Bryan's face on the cover of Sunday Roto magazine. "Academy Award ghost?" the caption read. "Guess again. This is an Akron ringer for the late James Dean—construction worker Bryan Mintz."

The reaction was immediate. Young women flooded the newspaper with mail, clamoring for details about the blue-eyed, brown-haired dreamboat.

"The Akron Beacon Journal is where I got started and it's very sacred to me," Bryan said.

The magazine found its way into the hands of producer Max E. Youngstein, who had just founded United Artists Records and was looking for new talent. He was pleased to discover the handsome construction worker could sing. Bryan had performed in high school plays, and knew how to play guitar. His voice sounded a lot like Pat Boone.

"They saw me and they said, 'I'm signing you up,'" Bryan said. "I was their first artist."

Goodbye, construction. Hello, pop music.

United Artists came up with the name Wes Bryan and booked the young singer into a New York studio, where he cut his first single: *Lonesome Love* with *Tiny Spaceman* on the B-side.

A big party was held at the 21 Club to celebrate the record company's launch, and Bryan got to meet another former Akron laborer: Clark Gable. "He shook my hand and said, 'What are you doing here, son? How are you?' I'll never forget that."

The publicity machine was in full gear when Bryan's record was released in late 1957. Bryan's mug was plastered on teen magazine covers and articles such as "Another James Dean?" and "Who Will Wear the Crown?"

"They sent me out to Fairmount, Ind., and I met Charlie and Emma Dean, Jimmy Dean's grandparents," he said.

The resemblance wasn't exact, but the Deans were impressed with the youngster. "They thought I had a lot of similarity, even walked like him quite a bit," Bryan said.

He followed Dean's footsteps in other ways, dating Christine White, a close friend of the actor. "That's what attracted the two of us together," he said.

Bryan began a national publicity tour of radio and TV programs, and traveled more than a year with Buddy Knox, whose big hit song was *Party Doll*.

After Bryan appeared on Wink Martindale's *Dance Party* show in Memphis, Tenn., Elvis Presley invited him to his house in December 1957.

"He idolized Jimmy Dean. . . . He sent a limousine to pick me up and he wanted to see what I looked like," Bryan said. "He had just finished *Jailhouse Rock*."

Bryan and Presley hit it off right away. "I met Gladys, his mother, and his father, Vernon, and had a toot," Bryan said. "We became pretty close friends all those years. I used to hang out at the house in the early '6os when I got off the road."

Presley was pleased when he heard United Artists was grooming Bryan for *The James Dean Story*, a movie about the late actor's life. "He said, 'You'd be perfect for it,'" Bryan recalled. "It never was to be, of course."

Bryan was visiting Chicago when he was confronted by a deranged fan who didn't want the movie to be made. "He threatened Max Youngstein's life," Bryan said. "So they got a restraining order against the guy and threw him in the calaboose and he stayed there for a while. When they let him out, we didn't know where he was. He found my hotel and shot at me. It just whizzed by me. That was the end of the beginning."

Police captured the man, but United Artists decided to shelve the movie. There would be no starring role for Bryan. "There's a lot of things that slid by me, but you've got to pick up the pieces, brush yourself off and go on," Bryan said.

He returned his focus to music, recording *Freeze!* in 1958 and *Honey Baby* in 1959. In 1960, Buddy Knox and Jimmie Rodgers (*Honeycomb*) persuaded him to join Roulette Records, where he did *Melodie D'Amour*.

"Elvis loved that record," Bryan said. "Of all the things I ever recorded, he liked that particular thing and had it on his jukebox for quite some time."

With the teen spotlight fading, Bryan joined American Music, where he worked as a staff writer in the early 1960s alongside Glen Campbell, Johnny Rivers and others. "We would write songs together," he said. "Being a staff writer, I used to have to turn 30 in a month."

In his lifetime, he has written 382 songs—and counting. "Fabian recorded a thing called *Break Down and Cry* and Frankie Avalon did a few things (including)

It's not James Dean! This is Akron construction worker Bryan Mintz, soon to be known as Wes Bryan, on the March 24, 1957, cover of Sunday Roto magazine in the Akron Beacon Journal.

I'm Forever Yours," he said. "Bobby Darin did *The Old Prospector*."

Pat Boone recorded *I Feel Like Crying*, which Bryan wrote with Presley bodyguard Red West. "The first big installment check that I got from that song, I went out and bought myself an XKE Roadster and took it up and parked it in front of Elvis' house."

It was right after Viva Las Vegas and Presley was dating Ann-Margret. "She came out and fell on the hood," he said.

Bryan still gets residual checks from the old songs. "It's kind of tapering down, but through the years, it's lasted a good run," he said.

He's hopeful that one song, *The Dying Ember*, will someday be heard. Presley recorded it in his home studio and it's still in the archives at Graceland. "Eventually they'll probably release it," he said.

Wes Bryan is as busy today as ever, working in studios and producing songs. He does a lot of projects for Capitol Records.

"I just finished an album for a kid up in Las Vegas," Bryan said. "Sam Hemingway is his name. He's quite a talent. He sounds a little like Bobby Darin.

Bryan also is proud of his daughter, Hollie, who has recorded a demo album and is being touted as a new L.A. diva. "She's a great singer," he said. "She likes rhythm and blues. She can sing opera. I wish I'd had the talent that she has."

Bryan is writing books about two late, great friends. The first, *The Lonely Idol*, is about Presley, who died at 42 in 1977. "He's one of the nicest people I ever knew in my life," he said. "He was one of a kind."

The book will take a spiritual look at Presley, which may be an eye-opener for fans, he said. "He was a very religious guy, you know. When he made the transition from rock 'n' roll into gospel, it was like night and day."

The second book, *Bogart of the Westerns*, is about Lash LaRue, the bullwhip-brandishing cowboy Presley idolized as a kid. Bryan met him at a western convention and the two remained friends until LaRue's death at 78 in 1996.

Bryan has been in the music business for 46 years and still loves his job. He thanks Akron for the life-altering experience. If it hadn't been for that 1957 photo, he might still be Bryan Mintz, building contractor.

"I've been able to be my own boss and stay free from punching a time clock," he said. Not many construction workers get to carve their initials in music history.

Guarding JFK

FORMER OFFICERS REMEMBER ESCORTING SENATOR KENNEDY IN AKRON

(Originally published Oct. 1, 2000)

Cheering and screaming, the frenzied crowd surged toward the Oldsmobile convertible as it rolled into downtown Akron. Men, women and children pushed for a closer look. About 50,000 people filled the streets, chanting slogans, holding signs and throwing confetti. The roar was deafening.

U.S. Sen. John F. Kennedy, D-Mass., sat atop the back seat of the white convertible, waving and smiling. Sporting a bronze tan, the 43-year-old presidential candidate looked debonair in his crisp gray suit and blue tie.

It was Sept. 27, 1960. Only the night before, Kennedy had faced Vice President Richard Nixon, the Republican candidate, in a Chicago television station for their first presidential debate.

Akron obviously liked what it saw on TV. Thousands of admirers greeted Kennedy when his airplane landed at Akron Municipal Airport.

Among the dignitaries were Gov. Michael DiSalle, U.S. Sen. Frank J. Lausche, U.S. Sen. Stephen Young, Akron Mayor Leo Berg and Democratic National Committee co-chairwoman Margaret Price.

Akron police provided security for the senator and led his motorcade from the airport to the Akron Armory, where he was to give a speech.

Officers Bill Boyce and Bill Wilson received the plum assignment of escorting Kennedy's convertible. They rode 1955 Harley-Davidson motorcycles alongside the auto during the entire route. "There were huge crowds everyplace," recalls Wilson, 70, a retired lieutenant who lives in Springfield Township. "They really were fond of him. The streets were just lined with people."

The motorcade traveled up Triplett Boulevard to Arlington Street to East Exchange Street. "We went up East Exchange, down past the Beacon, down to Main Street, turned to the north and went on down to the Armory," says Boyce, 70, who lives in Port Orange, Fla.

The crowds grew thicker and noisier as the motorcade neared downtown, making the job a challenge for the officers. "There was a big crowd down there on Main Street, and we were getting close to the Mayflower Hotel," Boyce says. "The crowds ran out into the street. I've got that 800-pound motorcycle and people ran right into the motorcycle.

"I fell over against the side of the car, right into just the front of it, and I was able to straighten the motorcycle back up again."

Many people tried to lean into the convertible to shake Kennedy's hand. "I remember being concerned for the people trying to get in as we were moving through, that somebody would get hurt," Wilson says. "You know, they did surge forward a lot on us."

The caravan slowly navigated the streets, squeezing between the tightening lines of spectators. "Oh, there was a lot of them," Boyce says. "Kennedy was sitting in the car up there at the Armory and I looked at him and I said, 'Fellow, you've got a lot of friends here.'"

Wilson, a lifelong Republican, says he couldn't help but be impressed with Kennedy. "I don't know exactly how to describe it," Wilson says. "You were drawn to him, and it was returned. He acted like you were the most important person in the world at that particular time."

Wilson recalls having "a nice long talk" with the senator when the motorcade finally stopped behind the Armory about 20 minutes ahead of schedule. "He was probably as charismatic a person as I've ever met in my life," Wilson says.

"He was telling us that his hands were raw from shaking hands, and he said how sore his hands were...."

"His personality just impressed me. You know, we sat there on the hood of the car and on the side of the motorcycles, and we'd talk like you'd talk with a gang of people you were golfing with."

The officers waited as Kennedy entered the Armory for his speech. A standing-room-only crowd of 5,000, loud and boisterous, had packed the arena.

Kennedy's 15-minute talk focused on reducing the jobless rate, strengthening the economy, building the military, improving education and meeting "the challenge of the 1960s."

An Oldsmobile convertible carrying presidential candidate John F. Kennedy squeezes through crowds on Akron's South Main Street in 1960. Akron police officers Bill Boyce and Bill Wilson rode alongside on Harley-Davidson motorcycles.

"This is a contest between those who say times are good and we who say they can be better," Kennedy told the crowd. "I can assure you, if I'm elected, the light that comes when society moves will burn in the United States again."

Thousands more gathered outside the Armory for a glimpse of Kennedy after his speech. The senator got back in the convertible and the motorcade inched its way through the phalanx of people.

Although the crowd was pushy and security was minimal, the officers never feared for the safety of the candidate. Those were different times.

"The thought never entered your mind," Wilson says. "I was more concerned for somebody running up and grabbing him, trying to kiss him, than for somebody trying to hurt him."

Boyce agrees: "They were so happy to see that fellow come down the street."

The motorcade picked up speed as the officers led the senator out of town. They drove Kennedy down Market Street to Canton Road past the Lakemore Shopping Center. Another police escort was waiting for Kennedy near Stark County. He was going to speak in Canton that night. "The Canton patrolmen picked him up and took him on," Boyce says. "We just took our bikes on back to the garage and that was it."

The historical significance of the day really didn't dawn on the officers until two months later when Kennedy defeated Nixon to become the 35th president.

"I escorted (Lyndon) Johnson, too, later on and Nixon as well," Wilson says. "None of them got the reaction that Kennedy did . . . He really was a nice gentleman. I enjoyed that very much."

Midway of Memories

MOGADORE WOMAN, 100, RECALLS WORKING IN A TICKET BOOTH AT SUMMIT BEACH PARK IN AKRON

(Originally published May 2, 2005)

When Sara Wohlford reminisces about Summit Beach Park, she hears the happy echoes of childhood. Laughter and screams. Horns and whistles. Sirens and bells.

A symphony of sound drifted over the Akron midway—the low rumble of roller coasters, the lilting melody of carousels, the metallic hum of machines. "Everything had its noise," she said.

The 100-year-old Mogadore resident has pleasant memories of growing up in the amusement business. Her father, Jack Kaster, designed every roller coaster in Summit Beach history. "The parks were just like home to us," she said.

Probably every child in America would have traded places with her. Not only did she spend the summer in an amusement park, but she also got to enjoy free rides. "Why, sure," she said with a laugh. "We always got the first one and the last one."

Being Kaster's daughter definitely had its privileges. Sara Kaster was born to Jack and Carrie Kaster on Dec. 24, 1904, in Hawthorn, Pa. Her father, the son of a lumber mill owner, made a name for himself as a roller coaster designer for the McKay Construction Co. "Dad built them all over the country," Wohlford said.

Kaster developed rides in Ohio, Pennsylvania, Indiana, Illinois, Maryland, Massachusetts and New Hampshire. His creations could be found at Cedar Point in Sandusky, Luna Park in Cleveland and Idora Park in Youngstown.

About 1910, Kaster was hired to design a coaster at Silver Lake Park, a 600-acre resort once nicknamed "The Coney Island of the West." When the job was complete, park managers persuaded Kaster to stick around and look after his new thrill ride.

Kaster managed the Silver Lake coaster while his wife cooked meals for park employees. He moved his family into a little cottage near the resort.

"Silver Lake was our home first," Wohlford said. "When I was a kid, we were down there. That's where I learned to swim. I'd help take the ponies over to the pony track."

Despite the investment in a new coaster, Silver Lake Park was near the end of the line. The park, which had operated since the mid-1870s, would shut down after the 1917 season and be sold for residential development.

After six years, Kaster jumped ship. His friend Ed Sheck, an Akron attorney, had won a contract to operate amusement rides at Summit Beach, a new park in Akron.

Sheck invited Kaster to design a roller coaster for the resort. Kaster responded with the mile-long Dixie Flyer. He would go on to design The Red Devil, Pippin and The Sky Rocket.

Summit Beach Park, "Akron's Fairyland of Pleasure," opened to the public in 1917. Its 50 buildings and 100 attractions included a Ferris wheel, merry-go-round, midway, dancing pavilion, roller rink, swimming pool, theater, picnic grove, penny arcade, shooting gallery, boat launches, a submarine, a twirling ride called The Whip and a motorcycle thrill show called the Motordrome.

The park was an immediate success. Residents arrived by the tens of thousands—in automobiles, streetcars and canoes.

"There wasn't hardly a day that went by that you didn't have crowds," Wohlford said. She wasn't yet 14 when she started working at Summit Beach. It was May 1918 and the United States was fighting in World War I.

Wohlford operated a ticket booth for a vendor who sold ice cream sandwiches. The wooden structure was painted white and had seating for only one person.

"I was a ticket seller. I sold a 10-cent ticket and a 1-cent ticket," she said. "The 1-cent ticket was a war ticket."

Every day, Wohlford caught a streetcar at the Silver Lake Junction of Hudson Drive and Front Street. She rode the car to Market and Howard streets in downtown Akron and transferred to a line that took her to Summit Lake. "That's quite a ways to go," Wohlford said.

It was a 5-cent fare from all points in Akron. Streetcars arrived every three minutes at the park. Summit Beach operated from 1 to 11:30 p.m. every day. There was no admission charge.

Mogadore resident Sara Wohlford, 100, holds up 1917 photographs of Summit Beach Park's carousel and Dixie Flyer roller coaster in 2005. Her father, Jack Kaster, designed every roller coaster in the Akron park's history. She started working in a ticket booth during World War I.

"I was down there from the time they opened until the time they closed," she said.

Wohlford recalls one summer day when her little sister Bernice came to the park for a visit. "We had a door on the back of the booth and she'd sit there," Wohlford said. "This man would make ice cream sandwiches. He got his ice cream in blocks, and he would cut off the ends and give them to my sister. She would sit on the floor in the back of my booth, eating her ice cream."

Wohlford also filled in for other workers as needed. "I sold tickets down at the roller rink for a while," she said. "Then there were times they'd need somebody to sell tickets over at the merry-go-round."

Ticket sellers were allowed to take breaks from their booths and could roam the park. One of the great perks was getting on amusement rides for free. "Oh, my gosh, I rode every one of them," she said.

Wohlford, who attended Crawford Elementary School and Cuyahoga Falls East School, spent at least three summers working at the park. But then the time finally came to go. Around age 17, she quit the resort to work full time at Eclat Rubber on Front Street in the Falls.

Just like a roller coaster, life took several twists and turns. In 1923, she married Francis C. Adams, whose father worked at Eclat as a firefighter. The couple had four children: Betty Adams Gallo, Viola Adams McKay, John E. Adams and Dorothy Adams Bumstead. When her husband died in 1940, she had to support the children on her own.

She worked at Firestone during World War II and then accepted a job at Lea Drugs, where she remained a fixture until retiring in 1969. She married her second husband, John Wohlford, in 1947.

Tragedy struck again in April 1948 when her father suffered a fatal plunge from a roller coaster at Summit Beach. Jack Kaster was inspecting the ride before the season opened in two days. The 72-year-old lost his footing and fell 35 feet to the ground. He died one day later.

Summit Beach Park began a steady decline over the next decade. The park lost its sparkle. Paint peeled. Metal rusted. The midway began to look rundown.

In 1958, the park closed down. Wohlford remembers it was a sad time for anyone who ever worked there. "It's like taking something out of your life," she said.

Following the death of her second husband in 1985, Wohlford moved to Mogadore to live with her daughter Betty Gallo. At 100 years old, she is cheerful and sharp. On a recent afternoon, she led a visitor on a tour of her home, using her cane to point out objects of interest. Her home is filled with beautiful quilts, rugs and wall hangings—all of which she created.

Her father wasn't the only designer in the family. "I made sweaters for my children and grandchildren," she said.

That must have taken a while. Sara Kaster Adams Wohlford has 13 grandchildren, 12 great-grandchildren and four great-great-grandchildren.

"She's always a happy person," Gallo said. "She's very thoughtful and caring. She is always thinking of everybody else before she thinks about herself."

Wohlford's eyes sparkle as she reminisces about Summit Beach. She thinks about the thrilling rides, the glittering lights, the exciting times—the park she once called home. "Yes, I liked it," she said. "Those were the days."

The Road to Akron

COMEDIAN BOB HOPE PAID TRIBUTE TO SUMMIT COUNTY'S WAR DEAD
AT RUBBER BOWL IN 1944

(Originally published Sept. 12, 2005)

A wisecracking comedian isn't the most obvious choice to land a serious role.

Akron officials were casting against type when they invited Hollywood jokester Bob Hope to be the keynote speaker at a World War II memorial service.

The Cleveland comic had never presided over such a solemn occasion, but Americans held him in the highest regard for traveling more than 200,000 miles to entertain and boost the morale of U.S. troops.

Community leaders were in the middle of planning a Rubber Bowl ceremony Sept. 24, 1944, to honor 600 Summit County men and women who had died in the war. A powerful speaker was needed to deliver the memorial address.

Someone, no doubt with a straight face, suggested Bob Hope, even though this was the same man who had hammed it up with Bing Crosby on the *Road to Singapore, Road to Zanzibar* and *Road to Morocco*.

The offbeat idea clicked. Mayor Charles E. Slusser mailed a formal invitation to the comedian, who had recently returned from a USO tour of the South Pacific.

The reply was immediate. "My being a fellow Buckeye, it will be a privilege to meet with the people of Akron and tell them some of the experiences I had with the men and women of your community in the war theaters," Hope wrote to Slusser. "Depend on my being at the Rubber Bowl Sept. 24."

For the next two weeks, a question lingered among some in Akron: Was Bob Hope capable of delivering a serious speech?

The mayor proclaimed Sunday as War Memorial Day. The city sponsored the free event with the assistance of industry, labor, veterans and religious groups.

Invitations were mailed to the parents and families of every local service member who died in the war. Special seating was arranged for Gold Star Mothers of World Wars I and II. Extra buses were scheduled to transport citizens from downtown to the Rubber Bowl.

The only thing that didn't cooperate was the weather. The temperature plunged into the low 30s on Sept. 24—

the earliest killing frost on record in Akron. That didn't stop nearly 25,000 people from paying tribute to Summit County's fallen heroes.

The Rubber Bowl ceremony began with a procession by the American Legion, Veterans of Foreign Wars, 314th Army Service Forces Band and a drum and bugle corps. An invocation was given. A benediction was pronounced. The 125-voice Akron Civic Chorus performed inspirational songs. Local actors offered a short play about the war.

Lt. Col. Kenneth D. Johnson of the Army Service Forces presented a war memorial plaque for Akron's mayor to place in the Municipal Building.

Mayor Slusser read a telegram from President Franklin D. Roosevelt: "I join with you in honoring the memory of those sons and daughters of Akron who have died in the service of their country. As a very minimum, we owe them the memorial of continued devotion to our home front tasks until the war is won. Beyond such service now we must dedicate ourselves also to the determination to make, beyond victory, enduring peace as their monument for the ages."

Organ music played gently while the roll of honor—a list of 600 names—was read to the crowd. Afterward, the audience stood for a moment of silence.

Then Bob Hope took the stadium stage. "Ladies and gentlemen, I wish the Akron Rubber Bowl were big enough so that every American could have been here to stand with us for that one silent minute of tribute to your sons and daughters," Hope said. "But even though that minute was silent, I'll bet many of the great thoughts inspired by other great moments in our nation's history were running through your heart. This is a big moment."

If there were any concerns about a comedian giving a serious speech, they quickly dissipated in the frosty air. Wearing a dark suit and speaking from a lectern, the 41-year-old Hope delivered a passionate, eloquent address.

He reminded the crowd about President Lincoln and Gettysburg. "On that day, a man made a short speech—more of a prayer than a speech," he said. "It was a prayer on a battlefield where American boys had

Screen and radio personality Bob Hope, who grew up in Cleveland, accepted Akron's invitation to be the keynote speaker at a World War II memorial service in the Rubber Bowl.

died, and he said: 'Let us here resolve that these honored dead shall not have died in vain.'

"You're thinking the same thing tonight, aren't you? We all are and want to keep on thinking it."

Hope recalled visiting Ohio natives from the 37th Infantry Division during a Pacific stop at Bougainville in the Solomon Islands.

"Some of you are relatives of those boys," Hope said. "I never saw a gang of fighting men in better condition. They look great. There is no outfit out there doing more to shorten the war than the 37th Division is."

He bestowed the highest praise on Akron for working nonstop to beat the enemy. U.S. service members were very much aware of the city's efforts, he said. "Whenever a B-17 sets down from a mission and the crew heaves a big sigh of relief, Akron's a part of that sigh, for once again Akron's big tires have come through," Hope said. "When a supply truck bounces over roads ruined by shell fire, Akron's trademark is written on that ground.

"Akron is in every battle, on the ground and in the sky. Yes, sir, you people here tonight have mixed your sweat with G.I. sweat in every battle since Pearl Harbor."

When the last battle is won, U.S. troops will come home, he said. They will want to meet those people who didn't forget them in the war, Hope said.

Then, turning to the Gold Star Mothers in front of the stage, he acknowledged that some had made the ultimate sacrifice for their country. "In the audience are the loved ones of hundreds of Akron boys killed in this war," Hope said. "Among you, too, as your guests are Gold Star Mothers . . . These are the mothers who so painfully have learned what a costly thing freedom is— how much one must be ready to pay.

"In paying our tribute to these mothers, let's tell them how thankful we are to them—the women who gave the men who gave America time to prepare for victory. Thank you."

A platoon of 24 soldiers fired three volleys in honor of fallen comrades. The ceremony concluded with a bugler sounding taps. On the other side of the hill, a second bugler played the mournful echo. An American flag was raised to full staff. The crowd joined in singing the national anthem.

Afterward, Bob Hope was whisked away to WADC radio downtown to appear on *We the People*, a live national program at 9:30 p.m. on CBS. The network had wanted him to go to New York for the Sunday broadcast, but the comedian had kept his promise to Akron.

In the studio, Hope met with Hollywood actor Jackie Coogan, who was in Akron as a featured celebrity at an Ohio model-plane competition. The two reminisced for a while about vaudeville. Coogan played a few tunes on a piano and Hope warbled a few songs.

Soon Bob Hope would be on the road again. The venerable comedian would circle the globe many times over, entertaining troops from Korea to Vietnam to the Persian Gulf—not to mention appearing in movies, radio programs and television shows. The Cleveland legend was 100 years old when he died in 2003.

Beacon Journal reporter Rayy Mitten was fortunate to snag a quick interview with Hope just before he left town in 1944. The newsman asked Hope what he thought about the memorial service at the Rubber Bowl.

"It was the finest program of its sort that I've ever seen anywhere," Hope replied. "I was really thrilled to have been included in it. It's the first time I've ever made a talk like that, you know. It's really way out of my line—but it was wonderful."

By Popular Request

(Originally published Sept. 9, 2002)

It wasn't rock 'n' roll, but it certainly was popular. Radio host Alan Freed's *Request Review* program ruled Akron's airwaves in the late 1940s.

The late show on WAKR was mandatory listening for the younger crowd. It played the coolest records, aired listener requests and allowed teens to dedicate songs to someone special.

The show's success belonged to its charming emcee. During a 4½-year reign in Akron, Freed was the king of the bobby-soxers and the lord of the hepcats. It was a dream come true for the fresh-faced kid from Salem.

Freed was only 23 when WAKR hired him in 1945—for $60.50 a week—to serve as host of the 11:15 p.m. show. It wasn't an ideal hour, but the energetic emcee turned the nightly program into something that could not be ignored on the radio dial.

He played pop and jazz records, and developed a snappy, engaging patter between songs. In that pre-rock era, the big acts included Frank Sinatra, Vaughn Monroe, Dinah Shore, Perry Como and Patti Page.

Freed was the only WAKR disc jockey allowed to select his own records. Station managers figured they had nothing to lose: Who could possibly be listening at that late hour? As it turned out: a lot of people.

"Oh, yeah, I did," said Minnalu Riley, 69, of Cuyahoga Falls. "I wasn't supposed to. I wasn't allowed to be up that late, but I would turn on that radio at night, real low so nobody could hear that I had it on, and I listened to him."

Riley, a 1950 graduate of Buchtel High School, remembers how she and her teenage friends got a kick out of hearing Freed croon into the microphone.

"He would play requests, and he always signed off with—I can't remember if he started or ended or maybe both—but he would sing himself: 'I don't know why I love you like I do. I don't know why. I just do.' He used to sing that every night," Riley said.

Freed's 45-minute program took off like a rocket. Within a few months, he was receiving about 500 letters a day from fans.

WAKR wisely turned that success into a franchise. In addition to his nightly gig, Freed began a 60-minute daytime show called *Request Matinee* and two 25-minute programs: *Jukebox Serenade* and *Music for Dinner*.

On Saturdays, *Request Matinee* aired from 2 to 5 p.m. and *Request Review* ran from 11:15 p.m. to 1:30 a.m. Somehow, Freed also found time to cover sporting events and serve as the master of ceremonies at dances.

Riley recalls attending a sock hop at Portage Path School when she was a Buchtel freshman. "Alan Freed was the emcee and he played records for us," she said. "Those who requested, he gave a record, and he signed a record for me."

A special thrill for Akron teens was joining the studio audience of *Request Review*. The show was broadcast from WAKR's studio in the basement of First Central Tower (later called First National Tower, now called FirstMerit Tower).

It was cramped, but Freed invited his young fans into the studio for Saturday shows. There was room for about 24. "Well, hi-ya, gang!" Freed greeted the group.

"Well, hi-ya, Alan!" the teens responded in unison.

Freed usually had the audience select a "studio queen." He then sang a romantic song to the blushing bobby-soxer.

During songs, he liked to chat and socialize with his visitors. "I was there," said Naomi Joyce, 71, of Barberton. "I remember it well."

Joyce, a 1949 graduate of Central High School, recalls visiting the show. "One of my friends had an older sister at Central, and we would go down and be in his audience," she said.

"We could also give requests while we were in his audience. He would just play his records and talk in between. That's basically what it was."

In the studio, teens filled out song requests on slips of paper. They could dedicate the song to a boyfriend or girlfriend. "To Billy from Nancy" or "To Mary from her secret admirer" or "To the girls in the front row from the boys in the back row."

There's no doubt who ruled the microphone on WAKR radio's *Request Review* program. Alan Freed is surrounded by young fans from the studio audience during a 1946 broadcast of his late-night show.

"I'm trying to think of a request that I made," Joyce said. "*Bali Ha'i* (from *South Pacific*) was one that he played."

In person, Freed was pleasant and charismatic, projecting a suave but rebellious aura. He was always well-dressed in a suit and bow tie, but liked to shake things up in the staid radio industry. He was polishing his act for the fame that awaited him.

"I don't even think we asked him for autographs," Joyce said. "We didn't realize that he was going to be something special."

Akron native Carroll Grant, 82, now a resident of Centerville, worked at WAKR from 1945 to 1950 and played an integral role on Freed's show.

"I was the control room engineer for a number of years there," Grant said. "I was there for five years. I think I might have been on that program for three or four years."

Freed wasn't the one actually playing those popular platters. It was Grant.

"We had a system," Grant said. "The control room engineer spun all the records and Alan Freed would sit there and talk about whatever. And when he introduced the record, then I'd just release the record."

On the nights without a studio audience, the program seemed relatively sedate.

"He'd talk about certain artists and introduce their music," Grant said. "He was in a studio with a microphone and a desk. And he had guests from time to time for interviews."

Grant said it was nice working with Freed. "He was lighthearted," he said. "He did a lot of joking around. He was very enthusiastic about music and all the chatter that went with it."

If things had worked out differently, Freed might very well have coined the phrase "rock 'n' roll" in Akron.

But he got into a contract dispute over his $10,000 salary and left WAKR in February 1950. He marched across Main Street to WADC radio, taking his listening audience with him.

WAKR filed a lawsuit, saying Freed had signed a no-compete clause and couldn't work for any other Akron radio station for a year. A judge banned Freed from the radio until the case was resolved. He lost . . . then he left.

In 1951, Freed joined the staff of Cleveland's WJW radio. He called himself "Moondog" and began to play rhythm-and-blues records, which he dubbed "rock 'n' roll." In 1952, he sponsored the Moondog Coronation Ball, the nation's first rock concert.

From there, Freed went to New York and became a superstar. He was a rock 'n' roll king until the 1959 payola scandal tarnished his crown. He admitted accepting money to play certain records.

He lost his job, his fortune and his will to live.

Alan Freed was only 43 years old when he died Jan. 20, 1965, in Palm Springs, Calif. He had suffered from uremia, a blood condition caused by failing kidneys.

But his music didn't die.

In 1986, Freed was inducted into the first class of the Rock and Roll Hall of Fame. The spark that ignited in Akron still burns brightly in Cleveland.

Time Is Deadly Enemy

WITH SECONDS TO ESCAPE TANK, 3 GUARDSMEN DIE

(Originally published April 27, 2009)

Precious seconds ticked away as the Ohio National Guard convoy rumbled through the streets of Barberton.

Time was the enemy. Unexpected delays and unfortunate circumstances put the armored military vehicles on a collision course with disaster.

When the locomotive's horn shrieked, it already was too late. An Erie Railroad passenger train slammed into a 33-ton Army tank on April 29, 1951, in a tragic accident that caught everyone by surprise.

"It sounded like the whole end of Barberton was blowing up when the train hit the tank," eyewitness Earl Lybarger told the Beacon Journal after the crash. "My wife fainted when she saw the locomotive would not miss the tank."

If only a few things had gone right, it would have been just another Sunday afternoon. More than 60 members from Company B of the 137th Tank Battalion in Barberton took a four-hour slog to Greensburg and back. In a pelting rain, a Summit County sheriff's cruiser led a "motor march" of National Guard trucks, jeeps and tanks to a practice field at state routes 241 and 619.

The reserve unit conducted maneuvers before beginning the return trip to Barberton. Near the city limits, the convoy sputtered. One of its three Sherman tanks ran out of gas because of a faulty fuel gauge.

The officers huddled and decided to leave the vehicle at the side of Route 619 until fuel could be brought back. The convoy resumed its march only to halt again at the city line as the sheriff's deputy turned over escort duties to Barberton police.

Because of load limits on bridges, the City Engineer's Office had recommended Fairview Avenue as the National Guard's best route to its tank storage garage on Norton Avenue.

The armored vehicles rolled west across the Tuscarawas River and Ohio & Erie Canal before stopping abruptly at a railroad crossing on Fairview. Warning lights were flashing.

There were four tracks. The first two belonged to the Pennsylvania Railroad. The second set, about 2 feet uphill, was shared by the Baltimore & Ohio Railroad and Erie Railroad.

Already running late for supper, the guardsmen had to wait 10 minutes as a slow-moving freight train passed. Finally, the caboose appeared, the blinking lights ceased and the police cruiser crossed.

A National Guard lieutenant stepped out of a jeep, walked over the tracks, looked in both directions and double-checked the warning lights. All was clear. He motioned the convoy to move. A ½-ton truck drove over the grade at 20 mph, followed by a tank traveling in low gear at 5 mph.

In the distance, a horn blasted a shrill warning. Guardsmen looked in horror as a six-car Erie Streamliner rounded a bend 3,291 feet away. It was hurtling 60 mph from Chicago to New York.

The five-man crew of the tank had little time to react. Sgt. Don W. Jameson, the tank commander, ordered the driver to stop. The tank lurched up the slope before halting on the rails. "I was coming around the curve and saw the tank pulling onto the tracks," train engineer J.F. Mason later explained. "But it was too late."

As the National Guard crew scrambled to escape, Jameson and Pfc. Carl Nichols leaped from the turret. Three of their buddies couldn't get out in time.

With a deafening roar, the 100-passenger train smashed into the tank at 5:45 p.m. The impact ripped off the turret and catapulted it 260 feet down the track. Rails bent as the diesel locomotive plowed the heavy tank about 130 feet. The train derailed, the locomotive uncoupled and the tank slid aside like a toy.

Erie passengers were tossed from their seats and beds as the Streamliner skidded 900 feet and came to a rest at a 45-degree slant on a hill.

The tank engine idled for 15 minutes following the crash. The three occupants had been killed on impact. One guardsman's watch was frozen at 5:45 p.m.

The dead were Sgt. Dale E. Cox, 27, of Akron; Col. William E. Livingston, 22, of Doylestown; and Cpl. Ronald L. Peterman, 19, of Barberton. Injured were Pfc.

An Ohio National Guard tank sits astride twisted rails after being struck by an Erie Railroad passenger train on April 29, 1951, at the Fairview Avenue crossing in Barberton. The turret is gone and the tread is missing from the far side of the tank.

Nichols, 20, of Akron, engineer Mason, 61, of Marion, fireman Francis Korte, 46, of Marion, baggageman Michael Korp, 49, of Youngstown; porter George Smith, 42, of New York; and passengers Estelle Hughley, 59, of Ravenna, Bernard McElroy, 72, of Highland, Ind., and Donnie L. Jackson, 35, of Chicago.

Guardsmen and police set up barricades to control the crowd that formed around the crash scene. An estimated 20,000 people watched the rescue, recovery, cleanup and repairs.

Three investigations—conducted by the Ohio National Guard, Public Utilities Commission of Ohio and Barberton Citizens Committee—began almost immediately. Careful measurements were taken. An identical tank was brought to the crossing to time its progress. It made it across the tracks in 18 seconds.

City officials had complained about the unlevel tracks since 1940. Vehicles often bottomed out while trying to cross. The railroads did not make improvements, however. They also ignored a city ordinance requiring trains to travel no faster than 20 mph in Barberton.

The warning system on Fairview Avenue was another issue. There were flashing lights, but no bells or gates. At least 19 guardsmen reported seeing blinking lights before the freight train passed, but none before the Erie Streamliner.

Barberton's inquiry declined to place blame for the tragedy on any single party. The National Guard's review faulted "the inadequate warning system of the Erie Railroad." The PUCO board demanded corrective action on "the grade differential."

The three railroads completed a $10,000 project that fall to make the tracks more level. In 1952, Erie paid $30,000 to the victims' families without admitting "any wrongdoing or liability."

Today, Barberton motorists travel back and forth across the Fairview Avenue tracks. Many drivers probably aren't aware of the tragic past.

Far from the battlefield, so close to home, three brave soldiers lost their lives in a tank.

Fun in the Sun

HI LOMA WAS POPULAR NESMITH LAKE BEACH CLUB IN THE 1960S

(Originally published July 30, 2007)

When David Bersnak hears the song, his mind drifts back to an endless summer on a sandy beach from childhood.

Ha ha ha ha ha . . .

Wipe out!

Drums pound, guitars wail. Once again, *Wipe Out*, the 1963 rock instrumental by the Surfaris, blasts out of the loudspeakers at the Hi Loma Beach Club.

"In the beach house, they had a jukebox," Bersnak said. "Somebody must have been addicted to that song. Every time I went over there, they would constantly play that song."

Bersnak, 57, vice president of the Kenmore Historical Society, can't drive on Manchester Road past Nesmith Lake without looking over to the west shore.

He doesn't see swimmers. Not anymore.

In the 1960s, Hi Loma Beach was a popular resort in Kenmore. Families packed picnic baskets and stayed all day. Kids splashed in the water. Teens dived off the floating dock. Bathing beauties soaked up the sun.

Summer at Hi Loma Beach was a whirl of picnics, luaus, birthday parties and sock hops.

"That was a place where the action was going on in Kenmore," Bersnak said.

Highland Park residents formed the private club in 1959 after acquiring 10 acres and a 200-foot beachfront on a 25-year lease from Castle Homes Inc.

For the first time in 15 years, Nesmith Lake was safe for swimming. Akron health officials lifted a ban from 1944, the year that tests revealed unhealthy levels of pollution in the spring-fed lake.

Starting with 30 charter members, the nonprofit club welcomed nearly 200 families in its first year. Members paid a $50 fee and could invite guests.

The gated grounds off Shoreline Drive included a swimming area, sandy beach, picnic tables, bathhouses, volleyball court and a red clubhouse about the size of a four-car garage. The clubhouse had furniture, equipment, a jukebox and vending machines.

Giant trees provided shade for picnic tables. Families brought lawn chairs or sat on beach blankets. Colorful pennants flapped overhead on ropes.

Beverly Fincher, 56, of Akron, was one of the first to join. Her father, Edward Leyh, was a club founder and board member. "It was the place to be," she said. "All of our friends were there."

In the summer, children stayed at the beach from open to close. Some went home for dinner but returned an hour later. "Sometimes my mom would pack a picnic and we'd eat down there," Fincher said. "We'd cook hot dogs or hamburgers on the grill. We'd be there all day. My dad worked at Firestone. He'd get off work at 2 o'clock and he'd come straight down there."

Retired Akron firefighter Greg Aschelman, 56, who belonged to Hi Loma in the mid-1960s, remembers walking a mile to the beach from his Castle Homes residence. "It was the first place I personally was allowed to go to by myself," he said.

The club was paradise for a 12-year-old boy. The vending machines offered soda pop, candy and ice cream. And the beach . . . well, it was even nicer. "Anything a young guy would want," Aschelman said. "Basically, girls."

During the baby boom, the neighborhood was a wonderful place to grow up. In Aschelman's allotment, there were thousands of children, he said. Most went to the beach.

Dr. Bob Fulton, 62, a Cuyahoga Falls dentist, worked as a lifeguard at Hi Loma Beach in the 1960s. His father, Samuel Pierce Fulton, was a charter member of the club.

The Kenmore teen was teaching Red Cross lifesaving courses at the Portage Lakes when he was recruited for the club. Most lifeguards made $4.50 an hour, he said.

One summer at Hi Loma Beach, he pulled in $1,200. "That was big money in those days," he said.

Fulton arrived at 10 a.m. each day and worked until 5 or 6 p.m. If there was a private party at night, he stayed until midnight.

Kenmore residents enjoyed hanging out all summer at the Hi Loma Beach Club on Nesmith Lake in the 1960s.

He sat in a lifeguard chair or atop a picnic table and scanned the water as dozens of swimmers frolicked. His gear consisted of a life ring, an oxygen tank and a bottle of Sea & Ski lotion.

In the three or four years that Fulton worked at the beach, he had to rescue only one person: A child tripped and was bruised.

Otherwise, it was just a matter of making sure that swimmers followed the rules. Everyone had to leave the water during safety breaks. Children often protested as they made their way back to land. "By and large, I didn't have a whole lot of trouble," he said.

A source of fascination was the floating dock and its diving board. The wooden platform rested on 50-gallon drums, which were tethered to steel pilings and filled with air. As weeks passed, the drums leaked, and the dock dipped in the water. "It was a big place to play hide and seek," Fulton said.

Bersnak, who belonged to the club from about 1961 to 1967, said his family went to the beach to cool off because his home didn't have air conditioning. "We couldn't wait to get in the water and start having fun," he said. "During the breaks, we couldn't wait to get up to the pop machines."

Fincher remembers going to teen dances on Friday nights. "The kids all went down for the dance," she said. "Once in a while they had a band, but most of the time it was the jukebox."

The Surfaris had little competition. Live entertainment was provided by amateur acts. "Usually it was just kids from the neighborhood that started up bands," Aschelman said.

Every once in a while, though, big stars did show up. Bersnak recalls when the TV cast of *Bonanza* took a break from its guest appearance at the All-American Soap Box Derby.

"One summer, I saw Little Joe and Hoss Cartwright walking across the beach in their bathing suits," he said. "That was back when I really liked Westerns on TV, and I got the thrill of my lifetime."

After a decade of fun in the sun, the beach club began to lose its glow. Many original members let their memberships lapse. The facility didn't seem to be maintained as well as it had before.

Cuyahoga Falls resident Roy King, 72, former vice president of Castle Homes, has a theory on why the beach club faded in the early 1970s.

"At the time we built the houses and the people were moving in, they had all young families," he said. "As their kids grew up and moved away, the parents stayed and they had no use for it, I guess. The club just kind of dissolved itself."

Once the group folded, the land was deeded back to Castle Homes. The clubhouse fell into disrepair and eventually burned. Castle Homes demolished what was left, King said.

A picnic area is what remains of the former resort. An old slab marks where the clubhouse stood. A grassy area reveals traces of beach sand. Hundreds of lily pads float offshore.

Out on the lake, steel pilings break the water's surface. The rusting metal is all that is left of the floating dock.

Former members will never forget the fun they had at the club on Nesmith Lake.

"Those were good times," Fulton said.

"It was just the thing to do when I was growing up," Fincher said.

Just as the Surfaris warned, Hi Loma Beach Club wiped out.

Ha ha ha ha ha . . .
Wipe out!

"Every time it comes on the car radio, I think of the Hi Loma Beach Club," Bersnak said. "It takes me right back."

It's Shirley Temple!

MOVIE PRINCESS MAKES SURPRISE TRIP TO AKRON IN 1938

(Originally published June 18, 2000)

Oh, my goodness! Child actress Shirley Temple was a ray of sunshine in the dark-and-gloomy days of the Great Depression. Her movies offered hope at a time when optimism seemed to be a rare commodity in America.

The curly-haired, dimple-cheeked actress was the nation's No. 1 box-office star in the 1930s—not to mention the most popular little girl on the planet.

No wonder Akron residents could hardly believe their eyes in June 1938 when "America's Sweetheart" showed up unannounced in the Rubber City.

The 10-year-old girl rolled into town about 4:30 p.m. June 22 with her parents, George and Gertrude Temple, three bodyguards, one maid and two dolls.

The Temples said they were taking a cross-country trip to Maine by automobile and Akron seemed to be a good place to stop between Chicago and Washington, D.C. They reserved the entire 16th floor at the Mayflower Hotel and then headed downstairs to the Puritan Room for dinner.

Word trickled out about the famous guest at the downtown inn. Newspaper reporters high-tailed it over to the hotel as a small crowd gathered in the lobby to catch a glimpse of the Hollywood star.

"All I had on the trip was some sandwiches and cookies we took in the car," Temple said as she sat down for dinner.

Akron Beacon Journal reporter Helen Waterhouse listened in on some of the VIP dinner conversation that night. "Oh, boy, look at those beets!" Shirley exclaimed at one point.

She dined on tomato juice, split pea soup, asparagus and pork chops, but set aside a piece of celery that she said had been "associating too much with a green onion."

The conversation turned to that night's heavyweight boxing match between Joe Louis and Germany's Max Schmeling in New York City.

"But what are they fighting about anyway, Mother?" Temple wondered. "Louis and Schmeling don't really hurt each other, do they?"

For the record, Louis knocked out Schmeling in the first round to win the heavyweight title.

Waterhouse watched as Temple played a practical joke on her Mayflower waiter. The actress used her cloth napkin to sop up water from a finger bowl on the table. Then she plunked an ice cube in the bowl and called the waiter over.

"Waiter, do you usually put ice in your finger bowls?" she asked with a straight face. The waiter hemmed and hawed over the apparent mistake, but was much relieved when the actress let him off the hook. "It's just a joke," Shirley said with a giggle. The waiter smiled, too.

Temple then noticed two little girls sitting behind her at another table. She took a box of candy over to them, saying: "Would you like one?"

The girls were Akron residents Catherine Johnston, 8, and her friend Nancy Osburn. Their presence was no coincidence.

Catherine is now 70 years old, lives in Aiken, S.C., and goes by the name "Kit" Bryant, but she still remembers the night she met Shirley Temple.

Her uncle, Bill Hall, was having dinner with his wife when the child star and her family sat down at the table next to them. He excused himself and raced to a telephone.

"He called my mother and my father and said, 'I'm at the Mayflower Hotel having dinner and Shirley Temple is here with her entourage. Get Puzzy'—my nickname was Puzz—'get her dressed up and bring her down here right away and she'll have a chance to meet Shirley Temple.' And so off we went," Bryant said.

Catherine and Nancy sat behind the actress, who turned around, offered them candy and quickly befriended them.

"We were both little girls about the same age," Bryant said. "We got to talking. I think she said 'Hi' and I said 'Hi' and she said, 'You want to come up to my room?' And I said, 'Sure.' So we went up to her room."

On the 16th floor, Temple handed one of her two dolls to Catherine. "The doll's name was 'Susie Block,'"

Catherine Johnston and Shirley Temple in Temple's Mayflower hotel room.

Bryant said. "How I remember that, I'll never know. She had 'Marcia' and I had 'Susie Block.'"

The girls chatted amiably about their pet dogs and other childhood subjects. Temple's parents allowed a news photographer to take pictures.

"She was adorable," Bryant said. "I was a picked chicken of a kid. . . . She was a dimpled darling and she was a plump little thing with all those curls and she was the cutest little girl you ever saw in your life. And then there was little me. I was pathetic."

Soon it was bedtime and Temple had to bid farewell to her new friend, leaving Catherine with fond memories and a story to last a lifetime.

The next day, Temple and her parents toured Saalfield Publishing Co.'s South Akron plant, casting some doubt on the family's assertion that their visit to Akron was by chance.

President A.G. Saalfield had the publishing rights to all books and paper products relating to Shirley Temple, a lucrative deal for the company and the actress.

Saalfield sold more than 50 million Shirley Temple books, including coloring books, paper dolls and movie tie-ins of *The Little Colonel*, *Curly Top*, *Dimples*, *Poor Little Rich Girl* and dozens of others.

Temple greeted Saalfield workers and watched in awe as one of the company's massive presses rolled off thousands of copies of one of her books.

"It's swell," she said.

After the tour, the Temples got in their automobile and prepared for the journey eastward. Akron Patrolman Art Adams revved up his motorcycle to give them an escort out of town.

Shirley Temple noticed an excited group of neighborhood children gathered in the Saalfield parking lot. She rolled down her window, leaned out and gave a cheerful hello to the fans.

It was time to hit the road.

"Let's get going, Mother," Temple said.

And with that, the automobile roared off and the greatest child star of all time was gone.

It Came from Mogadore

HALLOWEEN HAUNTED HOUSE WAS A MONSTER SUCCESS IN THE 1970S

(Originally published Oct. 13, 2008)

Halloween was a real scream at the Mogadore Jaycees' Haunted House. Ghastly creatures lurked in every corner of the old mansion. For those brave enough to enter, the dark corridors moaned with door-creaking, chain-rattling, bone-chilling fright.

The Jaycees had no idea what they were unleashing when the Halloween fun house opened in October 1971. The civic group's fundraising experiment turned into a monster that slithered across Ohio as other Jaycees copied the formula.

"We built it all ourselves," recalled Bob Martin, 68, of Brimfield Township, former Mogadore Jaycees president and retired executive vice president of Americhem. "Each person took a room and they did whatever they wanted. We had some pretty creative people."

The Jaycees warned visitors that the brick house had been empty for 100 years and once belonged to Bartholomew Sardonicus VI, a mysterious pioneer whose restless spirit roamed the village as a headless horseman. "We made that all up," Martin said with a laugh.

In reality, contractor Ray Garner allowed the Jaycees to use his house at 3376 Mogadore Road before it was torn down for an apartment complex.

The Jaycees moved walls, rewired electricity, built tunnels, painted rooms and cut a new entrance. After the renovations, the ominous building lured vampires, ghosts, zombies, skeletons, mummies, gorillas, mad scientists, spiders and assorted ghouls.

"All the costumes were being made down in our basement," said former Mogadore Jaycees treasurer Ted Oravecz, 67, of Akron, who taught math at the University of Akron in the 1970s. "At the time, we lived up on Sunrise Boulevard. Our children would not go down in the basement with all those costumes down there. They were scared."

His wife, Linda Oravecz, 65, who was in charge of costumes and portrayed a wicked witch, said Jaycee Wives spent weeks sewing scary outfits, making decorations and cooking food. "There was one room that was nothing but bugs," she said. "We had molds that we made all of these creepy-crawly things."

Organizers conducted a publicity blitz before the grand opening. They put up posters, bought newspaper ads, produced radio spots and mailed free tickets and fliers to high schools in three counties.

Admission was $1 for adults and 50 cents for children. The house, which operated for two weeks, was total pandemonium on opening night. Jaycees couldn't believe the traffic jams or long lines of excited teens.

Shrieks and laughter filled the house as monsters jumped out. Visitors entered through a musty basement, climbed a staircase to a bloody kitchen, worked their way through horrifying scenes, ascended to a series of macabre bedrooms and then ran screaming out the front exit.

"People would go out the front door and they would go back and get in line and come through again," Ted Oravecz said. "We had people come back every night for two weeks."

"They were coming from all over Northeast Ohio, and they were getting their money's worth," Linda Oravecz said.

SPECIAL EFFECTS

Mogadore had never seen anything like it. The house featured dry-ice fog, spooky music, black lights, scary mannequins, real coffins, glass jars filled with slaughterhouse parts and a faucet that appeared to pour blood.

Visitors walked through a dark tunnel with hanging threads that felt like cobwebs. As the ceiling slowly lowered, they hunched over, kneeled and finally crawled out the last few feet.

Martin worked as a monster in an upstairs bedroom. A grotesque mannequin was on one side of a bed while Martin lay next to it in identical makeup. "People would come in the room," he said. "It was kind of dark, not very well lit. They'd go: Those are dummies. Then I'd jump out of bed.

"A whole night of scaring people tires you out. You'd jump out of that bed 200 times a night."

Former Jaycee Roger McKissick, 67, of Springfield Township, was project manager while he taught art at Barber Elementary in Akron. His eerie artwork graced many walls in the house.

The vengeful spirit of Bartholomew Sardonicus VI, a headless horseman portrayed by Rod Brannon, gallops outside the original Mogadore Jaycees' Haunted House at 3376 Mogadore Road in 1971. The Halloween fun house moved to another site in 1973.

"We had a polka-dot room with a strobe light, and we had people who were dressed in costumes that also had polka dots on them," he said. "It was black with white polka dots. You couldn't see them coming at you until they were right on top of you."

Another favorite room had two open caskets that appeared to contain the recently deceased. The coffins rolled down an incline and halted just short of the patrons. Suddenly, the bodies sat up and reached out.

"They didn't expect the casket to be coming at them and they didn't realize the people in the caskets were alive," he said.

The success of the haunted house was a big jolt for the Jaycees. They hadn't expected the crush of customers. Jaycee Wives kept running out of food at the concession stand and had to hurry home to cook more.

"We expected a few people," Linda Oravecz said.

"That first night, I just remember being overwhelmed," Ted Oravecz said.

"I was going home every hour with pockets full of money to get out of there in case somebody robbed us," Martin said.

In fact, the Jaycees took turns sleeping in the house overnight because they were afraid vandals would try to sneak in. "That was kind of scary in itself," Martin said.

The Jaycees had hoped to raise $5,000. Instead, they raked in $50,000. The Jaycees donated the money to Mogadore High to build an athletic field house that stands today.

THE MONSTER GROWS

Mogadore's success inspired a slew of imitators. "I can remember people coming from other Jaycees chapters," McKissick said. "They had people coming through, making notes and copying our ideas."

Within a couple of years, Jaycees haunted houses popped up across Northeast Ohio: Akron, Hudson, Tallmadge, Canton, Canal Fulton, Medina, Massillon, Alliance, Manchester, North Lawrence, Jackson Township.

The Mogadore Jaycees moved their Halloween fund-raiser in 1973 to an old wooden house on North Cleveland Avenue near Mogadore Road.

Although many of the frights were the same, one of the new attractions was a room filled with packing noodles. As customers made their way through the crunchy material, monsters jumped up and grabbed them.

Fewer customers visited the second house—even though it had a better location and operated for a full month. The market was growing saturated and the economy was slowing. "That one wasn't near as successful," Martin said. "By then, everybody was copying it."

Despite having extended hours, the Mogadore haunted house made only $11,000 in 1974. It operated every October through 1978 until a fire damaged the house in June 1979 and Mogadore Jaycees decided to give up the ghost.

NOT SO SCARY NOW

Today, the formerly haunted site has a strip plaza with a Subway, Hungry Howie's and physical therapy office.

Many of the volunteers who worked on the Halloween house remain friends. Every October, they remember an old haunt. "I think we had 40 members and 40 wives that took an idea beyond our wildest expectations and made enough money to build a field house for the high school," Martin said. "That was all good, but I think the best thing was that we forged friendships to last a lifetime. That's why I think it was the mother of all haunted houses."

Requiem for a Diva

ECCENTRIC PORTAGE HOTEL DENIZEN LEAVES SHOCKING FORTUNE WHEN SHE DIES IN 1949

(Originally published Jan. 24, 2011)

Mezzo-soprano F. Louise Butler portrayed a tragic heroine in the opera of life. As the music built to a crescendo, audiences couldn't predict the dramatic final twist. For 30 years, the aging diva lived in a sixth-floor room at the Portage Hotel in downtown Akron, cultivating a reputation as being eccentric if not reclusive. She paid a special rate of $2.75 a day in the 1940s, eating food from cans instead of dining in the hotel's restaurant.

The red-haired Butler wore fur coats, shiny baubles and old-style gowns that hinted at a former place in East Coast high society. She kept a newspaper clipping from the 1890s that hailed her as "one of the most beautiful young women of New York."

She was born Frances Louise Butler in 1866 to a wealthy family in Olean, N.Y. Her father, Nelson S. Butler, owned a store chain and co-founded a bank.

Louise Butler, who despised her given name and never used it, graduated from Smith College in Northampton, Mass., and studied at the Boston Conservatory of Music. The singer won glowing reviews at the Olean opera house before moving to New York City and settling among the Park Avenue elite.

In later life, she told Akron acquaintances how delightful it was to appear at the Metropolitan Opera, playing the title character in Giacomo Puccini's *Tosca* opposite Italian tenor Enrico Caruso's Mario. In addition to Caruso, she counted opera stars Ernestine Schumann-Heink and Antonio Scotti as her friends.

Butler told tales about Hollywood stars Greta Garbo, Mary Pickford and Douglas Fairbanks, and claimed to have discovered Broadway actress Ina Claire. "I'll never forget the day Ina came in with her shoes holey at the toes, wanting me to introduce her to Oscar Hammerstein," she told the Beacon Journal in 1938. "She had a Harry Lauder vaudeville stunt she wanted to put on. I thought she had talent, so I saw to it that she got places."

BROTHER IN KENT

Butler often came to Ohio to visit her brother W.H. Butler, a Yale graduate nicknamed Benjamin, who set-tled in Kent in 1895 to develop and manage the Portage County Telephone Co.

She spent so much time in Akron that she rented Room 648 at the Portage Hotel while maintaining a home in New York. A skilled financier, Butler bought properties in Akron, eventually owning 75 homes and a few business blocks.

Akron businessmen jokingly referred to her as "The Capitalist." Butler rode out the Great Depression while living frugally in the hotel room, but she foreclosed on hundreds of tenants.

Was it all worth it? Butler once confided to a hotel employee: "I want all my money taken up in an airplane and scattered all over the ocean."

That would have been easier than what transpired. F. Louise Butler was nearly 83 years old when she died of pneumonia on Jan. 27, 1949, at Akron City Hospital. Authorities unlocked her hotel sanctuary and gasped at what they found.

FILLED WITH TREASURE

Treasure filled the room. Stocks, bonds, jewels and other valuables were hidden in closets, bureaus and valises.

On a closet shelf, searchers found $300,000 in government bonds wrapped in old newspapers. In a desk drawer, they pulled out sugar sacks filled with $20,600 in diamonds, pearls and jewelry. In a bureau, they found paper bags stuffed with $10,000 in uncashed dividend checks.

Passbooks showed $46,000 in deposits at First National Bank in Akron, $10,000 at Dime Savings Bank in Akron and $160,000 at a New York bank.

The diva's wealth topped $1 million (about $9 million today). Stripping the room, searchers found vintage gowns, satin slippers, stage costumes, old photos and pictures of composers.

About 40 people, mostly curiosity seekers, attended Butler's funeral Jan. 29 at Billow's chapel. Dressed in a lavender gown, Butler reclined in a $1,500 copper casket. The Rev. Harry Nicholson, pastor of West Congregational

Opera singer F. Louise Butler (1866–1949) was once described as "one of the most beautiful young women of New York," according to a newspaper clipping.

Church, presided. "She always greeted me with a smile, perhaps because I came only to administer to her welfare," he eulogized. "I had no interest in her money or her jewels. Irrespective of what others may have found in her, I found her a most interesting and fascinating friend."

After the ground thawed in April, Butler was buried in her family's plot at Mount View Cemetery in Olean, N.Y. Summit County Probate Judge Vincent Zurz appointed Akron attorneys Walton A. Woodling and Scott A. Belden and First National Bank trust officer Howard Milford to serve as administrators of Butler's estate.

They found a 1906 will that named Butler's mother, Elizabeth A. Butler, as the sole beneficiary, but she had died in 1921.

FINDING KIN

The diva had never married or had children, so finding her next of kin was a challenge. Butler's brothers, Benjamin and Nelson Jr., died decades earlier and didn't have any children.

Administrators contacted the Metropolitan Opera and were startled to find that there was no record of Butler singing there. Her stories about Caruso, Garbo and the rest could not be substantiated. Butler apparently had embellished her glittery career.

Meanwhile, letters and telegraphs poured into Akron from across the nation. More than 750 people claimed they were heirs.

Judge Zurz ordered claimants to answer 30 questions and file a formal application. Some claims were comical. Florence Ada Cease of Onaway, Mich., said she was Butler's long-lost sister who was put up for adoption at age 3 by Butler's father. Officials pointed out that the elder Butler died 12 years before Cease was born. The claim was dismissed.

Dan Chambers of Clay City, Ohio, requested $50,000 after weaving a tale about pulling Butler from the path of a speeding streetcar in Los Angeles in 1910. The claim was dismissed.

Earl Porsborg of Bismarck, N.D., furnished a will that named him as sole beneficiary. He said he saved Butler's life in 1922 when he scared off three bears that attacked her stalled automobile in Palouse, Wash.

The will, supposedly written by Butler, had misspellings and grammatical errors, including the sentence: "I want to pay for this great deed he done in saving my life." At the bottom, it was signed "Frances L. Butler," a name she never used. The claim was dismissed.

TAXES OWED

Investigators discovered that Butler had never paid income taxes. Judge Zurz ruled that the estate owed $80,000 in taxes to Ohio and another $17,000 to New York.

Next, he ruled that the remaining money—less legal fees—would be divided among 65 descendants of Butler's grandparents, Alexander and Lydia Butler.

That left $368,877 from the original $1 million. Receiving $13,860 each were Butler's cousins Blanche Morton Butler of Los Altos, Calif.; Juliet Butler Johnston, also of Los Altos; Alice Louise Wilsey of Chilli-

Authorities found a fortune in diamonds, pearls and other jewelry in cloth sacks in F. Louise Butler's hotel room in downtown Akron after she died.

cothe, Ill.; Leander Squires of Auburn, N.Y.; and Ethel Butler Golobay of Yates Center, Kan.

COUSIN STABBED

On the day the check arrived in 1951, Golobay was stabbed to death by her drunken husband, Joseph, who was angry that she didn't give him cash to spend.

Butler's other remaining heirs received $220 checks. Only a handful ever had met her. The estate finally was settled in 1952.

Mezzo-soprano F. Louise Butler created more drama in death than she had in life. When the final curtain fell, there was nothing but stunned silence.

The Swinging Bridge

FORMER AKRON NEIGHBORS REMEMBER RICKETY LANDMARK OVER LITTLE CUYAHOGA

(Originally published May 28, 2011)

Swaying back and forth over a rushing river, the creaky bridge was a rattletrap of splintered lumber and rusted metal. It didn't just bend the rules of architecture. It seemed to defy the law of gravity.

"The swinging bridge," as neighborhood kids called it, connected Akron's Otto Street to Ravine Street over the Little Cuyahoga River and served as a shortcut from Cuyahoga Street to Hickory Street, allowing pedestrians to avoid a two-mile hike down North Howard and across West North Street.

To the children who used it, the tiny span was as important a landmark as the North Hill Viaduct, which loomed to the east. "Nobody in the neighborhood can remember when the bridge was built," the Beacon Journal confided on April 3, 1931.

The unknown architects stretched steel cables across the river, wrapped them around wooden piers and secured them to tree trunks and a phone pole. Builders wired rough lumber across the cables and then nailed planks to the wood, creating "Akron's only suspension bridge" about 10 feet above the water. Cables served as handrails for the shaky structure, which sagged in the middle.

"You actually walked with your legs spread apart," recalled Stan Sipka, 76, of Cuyahoga Falls. "When you walked in a row, the bridge started moving. Eventually, you had to balance yourself."

When Sipka was a boy in the late 1930s and early 1940s, he lived at 155 Otto St. with his parents, Stan and Helen Sipka, and sisters, Rita and Arlene.

The swinging bridge beckoned like Shangri-La. At the dawn of World War II, Sipka and his young friends liked to play soldiers in the hills along the river, protecting their neighborhood from U.S. enemies.

"We used to cross it like it was nothing," recalled Sipka, who taught machine shop and skilled trades at Cuyahoga Falls High School before retiring in 1996. "I'm sure that bridge would be condemned like crazy now."

Sipka said there was one local character, a frequently inebriated fellow from the other side of the river, who often took the shortcut while drunk.

"He would be 'feeling good,' and we would always kind of see if he would fall in, because when he started sagging back and forth, the bridge would just go with him," Sipka said. "And he walked across! Everybody couldn't figure out how he never fell in, because he was weaving back and forth just walking down the street. Apparently, everything was timed just right."

After a heavy rain, kids raced to the bridge and witnessed the water level climb 3 or 4 feet. "Up on West Hill, if a kid lost a ball in the sewer, forget it," Sipka said. "The rain would wash it down the sewer system, dump it in the Cuyahoga River and it would go past the bridge."

Boys stood on the bridge and waited for baseballs, footballs and other toys to float toward the sewage treatment plant. "They had long poles with fish nets on the end, and as the ball came under the bridge, they would thrust the pole in the water and retrieve the ball," he said. "They would then throw the ball to those standing on land. I remember having more than enough balls to play with."

Akron resident Sonya Heckman, 71, who grew up in a house at 163 Mustill St., said the bridge was as scary as it was rickety. "We'd kind of tiptoe across it very carefully because we didn't want it to swing," said Heckman, a retired flight attendant for United Airlines. "And there was always a slat here and a slat there. I mean, there were so many that were missing. And we had to figure out a way to get around it. It was just terrible."

A child of divorced parents, Heckman lived with her mother Mabel Vrabel, but frequently visited her father John Suscinski, a South Akron Awnings player who lived on Hickory Street.

Heckman's big decision was whether to take the safe route, which took 30 minutes, or cross the bridge and get there in 10 minutes. She often traveled with her younger friend, Arlene Sipka.

"Nobody wanted to walk the long way," she said. She recalls that childhood pranksters Danny Gradisher and Donny Goliath liked to sneak up behind the girls after they stepped onto the wooden planks.

"I don't know why, but they thought it was funny to grab the end of the bridge there and shake it," Heckman said. "You know, make it go up and down, like a wavy effect. . . . Somehow or other, we managed to get across it, and we never got hurt."

Retired police officer Hank Petroski, 69, of Granada Hills, Calif., who grew up at 186 Cuyahoga St., has vivid memories of the swinging bridge in Akron.

"When I was 6 or 7, we used to go down to the river," he said. "Nowadays, parents don't want their kids to do anything. All we had to do is be home by dark in the summertime."

He had a convenient excuse to hang out at the bridge because his grandfather, John Petroski, lived on Mustill Street. He played there with his pal Larry Boser, who lived on Otto Street. "Larry Boser's family was quite poor—not that we were rich, but he was poorer than our family," he said. "I remember his dad bought him a new pair of shoes, which was a big deal."

The bridge had strange objects hammered to the bottom, including tin Coca-Cola signs with punched-out holes, he said. "Larry and I were running across the bridge and his foot goes down in one of those holes, and when he pulls his leg back up, his brand-new shoe went into the river," Petroski said. The stunned boy watched as the shoe floated downstream. It took a long time to gather the courage to go back home. "He said, 'I'm going to get killed,'" Petroski said.

An unpleasant incident at the bridge made a lasting impression that may have influenced Petroski's career. "The first dead body I ever saw, I was down there by myself," he said.

One day, he saw several police cars parked near the river and watched officers drag a man's corpse from the water. It had floated downstream after several days in the river. "When I saw that dead body when I was 6 years old or 7, it was probably an omen that I was going to be a homicide detective, and I didn't know it," he said. Petroski retired from the Los Angeles Police Department in 1990 after 25 years of service.

Over the decades, the Little Cuyahoga bridge underwent repairs as neighborhood tinkerers added

A schoolboy crosses the Little Cuyahoga River on Akron's swinging bridge between Otto and Ravine streets in April 1931. Ten feet above water, the precarious-looking bridge stood for decades. Cables served as handrails for the shaky structure.

boards and adjusted cables. An occasional flood washed it out, but people rebuilt it.

Although the bridge looked like it was ready to fall apart in 1931, it continued to accommodate pedestrians for at least 25 more years. Its precise demise is difficult to pinpoint. Heckman recalls it was still swinging in 1955 when she moved away. "I drove down there several years ago and I was surprised to see it was gone," she said.

Two old piers on the west bank are the only evidence that the structure ever existed. Its former users can't believe they took such a risk for a shortcut. "It was scary, but we did it anyway," Petroski said.

"Just talking about that stirs me up inside," Heckman said.

"I have grandkids," Sipka said. "If I ever saw a bridge like that, I would emphatically say, 'Don't you even think about crossing that bridge.'"

Archie Arctic

CHAPEL HILL MALL'S TALKING SNOWMAN FONDLY REMEMBERED

(Originally published Dec. 17, 2000)

Pssst. Hey, kids. Can you keep a secret?

We've discovered the identity of Akron's original talking snowman. But you can't tell anyone. It's a matter of national security.

In 1968, a mysterious figure debuted at Chapel Hill Mall, striking up conversations with holiday shoppers. His name was Archie Arctic, a 20-foot giant who wore a top hat and scarf, clutched a giant broom and lived in a landscape of artificial snow.

Young children looked up in awe as the smiling character greeted them and asked them questions about their lives.

The gentle voice belonged to Robert Koller, a 19-year-old student at Kent State University, who gave the snowman its name and provided its distinctive personality for two years.

Elisabeth "Libby" Buehl, the mall's first promotion director, came up with the idea for Archie. She asked her KSU sociology professor, Marvin Koller, if he knew any students who might be interested in supplying the character's voice.

The instructor knew just the person—his son Robert—although it took some coaxing when he got home.

"I was looking for a job across the Christmas break," recalls Robert Koller, 51, who now lives near Denver. "He thought I might enjoy it. The irony is, when he first mentioned that to me one evening, I felt terribly intimidated by it." Spurred by his father's encouragement, Koller went for an interview and Buehl hired him on the spot.

"The job began by me helping mall employees build Archie Arctic," Koller says. "I helped set him up. . . . It was basically plywood and chicken wire that was covered in cotton batten, and probably, if I remember right, some spun fiberglass."

Koller hid in a tiny, decorated house with tinted windows and spoke through a loudspeaker to Archie's visitors. "I'd start a dialogue with somebody that was passing by," Koller says. "Or I'd be absolutely silent. Ultimately, children would wander on up, and start poking around, and I'd start talking to them and catch them off guard."

Koller took inspiration from children's TV hosts like "Mr. Wizard" Don Herbert and Linn Sheldon, who treated their audiences with respect. "It's just my personality," he says. "I never truly appreciated people talking in a high, falsetto voice and down-talking to children."

So he'd ask questions: Where are you from? How are you doing? Where are Mom and Dad? Are they shopping?

"Now I would be silly," he says. "I would try to be entertaining and humorous. . . .

"When I was about to sign off, I'd say, 'Well, I gotta go back home to my wife, Ann. You know, Ann Arctic.'"

Children often came back to try to figure out where the voice really came from, but Koller never let kids see him get in or out of his hiding place. He would arrive at work early and stay inside until the mall closed. "We were very careful about that," he says.

An instant hit in 1968, the talking snowman continues to be a holiday tradition at Chapel Hill, attracting about 25,000 visitors every Christmas. The concept hasn't changed in more than 30 years, although the character's name was shortened to Archie and his appearance has evolved into a cartoonish look.

Koller's portrayal of the giant snowman was the start of a distinguished career. "I call it a career—bits and pieces," he says. "I've done a lot of different things." The KSU aerospace major joined the Air Force and became an intelligence officer at Wright-Patterson Air Force Base. "I set my sights to be an FBI agent, but I was found to be four months short of investigative experience," he says. "So I joined the CIA."

Koller served the agency for a year in Washington, D.C., and was on a team that provided weekly intelligence briefings to President Gerald Ford. "Once in a while, I'd have White House lawn duty," he says. "I enjoyed that."

After leaving the agency, he entered the aerospace industry, conducting work for General Dynamics, Grumman, Martin Marietta and Boeing. "When I went into aerospace, most of my assignments have been, as a result, involved in classified operations—things that I haven't been able to really talk about," Koller says.

Talking snowman Archie greets young visitors to Akron's Chapel Hill Mall in the early 1970s. The 20-foot giant debuted as Archie Arctic in 1968.

But there are a few things he is allowed to divulge. "For my first years at Boeing, I was their liaison to NATO for their AWACs aircraft, and that included the period through Desert Storm," he says. "That was probably my biggest single vocational accomplishment."

He also helped investigate the TWA Flight 800 crash off Long Island in 1996. "I was not a critical investigator," he says. "There was a cast of hundreds. I was involved in investigation of fuel system problems on 747s."

Strangely enough, Koller's training as Archie Arctic came in handy in the late 1980s at Boeing. A company set up an 800 number for children to phone Santa Claus, but mistakenly tied the calls into Koller's private line in Seattle, which was intended for commanders and maintenance crews in Germany.

"I would get calls from kids in Minnesota who wanted to talk to Santa Claus. Initially, I did say, 'Well, I'm sorry you've reached the wrong number.'"

But the phone kept ringing and ringing and ringing. "It didn't take long, a couple days, in fact: I surrendered. I just started playing Santa Claus," Koller says. "I went through at least one Christmas season playing AWACs liaison and Santa's helper."

At a certain mall in Akron, Archie was smiling.

Bell Tolls With History

KENT STATE FRATERNITY'S DONATION PEALS FOR 60TH YEAR, NOW WITH SOLEMNITY

(Originally published May 3, 2010)

The loud, metallic clang still sounds the same, but the tone has changed. Once it was a peal of joy. Now it rings with solemnity. Kent State University's famous Victory Bell has transformed into a symbol that its benefactors never intended.

The university is observing the 40th anniversary of the May 4, 1970, shootings, in which National Guardsmen fired into a crowd of people during an anti-war demonstration, killing four students and wounding nine others.

Housed in a brick-and-sandstone structure on the KSU Commons, the Victory Bell played a role in the events leading to the shootings. It will be a focal point today when KSU dedicates the 1970 site on the National Register of Historic Places.

Sixty years ago, the bell represented triumph. Alpha Phi Omega, a national service fraternity, donated it in May 1950.

"We had this idea that Kent didn't have a victory bell, and we thought that was something that we'd like to do," recalled the Rev. Gene Toot, 81, a retired minister from Trinity Presbyterian Church in East Liverpool.

A Dellroy native who graduated in accounting from KSU in 1951, Toot was president of the fraternity. The Epsilon Psi chapter began at Kent State's Canton division in McKinley High School and moved to the main campus in the late 1940s.

"I don't know if there was 25 of us or not," Toot said. "Maybe 30 at most." The group's motto, "Leadership, Friendship, Service," provided a true-blue clue about the membership's composition.

Nationwide Insurance retiree William Kohler, 81, of Canton, a 1951 KSU business graduate, said the fraternity members had a common background. "One of the requirements was that you had to be a former Boy Scout or currently an active member in scouting," he said.

The group's service projects included cleaning KSU bulletin boards, sponsoring barbershop quartet contests and holding dances such as the Hot Rod Hop. "We made a lot of money by raffling off an old car," Kohler said. "That's how we raised the money to buy the bricks."

CALLING UGLY MEN

Richard Barnard, 81, a 1951 KSU graduate in business administration who retired as director of Christian education and camp leader at Christ Presbyterian Church in Canton, remembers another fraternity fundraiser. "I think we ran an Ugly Man Contest," he said with a laugh. "Basically, it involved finding someone who would be willing to run in a contest to be the ugliest man on campus."

One year there was mock outrage when judges picked a woman disguised as an ugly man. Such a pageant might raise a few eyebrows in the 21st century. "That would somehow not work today, although we see lots of ugly people," Barnard joked.

Ravenna native Edward C. Stibbe Jr., 79, a retired dentist in Solon, attended KSU for three years before going to dental school in Cleveland in 1951. As an officer with Alpha Phi Omega, he helped procure the bell with his father, Edward Sr., who worked at Pyramid Rubber Co.

"He was a traffic manager who dealt with the railroads and trucking companies," Stibbe said. "When I mentioned the project to him, he said, 'Let me see if I can get you a bell off of one of the old trains.'"

BELL'S ORIGIN

The Erie Railroad donated a locomotive bell from the repair shop at the Brewster yards near Navarre in Stark County.

The fraternity won permission to place the bell in the atrium of the KSU Administration Building. Toot dreamed up a publicity stunt to post a giant question mark at the site where the bell was to be unveiled.

"Well, the good Lord didn't give me any artistic ability at all, but I couldn't find anybody to make the question mark," Toot said. "So, finally, with great labor, I made it myself and I put it up in there."

The poster hadn't been up for long when Toot heard razzing. To his embarrassment, he drew the question mark backward.

"That was the extent of my artwork at Kent State University," Toot said with a laugh.

Alpha Phi Omega member Arvid Johnson, an architecture student, designed a brick-and-sandstone frame to serve as a permanent structure for the bell.

PEACEFUL SETTING

Kent State President George A. Bowman gave his blessing for the monument to be built at the foot of Blanket Hill, where students enjoyed sunbathing and taking moonlight strolls.

The fraternity didn't know the bell-ringing tradition would be popular—given that winning seasons weren't guaranteed. "Heaven's no," Barnard said with a laugh. "We just hoped that we got to ring it enough." Unfortunately, the bell's wall took a few years to complete and the donors graduated before it was formally dedicated.

For more than a decade, KSU sports fans rang the bell to celebrate wins. In the turbulent 1960s, though, the monument took on another function. Students rang the bell to signal the start of political rallies.

Such was the case in 1970. Upset with the U.S. invasion of Cambodia, students organized a protest May 1 to bury a copy of the U.S. Constitution at the bell. Late that Friday night in downtown Kent, a mob broke windows and clashed with police. Mayor LeRoy M. Satrom called Gov. James A. Rhodes to send the National Guard.

On Saturday night, protesters torched Kent State's ROTC building across the Commons from the Victory Bell, and cut hoses when firefighters arrived. As students rallied Sunday night at the bell, police read the Riot Act and guardsmen fired tear gas to break up the crowd.

About 2,000 protesters gathered at noon Monday, May 4, on the Commons in defiance of an order prohibiting a rally. The Victory Bell rang. Guardsmen fired tear gas, and protesters hurled rocks and shouted obscenities. Anger, fear and chaos escalated. With bayonets fixed on M-1 rifles, guardsmen marched up Blanket Hill, forcing protesters to the other side of Taylor Hall. The Victory Bell was out of view at 12:24 p.m. when more than 60 shots rang out in 13 seconds. "It was just so unlikely that that would have happened at Kent," Toot said.

TIME FOR PRAYER

Earlier that day, a KSU dean had invited the minister to give the invocation and benediction at the June 13 commencement. The campus shut down after the shootings, and officials debated for weeks whether to have the ceremony. Amid tight security, exercises were held at Memorial Gym, and Toot led the prayer. "I was the first person to say something publicly on the Kent State campus after the kids were shot," he said.

Kent State University freshman Peggy Snyder of Akron is the first to ring the Victory Bell donated by Alpha Phi Omega, a national service fraternity, in May 1950. The railroad bell was later moved from the KSU Administration Building to a permanent structure on the KSU Commons.

Every May 4, the Victory Bell is the setting for candlelight vigils and political speeches. The bell is rung at 12:24 p.m. to honor the students killed or wounded.

ALTERED EMOTIONS

The 1970 shootings altered the landmark in the eyes of the men who donated it to KSU. Kohler's interest in seeing the bell has diminished "because it's related to such a sad situation."

"That's the unfortunate part about it," Kohler said. To this day, he blames the 1970 disturbances on "outside agitators" and believes KSU should have "set some parameters" to allow peaceful debate without letting violence erupt.

When he entered the Marine Corps in the early 1950s, none of his classmates at Quantico, Va., had heard of his alma mater. "Now everybody knows where Kent State is, thanks to the 1970s," he said. "It's a damn way to make a name for yourself, I'll tell you that."

Stibbe hopes that KSU can move beyond the shootings. "It's sure taken a long time," he said. Hearing about the 1970 events every May 4 is "one of my biggest sore spots," he said. Even so, the Victory Bell still reverberates for its 1950 donors. "It was a good project for us," Barnard said. "We're glad that it added something to the campus."

Designer Flattered by Listing

VICTORY BELL ARCHITECT CREATES A LANDMARK

(Originally published May 3, 2010)

Arvid Johnson was quite an architecture student at Kent State University.

One of the first structures he ever designed became a national landmark.

Johnson, 78, of Anthem, Ariz., was surprised to learn that his KSU Victory Bell is part of a historic site listed on the National Register of Historic Places.

"I'm flattered," he said. "I really am. I think it's wonderful."

An Akron native, Johnson attended Voris Elementary School and graduated from Garfield High in 1950. As an architecture student at Kent State, he got involved in the bell project as a member of the national service fraternity Alpha Phi Omega.

"Memory is a funny thing, but some things you never forget," he said.

He said he designed the bell's brick-and-sandstone structure with the assistance of classmate Roger Kettering. Johnson also helped build it.

"I actually did some brickwork in there," he said. "It came out very well."

The structure, which is 7 feet tall and 15 feet wide, was completed shortly before he graduated in 1955.

Johnson worked for architects in Canton and Barberton before leaving Ohio for Arizona in 1959. He founded Arvid Johnson Associates in Phoenix in 1961 and specialized in commercial and industrial projects.

"I couldn't even count them," he said. "Most of them are out here in Phoenix. Office buildings, shopping centers, everything."

He was shocked and saddened in May 1970 to learn that the Victory Bell played a part in the KSU shootings, in which National Guardsmen killed four students and wounded nine others during an anti-war rally.

"I heard that they had rung the bell when that riot started," Johnson said. "That was not at all what that bell was designed for. It's a victory bell."

Johnson regrets that he can't attend the dedication ceremony today for the national historic site.

"I think it's marvelous that they're going to do this," he said.

Students play football near the Victory Bell on the Kent State University Commons in October 1976.

Mighty Mud Maidens

AKRON BOASTS FAMOUS FIRST IN WOMEN'S PRO WRESTLING

(Originally published Dec. 27, 2010)

Be proud, Akron. You saw it first.

Although it's not commonly known, our fair city is the birthplace of women's professional mud-wrestling.

Hey, it had to start somewhere.

Magnificent Mildred Burke battled bodacious Babe Gordon on Jan. 7, 1938, at the Akron Armory in a slippery slopfest that made international headlines.

World champion professional wrestler Burke, a 5-foot-2, 128-pound Kansas native destined for the Pro Wrestling Hall of Fame, was only 22 when she agreed to compete in a "Hindu mud match" against vivacious grappler Gordon, 23, a Chicago transplant from Nebraska.

Akron wrestling promoter Carl A. Singleton inked the deal with Burke's cigar-chomping manager Billy Wolfe, who just happened to be her husband.

"It's a bout unique in the history of wrestling," the Akron Times-Press reported before the big event. "There have been Hindu mud matches before but always between men. Singleton's brainstorm is the first between women."

Auburn-haired Burke was "a husky and very capable tosser of holds," the newspaper reported, while Gordon was an "aggressive and fast little brunette" with "lots of color and courage."

For the winter match, the armory delivered 6 tons of mud, "the very best muck" from the banks of the Ohio & Erie Canal near Young's Restaurant off Manchester Road.

Akron's moral guardians clucked their tongues at the scheduled match and warned that the mud brawl would turn into a vulgar display. Despite the protest (or maybe because of it), more than 2,500 fans flocked to the armory that Friday night.

Three preliminary bouts—each about 30 minutes long—took place in a standard, dry ring at the center of the smoke-filled downtown arena.

In the first event, former Ohio State Big Ten champ Stacy Hall wrestled Texas strongman Jimmy Heffner to a draw. In the second bout, Kansas cowboy Orville

Brown used a headlock to defeat villainous heavyweight Nanjo Singh of India.

The evening turned decidedly theatrical when Lord Patrick Lansdowne Finnegan, a foppish character in a royal robe, entered the ring with his valet Tweedles for a match against Brooklyn roughie-toughie Pat Ryan.

In the middle of the fight, Tweedles sprayed the mat with insecticide, "accidentally" spritzing Ryan in the face. The enraged New Yorker tossed everyone out of the ring, including the hapless referee, who had no choice but to declare Finnegan the winner by disqualification.

If Finnegan's prissy act sounds familiar, it's because Texas wrestler George Wagner appropriated it a few years later to become the infamous Gorgeous George.

Finally, it was time for Akron's world premiere. Armory workers dismantled the ring to reveal a mud pit below.

As the crowd applauded, Burke and Gordon finished lacing up their shoes and emerged from their dressing room in one-piece leotards that revealed bare arms and legs. Flashbulbs exploded and newsreel cameras whirred as the scene unfolded.

Referee Ernie Maddock explained to the welterweights (and Akron audience) that the winner would be the first wrestler to hold her opponent's shoulders down in the mud for a three-second count.

SO IT BEGINS

The women shook hands, the bell rang and chaos ensued. Slipping and sliding, Burke and Gordon collided in the pit, dragging down the 240-pound referee and smearing his white uniform in mud.

The crowd howled with delight as Maddock sputtered with indignation and fell again.

Discovering that orthodox wrestling holds were nearly impossible, the wrestlers gathered handfuls of muck and hurled it at each other. The match spun out of control like a great pie fight.

"Their aim got poorer and poorer," Beacon Journal reporter Helen Waterhouse wrote. "Moving picture cameras clicked, reporters and photographers gave up trying to guard their clothing from the onslaught. Screams of laughter rose from a thousand throats. There was a general scramble and ducking behind a barrage of newspapers and blankets on the front rows."

Waterhouse got smashed in the face with an oozing mudball that spattered her green dress.

Again and again, the wrestlers hurled themselves at each other. Burke and Gordon soon were plastered from head to toe in shiny slime. The crowd couldn't tell them apart.

"Beyond the thick coating of mud that covered the two contestants and referee Ernie Maddock, there was nothing dirty or vulgar about the battle between the two 'mud hens,'" Times-Press Sports Editor Pindy Wagner wrote. "It was a clean wrestling match, much cleaner than most wrestling matches."

AND THE WINNER IS . . .

After 12 minutes of slithering, the bout ended when one woman pinned the other in 4 inches of mud. The sludge-caked referee raised the right arm of the victor, but no one in the audience knew who it was.

Only after she wiped her face with a towel did the crowd recognize Burke, who triumphantly retained her world title. She celebrated by splashing mud on her husband-manager Wolfe, who wore a three-piece suit. The crowd enjoyed one final laugh.

For the cameras, Burke, Gordon and referee Maddock took a shower together—fully clothed—to wash away the canal muck.

"The fad seems to be sweeping the country," Burke told a reporter after the mud match. "No one knows how long it's going to last, but while it does, I'm going to do it, for there's good money in it."

She also revealed her newly discovered key to victory: "No matter what part of you falls first, keep your head up always."

Gordon, understandably, was less enthusiastic.

"It was no fun, I can tell you that," she said.

Photos of Akron's match appeared in newspapers around the world. Later that month, Life magazine published a full-page pictorial and theaters showed highlights on newsreels.

Other promoters rushed to book similar bouts.

Clean or vulgar, real or not, women's professional mud-wrestling was a hit.

You made history, Akron.

Here's mud in your eye.

-.—.—-./——/ (Down to) -...../.—...-.. (the Wire)

AKRON'S LAST TELEGRAPH OPERATOR HAD WORLD
AT HIS FINGERTIPS FOR ALMOST 46 YEARS

(Originally published March 31, 2003)

Glen D. Benson knew it was time to retire when he reached the end of the line. For more than 40 years, the Kenmore man worked at the Western Union Telegraph Co. in downtown Akron. He was a maestro of Morse code, tapping out a staccato opus of dots and dashes on the telegraph key.

One day, though, he looked around. No one else was clacking. There were 40 Morse operators at the Akron office when Benson was hired in July 1918. Now he was the only one.

His mastery of the mechanical language was unparalleled, but it wasn't needed anymore. He might as well be fluent in Sumerian or Aramaic.

Telephones, teleprinters and teletypewriters had taken over the telegram industry. Operators had to adapt or face extinction.

"The ones who know only Morse? They're either out of the business or dead," Benson said in a March 1949 interview. "I watched lots of them go."

Benson was the last link in a long, long chain. Akron's first telegraph operations began in 1847, three years after inventor Samuel Morse had demonstrated the revolutionary technology. Morse created an alphabetical code of short and long signals—or dots and dashes—by interrupting the flow of electricity over a wire.

His first message, "What Hath God Wrought," was transmitted May 24, 1844, from Washington, D.C., to Baltimore. Akron's first message, unknown today but probably not as profound, was sent Nov. 12, 1847, by the Lake Erie Telegraph Co.

Postmaster Franklin Adams, the region's first telegraph agent, operated on South Howard Street. The Western Union Telegraph Co. arrived in Akron in 1856.

Glen D. Benson was born in Ravenswood, W.Va., in 1897, the 50th anniversary of Akron's first telegraph. He was raised on a farm in Pomeroy, Ohio, and attended school in Reedsville and Brilliant.

At age 15, he was hired as a messenger boy at the Western Union office in East Liverpool, where he learned the ropes and the wires. Five years later, he transferred to the busy Akron office to be a telegraph operator.

"Usual procedure was to take messages for a while and then send approximately the same number—usually 10 and 10," Benson told the Akron Beacon Journal in March 1959. "If you could type 40 words a minute, you could keep up with any operator."

Soft-spoken and gentle, Benson was not the flashiest of personalities. Although he stood no more than 5-foot-7, he was a giant in Morse code. By age 21, he had won the complete admiration of colleagues by sending crisp, clear messages, quickly and efficiently.

"Of course, the Phillips code helped," he recalled. "It was a system of abbreviations developed by press Morse operators. Like 'POUS' which means 'president of the United States.' They brought out an official book on Phillips code because it was such a timesaver."

His 46-year career had many interesting moments, alternately funny, sad and poignant. Benson recalled one time when a man walked into the Western Union office and plopped down a pair of shoes on the front counter. "I want to wire these shoes to Pittsburgh," the guy said.

"True as I'm standing here," Benson said. "And was he storming mad when he found out what a fool he'd made of himself. Never did find out who made him the butt of that prank."

Another time, an office colleague couldn't keep up with an outside operator who was transmitting Morse code too fast. "Let me cool him off," Benson told his co-worker. He jumped into the seat and captured every dot and every dash in the rapid-fire messages. Then he fired back: "Can't you go any faster? My stuff is starting to pile up."

Telegraph operators won praise for precision and clarity. If the signals ran together, the message was lost. Tapping techniques were as identifiable as nuances of speech.

One operator, for instance, always could be counted on to trip over the same word when sending livestock reports. "If you couldn't make it out, the word was 'cattle,'" Benson said.

Glen D. Benson of Kenmore took the Morse transmitter with him when he retired April 1, 1959, from the Western Union office in Akron. He was the last one who knew how to use a telegraph key.

Telegrams had a minimum of 10 words, and the Akron office sent out 1 million a year. Benson liked sending birth announcements, love notes and travel updates. Far less pleasant were the death notices, illnesses, disasters and other bad news that had to be wired, too. Every working day, the cycle of life played out at Western Union.

In his spare time, Benson did free-lance telegraph work for newspapers and rubber plants. "Goodrich particularly had a tough one…a really fast New York and Chicago wire with lots of code," he told a reporter. "It was a dandy to work."

In October 1920, he transmitted press accounts of the Cleveland Indians' World Series victory over the Brooklyn Dodgers at League Park. In the 1930s, he covered the launches of the Akron and Macon dirigibles at the Akron Airdock. "Sent a lot of heavy stuff out of that hangar at the airport," he recalled.

In the 1940s, he tapped out the results of horse races at Ascot Park, basketball games at Goodyear Hall and football games at the Rubber Bowl. "Never was interested in sports out of the ordinary," he confessed years later. "Guess I like racing best of all of them."

Morse code was his first love, but Benson could see that technology was improving. Teleprinters—telegraphs that worked like typewriters—were surely the future. So he learned to use the new machinery to retain his job at Western Union, then in the Ohio Building on South Main Street. He doubled as a switchboard operator, technician and supervisor.

Morse code requests grew fewer and fewer. By the late 1940s, the Akron, Canton & Youngstown Railroad was one of the last local companies still using Morse messages. Benson and Frank McGlinchey were the last two Morse operators, and then McGlinchey left the Akron office. A decade later, Benson would go, too.

The 61-year-old announced he would retire April 1, 1959. He and his wife, Zora, planned to abandon their 17th Street Southwest home and head for Pinellas Park, Fla., and that's exactly what they did.

Benson spent the rest of his life in sunny Florida. He died there in August 1972 at age 75.

In March 1959, a going-away party was held for Akron's last official Morse operator. Western Union superintendent Paul Ehret pointed out how much the city had changed since Benson's arrival in 1918. Not just the technology. Everything.

Ehret then gave Benson a special keepsake to remember his time at Western Union. He handed over the Vibroplex transmitter, the Morse code telegraph that Benson had used for decades. Of course, it had to go with him. He was the only one who knew how to use it.

Hello, Mr. Chimp

CHILDREN CONTRIBUTE SPARE CHANGE TO FUNDRAISER
TO BRING JOE COCO TO THE ZOO IN 1957

(Originally published May 9, 2011)

Pennies, nickels and dimes aren't necessarily chump change. Sometimes, they're chimp change.

Summit County youngsters poured out their hearts—and their piggy banks—in 1957 to bring a major attraction to the Akron Children's Zoo at Perkins Woods.

At the request of park officials, the Beacon Journal spearheaded a fundraising campaign to buy a "real live performing" chimpanzee for the menagerie now known as the Akron Zoo. Founded in 1953 with one cage and two bears, the zoo has grown into today's 50-acre complex with more than 700 animals.

Its early inhabitants weren't as exotic as the Humboldt penguins, Komodo dragons and Sumatran tigers of modern times.

"There are rabbits, ducks, alligators, turtles, pigs, deer, bears, buffaloes, coyotes—and even kangaroos—but not one of the most playful, fun-giving animals in the world—a chimpanzee—in the Akron Children's Zoo," the Beacon Journal noted in establishing the Mr. Chimp Fund in April 1957.

The newspaper set a goal of $600 (about $4,800 today) to purchase an African chimp that fund organizers described as "a real friendly animal" that "learns tricks easily" and "is a great pal."

No donation was too small. Promoters asked children to mail pennies, nickels or dimes to the Beacon Journal or drop off coins in person at the newspaper's front counter. If parents or other adults wanted to give a little money, that was fine, too.

Through movies and TV programs, Akron children were familiar with the antics of famous chimps such as Bonzo, Cheeta and J. Fred Muggs. The prospect of seeing a mischievous ape in Akron sounded really neat-o.

A great jangling began. Kids checked their pockets, shook their piggy banks and asked parents for change. They stopped at the Beacon Journal, sometimes dropping off a penny or two. Cub Scouts, Brownies, school clubs and church groups organized collections.

The newspaper published daily lists of donors. Some of the children included notes with their contributions, including messages such as these:

"I would like to send you three dimes that should go in my bank. I want a chimp in our zoo, so I'll give it to you."
—Dawn Kay Kupris, 1915 Hollis St.

"Here is my weekly 25-cent allowance my mother gives me. I'm sending it to help to get the chimp for the zoo."
—Linda Ann Unk, 172 Cedar St.

"I was going to buy some candy with this money, but I thought it would be much more fun to help the Children's Zoo than to buy any kind of candy."
—Edmund Blower, 593 Mineola Ave.

"Mr. Chimp: I've seen some of your relatives in other zoos and always enjoyed watching them. I think it would be fine to see you in our zoo."
—Ellen Holloway, 909 Greenwood Ave.

The response overwhelmed organizers of the Mr. Chimp Fund. Envelopes flooded the newspaper from 14 states and even a few foreign countries. Some children even mailed peanuts for the chimp to eat.

The $600 goal was surpassed within a few weeks, and still coins arrived daily. The fundraiser ended after a month with a grand total of $1,054.

"You've done it, kids!" the Beacon Journal cheered.

Children were invited to the zoo May 12 to witness the arrival of Joe Coco, a 2½-year-old, 21-pound chimp from Liberia.

A mug shot of the furry star appeared on the cover of the Beacon Journal's Sunday Roto magazine. Children were invited to keep the page as a poster.

A record crowd of 8,400 attended the welcoming reception on a gorgeous, sunny afternoon. Dressed in a little suit with a bow tie and suspenders, the chimpanzee arrived in the back of a convertible led by a police escort. Beacon Journal promotions director Ralph Iula presented the chimp to the zoo staff.

The audience went ape.

Joe Coco, the new chimpanzee at the Akron Children's Zoo, adorns the cover of the Beacon Journal's Sunday Roto magazine May 12, 1957.

"Everyone connected with the Children's Zoo is deeply appreciative for the wonderful response and cooperation with the Beacon Journal in raising the funds to bring Joe Coco here," Akron Service Director Leo Walter told the crowd.

"It is only through the warm-hearted support of the children in this area, who sent their pennies, nickels and dimes to the newspaper, that an addition like Joe can be made to the zoo."

Hundreds gathered around the chimpanzee's habitat and watched as the wary newcomer scaled a ladder, swung on bars, climbed a pole, swatted a ball and munched on peanuts.

"The weather and Joe combined to give us the finest day we've ever had," Superintendent Richard Barnhardt told the newspaper.

Akron Mayor Leo Berg proclaimed June 10–14 as Joe Coco Week. Children were admitted to the zoo for free in appreciation of their fundraising efforts.

The chimp helped boost 1957 attendance to more than 121,000 visitors—about 50,000 more than the previous year.

"I give all the credit to Joe Coco and to the Beacon Journal for conducting the campaign that brought him here," Barnhardt said. "We've had a marvelous year."

Behind the scenes, though, there were concerns. Joe Coco could be a miserable little beast.

The chimpanzee was as cute as could be, but his personality was sour. He didn't like interacting with people or being the subject of attention, and he increasingly fought with handlers.

Trainer Don Waddington tried to teach Joe Coco a few tricks over the winter to entertain children. On the zoo's opening day in 1958, the gruff chimp had a tantrum and refused to ride on the back of a donkey.

Joe became a second banana the following summer. In July 1959, the zoo introduced Suzy, a 1-year-old, 14-pound chimp who was outgoing and playful. She enjoyed being around humans, grinned at children and didn't mind being held. Suzy wore dresses and bonnets and was so docile that she rode in a convertible in the All-American Soap Box Derby parade.

Naturally, Joe Coco took an instant dislike to her. He gradually faded into the background as Suzy became the zoo's star.

It probably wasn't too surprising in January 1963, when the zoo announced that its original chimpanzee had left the zoo to pursue "a career in medicine."

Joe Coco was sold to the U.S. Department of Health, Education and Welfare and shipped to Bethesda, Md., to undergo "tests in connection with research in neurological diseases and blindness." Zoo officials said he was "happy and well cared for."

"Joe had reached the age of being just a bit too much to handle at the Children's Zoo," the Beacon Journal reported. "When chimps become 5 or so, they may be as strong as four men. . . .

"While Joe Coco gave many thousands pleasure over the years, he's in a position to contribute something important to medical research."

And just like that, he was gone. Goodbye, Mr. Chimp.

Death of an Officer

GANGSTER KILLED AKRON PATROLMAN IN 1930

(Originally published March 2, 2010)

In the final hours of life, Akron Patrolman Harland F. Manes helped solve his own murder. Detectives led two suspects into the officer's hospital room early on March 9, 1930, as he lay dying from a gunshot wound.

The first captive, 26, was a medium-built hoodlum with a deceptively boyish face. "Is that the man?" Chief Detective Edward J. McDonnell gently asked. Manes looked up. Too weak to speak, he shook his head no.

The second captive, 39, was a jug-eared brute with a cold stare. "Is that the man?" Manes gasped for breath. He nodded emphatically before sinking back into his pillow. That was the one.

About 24 hours earlier, Manes had stopped to assist vice squad officers in a 1:30 a.m. raid at 111 Kenmore Blvd. Officers saw two tipsy women leave a house of ill repute, cross the street and get into a sedan with two men. The driver tried to perform a U-turn, but crashed into an oncoming car.

Manes, 33, ran to the crash scene with Sgt. Steve Kovach while Patrolman Herbert Michaels and Patrolman Arthur Possehl watched from the curb.

Kovach yanked the male passenger from the car while Manes tended to the driver. The two women stepped out of the car, which reeked of bootleg liquor.

Without warning, the driver pulled a revolver and shot Manes in the abdomen. Then he fired crazily at the other officers. "There was no sign of trouble, but suddenly a shot rang out and I looked around in time to see Manes stagger a few paces and reach for his gun," Kovach reported. "As he fell, both Michaels and Possehl were shooting and I saw the one man jump from the small sedan and dash away. Michaels shot at him again and I believe wounded him."

The driver escaped, leaving behind Nathan King, 38, of Oklahoma City, also known as Jack Arnold and Jack Amos. King refused to identify the shooter or tell where he might have fled. The two women had disappeared during the gunfire. In a nearby alley, police found a discarded revolver with all six shells fired.

McDonnell rushed to Peoples Hospital to visit Manes after receiving the grim news at 2 a.m.

"I never had a chance," Manes rasped. "He pulled the gun before I could do a thing."

TO CANARY COTTAGE

Detectives scoured the Kenmore house and caught a lucky break when they found a phone number scribbled on a wall. Operators traced the number to a new listing on Lodi Street. Eight detectives armed with sawed-off shotguns sped to the two-story, yellow house—later dubbed Canary Cottage—at 447 Lodi St. in Goodyear Heights.

When an officer tapped on the door, the woman who answered was recognized as a passenger in the car crash. McDonnell pointed a gun to her head. "Make one move or let out one squawk, and I'll blow out your brains," he whispered. "Where are they?"

Nellie Denny, 44, aka Nellie Coleman, a Texas shoplifter, motioned to the second floor. The detectives crept upstairs and peeked into a bedroom where a baby-faced man was wrapping bandages around the arms of a middle-aged man.

When Detectives Patsy Pappano and Sherman Gandee stormed the room with McDonnell, the bandaged man froze. "Up with your hands!" McDonnell screamed. "Kill him if he moves, Gandee."

The younger man dived under a bed, but slid out after detectives threatened to shoot. Officers found an arsenal of weapons: a machine gun, shotguns, rifles and pistols. The license plate on a stolen Studebaker in the garage was traced to a Feb. 5 bank holdup in Sylvania.

Wounded Bert Walker, 39, also known as Bob Randall and Tom Alexander, was a wanted man from Kansas City, Mo. He had been tried in the 1920 murder of an officer during a robbery, but was acquitted. Walker was sentenced to 30 years for another heist in 1923, but escaped from a Missouri prison farm on Oct. 2, 1929.

His sidekick Frankie Mitchell, 26, also known as Frank Schultz and George Sanders, was a St. Louis bank robber who had met Walker in the slammer.

Ignoring the wounds to both arms, Walker denied shooting Manes. Police took him to Peoples Hospital for treatment.

Akron Patrolman Harland F. Manes, 33, was fatally wounded March 8, 1930.

SHOOTER IDENTIFIED

Officers led the men before Manes, and he identified Walker as the shooter—as did other police. Despite two surgeries and a blood transfusion, Manes died several hours later at 10:05 a.m.

A decorated hero of World War I and a six-year veteran of the force, Manes left behind his widow, Virginia, who received a police pension of $50 a month.

The funeral was March 13 at the Manes home at 80 Russell Ave. Color bearers, police officers, guardsmen and veterans marched in the procession. A flag-draped casket traveled up Main Street past the Summit County Jail, where Walker peered from his cell, then turned on Market Street for burial at Rose Hill cemetery.

Indicted on a charge of first-degree murder, Walker continued to deny everything. "I was drunk and don't know what happened," he said.

McDonnell prodded Walker, but the hardened gangster said he was being framed. He chuckled when asked about his pal. "You think I'm tough, but you haven't heard the last of that Mitchell boy yet," Walker said.

Police learned that Mitchell had another alias. He was none other than Charles Arthur Floyd, the notorious Pretty Boy Floyd. The suave bandit didn't seem so tough when he was cowering under an Akron bed.

Floyd and King were transferred May 20 to a Toledo jail, convicted of armed robbery and sentenced to 12 to 25 years in the Ohio Penitentiary. But Floyd escaped from a train Dec. 10 and led a four-year reign of terror.

FBI agents shot him to death Oct. 22, 1934, during a gunfight on an East Liverpool farm.

Walker took the stand at his murder trial in May 1930, and admitted only to being in the car that crashed in Kenmore. "Then I was jerked from my car by someone, my hat knocked off and someone struck me," he testified. "I wasn't allowed to pick up my hat so I began striking back. Then I heard some shots and ran."

Defense lawyer Robert Azar argued that Manes had been hit by friendly fire. However, ballistics tests linked the fatal shooting to the discarded gun in the alley.

A jury wasted little time in convicting Walker on May 21. Common Pleas Judge E.D. Fritch sentenced him to death May 24.

After exhausting his appeals, Walker faced the electric chair Nov. 10, 1930, at the Ohio Penitentiary in Columbus. "My record is the only thing that convicted me, but what the hell, I'll take my medicine like a man," he said.

He confided to his attorney Azar that Walker wasn't his real name. He was born James Bradley, the son of a prominent family from Texas. He said he hid his identity to protect his siblings.

FINAL MEAL

Walker spent his last day smoking cigarettes and reading newspapers. His final meal was a double sirloin steak with celery hearts and a crabmeat cocktail.

The Rev. Bill Denton of Akron's Furnace Street Mission tried to get the killer to repent in his final hours, but he declined. "He was hard-boiled to the last," Denton later recalled.

Walking to the electric chair, the sneering gangster couldn't resist making a wisecrack. "This is rather a shocking evening," he told witnesses.

With a flip of the switch, the lights dimmed. Walker was pronounced dead at 7:44 p.m.

He was buried in an unmarked grave in Lakewood Cemetery on West Waterloo Road in South Akron.

An eternal flame flickers in front of the Harold K. Stubbs Justice Center in downtown Akron. A memorial honors city police who died in the line of duty.

Harland F. Manes is the seventh name on a list of 21 officers. Etched in granite are the words "NEVER FORGET."

The Little Red Schoolhouse

PIKE TOWNSHIP BUILDING USED TO BE CLASSROOM

(Originally published Aug. 9, 1998)

Golden sunlight splashes off the red bricks of the old schoolhouse on the hill. It's a quiet place tucked between shade trees that sway in the breeze.

Green Ridge School, a one-room schoolhouse in Stark County's Pike Township, was built in 1871 next to a small cemetery where more than 30 early settlers are buried.

Time seems to stand still at the school on Greenhill Cabin Road. It isn't difficult to imagine children playing at recess or a teacher ringing the school bell to signal the start of lessons.

Nearly 60 years have passed since classes were taught there. Yet, the school is fresh in the minds of the pupils who once studied there—and the teacher who once taught them. Ruth Snedeker Williams was a child herself—in her late teens—when she began to teach at the school in the mid-1930s.

Despite her young age, the tall, thin woman with brown, shoulder-length hair had a flair for teaching. "I just absolutely loved it so much," said Williams, now in her 90s and retired in Plantation, Fla. "It was my first school. I taught all eight grades for four years."

The one-room school usually accommodated about 25 pupils, children from farming families in the rolling hills of Pike, she said.

Miss Snedeker, as she then was called, taught everything: reading, spelling, writing, mathematics, history. Younger children sat up front in single desks with inkwells. Older children sat in double desks in the back of the class.

"I heard that teachers up in Ohio were getting good money these days," Williams said. "I didn't make that much. I started at $2 or $3 a day, and it gradually went up."

Modern conveniences were few at the country school. There were no electric lights or running water. "I brought a jug of water every day," Williams said. "In the winter, I parked my car at the bottom of the hill and climbed. It was icy. Nevertheless, I got there."

Don McGrew, 73, graduated from Green Ridge's eighth grade in 1939, one of only three pupils at his grade level. "It's one of the soft spots in my heart," said McGrew, who lives in the house where he grew up. "We had to walk over the hills for a mile to get to school," he said.

His school memories include "the big old stove that you had to shovel the coal in . . . the outhouses . . . the blackboard up front . . . the pie and cake socials." He also remembers the desks in the back of the class: "You sat side by side in the double desks, and the boys hoped they would sit next to a girl and get a girlfriend."

Alice Van Voorhis, 80, another former Green Ridge pupil, was the daughter of Harry Garner, who taught at the school in the 1920s. She, too, has fond memories. "It was a very close group," she said. "We had such good times there. Everyone who went there turned out well."

She recalls eating lunch at her desk, playing outside at recess and competing in spelling bees at night by the glow of lamplight. And, of course, she recalls Miss Snedeker. "She had a sweet little face," Van Voorhis said. "She was dearly loved as a teacher."

After four years, Miss Snedeker was transferred to a larger school. She eventually married Tony Williams and retired in Florida after a 36-year teaching career.

Green Ridge School closed in 1940 as schools in East Sparta, Magnolia and Waynesburg began to consolidate to form the Sandy Valley Local School District. The old schoolhouse was empty until 1949 when a family known as the Blackburns moved in and raised 13 children there. Ownership of the school changed hands several times, but it never operated as an educational facility again.

Larry Barnes and Charles McFadden remodeled the inside of the building in the early 1970s, turning it into a cozy little home. Gary and Julie Babtist have lived there for 25 years, earning awards for historic preservation. Julie Babtist maintains an impressive history of the building, including old documents, clippings and photos of former pupils who sometimes stop by to visit.

Ruth Snedeker Williams can't see as well as she once did ("I'm a lot older than I was then"), but she can't forget the faces of the Green Ridge School pupils. "I never had children. They were like my children," she said. "They were so wonderful. I loved them so much."

The Pilgrim's Landing

GOODYEAR BLIMP SAILED TO AKRON STORE ROOF ON EXPERIMENTAL VOYAGE IN 1928

(Originally published June 7, 2004)

Go ahead and check your garage. Is there a car parked inside? Good.

Now go to your back yard. Do you see a moored airship? Didn't think so.

In the 1920s, it seemed reasonable, maybe even inevitable, that the highly advanced and technologically superior people of the 21st century would sail around Akron in personal blimps.

Well, not necessarily all people. Mostly just the affluent. A blimp would be a status symbol like a fancy automobile or a big yacht.

Goodyear President Paul W. Litchfield, a boating enthusiast, liked to think of blimps as "air yachts." He envisioned a day when mooring masts would be set up on private estates, public airports and country clubs. The sky was the limit.

In 1925, the Akron company introduced the Pilgrim, its first helium-filled, commercial airship. Expected to be "largely a demonstration ship" for use in "certain tests and experimental work," the silver blimp was 110 feet long and 32 feet in diameter with a gas capacity of 56,000 cubic feet. Its gondola had room for one pilot and two passengers.

The Pilgrim was inflated with hydrogen, a highly flammable gas, for its first test flight June 3 at Wingfoot Lake in Suffield Township, but switched to helium a month later before the formal dedication. Litchfield's wife, Florence, christened the ship July 18, 1925.

In the future, individuals and clubs, not just companies, would own blimps, Goodyear predicted. The company imagined airship clubs holding sky regattas and private owners sailing hundreds of miles to play golf at country clubs.

"The ships will probably be somewhat more expensive than high-class automobiles but not out of range for persons who now own yachts and big motorboats," Goodyear noted in 1925.

The Pilgrim became a familiar sight over Ohio. In its seven years of operation, it recorded 4,765 flights, logged 94,974 miles and carried 5,355 passengers.

One such flight turned into an iconic moment in Akron history. In June 1928, in an experiment designed to show the practicality of the "air yacht," Goodyear sent its blimp to the store.

The Pilgrim took off June 20 from Wingfoot Lake and set course for downtown Akron. Respected pilot Jack Boettner, "The Iron Man of the Airships," who had joined Goodyear as a teenager in 1916, sat at the controls. His sole passenger was James P. Lynch, advertising manager of the M. O'Neil Co.

Boettner's mission was to drop off Lynch on the department store's roof and return to the Wingfoot Lake hangar.

The event was highly publicized. National movie crews arrived in Akron to capture the event for newsreels. Newspaper photographers stationed themselves atop O'Neil's and the nearby Hotel Marne.

Downtown workers and shoppers gathered around the store's brand-new building at South Main and State streets while other spectators peered out windows.

Traffic halted on the roads. All waited to hear the whirring sound of the blimp. The Pilgrim circled the city like a giant shark in search of prey.

The word "AKRON" had been painted in giant letters on O'Neil's roof, along with arrows pointing to where the blimp should land.

Boettner spotted the target and began a slow, spiraling descent. The last time that a pilot had attempted to land on an Ohio building was back in May 1919 when the A-4 dirigible touched down on Cleveland's Statler Hotel.

For other reasons entirely, Boettner had painful memories of 1919. Somewhere in the back of his mind, as he floated toward the O'Neil's building, he may have been trying not to think about Chicago.

A tragedy occurred July 21, 1919, as Boettner piloted the Wingfoot Express airship over the Windy City. The hydrogen-filled dirigible spontaneously burst into flames. Boettner and his four passengers put on parachutes and jumped toward the rooftops below, but only the pilot and his mechanic survived the inferno. The fiery airship plunged through the skylight of the Illinois Trust & Savings Bank and killed 10 employees, a terrible day in Chicago history.

But that was a decade earlier, and The Pilgrim was filled with helium, not hydrogen.

The O'Neil's crowd murmured as the Goodyear blimp came into view. A landing party was waiting on the store's roof. Boettner guided the blimp down toward the roof. The landing crew reached up as the mooring lines drew near.

On the edge of the roof, The Pilgrim wobbled a bit and dipped backward. The rudder scraped hard against the building's parapet, and hearts skipped a beat as many observers worried that the tail section might break off.

The landing crew gave a mighty heave and brought the ship to a safe berth. For blocks around, the crowd cheered and clapped. It was 2:40 p.m.

Lynch, the O'Neil's advertising manager, stepped out of the gondola and reported for work. Store managers, city leaders, photographers and reporters rushed to greet the pilot and his passenger.

Boettner and Lynch proved that it was possible for the blimp to serve as an "air yacht" in the city. The practicality of such a voyage was debatable, though.

Over the next few years, Goodyear added the blimps Puritan, Volunteer, Defender, Reliance and Resolute to its fleet. The Pilgrim was decommissioned in 1932. Its gondola was donated to the Smithsonian Institution and is part of the collection at the National Air and Space Museum in Washington, D.C.

Jack Boettner, "The Iron Man of the Airships," remained with Goodyear until his retirement in 1952. He logged more than 10,000 flight hours over 35 years. He moved to Florida, where he died in 1961 at age 68.

The O'Neil's department store closed in 1989. Goodyear blimps fly over the building from time to time but never stop there.

The most amazing tale of the O'Neil's blimp landing was published in a small French newspaper in 1928. Something got lost in translation.

The Goodyear blimp Pilgrim wobbles slightly before touching down on the roof of O'Neil's department store in June 1928. The company wanted to demonstrate the practicality of the "air yacht." This photo was taken from the roof of the Hotel Marne in downtown Akron.

A French aviation buff named J. Foucault provided a photo of the Pilgrim along with this inaccurate-but-amusing account: "A rich proprietor of Akron, a little city in Ohio, owns a small dirigible," Foucault wrote. "And it is with this air balloon that he does his errands every morning.

"Here it is waiting for him near a store and the tradesmen are hurrying to bring him the orders which he has sent over the radio. It is a very modern vision, which without doubt we are not ready to see in our fields."

Paul W. Litchfield's dream had come true, if only for a day.

Alice Cooper

SHOCK ROCK BAND HAS AKRON LINKS

(Originally published Aug. 6, 2000)

Glen Buxton loved rock 'n' roll music. He loved it to death. The Akron native electrified the music world in the early 1970s as a founding member and lead guitarist of the "shock rock" group Alice Cooper.

The band conquered the Billboard charts, revolutionized stage theatrics and influenced countless other groups. And none of it would have been possible if a South Akron boy hadn't picked up a guitar.

Buxton was born Nov. 10, 1947, to Thomas and Geraldine Buxton at City Hospital. One of three children, he grew up at 898 Davies Ave. and attended David Hill Elementary School and Roswell Kent Junior High.

The road to rock stardom began about age 12 when Buxton started taking guitar lessons in downtown Akron. His studies continued in Arizona after the family moved in February 1961 because of Thomas Buxton's job transfer at Goodyear Aerospace.

At Cortez High in Phoenix, Buxton met future bandmates Dennis Dunaway and Vincent Furnier, a minister's son whom the world would know as Alice. "Without Glen, the band would have never happened," says drummer Neal Smith, 52, who now operates a real estate company in Westport, Conn.

"Dennis and Alice and Glen and a couple of their friends put a band together for a talent show. Glen was the only musician, the only guy who could really play. So he taught everybody else."

That band, the Earwigs, evolved into the Spiders, which became the Nazz and finally Alice Cooper, a name suggested in 1968 by Furnier, who adopted the moniker for himself as well.

"They were always stars to me," says Buxton's sister, Janice Buxton Davison, 47, who now lives in Bullhead City, Ariz. "The very minute they started playing, I knew this was going to be a really good thing. My girlfriends and I used to gather around the garage and keep the boys entertained and watered. It gets awfully hot in Arizona to have a garage band!"

The band featured Cooper on vocals, Buxton on lead guitar, Dunaway on bass and Michael Bruce on rhythm guitar. The original drummer wasn't working out so Buxton convinced the group to recruit Neal Smith, who played in the Holy Grail, a rival Phoenix band.

By sheer coincidence, Smith was from Akron, too. Born in Medina in 1947, Smith grew up in Akron's Wooster-Hawkins area and attended Schumacher Elementary School and Perkins Junior High, and spent two years at Buchtel High. When his parents divorced, he moved with his mother to Arizona in 1963.

Buxton and Smith were startled to discover they were from the same place. "You know, you start talking about Cedar Point, and you start talking about the Rubber Bowl and Derby Day and the airport and all the stuff that you can think of in Ohio," Smith says.

The two bonded instantly. "Neal and Glen were very close," Davison confirms. They were the 'Akron Boys.'"

"Not even friends," Smith says. "More like brothers."

After dominating the Phoenix music scene, the band moved to Los Angeles where it landed a deal with Frank Zappa's label, Straight Records. Alice Cooper released its first album, *Pretties for You*, in 1969 and followed that up a year later with *Easy Action*. The group found itself opening for The Doors and Led Zeppelin and hanging out with Jim Morrison and Jimi Hendrix.

Things heated up when Warner Bros. bought the label. The 1971 album *Love It To Death* featured Alice Cooper's first Top 40 hit, *I'm Eighteen*. The album *Killer*, also released in 1971, offered the radio staple *Under My Wheels*.

Attending an Alice Cooper concert was like going to some ghoulish carnival. The shows featured macabre makeup, outlandish costumes, strobe effects, glitter, bizarre props and, famously, a live boa constrictor. A highlight of each night's concert was the mock execution of the lead singer. Over the years, Cooper was led to the electric chair, gallows and guillotine as the crowd cheered.

Buxton's great triumph with Alice Cooper was the 1972 album *School's Out* and its title track, a rock anthem that captures the unbridled glee of children at the start of summer vacation.

"It was Glen's riff—duh da daah, duh da duuh—that was its opening," Smith says. "Glen wrote that and that was Glen 100 percent. Not only that, but that whole album—even though we all collaborated on it—it was really Glen's album."

As *School's Out* soared to No. 2 and its title track climbed to No. 7, Buxton and Smith had a happy homecoming in Akron. Alice Cooper rocked 30,000 fans at the Rubber Bowl on Aug. 5, 1972. "As a matter of fact, I still have the T-shirt," Smith says. "I have a T-shirt with 'Rubber Bowl, Akron' on it . . . That was a great show."

The band finally hit No. 1 in 1973 with the album *Billion Dollar Babies*, which spawned the classic songs *No More Mr. Nice Guy*, *Elected*, *Hello Hooray* and the title track. There would be no topping that record.

"Shock rock" group Alice Cooper, pictured about 1970, features (left to right) Michael Bruce, Dennis Dunaway, Alice Cooper and former Akron residents Glen Buxton and Neal Smith. *Courtesy of Warner Bros. Records*

Although the next two albums, *Muscle of Love* and *Greatest Hits*, both made the Top 10, the group broke up in 1974 and lead singer Alice Cooper went solo. The band's demise after selling 25 million records caught Buxton by surprise, Davison says.

"He told me he didn't even realize there was going to be a break," she says. "Alice went off on his own, and that's the last of it. He was somewhat bitter at times, but he wouldn't let anyone say anything bad about Alice. Alice was his friend."

Buxton, who had fallen victim to many of the vices of the rock 'n' roll lifestyle, was in frail health and endured some tough times over the next 20 years. He supplemented his music royalties by taking a job at Goodyear Aerospace. In 1990, he moved to Clarion, Iowa, to help a friend with his farm.

Alice Cooper fans were thrilled when Buxton reunited with bandmates Smith and Bruce on Oct. 12, 1997, for a show in Houston. Things seemed to be going the guitarist's way.

"He was going to be married in December of 1997," his sister says. "The band had decided in Houston that they would get back together and do some gigs. He was really excited about this."

But the Texas concert proved to be Buxton's last. "He was sick while he was there, but wouldn't go to the doctor," Davison says. "He had a pain in his side."

According to Smith, "Glen looked a little frail, but he never indicated to me that he was ill."

Buxton returned home to Iowa where his health ebbed. On Oct. 19, 1997, a week after the reunion concert, Glen Buxton died of pneumonia at age 49.

"I got a call from Janice," Smith says. "I couldn't believe it. We were just together. We had a great time."

Davison remembers her brother as "a loving and thoughtful person." "Glen was one of the funniest people I have ever known in my life," she says. "He could make you feel good just hanging out with him."

Friends, relatives, musicians and fans gathered Oct. 24, 1997, for the funeral in Clarion, Iowa. As Buxton's casket was rolled in before the start of the service, something remarkable occurred. Mourners got to their feet and began to applaud.

"He got a standing ovation," Smith says.

One last time.

Far Worse Times

SURVIVORS TELL HOW AKRON FAMILIES PERSEVERED IN THE GREAT DEPRESSION

(Originally published June 23, 2008)

There is no question that times are tough. Signs of economic distress are everywhere. In the last few months, Americans have endured a daily barrage of troubling news on home foreclosures, job losses, credit problems, record gas prices and soaring food costs.

Let's be realistic, though. As difficult as things seem, we have experienced far worse times. During the Great Depression, Akron residents coped with misery on an unprecedented level. Poverty, unemployment, debt and hunger were constant concerns for families in the 1930s.

"I remember it well as a kid growing up," said George W. Knepper, 82, distinguished professor emeritus of history at the University of Akron. "Everything that people were accustomed to doing or wanted to do was pretty much restricted.

"The whole society had to adjust. It was not like today's recession where some people, a very, very large percentage of the people, are living high on the hog, and others are in pretty desperate straits."

The turmoil of the 1930s affected nearly everyone: rich or poor, young or old. Some wealthy businessmen lost their fortunes and ended up selling apples and pencils on the street.

Jobs were almost impossible to find. Factories laid off workers or drastically cut back on hours. People stood in long lines outside soup kitchens.

"The industrial cities were hit extremely hard," Knepper said. "In Akron at the height of the unemployment, 1932–33, it's estimated that there was 60 percent industrial unemployment. That is factory unemployment. That's almost two out of every three people had zero jobs."

Knepper, who grew up on Beechwood Drive in West Akron, said his family was fortunate because his father, George, had a steady job as minister of High Street Church of Christ. "At the very worst of the unemployment, there were literally some families that had to depend on their little kid's paper route to make enough money to buy the essential food," he said.

FAMILIES MAKE DO

Virginia Nicholas, 84, of Akron, remembers moving from house to house with her parents, Roger and Nellie Casey. Homeowners would rent out rooms to help make ends meet.

"We'd sleep in upstairs bedrooms and come down and share the food with the people," she said. "Then we'd have to move someplace else. Years later, we finally got a home."

Despite the circumstances, people didn't seem to complain too much, she said. They tried to make the best of the situation. "You were grateful for everything," Nicholas said. "We were happy. We were poor and really didn't know it. We just made do with what we had and appreciated it so much."

When toys were scarce, kids learned to enjoy simple pleasures. Nicholas recalls splashing on Yale Street in South Akron.

"We loved to have it rain," she said. "When the streets flooded, we would wade in that dirty water and have the best time. Then the parents would have to wash us in the tub."

Every weekend, Nicholas and her friends from Lincoln School were allowed to splurge on a cowboy matinee at the Majestic Theater on South Main Street.

"We had a nickel to go to the show on Saturdays, which was a big, big thrill in our life."

STRETCHING FOOD BILLS

Bob Weyrick, 83, a lifelong resident of Ellet, remembers the cherries and peaches that he plucked from the trees outside his home. Depression-era families planted vegetable gardens and fruit trees to lower grocery bills and enjoy fresh produce.

"People took a lot of pride in their canned goods," he said. "Usually there was an area in the basement where jars of canned foods could be stored for the winter."

Weyrick's father, Clark, a carpenter, built a chicken coop on an adjacent lot so that the family could have a steady supply of eggs and chicken dinners.

Unemployed Akron men did a lot of standing and waiting in 1932 during the depths of the Great Depression. They lined up for soup. They lined up for bread. They lined up for relief. They lined up for jobs. Akron's industrial unemployment was roughly 60 percent in 1932, about two out of every three men.

"Every spring, you'd get a new group of small chicks," Weyrick said.

It wasn't uncommon for hobos to knock on the door to ask for something to eat. Weyrick's mother, Miriam, made sandwiches and handed them out to the hungry men. Even though the Weyricks had to scrimp, they still tried to share. "I think people realized that life was hard and it was even harder for many," Weyrick said. "As I remember, there was really a spirit of people trying to help one another as best they could."

CLOTHING MADE TO LAST

Eloise Schill, 81, of Copley Township, grew up on Herman Avenue off Diagonal Road in Akron. The whir of a home sewing machine was a frequent sound when she was a pupil attending Crouse Elementary.

"My mother made all of my dresses, and she did well, but I was embarrassed, you know, because everybody else went to the stores to get their clothes," she said.

Kids wore clothing until it couldn't be repaired. Socks were darned. Pants were patched. As little girls grew taller, mothers adjusted the hems on old dresses.

Such frugality helped Schill's parents, Gertrude and Willard Schill, keep their house. "A lot of people on that street lost their homes because they were all brand new," Schill said. "My parents survived."

Since money was tight, her favorite childhood memories involve activities that were free. She recalls riding a bicycle to the library to read books and climbing the Wooster Avenue hill to watch dirigibles over Akron.

"I never knew that we were in a Depression except I couldn't understand why we didn't do a lot of things that other people did," she said. "But we always had good meat and potatoes. We never went hungry."

Mel Hynde, 86, who grew up on Bittaker Street in East Akron, remembers how people used to look out for each other. "A family moved up from Alabama, and my mother went around the neighborhood, picking up clothes for them," he said. "And we were as poor as they were."

Neighbors had to find innovative ways to make a little extra cash during those difficult times. "A guy two doors up from us set up a barber chair in his house and he cut people's hair for a quarter," he said.

Parents Leonard and Evelyn Hynde had to reduce expenses after his factory job was cut back to three days a week. Their children were none the wiser.

"We didn't know," Hynde said with a laugh. "We didn't know we were doing without."

Except maybe for the clothes. Hynde was at the top of the ladder on hand-me-downs. "The fortunate thing was I was the oldest boy," he said. "My kid brother was a couple of years younger than me. So he got everything that I would wear."

MEN PUT TO WORK

Some Akron residents had to go on direct relief, receiving 12 cents a day from the state for each person in the family. Desperate people barely subsisted in crowded tenement houses. Some children couldn't go to school because they had no shoes.

The Works Progress Administration, a federal jobs program, helped alleviate some of the suffering in Summit County. Tens of thousands of people earned pay for working on hundreds of public projects. Unskilled laborers earned $55 a month while skilled workers took home $85.

In 1938, Ohio had about 238,000 workers on the WPA. Men dug ditches, paved roads, built bridges and constructed landmarks such as the Rubber Bowl and Nimisila Reservoir. Women canned vegetables, sewed garments and handled other domestic duties.

Most families depended on one income, usually a father who had been raised to believe he was the literal breadwinner.

"If he lost his job, not only did the family lose its income, but he lost his pride," Knepper said. "For that reason, even as a kid, I just knew that the New Deal programs that were putting people back to work were sensible. It gave them a little self-respect in earning the money."

Such programs kept people working until World War II started an industrial boom that ended the Depression.

LIFELONG FRUGALITY

Those who lived through that era never quite got over it. Many remained frugal for life.

The mantra "Use it up, wear it out, make it do or do without" was hard to break.

People saved butter wrappers to grease pans. They filled drawers with empty bread bags. They washed foil to use again.

Such thriftiness seemed amusing to later generations. In today's society, people throw away nearly everything in sight.

If the United States should ever fall into another depression, could we go back to the old ways? Would we learn how to save? Would we help each other?

"Sometimes it seems that life swings in cycles," Weyrick said. "Maybe you go from one end to the other. As the economy seems to be sliding down a little bit, we may see more of a tendency for people to try to be more helpful to others in need."

Nicholas, who refers to her childhood as "the happy days" despite the Great Depression, offers this advice for people coping with today's tough times.

"Just know that God will take care of us somehow or another," she said. "Just watch how you spend your pennies."

Depression Wisdom

(Originally published June 23, 2008)

Listen to your elders. They know a thing or two about surviving an economic downturn. Here are some Depression-era ideas on living more efficiently that still apply to the modern world:

Don't be wasteful.
Learn to make do with less.
Save your money for when you really need it.
Live modestly and avoid debt.
Learn a useful skill that will serve you for life.
Buy what you need before you buy what you want.
Don't throw away anything that can still be used.
It's cheaper to repair it than buy a new one.
Don't pay someone to do a job that you can do for free.
Plant a garden and reap the rewards.
Home-cooked meals cost less and taste better.
If you help your neighbors, they will help you.

LANDMARKS FROM 1930S

Even in the worst of times, good things can happen. Some of the Akron area's great landmarks were built during the Great Depression through private developers and federal programs. Here are some of them:

FirstMerit Tower, Mayflower Hotel, Rubber Bowl, Polsky's, Akron YMCA, Akron YWCA, Mogadore Reservoir, Nimisila Reservoir, Glendale Steps, Waterworks Park, Firestone Memorial Bridge, North High School, Buchtel High School, Goodrich Middle School, Voris Elementary School, Akron Times-Press Building (now the Beacon Journal), Highland Theater, Akron Fulton International Airport Terminal, Guggenheim Airship Institute, Broad Street Bridge.

BY THE NUMBERS

Some Greater Akron statistics about the Depression:

25,031 Number of rubber factory workers who lost jobs.
21,829 Peak WPA employment in October 1938.
10,249 Loss of city population from 1930 to 1940.
3,000 Number of families evicted from homes in 1933–34.
900 Number of people who applied to sell apples in 1930.
600 Miles of county roads improved by WPA.
381 Number of public buildings improved by WPA.
55 Number of bridges built by WPA.
40 Miles of sewer pipes laid by WPA.
12 Cents per day allotted for person on county relief.
3 Number of banks that failed: First-Central Trust Co., Community Savings Bank, Standard Savings Bank.
2 Number of daily newspapers in 1929.
1 Number of daily newspapers in 1939.

DEPRESSED PRICES

Here is a sampling of grocery prices from 75 years ago. A dime in June 1933 would be the equivalent of $1.50 today:

Lettuce—5 cents a head.
Cucumbers—6 cents apiece.
Oranges—25 cents per dozen.
Tomatoes—10 cents a pound.
Watermelons—35 cents.
Peanut butter—19 cents for a 2-pound jar.
Spaghetti—9 cents for 1-pound package.
Flour—73 cents for 24 ½-pound bag.
Sugar—45 cents for a 10-pound bag.
Hamburger—15 cents for 2 pounds.
Veal stew—15 cents for 2 pounds.

The Blizzard of 1978

OHIO RESIDENTS WILL NEVER FORGET BIG STORM

(Originally published Jan. 21, 2008)

The original forecast sounded harmless enough: "Rain tonight, possibly mixed with snow at times. Windy and cold Thursday with snow flurries."

People who went to bed early missed the bulletins at 9 p.m. Wednesday. They woke up to a screeching nightmare. A monster storm with hurricane-force winds slammed into Northeast Ohio early Jan. 26, 1978, spreading an icy coat of death and destruction.

The Blizzard of 1978, often called the Storm of the Century, killed more than 50 people in Ohio and caused at least $100 million in damage. Local residents will never forget the big storm of 30 years ago.

Retired meteorologist Bob Alto, 71, of Massillon, recalls arriving at work at 6 a.m. Thursday at the National Weather Service at Akron-Canton Airport. It became his home for the next 58 hours.

"Nobody could get in and nobody could get out," he said. "The roads were closed. So I couldn't be relieved. There were three of us there: myself, Phil Martin and Ed Heath. We rode it out there at the airport."

The trapped weathermen witnessed a record-breaking blizzard. The center of the storm was west of the airport. Around the clock, the trio updated forecasts, issued radio warnings and maintained contact with sheriffs in Summit and Stark counties.

They barely had time to nap.

Despite earlier projections, a low pressure area from North Dakota collided with a low pressure area from the Gulf of Mexico. Warm moist air slammed into bone-chilling cold. A satellite photo revealed a giant swirl of clouds over Ohio. It looked like a white hurricane.

Atmospheric pressure fell like a rock. A barometer registered 28.33 inches at 3:47 a.m., the lowest reading ever recorded at Akron-Canton Airport.

The weather service's barograph, a drum-shaped instrument that keeps track of barometric pressure, needed two charts for the measurement.

"Our trace on our barograph went down like a funnel," Alto said. "It looked like a big, sharp V. It just went straight down and it came straight up. But we had to change the chart because it was going off our chart. So we had to recalibrate it and put another chart on to get the rest of the trace."

Rain turned to ice and snow as the temperature plunged 21 degrees—from 34 to 13—between 5 and 6 a.m. Temperatures hovered around zero but the wind chill made it feel like 60 below.

Howling winds tore off roofs, knocked down trees and blew out windows. Thousands lost power, heat or phone service. The airport recorded a peak gust of 76 mph at 5:12 a.m., followed by sustained winds of 35 to 40 mph for the next 15 hours.

Nearly a foot of snow fell on top of a 16-inch storm from days earlier. The wind caused freakish drifts that swallowed cars.

Mary Jo Anderson, 61, of Springfield Township, remembers the high-pitched wail. "Oh, that was awful," she said. "Nobody slept much that night. We had never heard that kind of noise. You know, how your house rattles and squeals."

Her husband, Richard, tried to go to work that morning. He made it about a mile up the road in his Ford Pinto, but he couldn't drive any farther because the wind was too ferocious. "The ice was on the window of his car and he was trying to reach his arm out and scrape the ice off," she said. "He opened the car door and it almost ripped the car door off."

The vehicle spun around. Richard Anderson held the door shut and drove home. "He was happy to make it back," Mary Jo Anderson said.

Road crews could not keep up as blowing snow made streets impassable. Many motorists abandoned their vehicles.

Airports, schools, factories, offices, stores and other businesses closed. The Akron Beacon Journal published an edition, but delivery was nearly impossible.

Jack Edwards, 86, of Stow, remembers making it to his Goodrich job, only to discover that the building didn't have heat. Workers were sent back home on the treacherous roads.

Tossed around like a toy, a Cessna 150 rests upside down on the south end of Akron Municipal Airport near the Akron Airdock. The Blizzard of 1978 had sustained winds of 35 to 40 mph, with a peak gust of 76 mph in Akron.

"There was a large amount of snow," he said. "The wind velocity was so high and so steady that it just drifted absolutely, unbelievably deep."

To make matters worse, his home lost power and heat. He and his wife, Donna, huddled around a fireplace. "For a day or two, we were cooking with a little two-burner Coleman stove in the garage," he said.

Kevin Murphy, 56, of Barberton, described the blizzard as "something I will never forget."

"You literally had to hold on to things if you were going outside," he said.

He recalls watching in disbelief as his neighbors tried to put out their trash. "As soon as they set the bag down, it just took off," he said.

Murphy's family toughed it out with blankets when the furnace conked out. His son, 4, and daughter, 9 months, stayed cozy, but Murphy had to venture into the deep freeze. "I remember getting a phone call that day from my dad who worked at Ohio Bell," Murphy said. "He said, 'Hey, what are you doing?' I said, 'Well, we're trying to stay warm.' He said, 'Can you come down and get me?'"

The next thing Murphy knew, he was creeping along the Akron Expressway on a white-knuckle drive in a Chevy Nova. He made it downtown safely and used jumper cables to start his dad's car. "I told him, 'If I didn't love you, I'd kill you,'" he said with a chuckle.

Ruth Kohari, 87, of Akron, was a registered nurse working 11 p.m. to 7 a.m. at Barberton Citizens Hospital. The snow was deep around her home near Summit Lake.

"My husband (George) was working days at Goodrich," she said. "He had to shovel out to get to work. Then he came home and he shoveled out so my daughter (Marta) could get in from the university. Then he shoveled out again so that I could get out and go to work."

Road crews had been out all day and night. Kohari, who grew up in upstate New York, was no stranger to snowstorms.

She had no trouble driving.

"As a rule, most of the night shift made it—by hook or by crook," she said. "It was always busy on the medical floors during the winter. I worked a ward that had 42 patients."

The winds slowly began to diminish overnight. Blizzard warnings turned to travelers' advisories before dawn Friday. Bob Alto was able to leave the airport by 4 p.m. Saturday.

An abandoned car lies buried in a giant snowdrift on Jan. 27, 1978, off Eastern Road near Rittman in Wayne County. It took several days for Ohio residents to dig out after the storm.

It took Ohio residents several days to dig out. National Guardsmen rescued thousands of stranded people. Survival stories emerged from the frozen wasteland. A Cleveland truck driver was trapped for six days in a giant drift near Mansfield. He survived in his cab by eating snow.

Utility crews worked overtime to restore services. Kevin Murphy, who had been interviewing at Ohio Edison just before the blizzard, landed a job there soon afterward. He remained for nearly 25 years.

The blizzard helped make January 1978 the snowiest month in Northeast Ohio history. Akron-Canton Airport broke a record with 37.5 inches.

Meteorologist Alto kept the 1978 barograph charts as souvenirs and later let his grandkids borrow them for school projects.

The Blizzard of 1978 was one of the biggest calamities during his 34-year career—along with the 1963 Palm Sunday tornadoes and the 1990 Shadyside floods.

"I remember it very clearly," he said. "It was quite an event."

A Grave Secret

GRIEF-STRICKEN MOTHER'S COMMITMENT HONORS SOLDIER'S SACRIFICE

(Originally published Nov. 8, 2010)

Sophie M. Murray lost her beloved son in World War I.

She didn't lose her spirit.

For more than 30 years, the Cuyahoga Falls woman faithfully tended to the grave at Oakwood Cemetery, pulling weeds, removing leaves and placing flowers.

Pvt. John A. Murray, 28, a soldier in the 17th Infantry, 4th Division, was killed Sept. 27, 1918, in northeastern France on the second day of the Battle of Argonne Forest, an Allied offensive that punctured Germany's defenses on the Western Front.

He was one of 26,000 Americans killed in the devastating campaign.

The battleground was a sad coincidence for Sophie Murray, a European immigrant who was born in 1867 in the nearby town of Bischweiler in Alsace, France. She learned of her son's death one week before the signing of the Nov. 11 armistice that ended the Great War.

The U.S. government offered to return John's body to Cuyahoga Falls. Some families chose to have their fallen sons buried in French cemeteries, but Murray wanted her boy to come home.

After a delay of several weeks, the casket arrived for interment at Oakwood Cemetery.

"My relatives came from far and near to be here for the funeral," Murray later recalled. "It was to be the biggest military funeral the Falls had ever known."

A mournful city paid final respects to an American hero. The soldier was laid to rest with somber pageantry.

Following the military rites, Murray and her husband, John, a rubber factory worker, went back to their daily routines. They lived with their daughters, Frances and Helene, at 2360 Fourth St.—just a short walk from Oakwood.

Sophie Murray placed flowers every holiday at the standard government marker bearing her son's name. She cleaned the white stone and swept away acorns and leaves that fell from a towering oak tree next to the grave.

She wouldn't forget.

PRESIDENT OF CLUB

Murray became the first president of the Gold Star Mothers of Summit County, whose members lost sons in the war.

Wearing ceremonial white gowns and gold capes, the women marched in parades, gave speeches, raised money for veterans and sponsored patriotic functions.

Among their causes, the mothers purchased *The Spirit of the American Doughboy*, a 7-foot bronze statue of a World War I soldier, which was dedicated Nov. 11, 1934, outside the Akron Armory and stands today at the Summit County Courthouse. Gold Star Mothers placed roses at the statue's feet every Armistice Day.

In 1938, as the 20th anniversary of her son's death neared, Murray made a startling revelation at a monthly meeting of Gold Star Mothers. The news caught the attention of the Beacon Journal, which requested an interview with the local chapter's president.

Murray had a tale to share about her son's grave.

She told the newspaper how a Cuyahoga Falls undertaker had taken her aside after the casket arrived two decades earlier. It just so happened that the man was a friend of her son.

"He suggested to me the night before the funeral that we open the casket so that I could see my son for the last time," Murray recalled.

"But when we lifted the lid, it was not John. It was a boy with bright red hair. John's hair was black and very straight. It was a stranger.

"His bones were not formed like John's either. A mother knows."

The U.S. government had transported another soldier's remains from France to Cuyahoga Falls.

Murray was utterly stunned. How could this have happened?

With hours to go before the memorial service, she made a fateful decision.

"I said to the undertaker, well, I guess we will bury him anyway in the family plot," she said. "He is some

Cuyahoga Falls resident Sophie M. Murray, who lost her son John during World War I, clutches a silk banner with a gold star as she watches ROTC students march in 1940 near the University of Akron.

mother's boy. Some mother would be glad to have him have a decent resting place."

She held the funeral as planned.

MARKER ENGRAVED

With pomp and pageantry, the casket was lowered into the ground. A stone marker was engraved with Pvt. John A. Murray's name, but the tomb was that of an unknown soldier.

Murray decorated the grave as if her son were buried there. That was the least she could do for the other grieving mother who would never find out what happened.

"Afterwards, some of the boys from John's outfit told me the truth about John," Murray said. "You see, he was blown all to pieces by shrapnel."

There were no remains to send home. His final resting place was the Argonne Forest, not far from the town where his mother was born.

After her husband died in 1938, Murray stayed active with Gold Star Mothers. The club's membership grew,

steadily but sadly, after the United States entered World War II.

The gray-haired, bespectacled Murray was a common sight at parades, clutching a silk banner with a gold star.

Local veterans lovingly knew her as "Mother Murray." VFW members at Bob Appleman Post 3294 and Fred Reece Post 3310 adopted her as their own.

Sophie M. Murray was 82 years old when she passed away in June 1950.

Today, acorns and fallen leaves blanket the ground next to a towering tree at Section P, Lot 18, in Oakwood Cemetery.

It's a family plot.

A marble headstone reveals that Sophie and John Murray are buried between daughters and sons-in-law Helene and Roy Horning, Frances and Hubert Barnes, and a U.S. soldier whose real name will never be known.

Crash Test

GENERAL TIRE'S BLOW-OUT PROOF STUNT WAS A BIG SMASH IN MAY 1930

(Originally published May 22, 2006)

The advertising campaign hit a brick wall in May 1930. Fortunately, the marketing geniuses at General Tire & Rubber Co. hired a stuntman to do the work.

Hollywood daredevil Dick Grace, 32, made national headlines when he crashed a speeding automobile into a brick-and-concrete barrier on General Field in East Akron.

The publicity stunt—known as the General Tire Blow-Out Proof Test—demonstrated the durability of the Akron company's Dual-Balloon tires. It also demonstrated the durability of Hollywood stuntmen.

Grace, an ace pilot in World War I, gained fame for performing most of the thrilling stunts in *Wings* (1927), the first film to receive an Academy Award for Best Picture. He spent six months in the hospital after breaking his neck while filming a plane crash in the movie.

"But what's a broken bone now and then?" he told the Akron Times-Press. "I've had 68 broken in the last 10 years."

General Tire President William O'Neil paid a small fortune to lure the daredevil to Akron. Grace's minimum fee for stunts was $1,500—more than $17,000 in today's dollars.

O'Neil, who co-founded the Englewood Avenue factory in 1915, operated on a simple slogan: "Build tires that can be sold on merit regardless of competition and let volume take care of itself."

Company officials were especially proud of the Dual-Balloon, which they advertised as "Blow-Out Proof." The tire's patented construction was designed to run at extreme low pressure while providing "smooth, luxurious riding ease."

It would remain inflated under the roughest of rides, General assured buyers. The big test arrived May 17, 1930, on General's athletic field. Workers built a brick-and-concrete wall measuring 20 feet long and 10 inches thick. The barrier stood about 3 feet high, with another 2 feet sunken below ground.

Mechanics customized a touring car, tearing off the roof and windshield, and moving the axle and wheels forward so the front tires could absorb the impact of a head-on crash.

Dick Grace arrived in his usual stunt outfit, which included a leather helmet, an aviation jacket and knee-high boots. That was all he needed in those days before seat belts and air bags.

"There's a science in cracking up properly," he later explained to an Akron reporter. "I work each crackup out in detail and study it thoroughly before the time for making the actual shot comes."

Eight movie cameras rolled as Grace prepared for the stunt on a cool, overcast day.

The plan called for him to drive the vehicle toward the wall, bail out at the last second, hurdle over the bricks and land in a soft patch of dirt.

Hundreds of spectators stood on one side of the field while dozens of reporters, cameramen and company executives gathered on the other.

The stuntman entered the car and started the engine. He shifted the vehicle into gear and drove around and around and around.

"Grace let the machine pick up speed by circling the athletic field," the Times-Press reported. "Finally he charged down the 2,000-yard stretch, striking the obstruction at a speed of 37 miles an hour."

WHAM!!! Everything happened so quickly.

Witnesses reported seeing the wall shudder upon impact. The vehicle's hood crumpled. Grace couldn't—or wouldn't—bail out. His body hit the steering wheel and slammed into the dashboard. He was ejected headfirst through the passenger door and flopped into the grassy field on his hands and knees.

Only a complete cynic would have noticed that he landed directly in front of the newsreel cameras. The footage was spectacular.

Although the front section of the automobile was demolished, General's Dual-Balloon tires passed the test. They didn't blow out. They didn't even leak. The tubes maintained 40 pounds of air throughout the incident.

Hollywood stuntman Dick Grace, 32, stands with newsreel crews at General Field in East Akron before attempting General Tire & Rubber Co.'s Blow-Out Proof Test in May 1930. In 10 years of stunts, he broke 68 bones—including his neck in the 1927 filming of the Academy Award-winning *Wings*.

Meanwhile, the stuntman's wind was knocked out. "Grace was sent to City Hospital for medical attention, and after receiving treatment for cuts and bruises, was released," the Beacon Journal reported.

Over the next several days, he convalesced in a room at the Portage Country Club. His cut knee was bandaged, and he hobbled around with crutches.

"The racket is getting tougher and tougher," Grace told visiting reporters. At least he didn't break any bones this time.

News of the daredevil's injuries spread across the nation, generating tremendous publicity for General's tires. Movie theaters showed newsreels of the crash. Still photographs appeared in newspapers.

General produced a flip book so children could thumb through animated images of the Akron accident. When they turned the book over, the crash appeared in slow motion.

Needless to say, tire sales surged. "Our company did a larger volume of business in May this year than in the same month last year," President O'Neil announced in 1930. "Our unit sales during May were considerably larger." Unit sales were up for the year, too.

General continued to advertise its product as "Blow-Out Proof" until the Federal Trade Commission intervened in 1935. The FTC complained that the advertising slogan could not be true—no tire was blow-out proof—and labeled the claim as "unfair competitive advertising."

Gee, didn't they see the crash?

In 1936, General agreed to discontinue the advertisements until "such representations are an established fact."

Dick Grace retired from the stunt business and founded a freight and passenger airline in South America in the mid-1940s, according to the Internet Movie Database.

He died in 1965 at age 67.

General Tire maintained its world headquarters in Akron for nearly 70 years. The company was renamed GenCorp in 1984, sold to a German tire maker a few years later and moved to Charlotte, N.C., in 1996.

Three years later, the old complex was demolished.

Akron residents watched with sadness as another local landmark disappeared.

When the wrecking ball began to pound, the brick walls shuddered just as in the 1930 General Tire Blow-Out Proof Test.

Glitz at the Ritz

HOWARD STREET THEATER A HUB FOR MOVIES AND MUSIC IN EARLY '50S

(Originally published Feb. 25, 2008)

The Ritz Theatre was a jewel on Howard Street. It sparkled brightly from stage to screen, drawing big crowds with its glitzy mix of movies and music.

Film stars stepped off the screen into the auditorium. Recording artists stepped off the stage into music immortality. The Ritz was Akron's first big theater designed to serve African-American audiences.

When Howard Street was the center of Akron's black community, the Ritz took its place beside local landmarks such as the Green Turtle Cafe, Cosmopolitan Club, Benny Rivers Cafe, Coney Island Diner, Rhythm Bar, Elite Cafe and Oscar's Bar-B-Q.

The theater's owner was Maryland Theaters Corp., a subsidiary of District Theaters Co. of Washington, D.C., and Bijou Amusement Co. of Nashville, Tenn. The two companies operated more than 100 black movie houses in the East and South.

In 1948, Akron architect M.M. Konarski designed the 800-seat theater at 70 N. Howard St. The Howe Construction Co. of Cuyahoga Falls was general contractor. The project cost $160,000 or about $1.5 million today.

"Contracts already have been signed covering the use of films starring such actors as Louis Jordan, Cab Calloway, Lena Horne, Paul Robeson, Dusty Fletcher, Louis Armstrong and the King Cole Trio," the Beacon Journal explained during construction.

When the theater opened in 1949, neighbors flocked to see it. Richard Curling, 73, of Akron, remembers walking from his home on Hickory Street to the Saturday matinees as a child.

"Back in those days, they ran two features," Curling said. "Usually, one was a detective movie and the other was a cowboy flick. Then they would show the news and the sports reel and maybe a couple cartoons. All for one price."

The Ritz advertised standard Hollywood fare, including the latest films starring John Wayne, Clark Gable, Barbara Stanwyck and Johnny Weissmuller. However, the theater added features that weren't showing elsewhere. Some had all-black casts.

There was *Sepia Cinderella*, a romance starring Billy Daniels and Sheila Guyse; *Killer Diller*, a musical with Dusty Fletcher and Butterfly McQueen; *Professor Creeps*, a detective comedy with Mantan Moreland; *Look Out Sister*, a Western with Louis Jordan; and *Fight That Ghost*, a horror comedy with Pigmeat Markham.

The latest Tarzan and Jungle Jim movies occasionally shared the screen with older titles like *Harlem Rides the Range* and *Harlem on the Prairie*.

Cazzie Pryor, 75, of Akron, recalls being surprised when he went to the Ritz. "They had a lot of cowboy movies," he said. "A lot of the cowboy movies were black. I didn't know they made black cowboy movies."

The theater showed *All-American News*, a series about African-Americans. "They had true news," Pryor said. "A black did this and a black did that. Black inventors, and all that kind of stuff."

Sherman Roberts, 73, of Akron, remembers catching a bus with friends in West Akron and taking the long way to the Ritz. They went out Prospect Street to Federal Street, which put them in front of the theater. "Howard Street had a reputation, and your parents didn't want you to go down there," he said.

So the young moviegoers took an indirect route to avoid detection from their elders. "Grown-ups that knew you would see you," Roberts said. "They'd tell your parents, 'I saw Junior down on Howard Street.' And you would just be walking to the movies."

A big thrill for children was when comics such as Moreland or Moms Mabley appeared in person at the Ritz. Some attended film screenings, while others did vaudeville acts.

"I remember the comedians," Roberts said. "They had a guy called Pigmeat Markham. I saw him down there."

Curling remembers seeing Peg Leg Bates, a one-legged dancer who lost his limb in a childhood accident.

"With him and his peg leg, that was kind of awesome to us kids," Curling said. "The guy was an excellent dancer. He was a remarkable performer."

A 1948 drawing shows Akron architect M.M. Konarski's design for the 800-seat Ritz Theatre at North Howard and Beech streets.

Live entertainment was a big draw for the Ritz. Concerts cost 50 cents for matinees, 65 cents for evenings and 75 cents for midnight shows.

"When they had something at the Ritz Theatre, when they had somebody good that we knew, you could hardly get in there," Pryor said.

Blues guitarists B.B. King and John Lee Hooker played at the Ritz. Jazz singer Della Reese performed there a few months after signing a record deal.

Blues singer Wynonie Harris, R&B vocalist Larry Darnell and saxophonist Bull Moose Jackson made frequent visits.

Other notables were Lloyd Price, the singer of *Lawdy Miss Clawdy* and *Stagger Lee*; Big Mama Thornton, the first to record *Hound Dog*; and Johnny Ace, a crooner who shot himself to death a year after his Ritz show.

Audiences witnessed the birth of a cultural revolution at the Ritz. Some of the groups that played there were the Orioles, the Flamingos, the Larks, the Cardinals and the Swallows.

Others were the Clovers, the Checkers, the Counts, the Five Royales and the Five Keys. "Back then, rock 'n' roll was just kicking off," Roberts said. "They had most of the groups that got to be headliners later on come through there."

The Dominoes, which featured future superstars Clyde McPhatter and Jackie Wilson, performed regularly at the Ritz.

Deejay Alan Freed, who worked at Akron's WAKR radio until 1950, raided some of the talent for his Moon-

dog Coronation Ball in Cleveland in 1952. He lined up the Dominoes, Paul "Hucklebuck" Williams and Tiny Grimes, all Ritz veterans.

Akron's black community took pride in the theater. Seeing a movie or show hadn't always been convenient in town.

"It was one of the few movies that we could go into where we could sit downstairs," Curling said. "The rest of theaters, generally the blacks had to sit up in the balcony."

Roberts said the Ritz was a symbol of black empowerment. "If you didn't have nothing else, if you had a black movie theater called the Ritz, then that was something to look forward to. . . . When you have something like the Ritz, you can say 'This is ours. This is mine.'"

Unfortunately, the Ritz couldn't last.

Television was partially to blame. Movie attendance began to plunge across Akron as people stayed home to watch free entertainment. Neighborhood theaters began to fold all over town.

The Ritz, which relied on concerts, took an additional loss when rock went mainstream. Acts that used to appear on the small stage moved to the larger Akron Armory.

The Ritz shut down by 1955. As ownership changed hands, the building reopened in fits and starts. It became a dance club, a roller rink, a tabernacle and a contractor's office. The Summit County Society of the Blind used it for a workshop.

Urban renewal erased most of the old theater's surroundings. Landmarks fell one by one in the 1960s and 1970s, making the block virtually unrecognizable. Construction of the Akron Innerbelt barely missed the Ritz.

The building still stands at Howard and Beech streets. Since 1988, it's been called the Interbelt Nite Club.

For those who went there in the 1940s and 1950s, it will always be the Ritz Theatre. "Every time I go by there, I tell my wife, who came from Florida, 'Boy, did we have a good time down there,'" Pryor said.

"People talk about the good old days," Curling said. "I guess every generation had their good old days. But I feel like I grew up at the right time, and it was a lot of fun."

Don't Take My Home!

ELDERLY WOMAN REFUSED TO FOLLOW EVICTION ORDERS
AT AKRON MANSION IN LATE 1930S

(Originally published May 3, 2004)

Just because it was legal didn't make it right.

Augusta Kaiser's signature was on the documents. The deed had been notarized and duly witnessed. Everything seemed to be in proper order.

It was all a swindle, though, the elderly woman insisted. She hadn't understood what the papers meant when she signed them. She thought she was merely clearing up a bank debt. There's no way on earth she would have agreed to sell.

This was her home. "I am going to stay here till I die," she promised.

The 80-year-old Akron native had resided for nearly 60 years in the gray stone mansion on the northeast corner of Exchange and High streets. The 10-room house, built in 1879, was obviously too large for its single occupant in the 1930s.

The main floor featured a master bedroom, living room, parlor, dining room, kitchen and grand hallway. A winding staircase rose from the first floor to the attic. The second floor had four spacious bedrooms. The third floor, designed as servants' quarters, no longer was in use.

The last remaining servant, a handyman with the memorable name of William Shakespeare, resided over the old carriage house on the property. Augusta Kaiser hadn't always lived alone. She was one of seven children born to Joseph and Johanna Kaiser, German immigrants who settled in Akron in the 1840s.

Joseph Kaiser made a fortune in the hardware business, specializing in stoves, tin, copper and sheet iron. In 1871, he constructed the three-story Kaiser Block, a landmark building that still stands on South Main Street near East Exchange.

He built the gray mansion eight years later only a block from the family business.

Sadly, neither he nor his wife would enjoy it for long. Joseph Kaiser died in 1882 at age 65. Johanna died in 1884 at 63.

Augusta, who never married, continued to live in the family home long after her siblings moved out. She watched the residential area turn into a business district. Old homes were razed, and businesses sprouted along High and Exchange.

Her new neighbors included German-American Music Hall, Peoples Savings Bank and the Akron Canton & Youngstown Railroad.

Businessmen were interested in buying Kaiser's home because of its prime location. For decades, Kaiser turned down offers, including a $250,000 pitch in 1925. Even in the lean years of the Depression, she held firm.

But something went terribly wrong in 1935. Alden K. Crawford and Calvin G. Wilson, employees in the liquidation of First Central Trust Co., approached Kaiser with documents. She knew Wilson and thought she was signing a routine bank note, but it turned out to be a real estate deal.

Kaiser unwittingly gave up the family estate.

It was announced that Carrie Pfeiffer, wife of former Miller Rubber President William F. Pfeiffer, had bought the Kaiser property for $59,000 (about $807,000 in today's dollars).

Crawford and Wilson shared about $16,000 in commissions from the sale. After Kaiser's debt was subtracted and the commissions were added, she made less than $1,000 in the deal.

Kaiser may have looked frail, but she was plenty tough. She refused to leave the mansion. "This is my home," she said. "I ain't going to let them have my own home. They can't steal it. I've worked for it since I was a child."

For two years, she battled in court. She became something of a folk hero as newspapers described the "doughty old spinster" who fought for her home.

Although Wilson and Crawford were indicted on charges of embezzlement, their real estate deal was ruled to be legal. Lower courts decided Pfeiffer was the owner. The Ohio Supreme Court refused to hear an appeal.

"Miss Augusta Kaiser, the court has ordered you to vacate and leave your premises," Municipal Bailiff Justin Gardner warned in early 1938. "If the property is not

The Kaiser family's gray stone mansion at Exchange and High streets is shown in 1929. The five-bedroom house was built in 1879.

vacated by Sunday, Jan. 8, your furniture will be set into the street without further notice."

Kaiser wouldn't budge. She had 5 tons of coal delivered in her basement, enough to last a year. She filled her pantry with food. She locked her doors.

"The Lord can change the whole thing in a twinkling of an eye," she said. "I'm not going to move."

Blanche Hower, a state legislator who lived in Hower House on Fir Hill, was among those who rushed to Kaiser's defense. She had known Kaiser since childhood and appeared in court to testify on her behalf.

Local authorities took Hower aside and begged her to help them get Kaiser out of the home. "Help you get her out?" Mrs. Hower said. "I'm helping to get her to stay in it."

Municipal Judge Don Isham extended the eviction deadline, but made it clear that the law was the law. "If we can't get cooperation from her friends to persuade her to leave, we eventually will have to do that which no one wants to do—force her out," Isham said.

The standoff continued all winter and into spring. Kaiser refused to let anyone into her home except for Hower and a few other close friends. She nervously peeked out the window from time to time. "Every time the doorbell rings, my heart goes into my mouth," Kaiser admitted.

The moving van pulled up on May 4, 1938. Court bailiffs Nick Williams, Roy Purdy, James Miller and Nick Mancuso stepped out. They were carrying crowbars.

Akron Policewoman Mabel Kruse and Dr. W.I. Jenkins arrived on the scene. All walked up to the mansion. The front door was locked. They pried it open.

"Get out! Get out!" Kaiser screamed as the intruders smashed into the house. The 82-year-old woman was wearing an old dress and apron. She cried and kicked as Miller and Mancuso cornered her, picked her up and carried her toward the door. "Help! Murder!" she cried.

A crowd of onlookers watched the pitiful scene as Kaiser was carted away and her furniture was piled into the van. "This is my home," she cried. "I've been a taxpayer in Akron all my life. Why, I didn't know there were such people as you—you get out!"

They took the distraught woman to the Hower mansion, where her good friend promised her a place to live.

Kaiser lived at Hower House for less than 24 hours. A day after being evicted, she fell on a step in the unfamiliar home and broke her hip.

She spent the next six months at Akron City Hospital. Hower visited her friend regularly at the hospital, but the trips were heartbreaking.

"I wonder if my house is open," Kaiser asked at one point. "What will they do with my things? They won't go into my closet, will they? It's locked."

No one had the heart to tell her that the mansion had already been demolished.

Kaiser's health improved a little that summer but faded by fall. During a court deposition at her hospital bedside, she was completely confused. She didn't recall signing away her home. Charges against Wilson and Crawford were dropped.

The trauma of the year finally caught up with Kaiser. "If only I were back in my little old kitchen again," she mused in a visit by Hower. Three days later, she died.

Augusta Kaiser passed away Nov. 29, 1938, at age 83. Old age, the hip injury and the eviction were cited as the main causes.

Her last will stipulated that a $15,000 estate be shared by former servant William Shakespeare, St. Paul's Episcopal Church and a handful of nieces and nephews.

If anyone was hoping to make a quick buck off the former Kaiser property, it didn't work. The corner stood vacant for nearly 10 years until Christe A. Philios bought the lot for $90,000. In 1949, he opened the popular Western Drive-In, which erased sad memories of the corner. Today, the site is an Akron Beacon Journal parking lot.

Augusta Kaiser was buried next to her family in the Kaiser plot at Glendale Cemetery. She finally can rest.

No one will disturb her now.

Sole Survivor

CIVIL WAR VETERAN PAYS FINAL RESPECTS TO LOST COMRADES

(Originally published Nov. 12, 2000)

Alvin D. Miller lost many friends in the Civil War. Illness and old age took the rest. In 1940, the 92-year-old man found himself alone, the sole survivor of the Akron post of the Grand Army of the Republic.

In the late 19th century, nearly every local town had a GAR, a Union veterans group that was the VFW of its day. Summit County's largest chapter was Akron's Buckley Post 12, which was founded March 21, 1867, with nearly 1,000 members.

The post was named for its first commander, Lewis P. Buckley, a colonel in the 29th Ohio Volunteer Infantry who died a year after organizing the chapter. Meetings were held once a week in a hall at the northeast corner of South Howard and Mill streets. Walls were decorated with photos of Abraham Lincoln, Ulysses S. Grant and other Union heroes.

Wearing blue uniforms, veterans united in prayer and sang patriotic songs. Rites featured bugles, fifes, drums and the clanking of sabers.

When Grand Army members marched in Akron's parades, the regiments stretched for blocks and blocks. On patriotic holidays, Union veterans decorated soldiers' graves and held memorial services at Glendale Cemetery's chapel, a Gothic shrine built by the Buckley Post in 1876.

Alvin D. Miller, a charter member of the post, was born May 26, 1848, in Pennsylvania and raised on a farm near Wadsworth in Medina County.

In 1864, the 16-year-old boy enlisted in Company B of the 180th Ohio Infantry. He fought in the battles of Wilmington, Port Fisher, Wise Forks and Nashville, and trudged across Georgia during Gen. William T. Sherman's "March to the Sea."

One of Miller's proudest moments was parading before Lincoln when the president made a surprise visit to inspect the troops. "His eyes were very kind and sad, due probably to worry," Miller recalled in 1929. "Every soldier was true to him to the last."

Miller returned to Ohio after the war and found work in Akron at the Empire Mower & Reaper Works.

He became deeply involved in Buckley Post activities, enjoying the company of other veterans at the chapter's banquets, parties and dances.

As the years marched by, the Grand Army's ranks dwindled. Dark hair turned gray, sturdy bodies grew frail, old soldiers faded away.

The aging veterans watched as the United States entered the Spanish-American War in 1898 and then World War I in 1914.

"I fought in one war and lived through two others, and they were useless," Miller told the Akron Times-Press in 1933. "The people back home who want to get rich make them, and the lads who feel so brave fight in them. If people would just be reasonable, they could settle everything without fighting."

When Miller was named post commander in 1920, there were only about 100 members left. A decade later, only 40 survived.

Soon there were 10.

A handful of octogenarians met each week at the Akron Armory to play a game of pinochle and reminisce about the old days. One by one, they died, too.

After 95-year-old George Limric passed away in January 1940, Miller was the last man standing, the commander of a post that no longer existed.

The Buckley Post officially folded in May 1940 when Miller unveiled a monument to his old friends.

Surrounded by the graves of Civil War veterans, a marble memorial was placed atop a hill at Glendale. The white-haired Miller used a cane to climb the slope at the dedication service. "I come here today to dedicate this memorial to my departed comrades," Miller told those gathered. "May they rest in peace."

The monument, which still stands today, bears the inscription: "This memorial erected in memory of its departed comrades by Buckley Post Grand Army of the Republic by order of A.D. Miller, commander and sole survivor."

It wouldn't be long before Miller joined his friends. In December 1940, the veteran was confined to his

Civil War veteran Alvin D. Miller, 92, attends the dedication ceremony for the Grand Army of the Republic Monument at Akron's Glendale Cemetery in 1940. Miller was the final commander of Buckley Post 12.

Rhodes Avenue home after becoming seriously ill. He lingered through the winter, but died March 6, 1941, two months shy of his 93rd birthday.

More than 1,000 mourners, including members of the VFW and American Legion, attended Miller's funeral at Loyal Oak Evangelical Lutheran Church (now called Trinity Lutheran Church).

For the final time, the Grand Army of the Republic's burial service was recited for a Buckley Post member. A firing squad provided a rifle volley. A bugler sounded taps.

Miller's bronze casket was lowered into the ground at the church's cemetery. And Akron's final meeting of the Grand Army of the Republic was adjourned.

A Brush With Greatness

CUYAHOGA FALLS TEENS PAINTED ICONIC MURAL IN 1975

(Originally published July 19, 2010)

A patriotic mural captured the golden summer of 1975 in bold splashes of acrylic paint. The Cuyahoga Falls teenagers who created it didn't realize they were producing an iconic image to be viewed around the world.

Bathed in yellow-and-orange rays from the Statue of Liberty's torch, the mural beamed "SHINE ON AMERICA," a slogan that unexpectedly illuminated a new wave of Akron music.

The painting was roughly 90 feet wide and 50 feet tall and covered the brick side of the former Great Falls Employment Agency, which operated at 2091 Front St. in an 1832 building.

City officials approached Cuyahoga Falls High School art teacher Ron Simon about having students create murals for the U.S. bicentennial in 1976.

"The city actually paid for the thing," recalled Simon, 76, who taught for 27 years in the district and retired in 1986 as Cuyahoga Falls Teacher of the Year. "It was their concept. We brought together the kids."

Through the Student Temporary Employment Program (STEP), Falls students earned $2 an hour to paint that summer. Simon picked a core group of eight talented artists, most of whom were June graduates.

Participants were Lynne Condley, Ann Cisco, Tony Giannini, Barbara Hapanowicz, Karen Ann Jones, David Kanios, Nancy Reilly and John Stewart. "The kids were like heroes," Simon said. "Everybody knew about them."

Lynne Vanhorn, 52, of Columbia Falls, Mont., the former Lynne Condley, said the teens enjoyed the project. She remembers sketching the Statue of Liberty's torch-gripping hand and penciling "Shine On America" while brainstorming with classmates at the library.

"As I recall, I came up with the basic design," she said. "We were trying to find something fairly simple that would be not too hard for us to put up there."

A radiating torch wasn't enough, though. "They thought it was too plain, so they had us add the faces," she said.

The students incorporated images of Abraham Lincoln, Benjamin Franklin and Chief Joseph on the left side of the mural. At the last minute, Simon suggested adding the U.S. Apollo and Soviet Soyuz spacecraft, which docked July 17–19, 1975.

Robert Mothersbaugh, 84, of Akron, who owned the employment agency, remembers how the mural ended up on his wall 35 years ago. "The art director, Mr. Simon from Cuyahoga Falls High School, approached me and asked me if some students could put this sign on the side of the building," he said.

Mothersbaugh was a bit ambivalent about the soon-to-be-famous painting, which faced Broad Boulevard and caught the eyes of drivers on state Route 8. "I thought it was interesting," he said. "I was in the job shop, you know, headhunting, so I was more concerned with that. At least it cleaned up the side of the building."

It might be difficult to fathom in today's litigious society, but city officials allowed the teens to operate wooden scaffolding 40 feet in the air. The artists laid out the mural with chalk and string before painting it.

Barbara Swysgood, 53, of Sunbury, the former Barbara Hapanowicz, remembers the process. "We worked on it a section at a time," she said. "If you had three people on a section of scaffolding, you moved around pretty good."

At night, the scaffolding was parked atop the building so no one could get to it. In the morning, the teens climbed a fire escape to retrieve the platform.

The high-rise artists endured sunburns and spattered paint as they worked all June and July. "We were pretty fried," Swysgood said.

David Kanios, 54, who now lives in Palmetto Bay, Fla., doesn't recall any rainstorms interrupting the work. "It must have been one of those beautiful Ohio summers," Kanios said. "When you're young, all summers are great."

The project felt like a "last hurrah" to him. He knew he wouldn't see most of his classmates as they headed to college. "While we were painting the wall, I walked over to the naval recruitment center on Front Street . . . and I actually signed up for the service," Kanios said.

Supervising from the ground, Simon watched with pride as his students finished their masterwork. He couldn't get over what a great time they were having.

The "Shine On America" mural takes shape in July 1975 on the side of the Great Falls Employment Agency building at 2091 Front St. in Cuyahoga Falls. Paid $2 an hour for their work, teen artists painted from scaffolding 40 feet above the ground.

"They were always hollering and screaming at each other, just laughing," he said. "It could have been just the opposite, but they were all into it so much. That's what I remember about it."

Completed in late July 1975, the mural was barely dry when it became an unusual backdrop. Building owner Mothersbaugh's sons, Mark, Bob and Jim, were in a little band called Devo. The Akron group was working on a 10-minute film, *The Truth about De-Evolution*, which maintained that humankind regresses as it moves forward.

In a 30-second segment introducing the song *Jocko Homo* ("Are we not men? We are Devo!"), Mark Mothersbaugh's Booji Boy character, a man-child in a cherub mask, ran the length of the "Shine On America" mural and raced up the fire escape behind the building.

The video sequence entered the U.S. spotlight when Devo performed the song Oct. 14, 1978, on NBC's *Saturday Night Live*.

Simon remembers his reaction: "Oh, my God, look!" Swysgood was surprised, too. "We didn't expect it to get that kind of attention," she said.

Kanios was stationed in South America when a Navy pal received a shipment of videotaped television programs. "I remember my buddy saying, 'Aren't you from Akron? Didn't you say you painted some wall?'" Kanios said. "He said 'You've GOT to see this.'" And

that's the first time I saw the Devo video. "I was like, 'You've got to be joking me.'"

That same year, Stiff Records used a photo of the "Shine On America" mural as the cover for *The Akron Compilation*, an album featuring local acts such as Rachel Sweet, the Waitresses, Tin Huey, the Bizarros, Rubber City Rebels, Chi Pig and others. (Today, a replica of the mural is on a wall at Square Records in Akron's Highland Square). The album cover revealed that the mural hadn't aged well after enduring the wicked winters of 1977 and 1978. Giant swaths of paint had fallen off, leaving exposed brick. "Shine On America" became an ironic statement of urban decay.

Just as the mural gained global attention, Cuyahoga Falls workers sandblasted the wall to remove the eyesore. The painting was gone by late 1978.

The wall remained blank until an abstract blue-and-white mural of a waterfall was added about 20 years ago. That painting has been blocked from view since the adjacent Pavilion at Falls River Square was built in 2003.

No amount of sandblasting can eradicate the memories of the artists from 1975. "It was a fun project," Vanhorn said. "How could it not be?"

"I think we all felt pretty proud of it," Swysgood said. "It was one of those experiences," Kanios said. "It was outstanding." Shine on, America.

Dead Parrot Society

EXOTIC BIRD MAINTAINS PERCH AT AKRON CIVIC THEATRE AFTER 75 YEARS

(Originally published April 19, 2004)

She stands in rapt attention, casting a quizzical eye on all who pass. Not much has escaped that steady gaze in 75 years. If these walls could talk, they surely would squawk. The beautiful parrot maintains a dead silence, though. She's too stuffed to move.

The legend of Loretta is as much a part of the Akron Civic Theatre as the twinkling stars, floating clouds and Mighty Wurlitzer pipe organ.

When the Civic opened its doors April 20, 1929, as Loew's Theatre, the colorful bird was very much alive— and chewing up the scenery. Parrots and doves nestled among the classical statues and blended with the lavish decor in the 3,500-seat Moorish theater at 182 S. Main St.

The Akron Times-Press, upon taking a sneak preview of Loew's, announced that it was "difficult to describe" the place: "Difficult because one cannot faithfully describe the swaying of a palm leaf, the flutter of a bird's wing, the twinkle of a tiny star, the grandeur of a floating cloud, the deep shadows of a lovely garden. Yet all of these are in the new theater."

More than 14,000 people showed up for the gala opening. The bill, presented four times a day, included the "all-talking movie" *The Voice of the City*, five vaudeville acts, newsreels, comedy shorts and organist Estelle Ruth.

Loretta, one of at least two parrots at the theater's debut, began an unlikely rise from ill-tempered bird to beloved mascot after taking a perch in the Grand Lobby near the main entrance.

"I remember the days when we first opened there," said West Akron resident Raymond Tyulty Sr., 90, who was hired as a Loew's usher in 1930 and moved up to head usher and floor manager. "We had people lined up all the way down to Bowery Street to get tickets to get in the theater."

Customers entered the lobby and often stopped to gawk at the multicolored, long-tailed macaw preening in the corner. If they were lucky, the bird would greet them with a shrill "Hello" or a "Hiya, Toots."

Loretta was an old pro in show business. Before arriving in Akron, she had spent seven years in a Baltimore theater and 11 years in a Columbus theater.

She was a beauty, but it wasn't a good idea to get too close to her. Loretta liked to bite.

Tyulty discovered the bird's devilish nature while trying to befriend it with an offering of sunflower seeds. "Instead of thanking me, he took a bite out of me once," he said. "So I punched him one in the beak. Lightly."

Other than the occasional bite, Loretta remained extremely tight-beaked around Tyulty. "I couldn't get him to talk, that son of a gun," Tyulty said. "I did say 'Ouch' once, and I thought he'd say it right back, but he didn't."

It's the only bird he remembers seeing at the theater. "That was enough," he deadpanned.

Kent resident John Leidal, 88, a former doorman, was hired at Loew's about 1934 and worked there for 3½ years. He, too, recalls having a few run-ins with Loretta.

"All I can tell you was she was noisy," he said. "You couldn't handle her, I tell you. She'd bite you. People would come by there and look at the bird. She'd put her head down, and feathers would go up like a mad dog, you know. She'd start squawking and squawking and squawking."

Even more aggravating for the theater staff was having to catch the bird. Loretta's wings had been clipped, but she could still travel short distances.

"A lot of times, she would fly up to the ceiling," Leidal said. "We had a hell of a time getting her. In fact, the night crew used to come in, and they had to get her. They put a ladder up there."

Assistant manager Fred Clover sent the bird to a downtown pet shop for a weekly grooming. She was primped and powdered. Her beak was polished, and her feathers were cleaned. She came back to the theater—all dolled up and ready to peck.

Some customers apparently got what they deserved. "Everybody used to come up there and tease him and put their fingers towards him," Tyulty said. "Eventually, he'll grab you."

According to local legend, a Cleveland man sued the Akron theater in the 1930s after suffering a vicious bite. An out-of-court settlement supposedly was reached with the patron, but details are sketchy, and documentation remains

Loretta the parrot has been a mainstay at the Akron Civic Theatre for 75 years, although she's not as animated as she used to be.

By the 1940s, the bird was placed near the grand staircase on a mezzanine-level perch overlooking the Grand Lobby. And that's where she stayed.

For decades, she stared with glassy eyes as the great old theater slowly fell into disrepair. Fewer and fewer patrons were coming downtown. Loew's Inc. finally unloaded the property in 1964. The plan was to demolish the theater and build a parking lot, but cooler heads prevailed. The theater was rescued in 1965 and renamed the Akron Civic Theatre. Crowds eventually found their way back to the downtown landmark.

Age played a cruel joke on Loretta. By the 1970s, the symbolic parrot was disintegrating. "She wasn't very pretty close up, actually," Eddy said. "Obviously, she had been stuffed, and it looked like she had been painted or something."

Adding to the indignities, Loretta was briefly turned into a theater prop. Eddy recalls lending the parrot to Weathervane for the full run of a play. She dangled the bird's swing on a ceiling clip in her car and then drove to the playhouse. "It was kind of weird because she kept bumping against the window all the way down to Weathervane," Eddy said. "I don't think I handled her very nicely."

Loretta returned to her perch and continued to fall apart for two more decades. When the Akron Civic Theatre recently underwent its $22.5 million renovation and restoration, the parrot almost didn't make the final cut.

"We actually looked at getting a brand-new bird and just keeping the story going," said Dan Dahl, executive director of the Civic. But the plucky parrot persevered. Its history was too rich.

A Ravenna taxidermist was hired for a couple of hundred dollars to give her a makeover. "While the building was being done, Loretta went to the 'spa' and came back with new, bright feathers, and looking better than ever," Dahl said.

The results are extraordinary. The parrot glows in hues of red, green, blue and yellow. Dahl described it as one of the best, most affordable things the theater did during renovations. "She was a mess," Dahl said. "There wasn't a lot there to work with."

Loretta is back on her perch over the Grand Lobby and will quietly observe the Civic Theatre's 75th anniversary. The beloved icon is well-preserved—just like the theater around her.

elusive. It may have been the final straw, or at least the last finger. Loretta is said to have died under suspicious circumstances shortly after the incident, possibly because of the litigation. "I just remember the rumor was that after it bit the party in question that it mysteriously expired," said Patti Eddy, director of the theater from 1984 to '91.

New York City resident Randall J. Hemming, who managed the Civic from 1977 to '81, has heard the legend but is skeptical. "My gut feeling is it never happened," he said. He recalls sorting through boxes and boxes of information while cleaning out an attic area above the lobby. "We went through everything with a fine-toothed comb," he said. "I don't remember ever seeing anything like that."

One thing is certain, however. Loretta did die. Instead of going to a pet shop for grooming, she went to a taxidermist. "It was such a beloved icon of the theater that they just stuffed it," Hemming said.

"Just like what Roy Rogers did with Trigger."

What's the Score?

AUTOMATIC PLAY-O-GRAPH OUTSIDE BEACON JOURNAL HEADQUARTERS KEPT AKRON
BASEBALL FANS UPDATED ON WORLD SERIES GAMES IN 1920S

(Originally published Oct. 2, 2006)

Akron baseball fans enjoyed every minute of the World Series without going to a single game. Through the wonders of technology, major-league championships transfixed audiences on downtown streets in the 1920s.

Large, enthusiastic crowds gathered every October around the Beacon Journal's Play-O-Graph, an automatic scoreboard that charted game progress.

The giant board provided team rosters and box scores. It recorded who was pitching and who was at bat, and it duplicated strikes, balls, outs and runs as they occurred. The experience was so realistic that fans broke out in applause during important plays.

"The Play-O-Graph keeps a complete record of the game," the Beacon Journal explained Oct. 2, 1928. "As it depicts the flight of the ball, it also shows the progress of the runner from base to base.

"By an ingenious invention, a large white ball is suspended in front of the playing field and as the ball is pitched, batted or fielded in the actual game, so the ball on the Play-O-Graph travels to all parts of the playing field in exact duplication."

OK, the "ingenious invention" got a little help from a guy hidden behind the machine, but the crowd didn't have to know that. In essence, it was a marionette show with flashing lights. During a game, each play was telegraphed to the Akron newspaper office, announced by megaphone to the crowd and simultaneously updated on the Play-O-Graph diamond.

To fully appreciate the mechanism today, it's important to remember that television didn't exist and radio was still in its infancy. Fans had to wait for the Beacon Journal's World Series extras—published on green paper—to get game coverage.

The newspaper began holding World Series parties in October 1919 outside its headquarters at East Market Street and North Broadway.

In those years, the series began in early October as soon as the regular season ended. The team with the best record in the American League played the team with the best record in the National League. In the event of a tie, a one-game playoff determined which team would advance to the title series.

Games always were held in the afternoon, so Akron's baseball parties began around 1:30 p.m. Police roped off Broadway to accommodate throngs of onlookers for each game.

Organizers went a little overboard for the first extravaganza Oct. 4, 1919. The lineup included boxing matches, vaudeville comedians, Parker Lowell's Jazz Orchestra, the Goodrich Male Chorus, Grand Theater chorus girls, Egyptian dancer Cairo Shira and sports cartoonist Lawrence Redner.

Oh, there was baseball, too. The newspaper borrowed a rudimentary scoreboard from East Market Gardens and posted the rosters of the Chicago White Sox and Cincinnati Reds. "The party can readily be classed as a climax to the greatest baseball season in history," the newspaper boasted.

It was a World Series to remember, but for the wrong reasons. The Beacon Journal's first baseball party coincided with the Black Sox scandal in which eight Chicago players, including "Shoeless" Joe Jackson, were accused of throwing the series.

The following year, Akron baseball fans put the scandal behind them, cheering on the Cleveland Indians against the Brooklyn Robins.

The 1920 street party included more boxers, comics, dancers and musicians. Former heavyweight champion "Gentleman" Jim Corbett milled about the crowd with two actor friends.

"If you hadn't invited us to the party, you couldn't have kept us away from watching the games on the scoreboard," Corbett said.

The Beacon Journal's new, improved scoreboard—the Star Ball Player—was said to have an "almost human ability to accurately describe, play by play, a baseball game."

How it didn't spontaneously combust in Game 5 is anyone's guess. The scoreboard had to keep track of three remarkable feats by Indians players: second base-

Akron baseball fans watch the Beacon Journal's Play-O-Graph automatic scoreboard and listen to Sun Radio's public address system in 1929, during a World Series party on Summit Street. In real time, the scoreboard tracked progress between the Philadelphia Athletics and Chicago Cubs.

man Bill Wambsganss' unassisted triple play, outfielder Elmer Smith's grand slam (the first in a World Series) and pitcher Jim Bagby's home run (the first by a World Series pitcher).

The Indians beat the Robins in seven games.

As the decade progressed, the newspaper eliminated the sideshows and concentrated on baseball. Fans jammed the street parties to see the World Series, not Egyptian dancing girls.

The events took on more of a game atmosphere. Vendors sold peanuts and soft drinks. The crowd even stretched in the seventh inning.

In 1925, the Beacon Journal introduced the Play-O-Graph, the ultimate scoreboard. "It's as near like actually being at the game as is humanly possible to make it," the newspaper advertised.

The device—featuring a white ball on a string—was updated "just a few seconds after the play actually takes place."

Some great names in baseball appeared on that board, including Casey Stengel, Leo Durocher, George Kelly, Rogers Hornsby, Goose Goslin, Herb Pennock and Roger Peckinpaugh.

Most famous was the New York Yankees' "Murderers' Row" lineup of Babe Ruth, Lou Gehrig, Tony Lazzeri, Bob Meusel, Earle Combs and Mark Koenig.

As Akron fans watched from afar, the New York Giants won the series in 1921 and 1922 while the Yankees won in 1923, 1927 and 1928. Other winners were the Washington Senators (1924), Pittsburgh Pirates (1925), St. Louis Cardinals (1926) and Philadelphia Athletics (1929).

When the Beacon Journal moved its headquarters to East Market and Summit streets in 1927, it took the scoreboard with it. Police closed Summit Street to traffic, and the parties shifted one block east.

The Play-O-Graph completely captivated crowds. For hours, fans stared up at the electronic board, watching every move with blank stares that foreshadowed the arrival of television in a couple of generations.

"They stood before it, gazing upon it fixedly until hypnosis took charge of them, and they were no longer standing on Summit Street in a Midwestern city, but were standing at the edge of eternal conflict, watching," Akron journalist Jake Falstaff reported Oct. 5, 1928.

"So complete was the illusion—so thorough was the telepathy—that the swing of a bat in New York City brought a cry to a thousand throats in Akron."

In 1929, Sun Radio supplied a $50,000 public address system that blared play-by-play coverage as the Play-O-Graph charted games between the Philadelphia Athletics and Chicago Cubs.

The days of the megaphone were over. The days of the Play-O-Graph were numbered, too.

Most Akron households owned radios by the late 1920s, so citizens no longer needed to attend parties to follow games. Fans could hear live broadcasts from the comfort of home.

The Beacon Journal dusted off the Play-O-Graph one last time as the Athletics beat the Cardinals in 1930.

When that World Series ended, the game truly was over for Akron's automatic scoreboard.

Mystery Mound

(Originally published Aug. 5, 2002)

The law of gravity didn't seem to apply at Mystery Mound. Water flowed uphill. Strings dangled sideways. People stood at crooked angles.

Visitors couldn't believe their eyes at the Green Township tourist attraction. That's because the strange phenomenon wasn't exactly on the level.

An out-of-kilter fun house was constructed in the 1960s as a sideshow for Wonderland Acres Miniature Golf at 571 E. Turkeyfoot Lake Road.

Dr. Charles Keller and his wife, Goldie, both ordained ministers, operated Wonderland Acres for about 25 years next to their house on state Route 619.

"They built it as a Christian recreation center," said son David Keller, 61, of Barberton. "They had a very nice miniature golf course for years."

The Kellers purchased the 31-acre site in 1952 and opened a nine-hole course in 1953 that expanded to 18 holes in 1954. As an archery range and other features were added, Wonderland Acres became a suburban fun land attracting 15,000 visitors each year.

About 1960, Goodyear Aircraft technical writer Curtis Lovely, a former newspaper reporter, approached the Kellers with an unusual idea.

"He came out and asked my parents if he could put in the Mystery Mound next to the golf course," Keller said. "So they leased him some land to do that."

What was Mystery Mound?

Well, it was a mystery. But after all these years, we probably can reveal the secret. It was a wooden structure built on the side of a hill. "They build a room that's on a 20-degree angle, and when you walk into it, you think that the room's upright," Keller said.

"You're walking at an angle so it makes you really dizzy and you tend to want to fall against the one wall. You want to stand upright and everything else is telling you that this 20-degree angle is vertical."

Judy Lind Walters, 58, of Stow remembers the angle well. She worked for two summers as a teen guide at Mystery Mound. She was Lovely's stepdaughter.

"You were crooked," Walters said. "When you stood in the house, you were crooked. It was a pretty good optical illusion."

A tall fence enclosed the house so visitors weren't able to scan the real horizon. Their eyes told them that the floor and ceiling were level, but their bodies felt strangely out of balance.

"The idea that Curt got this from was a place up in Port Clinton called Mystery Hill," Walters said. "That's where he saw it and got the idea and then came back and built his own."

The front of the building seemed innocent enough as visitors lined up to pay admission. "From the outside, it looked normal," Walters said. "I guess if you want to compare it to something, it was kind of like the western movies where you walk down Main Street, and you have all the fronts of the stores," Keller said.

Inside, though, was a topsy-turvy world like something out of *Alice in Wonderland*.

One demonstration that never ceased to amaze viewers was when the Mystery Mound guides pumped water into a wooden trough. The water appeared to run up a steep incline and pour into a tub. It was actually trickling down, of course, but the house's odd angle changed the perception.

"It was very much a fooler," Walters said.

A second room at Mystery Mound created a grand illusion for visitors peering through two holes in a wall. When a person walked from one side to the other, he or she appeared to get shorter or taller, depending on the direction.

There was a big door at one end and a small door at the other. Oversized furniture and giant decorations seemed to diminish as the ceiling sloped down toward the smaller door.

"As you went across the room, things in the room got smaller, which makes you look big," Walters said.

The young guides were instructed not to give away the secrets of Mystery Mound.

Which way is up? A group of boys from Stow Alliance Fellowship Church enjoy an off-balance outing in 1962 to Mystery Mound on East Turkeyfoot Lake Road in Green Township. The tour guides are (from left) Maria Polumbo, Mary Kirkland and Judy Lind.

"We did not tell people it was an optical illusion," Walters said. "We said that this was just a 'strange phenomenon.' We 'didn't know' what caused it "We were told: Don't tell them exactly what it is. I don't know if that was right or not, but that's what happened."

Some gullible visitors, amazed by the experience, really thought that strange, unearthly powers were at work. "Beside Mystery Mound, there was a gravel pit, where they sold sand and gravel," Walters said. "Some of the people walked over to that pit, and they came back and said, 'Do you know it feels funny up there, too?'"

Today, the ramshackle simplicity of Mystery Mound would probably be the subject of liability concerns. "Back then, liability wasn't as critical as it is now—otherwise, we wouldn't have had an archery range," Keller said with a chuckle. "But we always did watch safety on it."

Mystery Mound operated from about 1960 to 1964. It was quite popular at first, especially with church groups, but the number of visitors dwindled as the novelty wore off.

"A place like that I'm sure would probably be more of a success had it been in a tourist town," Walters said.

Finally, Curtis Lovely closed the venture and dismantled the building. In 1969, he died of cancer at age 58. The Keller family continued to operate Wonderland Acres as a miniature golf course and recreation center until 1978.

"Dad turned about 70 It was too much for him to take care of," Keller said. "He had people that wanted to take it—either buy it or rent it from him—but he felt very strong.

"He had certain principles that he ran it by, and he didn't want those to be compromised, so he closed it."

Charles Keller died in 1983 at age 77. His wife, Goldie, passed away in 1997 at age 89. The Wonderland Acres property was sold to developers. Now located in the city of Green, the land is home to the Liberty Business Park.

If you want to visit Mystery Mound today, you have to use your imagination. "They leveled a lot of it off, but there's still kind of a ridge up on a hill," Keller said.

Gravity seems to have regained control of the land. "It was fun while it lasted," Walters said. "It was different."

A Sultan Visits Akron

BASEBALL GREAT BABE RUTH GAVE AKRON FANS A REAL POWER SHOW IN 1921

(Originally published July 21, 2008)

Seriously, Harvey S. Firestone. Did you need to throw in the free tires? Your baseball team already was an underdog—to say the least—when it challenged the New York Yankees to an exhibition game in 1921.

The founder of Firestone Tire & Rubber Co. couldn't resist offering a bonus to any batter who hit a homer that day at Akron's League Park. It was good publicity for the company.

"Mr. H.S. Firestone has said that he wants to see as many home runs as either side can slam out," reported the Firestone Non-Skid, an employee publication named for one of the company's early tires. "As an incentive to the players to knock 'em over the fence, he offers a tire—one to fit the player's car for every bingle that goes over the high board fence at the rear of the lot."

Yankees superstar Babe Ruth, 26, who already was enjoying one of the greatest seasons of his career, suddenly had an extra reason to beat Firestone's industrial team, also named the Non-Skids.

His car needed new tires.

More than 6,500 fans gathered under sunny skies July 22, 1921, in the baseball park at Beaver and Carroll streets. Bleacher seats cost 50 cents—about $5 in today's money—for the 4 p.m. game. A few crafty youths climbed telephone poles to peer over the fence and watch the game for free.

With all due respect to the home team, Akron residents were excited to see the "The Sultan of Swat" in action. The genial, stocky, hard-hitting player was a living legend in his second year with the Yankees.

"Today will be the greatest day in the lives of hundreds of Akron kids," the Akron Evening Times predicted. "Babe Ruth is the idol of the American youth and the future home run clouters of Akron will be there in droves to see Bambino swat 'em."

The Yankees had the day off between games against the Indians at Dunn Field in Cleveland. The day before, the Yankees lost 17–8 to the defending World Series champions.

A crowd was waiting outside Union Depot when the New York team arrived in Akron shortly before noon Friday. Ruth was wearing white flannel, blue twill and a straw hat when he stepped off the train.

Akron Press reporter Betty Brown waded through the gawking fans and snagged a brief, amusing interview:

"How many home runs are you going to make this summer, Mr. Ruth?"

"Oh, I don't know about that."

"Well, how about the game this afternoon? What are you going to do there?"

"I can't say about that."

"What do you think of Akron, Mr. Ruth?"

"Don't know. I haven't seen it yet."

"Haven't you ever played or been here before?"

"Well, not that I remember of."

Firestone pampered the visiting team from the moment it arrived. The Yankees were whisked away to the company headquarters, where the players took a tour of the factory, dined in the cafeteria and enjoyed a swim at the clubhouse.

The players were feeling relaxed and refreshed for the game. The Non-Skids weren't going to have much of a homefield advantage.

Before the first pitch, F.F. McCarthy, grand knight of the Akron chapter of the Knights of Columbus, presented a $100 check to Ruth to help rebuild St. Mary's Industrial School for Boys. The Baltimore school, where Ruth had learned to play baseball, had been destroyed by a fire in 1919. Flash bulbs exploded as news photographers captured the check presentation.

Then it was time to play ball.

Joining Ruth were Yankees teammates Frank "Home Run" Baker, Ping Bodie, Tom Connelly, Al DeVormer, Alex Ferguson, Harry Harper, Chicken Hawks, Fred Hofmann, Mike McNally, Johnny Mitchell, Bill Piercy and Wally Pipp. Their manager was Miller Huggins.

The Non-Skid roster featured Chester Blue, Art Bond, Roy Broadbent, Clarence Butts, Howard Camp-

Akron Beacon Journal news carriers meet Babe Ruth after a July 30, 1928, game between the Indians and Yankees at Cleveland's Dunn Field. The boys are (front row) Donald Bush, William Baum, Victory Pistney, Chester Rector, Earl Crouse, Carlos McKinley, James Whitmer, Adrian Jones, Robert Harner, Joseph Aylward, John Fasnacht, (back row) Frank Long, Charles Edwins, Babe Ruth, George Brittain and newspaper district men Paul Coudriet and Donivan McCombs.

bell, Eddie Dobscha, Kenneth Edwards, Herschell Gaffin, Dixie Lessley, Percy "Mac" McKinstry, Sam Mercer, Jerry Newkirk and Tim O'Laughlin. Their manager was Paul "Pepper" Sheeks.

The Non-Skids were in first place in the Industrial League. Pitcher Mac McKinstry, who had lost only one game that season, squared off against Ruth in the first inning.

Strike. Ball. Ball. Strike. A cry arose from the crowd when the Akron left-hander struck out the Yankees slugger on a called third strike. "It was a foot outside," Ruth joked as he returned to the bench.

Ruth, a first baseman and pitcher in this game, walked in the third inning, singled in the fourth inning and walked in the sixth inning. Expectations were soaring by the time he stepped up to the plate in the seventh inning against Non-Skids reliever Art Bond. The moment had arrived.

CRACK!!!!!!

With a mighty swing, Ruth smashed the pitch on a 1–2 count. Pandemonium swept the crowd as the ball rocketed 370 feet and cleared the right-field fence by 2 feet. It fell into the Standard Oil Co. yard and was last seen rolling south. Gleeful children cleared the stands and mobbed the diamond.

"When the ball sailed over the fence, a thousand or more youngsters started to race across the field from all corners of the lot to greet Babe when he crossed the plate," reporter Lynn F. Wagner wrote in the Akron Evening Times. "When he touched the last base on his circuit tour, every kid who could get within reaching distance of the Swat King patted him on the back or shook his hand.

"The kids swarmed onto the field and play was held up while Babe pushed his way, good-naturedly, thru the throng of future Babe Ruths to the Yankee bench."

Akron fans were witnessing the rise of a dynasty. Babe Ruth (1895–1948) finished the 1921 season with 59 homers and a .378 batting average, and led the Yankees to their first World Series appearance. They would win it all in 1923, the year that Yankee Stadium opened. It was the first of 26 titles for the team.

The Sultan of Swat qualified for a free Firestone tire with the longest shot ever recorded at League Park. The three-run blast was the only homer of the game—a little surprising since the final score was a jaw-dropper.

Yankees 22, Non-Skids 3.

Oh, well. It was only an exhibition game, right?

For all we know, that ball might still be rolling south.

Lair of the Bears

NELLIE AND GROUCH DRAW VISITORS TO PERKINS WOODS FOR 35 YEARS

(Originally published Oct. 19, 2009)

Giant bears prowled for food along the craggy hillside in Perkins Woods Park. With sharp claws and glistening fangs, the hungry beasts caught a scent, rushed downhill and pounced on hapless prey. The poor peanuts never knew what hit them.

Alaskan brown bears Nellie and Grouch were a popular outdoor attraction for 35 years in the Akron park. Hardware magnate W.E. Wright, a big-game hunter, donated the sister cubs to the city in July 1916 after making a trophy out of their mother during an Alaskan expedition. The Beacon Journal hailed the gift as "the nucleus of a brand-new zoo."

"A special cage will be built, and the bears will be treated with baths, deodorizers and—perhaps—toilet water, so that the atmosphere of the park will remain in its natural condition," the newspaper reported in 1916.

The Ornamental Iron Works Co. fashioned a permanent home for the bears. A 10-foot iron fence, curved inward at the top with two rows of bars, surrounded the den. Built into the hillside, the three-level enclosure had a rock terrace, cave, dipping pool and brick floor. The habitat was roughly 40 feet by 80 feet—too small by today's standards, but fairly spacious for the era. Some parks in other cities exhibited bears on concrete slabs in small pits.

Nellie and Grouch lived there for the rest of their lives. Sun, rain, sleet or snow.

Perkins Woods Park was Akron's answer to New York's Central Park. Col. George T. Perkins, president of B.F. Goodrich Rubber Co., donated the 79-acre preserve in 1900. The park had a shelter house, rock garden, bandstand, fountain, wading pool and memorial to abolitionist John Brown.

Perkins Woods caretaker Ed Muckensturm looked after the 450-pound bears for 25 years. The only way to tell them apart was by their claws: Nellie's were white and Grouch's were black. Each week, the bears gobbled 15 pounds of meat and 15 loaves of bread, plus fish, honey, carrots, parsley, apples, parsnips and grass. Their favorite treat was peanuts in the shell.

Robert M. Kraus Sr., 89, of Akron, who grew up on Fernwood Drive off Copley Road, remembers visiting

Nellie and Grouch in the 1920s. "When I was a youngster, every summertime Sunday afternoon, my parents and I walked from home to Perkins Park to see the bears," he said. "We always took along a bag of peanuts."

In the winter, he and his two brothers liked to sled down the park's hills. After spending an afternoon dodging trees, the boys capped the adventurous day with a visit to the iron cage. "Those bears were a fascination for us," Kraus said. He recalls standing beyond the outer fence and tossing peanuts to the shaggy creatures.

"Sometimes they'd grab them with their paw," he said. "Sometimes they'd get them in their mouth. You'd try to hit their head. They'd bite them and spit them out just like a squirrel spits out the shell of a nut."

Cyrus Thornton, 92, of Fairlawn, who grew up at Waterloo Road at South Main Street in Akron, remembers going to Perkins Woods with his parents. "It was not a national park like your Cuyahoga Valley, but it was considered a Sunday afternoon park for the families to go to and see the bears," he said.

The Thorntons packed picnic lunches, found a suitable location to spread a blanket and enjoyed dining outdoors. Afterward, the family followed a walkway toward park benches in front of the iron cage.

"I remember the bars were a good 4 inches apart, really," Thornton said. "They could get their paw out between them. They weren't real tight cages."

One thing that has stuck with him all these years is that one of the bears died young. That was the third bear.

Akron businessman Anthony Masino donated a black bear cub to the park in 1928 after bagging its mother on a hunting trip in Quebec, Canada. The female bear was about 5 months old and weighed 75 pounds.

Masino brought the cub to Akron on Columbus Day, so he named her Chris. Unfortunately, Nellie and Grouch didn't get along with the newcomer, so park officials built a separate enclosure. Chris lived to be 9 years old and 300 pounds. She died of heart disease in 1937.

Nellie and Grouch spent their days wrestling, sleeping, feeding and taking dips in the pool. They were frisky as cubs, but they slowed with age.

Children reach through iron bars to offer snacks to Nellie and Grouch at Perkins Woods Park in 1943.

LeRoy Teeple, 70, of Suffield Township, grew up on Douglas Street, two blocks away from Perkins Woods, and recalls playing baseball there in the 1940s. "A bunch of us would walk up," he recalled. "There was a drinking fountain up that way, and we'd be nice and dry, so we'd go up there and get a drink and see the bears."

Park officials stationed a peanut vendor near the iron cage so children could buy snacks to give to Nellie and Grouch. "There was an inner set of bars and an outer set of bars," Teeple said. "I'd reach my little arms through there and throw a peanut at them. It was about the only way people could get any action out of them because they were pretty old by then."

As dangerous as the feeding looked, biting and clawing incidents were rare. A few children had to get stitches and tetanus shots after suffering bites to their hands in the 1930s and 1940s.

Teeple recalls discovering an empty cage one day. "In the bottom section, set back into the rocks, was a steel door," he said. "These two guys came out with mops and buckets and brooms, and they were cleaning the whole cage. I don't know what was behind that door, but obviously the bears must have been in there."

In 1949, Akron Parks Superintendent Richard Barnhardt proposed establishing a natural history museum on land near Nellie and Grouch's habitat. The park district converted a former service building at Perkins Woods into a museum with plant and wildlife displays. After it opened in 1950, the museum attracted 30,000 visitors in six months.

They were among the last to see Nellie and Grouch. The 35-year-old bears suffered declining health. Nellie, in particular, could barely hobble around the cage. She stopped chasing peanuts. In 1951, the park district made the difficult decision to euthanize Nellie. The loss devastated Grouch, who stopped eating after losing her lifelong companion. She died two months later.

The Cincinnati Zoo donated 2-year-old Russian brown bears Ivan and Triska to replace Akron's loss. Crowds showed up to see the playful new animals. In 1953, the Akron Children's Zoo (now Akron Zoo) opened in Perkins Woods. It grew from one cage with two bears into today's 50-acre site with more than 700 animals.

Zoo spokesman David Barnhardt, grandson of the founder, said the old iron enclosure still stands, but it's in an area that isn't accessible to the public. The habitat held bighorn sheep in the 1980s and a turtle exhibit in the 1990s, but now it's empty. "We don't know exactly yet what that area is going to become," he said. "We have talked about preserving a piece of that because it's so historic."

Nellie and Grouch have been gone for nearly 60 years, but their peanut-munching exploits bring happy memories to mind. "Those were the days," Kraus said.

"We'd always go over and watch the bears," Thornton said.

"As a kid, you take all this stuff for granted," Teeple said. "Then when you get older and you look back, you say, 'Wow. That was pretty terrific.'"

Cry-Baby Bridge

LEGENDARY STRUCTURE HAS CHILLING TALE IN ROGUES' HOLLOW

(Originally published Oct. 29, 2000)

Legends never die. Details may change, settings may differ, but spooky tales continue to haunt generation after generation. The legend of Cry-Baby Bridge has been frightening youngsters in Northeast Ohio for so many decades that its origin is lost in the shadows.

The folklore, however, is distinct: If you stand on the bridge at midnight, especially during a full moon, especially when it's foggy, you can hear the wails of a baby who drowned more than 100 years ago.

Rogues' Hollow in Wayne County's Chippewa Township is fertile ground for ghost stories. The picturesque valley south of Doylestown earned its roguish name in the 18th century from the hard-drinking, barroom-brawling men who worked in the hollow's many coal mines.

Ghostly tales flowed as easily as liquor, and legends spread into the surrounding woods. Saloon patrons swapped stories of "The Headless Horse," "The Ghost Oak Tree," "The Haunted Mill" and "The Ghost Train."

Other stories swirled around a small bridge that crosses Silver Creek on an unmarked section of Galehouse Road. "A common tale is that a family was coming down the steep hill approaching the bridge and lost control of their buggy and a baby was thrown overboard into the creek and was drowned," says Charlie Cummings, vice president of the Chippewa-Rogues' Hollow Historical Society.

Another version of the story is that a woman killed her baby by throwing it off the bridge. The legend persists even though there is no record of any murder in Rogues' Hollow or any buggy crash in the creek.

"Teenagers and others have been visiting the bridge for at least 60 years hoping to hear a baby cry," Cummings says.

Frank Fox, 50, of Chippewa Township recalls visiting Cry-Baby Bridge in the 1960s with his teenage buddies. "You didn't go down there by yourself," he says.

It's a spooky place in the dark, especially if young imaginations run wild and nearby trees seem to come alive in the wind.

"The first year, you wouldn't get out of the car," Fox says. "You'd roll the windows down, turn the radio off in the car and listen. Then you'd get a little braver, and you'd get out on the bridge and listen."

Sound carries in the hollow. Every noise is amplified. At first, the rippling water of Silver Creek is all that's heard, but creaking tree limbs and hooting owls might cause a young heart to skip a beat.

"Personally, I never heard the baby, but somebody in the group would always say, 'Yeah, I hear it,'" Fox says. "If four of us were in the car, I guarantee you that one or two or maybe even three heard it."

Skeptics, of course, would attribute this to mass hysteria, the power of suggestion, a practical joke, animal noises or some other rational explanation.

"I think that most of the local people who aren't overcome with romanticism reject the ghost stories and the tales of violence, and probably reject the tales about Cry-Baby Bridge," Cummings says.

Although Fox never heard the crying baby, he's not so sure about "The Ghost Train."

One night in 1969, Fox was driving near the hollow when he heard a train approaching an unmarked crossing. "I could hear wheels on the rails, a horn blowing and everything, so I stopped," he says.

He sat in his car for a few minutes, switching the AM radio back and forth from WHLO to WAKR, listening to music.

"After I sat there for a while, it dawned on me: Whatever happened to that train?" he says.

He looked down the track in both directions. "There was no train nowhere," he says. "You could see for miles."

Members of the historical society aren't particularly fond of the ghost stories.

"The historical society's museum is a couple of hundred feet from Cry-Baby Bridge and has been the victim of vandalism on a number of occasions," Cummings says. "The tales of the bridge attract people who have parties and drink and become rowdy and smash things, and the historical society pays the price for that . . ."

The scent of fallen leaves and wet wood fills the autumn air over Cry-Baby Bridge in Wayne County's Chippewa Township. Some people swear they can hear a baby crying when they visit the spooky structure.

Visitors have spray-painted or scratched their names into the bridge's rusty guardrails. The underbrush is littered with empty beer cans.

Sheriff's patrols, the posting of "No Trespassing" signs and the installation of two street lamps are intended to sober the mood near Cry-Baby Bridge.

Meanwhile, a simple review of the facts spoils the eerie fun, pulling the sheet off the ghost.

First of all, this isn't the original bridge. Its steel beams offer proof that it was built more recently than 100 years ago. Rubble from an earlier bridge is scattered in the creek.

Second, there are serious doubts about the story. You see, there are people in Stark County who swear that the "real" Cry-Baby Bridge is in Canal Fulton.

There is also a Cry-Baby Bridge in Butler County. There is one in Logan County. There is another in Darke County.

Outside of Ohio, you can find Cry-Baby Bridges in Luling, Texas; Jenks, Okla.; Hartselle, Ala.; and Crescent, Iowa; not to mention Howard County, Md.; Franklin County, Ga.; and Lancaster County, S.C.

All are linked to the eerie tale of a baby ghost wailing at night.

Since it's improbable that infanticide occurred at every other bridge in the United States, it would seem that the story of Cry-Baby Bridge in Rogues' Hollow is nothing more than an urban legend, or in this case, a suburban legend.

"There are many tales of violence and ghosts in the hollow, and the tales are controversial today," Cummings says. "Some people believe them passionately and others deny them just as passionately."

Professor Jack

FORMER CHILDREN'S SHOW HOST RECALLS EARLY DAYS OF AKRON TELEVISION

(Originally published March 5, 2000)

Anything could happen. Jack Bennett thrived in the electric atmosphere of live television. Beneath the hot studio lights at WAKR-TV, he performed five nights a week as the zany host of *The Professor Jack Show.*

The children's program, which featured a studio audience, danced across Akron's cathode-ray tubes from 1963 to 1966.

"TV was much more exciting back then—the urgency of it, not knowing what was going to happen," said Bennett, 66. "It was live. If you made mistakes, you made mistakes."

Bennett, a graduate of Buchtel High and the University of Akron, got his start in television on WAKR's *The Teen Who Club*, a 1950s dance program he describes as "a poor man's Dick Clark." Akron youths danced at the TV station's original studio in the First National Tower basement.

Bennett was "discovered" while hanging out at the station. He was hired for $5 a week to do comedy sketches and lip-sync to records. Gene Davis was the show's host.

Although the work was fun, Bennett halted his fledgling TV career to work as a piano salesman at the downtown O'Neil's store. It was there that he landed a Christmas gig as emcee of the "Breakfast with Santa" program in the Georgian Room at O'Neil's.

Bennett's job was to entertain children until Santa Claus arrived. "I came out in a funny costume: big burlesque hat, big glasses, everything overdone," he said. "I took the hand mike and went around interviewing the kids."

All that was missing was a name for the colorful character, and Santa Claus provided that upon arrival: "Thank you, Professor," he said. The name stuck.

It just so happened that WAKR-TV operations manager Robert Bostian was in the audience one day with his young son. The boy was fascinated with Professor Jack and Bostian quickly realized the character's potential. *The Professor Jack Show* debuted at 6 p.m. Feb. 25, 1963.

The 60-minute show featured comedy skits, interviews and scratchy old Betty Boop cartoons. "Anything went," Bennett said. "There was no script."

The TV station, which had moved to the former Copley Theater on Copley Road, usually had a studio audience of 30 to 40 kids.

On the first night, however, there was no audience. Professor Jack ran out of material after 45 minutes. "I had 15 minutes left with nothing to do," he said.

Thinking quickly, Bennett asked a stagehand to bring him a newspaper. He then announced that he was going to teach viewers how to make a paper hat.

"Now, I had no clue how to make a paper hat," Bennett said. He folded pages every which way, making up instructions as he went along. "The studio crew was roaring," he said. "By the time it was over, I took a wad of paper, put it on my head and said, 'There's your paper hat.'"

It didn't dawn on Professor Jack that kids across the city were destroying that day's Akron Beacon Journal. Bennett was scolded the next day by a boss whose kids had torn apart his newspaper. "That's when I realized the power of television," Bennett said.

The studio audience usually featured Cub Scouts or Brownies or school groups. Bennett enjoyed interviewing the children. "Kids came up with great answers," he said. "You never knew what they were going to say."

A regular guest on Professor Jack's show was Jungle Larry, whose wild animal act was then housed at Chippewa Lake Park. He brought exotic animals to the WAKR studio, including pythons, tiger cubs and bear cubs.

"One day he brought a huge iguana, a mean-looking thing, and it got away from him," Bennett said. "It went under the bleachers where the kids were. The kids were yelling and I thought, 'This is gonna be one of the best bits we ever had on television: Jungle Larry capturing his own beast.'"

Jittery studio bosses, however, ordered the director to switch to a commercial. The iguana was snared without incident, but the TV audience missed the action.

Jack Bennett portrayed Professor Jack on Akron television from 1963 to 1966.

Bennett made $50 a week as the professor, but that climbed to $75 and finally $125.

"They started getting sponsors and I got a cut of that," he said. "The reason they gave me the raise was because I was buying my own props."

Northeast Ohio was crowded with children's hosts in the 1960s. Professor Jack's Cleveland TV counterparts were Captain Penny (Ron Penfound), Barnaby (Linn Sheldon), Franz the Toymaker (Ray Stawiarski) and Woodrow the Woodsman (Clay Conroy).

At one point, Bennett was hired to replace Barnaby at KYW (Channel 3) because Sheldon was leaving the station. A contract was drawn up that would have paid Bennett $390 a week to do a 15-minute program, five days a week.

A week later, however, the Federal Communications Commission ruled that NBC had coerced Westinghouse to swap its Philadelphia station in 1955 for NBC's Cleveland station. The FCC reversed the trade in 1965, sending KYW and its staff to Philadelphia and bringing WKYC to Cleveland.

After his Cleveland deal fell apart, Bennett asked his WAKR bosses for a raise. "I'm only looking for a living," he told them. "I need to make a living."

His pleas were ignored, though, and he gave notice that he was quitting. *The Professor Jack Show* went off the air on April 1, 1966. "It was a good time," Bennett said. "I just wish it was more lucrative."

Bennett was hired as the executive director of the Akron chapter of the March of Dimes, a post he held for nearly five years. After that, he worked in retail at Montgomery Ward and other stores, including his present job at Cigarette Outlet in Cuyahoga Falls.

Although, Bennett no longer is on television, he's still involved in entertainment. He has acted at Weathervane Playhouse and Coach House Theatre in such plays as *The Odd Couple* and *Our Town*. He also has acted in Eileen Moushey's murder mysteries.

For four years, Professor Jack Bennett has been in charge of the Coach House Theatre box office. "My hand is still in there—whether it's in the box office or a murder mystery," he said. "It's more of a hobby now."

And he no longer has to make paper hats.

Big Brother

BOXER SAMMY CRANDALL BATTLED HIS WAY OUT
OF POVERTY TO BECOME NATIONAL CONTENDER

(Originally published Feb. 18, 2008)

A championship definitely seemed possible. The muscular fighter was quick and strong and smart and brave. He seldom lost a bout.

"Big Brother," as his siblings called him, was a handsome kid whose cheerful personality could brighten any room. Since the Crandall home had no electricity, that was a powerful gift.

One of seven children, Samuel A. Crandall was born in 1927 to Samuel and Lydia Crandall in South Akron. His siblings were William, Helen, Marjorie, Russell, Marian and Constance. When William died young, Sammy took on big-brother duties.

"He was a kind, generous person," recalled his sister Constance P. Evans, 75, of Akron. "He was a lot of fun. He had a lot of friends. Everybody just loved him."

The family had to go on relief during the Depression. Their father worked odd jobs and helped build the Rubber Bowl with the WPA. He later was an auto mechanic and rubber worker, but money was still tight.

The Crandalls rented a small home at 405 Washington St. near the tracks. There was no power or running water. The family used kerosene lamps for light. "It wasn't a very nice place," Evans said. "There wasn't enough room for all of us piled up in there."

The children attended Spicer and Leggett elementaries and Central High School. Around age 12, Sammy began to hang out at Rice's Gym to practice boxing.

He saw the ring as a way out. Trainers were impressed with his natural ability. He began to compete in the 1940s, compiling an amateur record of 48 wins and three losses.

As a welterweight, Crandall won local Golden Gloves championships and advanced to the 1945 quarterfinals of the National Amateur Athletic Union tournament in Boston. New York boxing promoter Michael Spinelli approached the 140-pounder about turning pro and offered to be his manager.

Evans remembers when Spinelli and two other well-dressed men arrived in 1946 at the family's home. They brought a contract for the parents to sign.

"They all looked wealthy to us back during that time because we were poor," she said. "Everybody looked wealthy—and very seldom would you see a white man in the neighborhood, a big shot driving a big fancy car."

Spinelli, whose middle name was Baroudi, dubbed his new fighter "Sammy Baroudi."

"But that's not important," the boxer told the Beacon Journal at the time. "As far as Akronites are concerned, I'm still Sammy Crandall."

Baroudi made a big splash. Within a year, Ring magazine ranked him as one of the top 10 middleweights. He won 40 of 46 professional bouts, including 23 knockouts. One of his triumphs was a win over Bobby Dare at the Akron Armory.

Former heavyweight champion Jack Dempsey was a fan of Baroudi. "Although comparatively a newcomer, Baroudi must be reckoned with in middleweight circles," Dempsey wrote in 1946. "An aggressive, willing mixer, and a stiff two-handed puncher, Baroudi capped an impressive year by whipping Holman Williams, Coolidge Miller and Jose Basora in successive matches."

Baroudi wanted a shot at Jake LaMotta's middleweight title. "Give me that, and I'll bring Akron a world's championship," he vowed. But Baroudi was pushing 170 pounds, too heavy for middleweight fights.

His manager arranged a light heavyweight bout Feb. 20, 1948, with Cincinnati's Ezzard Charles at Chicago Stadium. The more experienced Charles outweighed Baroudi 176 to 169 pounds. He was 26 while Baroudi was 20.

In Illinois, a boxer had to be 21 to fight in a bout longer than six rounds. Spinelli told the boxing commission Baroudi was 22.

Evans remembers listening to the broadcast 60 years ago. Neighbors strung extension cords to the Crandall house so the family could hear the fight on a beat-up radio on a table. "All of us were crowded around that little radio and we heard the fight that night," she said.

Baroudi won the first two rounds against the heavier opponent. The next seven rounds were considered evenly matched. The 10th and final round would be decisive.

Akron boxer Sammy Crandall, who fought under the name Sammy Baroudi, won 40 of 46 professional bouts in the 1940s. He became a prize fighter to help his family get out of poverty.

When the bell rang, Charles began a ferocious barrage on Baroudi's body. The crowd booed when Charles landed an apparently low blow, but the onslaught continued. Only 47 seconds into the round, Charles fired a left into Baroudi's chin. The Akron boxer, who had never been knocked out in a fight, fell to the canvas.

Baroudi didn't get up. Attendants couldn't revive him.

They carried him on a stretcher to his dressing room and then took him to a hospital.

The radio report upset the Crandalls. While Baroudi's father made plans to go to Chicago, devastating news arrived at the home. Sammy Baroudi had died of a cerebral hemorrhage at 5:48 a.m. Akron time.

"Couldn't believe it," Evans said. "Couldn't believe it. We could not believe it. He was so young."

Akron's Second Baptist Church overflowed with grief Feb. 26, 1948, as the world bid farewell to a young boxer. Boxing commissioners, managers, fighters, reporters, students and fans were among those paying their respects. He was buried at Mount Peace Cemetery.

"That was one of the biggest funerals in the city of Akron," Evans said. "Dignitaries came from everywhere." Notably absent were Spinelli and Charles.

According to an Illinois investigation, the manager left the stadium with the purse money while Baroudi was unconscious. The cash was seized. A coroner's jury recommended that Spinelli be barred for life from boxing.

In the Crandall home, there was no love lost for Charles. Witnesses told the family that he used kidney punches and rabbit punches (blows to the back of the head and neck) on Baroudi.

Charles initially pledged to stop fighting, but then held a benefit to raise money for the Crandalls. A year later, he beat Jersey Joe Walcott for the American Boxing Association world heavyweight title. He died in 1975 at age 53.

Sammy Crandall kept his promise. Following his death, his family was awarded $5,600, including the $4,000 Chicago purse. The Crandalls used the money to buy a house on Charles Street in North Akron.

The death helped inspire rule changes in boxing, including better gloves and a mandatory nine count on knockdowns.

Sammy Baroudi Crandall wasn't the only one in his family to make a difference. A school is named for his sister Helen E. Arnold, an Akron educator. A community center is named for his sister Marian T. Hall, a welfare rights activist. His sister Constance P. Evans, a deaconess, will be honored March 7 at the Harold K. Stubbs humanitarian awards banquet.

Evans recently wrote *Pushed Beyond His Years*, a book about her brother Sammy. She wanted her children, Candace B. Crandall and Russell E. Crandall, and her nine grandchildren and 10 great-grandchildren to learn the history. "I'm the last one of my siblings that's living," she said. "When I'm gone, the story is gone."

So she told the story. Now the next generation knows about "Big Brother," too.

East Market Gardens

AKRON'S POPULAR DANCE HALL IS LONG GONE,
BUT FOND MEMORIES STILL WHIRL ABOUT THE PLACE

(Originally published April 26, 2004)

The last dance was long ago. The music ended, the floor cleared, the lights switched off.

There's still an echo. Happy tunes and pleasant times ripple through the memories of those who were there. They recall when live orchestras filled the radio and big bands ruled the night. They recall when East Market Gardens was the place to be.

The dance hall at 264 E. Market St. was one of Akron's most popular attractions in the 1920s and '30s. Couples crowded the floor and danced all night to the greatest bands of the era. Cab Calloway, Tommy Dorsey, Jimmy Dorsey, Benny Goodman, Harry James, Stan Kenton and Woody Herman were some of the greats who played at East Market Gardens.

However, the hall's most important band leader may have been Wilbur F. Stickle.

Who?

Wilbur F. Stickle. He and his business partners built the place—or at least its predecessor.

Stickle conducted Stickle's Orchestra and operated Stickle's School for Dancing in downtown Akron. In 1905, he and his colleagues decided to cash in on the roller-skating fad by organizing the Akron Skating Co.

They constructed a 100-by-200-foot skating floor, billed as "the largest rink in Ohio," on the south side of East Market between South College and South Union streets. A $3,000 organ would provide the rollicking music as wobbly skaters rolled around the wood floor.

More than 2,000 people turned out for the rink's opening. It cost a dime to enter and another 15 cents to rent skates. Within hours, the rink had rented out all 800 pairs of its skates. It was the first of many sold-out events at that address.

THE OLD GARDENS OPENS

The business operated for a decade until the skating fad grew tired. In May 1915, the rink was converted into "a summer garden and dancing pavilion." A crowd of 2,500 attended the opening of East Market Gardens on May 20, 1915. Once again, it cost a dime to enter.

Herman Kline's 12-piece orchestra furnished music in the pavilion. Professor F.B. Conklin offered dance lessons.

Water gurgled from a fountain in the beautiful garden. Japanese lanterns provided illumination. Motion pictures flickered in an open-air auditorium. If this wasn't paradise, patrons didn't know what was.

The dancing pavilion was open Saturday afternoons and every evening—except Sundays, of course. In Akron, it was illegal to dance on Sundays.

Some dances were illegal, too. In 1917, a controversy erupted over the one-step, a dance that involved quick walking steps.

Mrs. Gertrude Hoffman, city dance inspector and probation officer, was horrified: "Anything that is not scientific is immoral," she announced. "If the one-step is not founded on a scientific principle, it is not moral."

Her job was to enter nightspots and make sure that couples weren't dancing too closely. Offenders could be thrown out. "I don't dance," she explained. "Bar the one-step, and there will be less ruined girls. During my experience as probation officer, I have come to learn the evils of the dance."

Akron Mayor William J. Laub finally resolved the crisis by issuing an edict. Dancing couples were required to:

–Assume a proper position.
–Remain one foot apart.
–Use the feet and not the body.

THE NEW GARDENS

It's safe to assume that Mrs. Hoffman's job didn't survive the Roaring Twenties. Neither did the original East Market Gardens. A massive fire destroyed the wood pavilion in February 1920. The hall remained closed for a year before rising from the ashes as a steel-and-brick building with a stucco exterior.

That is the building that's remembered today. For the next 30 years, it was home to social galas, charity events, dance marathons, beauty contests, radio shows and a long string of concerts.

Akron's East Market Gardens at 264 E. Market St. was a popular dance hall in the 1920s and '30s. The hall started out as a roller rink and ended up as a bowling alley—with lots of dancing in between.

East Market Gardens decided to end its summer hours, allowing Summit Beach Park to take over the dance season from Memorial Day through Labor Day. But it reopened every September, and good times rolled.

"I remember East Market Gardens," said Gene Abdenour, 86, of Akron. "We had more fun there. That was the hub."

Young men and women converged on the dance hall from all parts of the city. They took streetcars, piled into cars, hitched rides or walked.

On Saturday evenings in the 1930s, admission cost 50 cents for gentlemen and 35 cents for ladies. On Mondays, though, it cost only a dime, and that's when high school kids turned out.

"My sister and I went there every Monday," recalled Lucille Hageman, 88, of Cuyahoga Falls. "Oh, it was packed. You stood in line to get in."

Hageman's sister, Jean Edwards, 86, of Cuyahoga Falls, said Dime Night was always fun. "Of course, I'd rather dance than eat," Edwards said. "When my mother really wanted to punish me, she'd say, 'All right. You can't go to the dance on Monday night.'"

Victor Palitto, 91, of Fairlawn, recalls meeting up with four or five pals at Walnut and Maple streets, and then taking a hike. "We walked all the way up there," Palitto said. "We'd all go dancing. We didn't have no cars, so we couldn't date no girls or take any girls home."

But while they were there, it was a great time.

THE PREDANCE RITUAL

Most of the dancers gussied up in nice outfits and primped carefully for the occasion. "They all dressed up pretty good," Palitto said. "No jeans or shorts, you know."

"You wore a suit and tie," Abdenour said.

"We'd have our clothes ready," Edwards said. "We thought we were something else."

At the hall, an elaborate ritual began among dancers, wallflowers and those somewhere in between. Boys gathered up the courage to go up to a girl. Girls wondered what was taking the boys so long.

"You'd stand around waiting to be asked to dance," Edwards said. "If you didn't get a dance at that one, you stood out. You sometimes would walk into the ladies room and fiddle around until the dance was over, and then back out you'd go."

Waltzes, fox trots, jitterbugs and two-steps were among the most popular dances at the Gardens. The floor was crowded, and the joint was jumping. "I danced until my suit jacket was wet," Abdenour said. "That's the way it was back then."

BIG NAMES

East Market Gardens was treated to some of the finest musicians of the 20th century. "Cab Calloway was the first one that I remember there," Abdenour said.

"All those name bands, like Harry James, Cab Calloway, Duke Ellington, the Dorsey brothers," Palitto said.

"You name any one of them," Edwards said. "They came to these places." She and her sister didn't realize they were in the presence of music legends. It dawned on them only as they got older.

"At 14 and 15, we didn't read the papers much to find out who was who," Hageman said. "We just went."

Nothing lasts forever. By the late 1930s, change was in the air. The crowds just weren't what they used to be. Akron nightclubs had siphoned away many of the hall's dancers.

In 1940, East Market Gardens reverted to a roller rink. After the United States entered World War II, the hall was leased to B.F. Goodrich to store tires.

"I was disappointed when I came home from the service and it was no longer there," Abdenour said.

The ballroom would reopen in 1946, advertising such bands as Vaughn Monroe, Tommy Dorsey and Tex Beneke. The golden years were over, though. On Memorial Day 1951, East Market Gardens closed forever.

It was born as a roller rink, and it died as a bowling alley. The building was converted into the Garden Bowling Lanes, an amusement center that continued until the late 1970s.

The name changed briefly to Rubber City Lanes before it shut down in 1982. Akron's big-band lovers lost an old friend when the building was demolished in April 1984.

"It was a nice, big ballroom," Abdenour said.

"Ten cents a night to dance!" Palitto chuckled.

"Really and truly, it was just wonderful," Edwards said.

The Battle of Summit Lake

CIVIL WAR VETERANS RE-ENACTED 1862 NAVAL CLASH
DURING FOURTH OF JULY FESTIVITIES IN 1888

(Originally published July 4, 2005)

One of the greatest battles of the Civil War took place on Summit Lake. The ironclad warships Monitor and Merrimac exchanged cannon fire during a fierce clash on choppy waters.

More than 30,000 people watched from shore as bombs exploded, vessels burst into flames and smoke filled the sky. Then everyone clapped and cheered.

It may not have been a real conflict, but it was impressive. Akron veterans staged an elaborate re-enactment of the famous 1862 naval battle for Independence Day 1888. For decades, those in attendance would remember it as "the greatest Fourth of July celebration ever witnessed."

The Buckley Post of the Grand Army of the Republic, a Union veterans group, sponsored the event as the grand finale of a daylong commemoration.

Festivities began in the morning with a huge parade that formed downtown at Main and Mill streets. Uniformed veterans and militias marched in regiments along Union, Market, Howard and Exchange streets.

The colorful procession featured brass bands, horse-drawn carriages, decorated wagons, balloons, fireworks and costumed characters, including a young woman dressed as the Goddess of Liberty. Spectators waved American flags as the parade traveled past businesses and homes decked out in red, white and blue.

When the units disbanded at the Exchange Street railroad tracks, marchers boarded a train for Summit Lake while carriages rolled on toward Lakeside Park. Some parade watchers followed on foot in the 2½-mile journey.

By midafternoon, crowds were beginning to swell at the park. The Great Western Band performed *Yankee Doodle* and other star-spangled tunes while politicians gave patriotic speeches to anyone who would listen.

Petticoat-clad ladies from the Women's Relief Corps, auxiliary to the Grand Army of the Republic, dished out more than 300 gallons of ice cream and ladled barrels of homemade lemonade.

The turnout exceeded all expectations. Today, 30,000 people would be considered a good crowd, but in 1888, it was greater than the city itself! Akron's population was only about 27,000.

Onlookers claimed every vantage point around the lake. They gathered on hills, climbed trees and swarmed the shoreline.

The first action of the afternoon was a sham battle on land. Hundreds of Union troops laid siege to a Confederate fort that had been built on a hill for the occasion. A general on a black steed led the charge. While cannons blasted away, the soldiers battled with rifles, bayonets and sabers.

This being a northern town, there was little doubt which side would win. When the smoke cleared, the bodies of uniformed rebels were strewn about the battlefield.

Well-timed explosions had provided the illusion of cannon fire. Guns fired blanks. The only real casualties were spectators who passed out in the heat and a soldier who accidentally gashed his hand on a bayonet.

"The charge was a most brilliant spectacle, and the entire battle was most realistic," the Summit County Beacon reported. "Old veterans were heard to say that they lived over again many a hard-fought battle during that hour, so real was it."

The main event—Monitor vs. Merrimac—began at 7 p.m. Event organizers offered a condensed version of the March 9, 1862, battle between armor-plated ships in Hampton Roads, Va.

In reality, Union ironclad Monitor and Confederate ironclad Merrimac (known in the South as the Virginia) battled for more than four hours. In Akron, the clash lasted about an hour. The show began with the Merrimac (actually the Dauntless steamboat in a convincing disguise) attacking rowboats dressed to resemble the Union ships Cumberland, Congress and Minnesota.

"As she plows through the water with that deadly iron beak, the cannons showing like grinning teeth from

An 1862 lithograph depicts the Civil War naval battle between the Union ironclad Monitor and the Confederate ironclad Merrimac at Hampton Roads, Va. A similar clash took place in 1888 on Akron's Summit Lake, although the stakes were not as dire. More than 30,000 people watched the re-enactment from shore during Fourth of July festivities that day.

the row of portholes in her black sides; with the skull and cross bones at her bow and the Confederate flag at the stern, she looks like some great iron devil, bent on destruction," the Summit County Beacon reported.

The Merrimac bombarded the hapless Union ships. Small explosives with short fuses were tossed into the lake, making it look like shells hitting the water.

Suddenly, a commotion erupted on the north side of the lake. The crowd began to cheer as the Monitor emerged from the Ohio & Erie Canal.

"But what is that strange craft which slowly steals out into the bay?" the Beacon reported. "Her deck, surrounded by a light railing, scarcely shows above the water, while in its center is a revolving turret showing two portholes."

Famously described as a "cheesebox on a raft," the Monitor (actually the Juniata steamboat fitted with a new deck) raced toward the Merrimac.

Cannons roared as the two ships blasted away at each another. Plumes of smoke drifted over the vessels while they circled the lake. One errant explosion, apparently not part of the act, set the Monitor on fire, but the Union crew quickly doused the blaze before history had to be rewritten. The ships slugged it out until both vessels were battered.

In real life, the battle was considered a draw. In Akron, however, history was revised a bit. The re-enactment ended with the Monitor chasing the Merrimac away. The crowd, of course, went wild.

"Suffice it to say, that unless the guns had been actually loaded and the ironclads engaged in a genuine struggle, the battle could not have been more real," the Summit County Beacon noted. "And of the thousands who witnessed the mock naval engagement there is not one, excepting those who saw the real fight in 1862, who did not go home with a better idea of that most celebrated of all naval encounters, the battle of the Monitor and the Merrimac."

There was only more thing left to do that Independence Day. The program concluded with a $600 fireworks display—about $15,590 in today's dollars.

Rockets fired in all directions. Twirling wheels shot off sparks. Silver and gold fountains gushed. Colorful stars exploded.

"The greatest Fourth of July celebration ever witnessed" ended with a glowing tableau of giant phosphorescent letters. They spelled out "Akron," "Buckley Post" and "Good Night."

Akron's Big Bonanza

CARTWRIGHTS GALLOPED INTO AKRON FOR DERBY IN 1960S

(Originally published July 23, 2001)

Akron was a long way from the Ponderosa ranch, but the Cartwright family felt right at home in the Rubber City.

When the cowboy heroes ambled into town, the welcome was wild. Confetti streamed from the skies while boisterous crowds applauded and waved. Cheers rolled down South Main Street like a flash flood crashing through a canyon. It was enough to make even the toughest hombre smile from ear to ear.

The cast of NBC television's *Bonanza* was the star attraction at the 27th annual All-American Soap Box Derby in August 1964. Patriarch Lorne Greene (Ben Cartwright) and his TV sons Michael Landon (Little Joe Cartwright), Dan Blocker (Hoss Cartwright) and Pernell Roberts (Adam Cartwright) turned the weekend into one of the most fondly remembered in Soap Box Derby history.

Actually, it was a summer rerun for three of the actors. All but Roberts had attended the 1962 festivities in Akron. During the two-year interim, though, the Sunday night program had soared to No. 1 in the ratings. This was the only time all four appeared together in Akron.

"Now I know what the others were talking about," Roberts said as motorcycle deputies escorted him through a gantlet of fans on South Main Street.

"This welcoming crowd is always very enthusiastic," Landon told a reporter. "I'm glad my wardrobe is made of strong material."

"It's an astounding turnout," Blocker agreed.

"It's really the only way people who like a television performer can say 'thank you,'" Greene said. "This is the only audience we really know."

The actors arrived in character—cowboy hats, vests, boots and holstered guns—with the exception of Roberts, who embellished his dark, signature outfit with a fishing hat and sunglasses.

A year later, Roberts would quit the series in the middle of its 14-season run. The fishing hat may have been a sign of his growing discontent, but if that was the case, he didn't let on.

"They were all great guys, really. Very down to earth," remembers Tony DeLuca, 64, executive director of the derby. "We got to talk to them quite a bit because we were part of their security and their escort."

DeLuca, a former Summit County sheriff's deputy who was in charge of derby security in 1964, says the actors were obviously impressed with Akron.

"Back then, they got treatment that they probably didn't get anywhere else in the country," he says.

Former Akron police officer Bill Kuntz, 74, of Fairlawn has worked at the derby since the 1950s. Today, he is in charge of transportation, a logical progression from the early 1960s when he drove a courtesy car for the Bonanza cast.

"They pretty much played themselves on the television program," Kuntz says. "I mean, I still watch it now and then, having met them all. The type of people they portrayed on *Bonanza*, they were really that kind of people. That's who they were."

In particular, he recalls how Landon enjoyed blending in with the crowd after arriving at the Mayflower Sheraton Hotel in full cowboy regalia.

"After they got their welcoming, Michael Landon went upstairs and he put his civilian clothes on," Kuntz says. "And he came down on the corner and just stood with us on the corner and watched all the festivities go on. Nobody recognized him."

He also remembers driving Greene to Camp Christopher on the night before the race to give a pep talk to the contestants. "He told them that they were all champs, that only one of them would come away a winner here, but they were all champions," Kuntz says. "He gave a tremendous talk to the boys."

Among children, the most popular cast member was Blocker, a gentle giant with a warm smile. Kids gazed up in awe at the 285-pound, barrel-chested actor, who liked to tip his 10-gallon hat to young fans, and greet them with a "Hiya, little fella."

Everyone seemed to be fascinated with Hoss' headgear.

Bonanza patriarch Lorne Greene (left) watches as his television sons (from left) Dan Blocker, Michael Landon and Pernell Roberts jostle for the Oil Can Derby trophy. Blocker, who played Hoss Cartwright on the program, won the celebrity race at the Soap Box Derby in 1964.

"It appeared to me if I would have put Dan Blocker's hat on, it probably would go on right down over my shoulders," DeLuca says. "It was huge."

Unfortunately, the trademark hat played a role in the weekend's only controversy. Hundreds of enthusiastic fans rushed up to Blocker's convertible during the Friday parade on Main Street. Amid the frenzy, the hat disappeared into the crowd and never was seen again.

Despite a plea in the Akron Beacon Journal, no one came forward with the ill-gotten souvenir. It's probably collecting dust today in some Akron attic.

Somehow, Blocker found a substitute hat in time for the next day's events. He and his TV brothers competed in the Oil Can Derby with Greene serving as flagman at the finish line.

Blocker's size presented some difficulties. He couldn't quite fit into his derby car. "They had to take out the whole steering wheel," says Jeff Iula, general

manager for the derby. "So they had to take out the steering cable and all that, put him in it, then slip the steering wheel back in and then hook up all the cables so he could go down the hill."

The Derby Downs crowd roared as the *Bonanza* boys rolled down the track.

The law of gravity smiled upon Hoss Cartwright's bulky frame. Blocker easily captured the checkered flag, followed by Landon and Roberts.

"I think they basically just picked him up and put him on the trailer and took him back to the winner's circle," Iula says.

After derby crews finally extricated Blocker from his car, he triumphantly raised the Oil Can trophy above his head—out of the reach of Landon and Roberts who were jokingly trying to wrest it from his grasp.

Blocker lost the hat, but he won the race. Just like on television, there was a happy ending.

The Red Peppers

AKRON FOOTBALL TEAM WAS SIZZLING HOT IN 1930S

(Originally published Oct. 15, 2007)

When Richard Dieringer has trouble falling asleep, he doesn't need to count sheep. He visualizes a vast green field under bright lights. He sees his buddies in padded uniforms, canvas pants and leather helmets. He hears the crowd's roar and referee's whistle.

Just before he drifts off to sleep, Dieringer calls another play for the Red Peppers. The 90-year-old Akron man likes to reminisce about the football games of his youth. The bantam team was a shining star in the dark days of the Depression.

"I started out as a halfback. By the time I finished three years later, I was a quarterback. There was a lot of talk about whether I was a good one or not, but I don't care what they think now," he said with a chuckle.

A lifelong resident of Firestone Park, Dieringer was an original player for the Red Peppers in 1931. His friend Joe Lampasone had tipped him off that Firestone Tire & Rubber Co. athletic director Paul "Pepper" Sheeks and former University of Akron star halfback Kenneth "Red" Cochrane were planning to form a team for the Ohio Bantamweight Football Association.

The 14-year-old Garfield student wrote a letter to Sheeks, and the coach invited him to tryouts at Firestone Stadium. "Judas Priest, you ought've seen the pile of kids that was there," Dieringer said. "It was a couple hundred kids."

The bantam league was designed for boys who were too small for high school teams. When the Akron squad formed, players had to be 16 or younger and weigh less than 116 pounds. Boys ran football drills in the clothes they wore to practice. After weeks of training, the field narrowed from 250 players to 45.

The 5-foot-6 Dieringer watched as the coaches selected players around him. He began to worry that he might get cut, but he refused to give up. "Finally one night I went to practice, and they gave me a uniform," he said. "I thought, 'Oh, man, I've finally made the grade.'"

The Beacon Journal sponsored the team, donated uniforms and paid expenses. Money raised at games benefited a charity fund that donated eyeglasses, shoes, wheelchairs, leg braces and hot meals to the needy.

Beacon Journal sportswriter Eddie Butler supplied the team's cheerful name. He suggested combining the nicknames of "Red" Cochrane and "Pepper" Sheeks into the "Red Peppers."

The team's first season was played at League Park near Summit Beach. Admission ranged from 10 cents for bleachers to $1 for box seats. It was a novelty to watch football games at night under stadium lights.

After a month of training, the players felt confident, but they didn't realize their skill until the first game. They crushed the Salem Sheen Bulldogs 53–0. The following game, they clobbered the Cuyahoga Falls Eclat Rubbers 24–0. "We had a good team," Dieringer said. "We were always trying hard."

The Red Peppers played such teams as the Cleveland News Skippies, Cleveland Press Bearcats, Columbus Red Birds, Dayton News Rinkey Dinks, Niles King News, Toledo Silver Streaks and Ravenna Golden Bears. No Ohio team scored on them in the first season. No Ohio team beat them in the first three years.

The Red Peppers found stronger competition elsewhere. Sheeks scheduled games against the Mooseheart Red Streaks of Illinois, the Charlottesville Fives of Virginia and the Erie Times Blue Streaks in Pennsylvania.

Mooseheart proved to be the Red Peppers' biggest rival. "That's probably the only team that ever beat us more than once," Dieringer said.

He recalls riding a bus to Charlottesville on mountain roads. A few times, the curves were so sharp that the team got out and walked. "The coach drove around and we got back on and went on our way." It was a scary trip for Charlottesville, too. The Virginia team, which claimed to be national champions, lost 26–0 to the Red Peppers in 1932.

In its five-year history, the Akron team was loaded with talent. Some of its big names were Gerald Ball, Bruce Dando, Albie Davis, Mitch Filing, Bennie Flossie, Dick Hart, Al Huey, Al Gorup, Bony Juhasz, Eddie McGlinchey, Russell Plappert, George Nichols, Bobby Roberts, Ed Roe, Carl Stager, Lyle Stemple, Eddie Suscinski, George Webb and Carl Whitten.

These boys carried out the brunt of the attack. The Red Peppers' front line in 1933 featured (left to right) Eddie Suscinski, Bobby Roberts, Dick Hart, George Hensal, Al Buzzelli, Lyle Stemple and Joe Natoli.

"Oh, my God, there were so many good ones," Dieringer said. Large crowds followed when the team moved to Buchtel Field near the University of Akron. Former running back C.P. Chima, 87, of West Akron, remembers hearing the spectators cheer from the grandstands.

"We drew as many as 8,000 fans on a Thursday night at the old Buchtel Field," Chima said. "The University of Akron on a Saturday would draw 1,200."

Chima was a Red Peppers second-stringer whose football career was cut short by a knee injury. The Garfield student began practicing with the team in 1934, an undefeated season. "It was just a tremendous program," he said. "Paul Sheeks was one hell of a coach. A little tough, but he told it like it was: 'Get your butt in there and play this game properly.'"

Phil Schweigert, 87, of Springfield Township, recalls trying out for the team when he was growing up in Goosetown. He didn't make the team, but he remained a big fan. Most of the neighborhood kids were trying to emulate the Red Peppers. Schweigert, a student at Hower Vocational School, practiced with a squad named the Goosetown Bobcats.

"You didn't have uniforms so you had to make up your own uniform with maybe three pair of sweaters and two pair of pants," he said. He and his friends belonged to the Knothole Gang, a YMCA club. Members received tickets to Red Peppers games.

"The crowd applauded the hometown heroes. The Red Peppers lifted people's spirits during the Depression," Schweigert said. "Everybody turned out and watched the games," the Goodyear Aerospace retiree said. "It was a big thing at that time."

"Yeah, we lost a couple," Chima said. "Not too many. We were pretty damn good."

Dieringer lost track of the Red Peppers after he became Garfield's quarterback in 1934. "I only saw one game after that," he said. The team finished the 1935 season without knowing it was the last. The Beacon Journal noted in 1936 that the team would "take a vacation" because of a "lack of adequate opposition."

Most Ohio cities had dropped out of the bantam league. Nobody wanted to get creamed by Akron. Even Mooseheart and Charlottesville called it quits. The Red Peppers were done.

Sheeks helped organize a new bantam league in the 1940s. Soon football fans were following the Kenmore Gremlins, St. Vincent Shamrocks, Eastside Corsairs, South Rangers, Central Flyers, West Hornets, North Commandos, Portage Lakes Panthers and Barberton Barons.

After World War II, former Akron player Louis "Bony" Juhasz opened the Red Pepper Steak House. The restaurant, which featured memorabilia from the 1930s team, was a popular hangout for 50 years. "It was a nice place to go eat," Chima said. "You always met somebody who used to play."

Dieringer stayed in touch with teammates for a few years, but they lost contact as the players grew up, got married, had families and moved. He wed his high school sweetheart, Paulyne Pershing. The two have been married for 67 years.

Most of the Red Peppers have passed away in the last 75 years. Dieringer said only a few are left. "People just fade away, it seems like," the Firestone retiree said. He often thinks about his great team. Sometimes when he can't sleep, his mind replays key moments on the football field. "You have no idea how much enjoyment I've got reliving those games over the years," he said.

A Man of God

RELIGIOUS PILGRIMS TRAVEL TO ELLET CEMETERY TO SEE A.W. TOZER'S GRAVE

(Originally published April 17, 2006)

They pray at the grave of a man they never met. Out-of-town visitors make a special pilgrimage to Ellet Cemetery to honor a 20th-century prophet whose writings inspire them.

Evangelical author Aiden Wilson Tozer, pastor of a Chicago church for more than 30 years, wrote nearly 40 books about faith. Two of his titles—*The Pursuit of God* (1948) and *The Knowledge of the Holy* (1961)—are considered classics in evangelical Protestant theology.

Many Akron residents may not know that the minister is buried in Ellet, but the word has spread beyond Summit County. Almost every month, small groups of Tozer's admirers wander into the historic cemetery behind North Springfield Presbyterian Church at Canton Road and Albrecht Avenue. "There's probably a hundred people, I'd say, that have been there to see that grave since about a year ago," said Robert Dishman, the church's custodian for 33 years.

At the cemetery, Dishman digs graves, mows grass, trims trees and handles other duties. When he works outside, he occasionally runs into visitors. "I'll see people up here walking around, and I'll ask if I can help them," he said.

Quite often, they're looking for Tozer. He guides them to the back corner of the cemetery—Tier 23, Lot 57, Grave 4—to a rose-colored granite marker with a simple inscription:

A.W. TOZER
A MAN OF GOD
1897–1963

"The people that come here are ardent readers of his books," said Jerry Schrop, Ellet Cemetery superintendent. "They really respect his theology."

Some bring flowers. Some take pictures. "A few of them have stayed by his grave for several hours and prayed," Schrop said.

Nearly a century ago, Tozer found his calling in Akron. He was born April 21, 1897, in La Jose, Pa., and moved with his family to the Rubber City in 1912. Jacob and Prudence Tozer and their six children—Zene, Essie, Aiden, Mildred, Margaret and Hugh—lived in a crowded house at 108 Roger Ave. in Middlebury.

Aiden enrolled briefly at Akron High School but left at age 15 to support his family. He found jobs in the rubber shops at Goodrich, Goodyear and Mohawk.

According to biographer James L. Snyder, the defining moment of Tozer's life arrived in 1915 as he walked home from work one day. A crowd had gathered around a street preacher, and Tozer stopped to listen. "If you don't know how to be saved, just call on God, saying, 'God, be merciful to me, a sinner,' and God will hear you," the old preacher said.

The words resonated with the teen. When he got home, he climbed to the attic and prayed. In his mind, a light clicked on.

Tozer started paying closer attention to sermons at Grace Methodist Episcopal Church on East Market Street. He studied the Bible, memorized passages and practiced preaching.

He discovered something else at church, too: Ada Pfautz, a 16-year-old parishioner. He asked to walk her home to 1458 Malasia Road in Goodyear Heights. The afternoon stroll led to a courtship, and the courtship led to marriage April 26, 1918. By then, Tozer knew he wanted to be a full-time preacher.

Aiden and Ada Tozer joined the Christian and Missionary Alliance church on Locust Street. Tozer worked to save souls on Akron street corners and traveled with his brother-in-law to preach in West Virginia.

The young evangelist left Akron in 1919 to serve as pastor of Alliance Church in Nutter Fort, W.Va. Over the next decade, he led churches in Morgantown, W.Va., Toledo and Indianapolis—each congregation a little bigger than the previous.

His immediate family kept growing, too. The Tozers welcomed six sons and a daughter.

By the time Tozer arrived at Chicago's Southside Alliance Church in 1928, he was one of the most influential U.S. evangelists.

Tozer's sermons were simple, yet powerful. Despite having little formal education, Tozer crafted beautiful prose that stirred audiences.

"A.W. Tozer had the gift of taking a spiritual truth and holding it up to the light so that, like a diamond, every facet was seen and admired," Chicago author Warren Wiersbe once noted.

In 1943, the evangelist wrote his first book, *Wingspread*, a biography of Christian and Missionary Alliance founder Albert Benjamin Simpson. He drafted his most famous work, *The Pursuit of God* (1948), during an overnight train trip to Texas.

"I think a new world will arise out of the religious mists when we approach our Bible with the idea it is not only a book which was once spoken, but a book which is now speaking," he writes in the best-seller.

Other Tozer titles include *Let My People Go* (1947), *The Divine Conquest* (1950), *The Root of the Righteous* (1955), *Keys to the Deeper Life* (1957), *Of God and Men* (1960) and *Paths to Power* (1964). Tozer's sermons, letters, radio addresses and newspaper columns have been collected in dozens of other books.

"Secularism, materialism, and the intrusive presence of things have put out the light in our souls and turned us into a generation of zombies," Tozer warns in *The Knowledge of the Holy* (1961). "We cover our deep ignorance with words, but we are ashamed to wonder, we are afraid to whisper 'mystery.'"

Tozer retired from the Chicago church in 1959 and accepted a pastorship at the Avenue Road Church in Toronto, Ontario.

His final years were spent in Canada. A.W. Tozer died of a heart attack May 12, 1963, in Toronto. He was 66 years old.

The author was buried in Chicago, but his widow had second thoughts. In 1976, she had the remains disinterred and moved to Ellet Cemetery in Akron, the town where they met.

Ada joined her husband in 1987. She was 87 years old. Robert Dishman, custodian at North Springfield Presbyterian Church, dug both graves.

Within the last two years, religious pilgrims began to ask about Tozer at the cemetery. "I had never heard of him," said the Rev. Janet Lowery, church pastor since 1999. Tozer's writings aren't as well known in the Presbyterian Church, but she set out to learn more.

The grave's location was disclosed in James L. Snyder's 1991 biography *In Pursuit of God: The Life of*

A.W. Tozer (1897–1963) was buried in Chicago, but his widow had his remains moved to Ellet Cemetery in Akron in 1976.

A.W. Tozer. The Ellet inquiries multiplied after excerpts appeared on the Internet.

Some visitors have tried to convey how much Tozer's work means to them. "One particular young man was in an accident and had some injuries," said Jerry Schrop, the cemetery superintendent. "He considers himself a disciple of Tozer. He works down in Tijuana, Mexico, passing out tracts."

The man's last wish is to be buried near the pastor. "To pacify the guy, I told him if he was cremated and brought his ashes, I'd put him somewhere near there," Schrop said.

The Rev. Jonathan Carey, pastor of Ellet Grace Brethren Church near the cemetery, grew up reading Tozer's books and owns several titles. His favorite may be *The Pursuit of God*. "He comes across very passionately," Carey said. "A 20th-century prophet is how he's been described. He read the church fathers and the mystics and applied that to the 20th century."

Carey was surprised when he learned that the author's grave was across the street, but he wasn't surprised by the public's interest. He wanted to look, too.

He joined a visiting Brazilian missionary who had asked about the grave. "We were moved by the simplicity of it," Carey said. "It's just a ground marker."

The epitaph "A Man of God" couldn't be more precise. "Something simple, and yet so profound," Carey said. "That seems to be the testimony of his life."

A Token of Appreciation

ARCADE FAN REMEMBERS FUNSVILLE USA IN FALLS WHEN IT WAS POPULAR 1980S HANGOUT

(Originally published Aug. 17, 2009)

When I peer through the dusty windows, the game room is dark and deserted. The rows of machines are gone. There is no more joy at Funsville USA.

I don't recall the last time I went to the video arcade at the State Road Shopping Center in Cuyahoga Falls. It must have been around 1990, a few years before the business closed.

The final visit should be etched in my mind forever because the place meant so much to my friends and me. Maybe I didn't realize the end had arrived. Maybe I thought I could always go back. When demolition begins next week on the abandoned plaza, I'll try again to remember.

Funsville USA, which opened in 1982 during the golden age of video games, operated for more than a decade at 2711 State Road. Unlike gritty, smoke-filled arcades of the past, Funsville was bright, clean and family-friendly.

The complex offered video games, pinball machines, skee-ball lanes, kiddie rides, novelty prizes and a pizza shop. Open seven days a week, Funsville reigned from 10 a.m. to 11 p.m. except Fridays and Saturdays, when it closed at midnight.

Customers risked sensory overload when they walked through the front door. The arcade was a cacophony of electronic bleeps, robotic voices, synthesized tunes and blaring rock songs. As colorful lights flashed and whirled, game monitors glowed in upright cabinets with gaudy marquees.

My buddies and I were in our late teens when we started going to Funsville. Our core group included Doug Caswell, Joe Del Medico, Paul Mancini, Steve Neff, Mark Ohm, Tim Ricks, Chris Scott, Paul Sink, Doug Smith and Glenn Stephenson. We congregated at the arcade almost every weekend and played games all night until cathode-ray images seared our retinas and pixelated ghosts floated when we blinked.

Per usual, the place was jammed. Kids were decked out in 1980s regalia: concert jerseys, parachute pants and head bands. No, wait. That was me.

I imagined myself as John Travolta's Tony Manero character from *Saturday Night Fever*, although Funsville didn't seem to attract as many women as the 2001 Odyssey disco. When girls did enter the arcade, we often were too engrossed in games to notice.

Instead of quarters, Funsville used clown-faced tokens—five for $1—dispensed from dollar changers. A lot of college tuition got fed into those machines.

Some of the classic games we enjoyed were Arkanoid, Asteroids, Battlezone, Berzerk, Centipede, Defender, Dig Dug, Donkey Kong, Dragon's Lair, Elevator Action, Frogger, Galaga, Joust, Jungle King, Missile Command, Moon Patrol, Mr. Do, Ms. Pac-Man, Pole Position, Qix, Robotron: 2084, Sinistar, Spy Hunter, Tempest, Tron, Tutankham, Wizard of Wor and Zaxxon.

I can still see and hear every game. I even remember where they stood in the arcade. My favorite was Q*bert, a snorkel-nosed creature dodging monsters on a three-dimensional pyramid of color-changing cubes. I became so good at it that I could play on a single token for hours—and I often did. Sadly, I found few real-life applications for this particular skill.

One of the great moments in Funsville history was when our friend Paul Mancini landed a job as a game attendant. In our eyes, he transformed into Willy Wonka, a benevolent figure who held the keys to the kingdom. Sometimes at closing time, he locked the doors and let us play games as he swept the arcade.

Eventually, we had to grow up. The guys found jobs, got married, moved away, reprioritized their lives. We stopped going to Funsville, and it closed about 1993, no doubt a victim of home computers and video game consoles.

I haven't seen some of my arcade pals in years. In my mind, they look just like they did in the 1980s. That can't be, though. The face in my mirror doesn't quite match that long-ago reflection from a Q*bert machine.

From time to time, I still find clown-faced tokens while rummaging through my belongings. How I wish I could go back to Funsville USA to spend them.

Game over. Game over. It was fun while it lasted.

Flight to Eternity

AMERICAN AVIATOR AMELIA EARHART TOLD AKRON THERE WAS NOTHING TO FEAR

(Originally published July 2, 2007)

If Amelia Earhart knew she was doomed, her calm voice didn't give her away. "We must be on you, but cannot see you," she spoke into the radio. "Gas is running low. Been unable to reach you by radio. We are flying at 1,000 feet."

The famous American aviator and her navigator Fred Noonan had traveled 22,000 miles in an attempt to circle the globe. The epic journey in Earhart's twin-engine Lockheed 10-E Electra was three-quarters complete.

After flying all night from New Guinea, they were searching for Howland Island, a speck of rock in the South Pacific. Earhart exchanged messages with the U.S. Coast Guard cutter Itasca, but radio operators couldn't get a fix on her position. She thought she was 200 miles away, then 100. When she didn't see the 2-mile island, she circled. Then she lost the ship's signal.

Radio operators listened helplessly as the last transmission arrived about 8:55 a.m. July 2, 1937. "We are now running north and south," Earhart said.

Seventy years ago today, Earhart journeyed into oblivion. In doing so, she broke her promise to Akron. She told us there was nothing to fear.

"My best recipe for success in long-distance flying is 'Don't worry,'" Earhart told an Akron audience only seven months before her fateful trip. "That is, do all your worrying about the flight a couple of months ahead. Worry retards your reactions."

Earhart was a frequent visitor to Akron in the 1920s and 1930s. She liked the city because "Akronites did things in aviation."

The Kansas native catapulted to fame in 1928 as the first woman to cross the Atlantic in an airplane. She was a passenger on that flight from Newfoundland to Wales. She later repeated the feat on her own terms.

Her first big visit to Akron was in 1929. She arrived by train at Union Depot and stayed at the home of Rayburn and Kathryn Hemphill at 514 Merriman Road.

Hemphill was secretary of Colonial Insulator Co. and a member of the Akron Business Club, which invited Earhart to speak at the Akron City Club.

Akron reporters peppered the "tousle-headed aviatrix" with questions about domestic life. The willowy blonde was still single. Did she sew? Did she cook?

"I wouldn't make a good wife, and I doubt if any man would have me," she said. "I'd be a fine wife, wouldn't I, if I traveled all around the country most of the time?"

Following a luncheon in her honor at Portage Country Club, Earhart was invited to ride the Goodyear blimp Puritan, which waited on the lawn. She preferred heavier-than-air machines, but was willing to try an airship.

Pilot Jack Boettner set course for Akron Municipal Airport and had Earhart slide behind the controls. Afterward, she had to admit: "It was wonderful."

Earhart congratulated Akron on its new airport, which she inspected from the air and ground. She predicted it would "compare favorably" with the nation's best.

Speaking at the City Club that night, Earhart said she would never undertake a hazardous trip just for the danger of it. Each trip had to be of value to aviation. "I believe in taking every precaution before one attempts a flight," she said. "Naturally, there is danger in everything."

Earhart came back to Ohio in the fall of 1929 to christen the Goodyear blimp Defender at the National Air Races in Cleveland.

VISITS AIRDOCK

In August 1931, she returned for the christening of the USS Akron, the Navy dirigible built in Goodyear's airdock. "I like Akron," she said. "You're doing some wonderful work here in lighter-than-air pioneering."

The visit was notable for two reasons. She arrived by autogiro after making a cross-country trip. She brought her husband, George Putnam, a New York publisher. OK, she had changed her mind about marriage. They stayed at the Mayflower Hotel.

Earhart's popularity soared in May 1932 when she became the first woman to fly solo across the Atlantic. "Lady Lindy" traveled from Newfoundland to Northern

Pilot Amelia Earhart (1897-1937), the first woman to fly solo across the Atlantic Ocean, was a frequent visitor to Akron. Below, she stands in front of the twin-engine Lockheed 10-E Electra that she was flying July 2, 1937, when she and navigator Fred Noonan disappeared over the Pacific Ocean.

Ireland in two days. Three years later, she flew solo from Hawaii to California.

The next Akron visit was a little embarrassing. Earhart didn't realize an air show was scheduled at Municipal Airport when she stopped for fueling in August 1935. A crowd of 100,000 was enjoying aerial acrobatics when the famous aviator showed up unannounced.

B.E. "Shorty" Fulton begged her to talk over a microphone, but Earhart was taking mail to Pittsburgh and running late. "This plane is on regular schedule," she said. "Nothing must be allowed to hold up the mail. I am sorry. But we must go on."

Earhart's last big appearance in Akron was as a featured guest at Air Progress Week in 1936. She set up shop at the Portage Hotel and traveled to Municipal Airport to meet Akron brothers Joe and Howard Funk, who had designed a plane. She inspected the craft, made a few suggestions and took it for a test flight. "I am going to keep my eye on you," she told them.

A PACKED HOUSE

She delivered a lecture to a packed house Oct. 28 in the Akron Jewish Center at 220 S. Balch St. In a speech titled *Aviation Adventures*, she talked about her new plane, which she insisted was safer than an automobile.

"Based on the average flying which the average person will do on regular airlines, he would have to reach 128 years old before any kind of airplane accident happened to him," she said.

She described her solo flights, saying she originally believed she had only a 10 percent chance of crossing the Atlantic and a 50–50 chance of crossing the Pacific.

"I took many Akron products along on that Pacific flight," she told the crowd. "After the public became very nervous about the idea of my going at all, I added to my equipment a collapsible rubber boat which could be instantaneously inflated. I also wore a rubber vest, instantly inflatable."

Made with rubber-coated canvas, the B.F. Goodrich raft folded up into a small bundle. In the event of an emergency, the pilot could pull a trigger that released a gas cartridge to inflate a rubber bladder. The boat would be ready to use immediately.

Earhart jokingly referred to the raft as her "one last hope." She said she also carried a bright balloon on which she planned to tie a bright red flag if needed. Those words haunted Akron.

In early 1937, the 39-year-old pilot announced she would attempt to fly around the globe. She and Noonan, an experienced navigator, began the historic trip May 30, 1937 in Oakland, Calif.

BANNER HEADLINES

The journey made banner headlines everywhere. The west-to-east route roughly traced the equator, hopping from North America to South America to Asia to Australia.

Earhart and Noonan landed June 30 in New Guinea. They rested, refueled and took off July 1 on a 2,600-mile course to Howland Island. They never made it. The U.S. Navy searched for two weeks, but found no sign of the airplane.

Earhart's disappearance is one of the world's greatest mysteries. Many theories abound, but most involve an out-of-fuel plane crashing into the Pacific.

It's down there. Somewhere.

If the wreckage ever is found in the murky depths, Akron residents will want to know: Is our raft still folded up in a small bundle? Or did Amelia Earhart use her one last hope?

The Lost Campus

UNIVERSITY OF AKRON NEARLY MOVED ACROSS TOWN IN LATE 1920S

(Originally published Oct. 8, 2007)

The University of Akron desperately needed space. The six-acre campus had grown so crowded that school officials raised entrance requirements and turned students away.

As enrollment climbed to an astounding 3,000, the university made a drastic decision. It agreed to transfer.

In one of the zanier moments in local history, the venerable institution on the hilltop nearly moved to the outskirts of West Akron in the late 1920s.

President George F. Zook, who led the university from 1925 to 1933, was one of the chief proponents of moving the campus. "For the first time in the history of the school, the enrollment was stationary this year," Zook told reporters in 1928. "The reason was not that students were not available, but because we could not accommodate them. There was no room to teach them."

Founded in 1870 as Buchtel College, the school had witnessed the rise of Akron from canal town to industrial city. There were 200 students when Akron converted the ivy halls into a municipal university in 1913. Within 15 years, enrollment climbed to 1,200 day students, 1,300 night students and 400 summer students.

Every classroom was packed from dawn to dusk. Desks had to be set up in old storage rooms. "We have chased every student activity but the Women's League off the campus," Zook said. "The men have no social rooms on the campus at all. The physical activities for women are limited to two hours a week for freshman girls."

After several years of frustration, UA officials seriously began to consider moving the school from its landlocked site. A committee studied property on East Avenue, Merriman Road and North Howard Street before settling on an ideal location: J. Edward Good Park.

Good, an Akron businessman, had donated his 180-acre farm to the city in the early 1920s. The park at South Hawkins Avenue and Sunset View Drive was home to an 18-hole golf course.

With great fanfare, the UA board of directors voted unanimously in favor of a 1928 resolution to build a campus on 72 acres of the park.

The nine-member board had tremendous clout. Its directors included Goodyear President Paul W. Litchfield, Firestone Chairman John W. Thomas, Polsky's Department Store President Bert A. Polsky, Central Hardware President James B. Pergrin and Akron attorney Cletus Roetzel.

"The university's service has expanded far beyond the limits put upon it by the present wholly inadequate buildings and equipment, and if the university is to live up to its purpose, it must move to a new site where it can be added to as needed," Thomas said.

"It was only after four years of careful thought and study of sites that the board of directors decided to make the move to the new site," Polsky said. "It is a most wise move and one that will show actual money saved."

Architect M.M. Konarski sketched a preliminary design for a handsome campus. In addition to a library and administration building, the complex would offer halls for liberal arts, commerce, law, engineering, rubber research, chemistry, physics, biology, home economics, education, nursing and secretarial service. The design also featured a stadium, public auditorium, art museum, music conservatory, open-air theater, gymnasium and power plant.

Business owners and civic leaders reacted with great enthusiasm to "the New University." The Akron City Council approved the plan. Students and faculty members raised $25,000 to help build a gym. When they reached the goal, they celebrated with a three-mile parade to Good Park.

Alumni launched a $200,000 campaign to establish a building fund and topped the mark after less than a month of fundraising. Polsky and Thomas pledged $10,000 apiece to the drive. Zook praised the effort as "the beginning of the greatest era in the history of the college."

It was a good start, but more money was needed. The city council agreed to place a $3 million bond issue on the ballot. Supporters kicked off the campaign with a pep assembly Oct. 7, 1929, at Central High School. Football cheers and band music filled the auditorium.

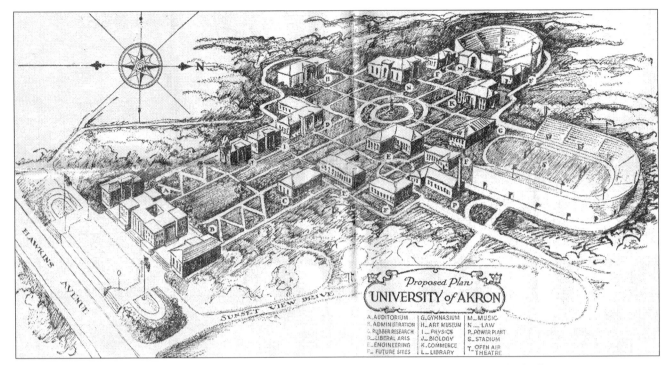

Behold the new, improved University of Akron. A 1928 illustration depicts how the campus would look after its move to a 72-acre site at J. Edward Good Park at South Hawkins Avenue and Sunset View Drive in West Akron. The design included an art museum, music conservatory, stadium, open-air theater, gymnasium and public auditorium.

Akron Public Schools stood to gain from UA's move. The old campus was expected to be awarded to the district, which hoped to turn the engineering building into a vocational school.

Amid the chorus of praise, there were a few prominent boos. Former Mayor William T. Sawyer, a Buchtel College alumnus, called the move illegal. He cited 1913 legislation that allowed the city to acquire the college. The measure stipulated that Akron "devote perpetually the funds and plant thus turned over to it to the uses of a municipal college or university."

"I do not see how the word 'perpetually' can be construed any other way than to mean that the school must be kept where it is now," Sawyer said. Dismissing the complaint, UA supporters continued to campaign for the bond issue.

Their timing was terrible. The U.S. stock market crashed Oct. 29, 1929, ushering in the Great Depression. The Akron election was held Nov. 5, the Tuesday after the plunge. Worried voters rejected the bond issue 22,745 to 18,923.

The "victory party" at the Akron Palace Theater turned glum, but UA students cheered when Zook addressed the crowd. He called the ballot loss "a small skirmish."

"Of course, we'll cope with conditions and triumph over them," he said. "I'm sad about this thing, and we're all sad about it, but there is no occasion to despair."

The Depression and World War II ended all discussion of moving the school. Instead, the University of Akron retrenched at its original site. Over the decades, UA systematically bought land near its campus and constructed dozens of buildings. The school eventually closed Buchtel, Union and Carroll streets to create a pedestrian-friendly campus with a more collegiate feel.

Today, more than 24,000 students attend UA, a state university with more than 80 buildings on 218 acres. It soon will expand to include Quaker Square and a new football stadium.

Zook Hall, which houses the College of Education, honors the former president who left UA to become U.S. commissioner of education and later served as president of the American Council on Education. He died in 1951.

In retrospect, he had the right idea. It was just the wrong time and place. The university couldn't move to a better campus, so it had to become a better campus.

"Although we are not sure about our next move, the spirit that we have shown proves that we cannot be stopped," Zook told UA students in 1929.

His Mother's Voice

1943 RADIO BROADCAST STUNS WORLD WAR II SAILOR AT SEA

(Originally published Dec. 1, 2008)

World War II sailor Dick Snader was tired and homesick. The 20-year-old Akron radioman worked the midnight shift aboard the oil tanker M.S. Brunswick, sending and receiving messages in a tiny room filled with electronic equipment. The giant ship had just dropped off a load of Venezuelan oil in Portland, Maine, and was traveling down the Atlantic coast toward New York in December 1943.

Sunrise signaled the end of Snader's shift as the tanker cruised about 75 miles offshore. After the morning crew arrived at 8 a.m., Snader took off his headset and wandered over to the galley in search of hot coffee.

At first, he didn't notice the small radio playing softly on a wooden shelf in the galley. It was picking up a live broadcast from Manhattan, but no one was paying much attention.

"I heard this woman on there," recalled Snader, a Fairlawn resident who is now 85. "It was just on in the background. I heard her saying something about 'Mrs. Snader.' I went, 'What the hell is that?' I turned it up a little bit and listened to it."

The commentator was Adelaide Hawley, whose NBC program attracted an audience of 3 million people. The pleasant-sounding Hawley, a broadcasting pioneer, was destined to become a cultural icon as television's original Betty Crocker in commercials from 1949 to 1964.

Snader's jaw dropped when Hawley introduced a special guest at the WEAF studio in New York. The visitor's voice was unmistakable. "She was interviewing my mom," he said.

Mary Snader, age 46, a mother of five and grandmother of two, entered the national spotlight that week for her contributions to the U.S. war effort. An airplane tire builder at Firestone in Akron, Mrs. Snader was one of six women honored on Dec. 9, 1943, at the War Congress of American Industry sponsored by the National Association of Manufacturers. Each "Rosie the Riveter" represented a vital industry in the war effort: aircraft, chemistry, steel, shipbuilding, transportation and rubber.

The radio show bewildered Snader, who couldn't believe his mother was in New York. "My mom had never been out of Akron," he said. "What's she doing here? It was completely out of the world for me."

Mrs. Snader told the interviewer that she had a boy in the Navy, but she didn't know where he was. He had enlisted in January 1943 and she hadn't heard from him in a while. "Some of the other sailors gathered around," Snader said. "They were laughing and joking."

Harvey Firestone Jr. selected Mrs. Snader to represent his company and the rubber industry. The small, bubbly, blue-eyed woman had a compelling story.

Mrs. Snader, the former Mary Rininger, was raised on a farm in Greentown, the eldest of 12 children. At age 16, she went to work at the Hoover plant in North Canton, but quit to take care of her siblings when a fire destroyed the family home.

After high school, she married Roy Snader and moved to South Akron. The couple raised five children—Irene, Margaret, Lois, Dick and Bill—in a tiny home on Hillcrest Street. A sixth child, Robert, died in youth.

When a 1929 industrial accident seriously injured Roy Snader, his wife became the breadwinner during the Great Depression. She turned out to be very resourceful at making money, Dick Snader remembered.

"My mom would bake doughnuts in the kitchen, put them in bags, and we would go out and try to sell them door to door," he said.

Then one day, she saw a newspaper ad that Old Dutch Cleanser was hiring a saleswoman to imitate the Dutch girl pictured on the container. "They gave her one of those Dutch cleanser dresses, and she'd go door to door dressed as a Dutch cleanser girl," he said.

In 1934, Mrs. Snader found a steady job in Firestone's tire division. She made miniature tires for wheelbarrows and gardening equipment, and eventually became the first female supervisor in the department. When the war began, she moved to the midnight shift—seven days a week—and became the first woman to build airplane tires.

"It is a great satisfaction to know that the tires I build make possible the operation in war zones of a wide variety of planes, from the Grumman 'Hell Cat' fighter to medium and heavy bombers," she noted at the time.

Left to right: Akron resident Mary Snader, an airplane tire builder at Firestone, was honored in 1943 at the War Congress of American Industry sponsored by the National Association of Manufacturers in New York. Dick Snader is pictured as a World War II sailor in 1943 and as a real-estate agent today.

Mrs. Snader never was tardy in 14 years on the job as a tire builder. After Pearl Harbor, she labored for an entire year while taking only two days off.

New York Mirror columnist Emily Cheney sized up the Akron worker in a 1943 profile: "Her littleness might be deceptive: More than anything else Mrs. Mary Snader is square, square-faced, square standing. And she has tough, square hands that grip yours in a handshake that almost hurts."

Mrs. Snader took the train to New York for the National Association of Manufacturers forum. More than 1,500 industrialists attended a banquet at the Waldorf-Astoria Hotel.

Radio announcer Jim Backus, future star of television's *Gilligan's Island* and *Mr. Magoo*, served as the emcee. "It gives me great pleasure to present Mrs. Mary Snader from the Firestone Tire & Rubber Co. in Akron, Ohio," Backus told the crowd. "Mrs. Snader has nine years of continuous service with Firestone—three of them as an expert airplane tire builder. You will want to know that she supports her invalid husband and three of her five children by working the graveyard shift." Backus hailed her as "American womanhood at its finest."

The next day, Mrs. Snader was interviewed on NBC radio, and that's when her sailor son tuned in offshore. She mentioned that she was staying at the Shelton Hotel in New York. "The ship got in probably about 3 o'clock in the afternoon," Snader said. "I got off right away and I shot over to that hotel." His mother hadn't returned, so he sat down in a lobby chair and fell asleep.

When the sailor awoke, it was dark outside. He jumped to his feet and raced upstairs to Mrs. Snader's room. "I was just getting ready to knock, and she came out," he said.

Now it was his mother's turn to react with disbelief. A look of joy washed over her face as she recognized the man in uniform. She had experienced many wonderful moments during her trip, but reuniting with her son was the happiest of all. "She was tickled to death," Snader said. "She never expected to see me, naturally."

The six honorees were leaving for dinner in the Hawaiian Room of the Lexington Hotel, and they invited Snader. He couldn't stay long because the ship was in dry dock, but he grabbed a few bites and caught up on current events before hugging his mother goodbye and running back to the tanker.

After the war, Mary Snader bid farewell to Rosie the Riveter. She quit Firestone, got a real-estate license and worked for Sanders Home Corp., which is where she retired. She was 96 when she died in 1993.

Dick Snader returned home from the Navy in January 1946. He married Pauline Marhevsky, worked as a taxi driver, served as an Akron firefighter and won election as a Fairlawn councilman. Today, he is a Realtor for Ederer Real Estate.

It has been 65 years since that remarkable morning when he heard his mother on the radio. A friendly voice soared across the waves and comforted a tired, homesick sailor on a giant ship. "It surprised the hell out of me, I'll tell you that," Snader said.

Mystery of Charlie Chan

FICTIONAL DETECTIVE FOLLOWS TRAIL OF CLUES FROM AKRON

(Originally published May 5, 2008)

There is no smoking gun, crimson dagger or coiled rope. Yet there is tantalizing evidence that a fictional detective has close ties to Akron.

Mystery novelist Earl Derr Biggers (1884–1933), a Warren native who created Charlie Chan, seems to have left a trail of clues in Northeast Ohio.

Biggers wrote six books about the brilliant Chinese-American sleuth, an unusual protagonist for the United States in the early 20th century. "I had seen movies depicting and read stories about Chinatown and wicked Chinese villains, and it struck me that a Chinese hero, trustworthy, benevolent and philosophical, would come nearer to presenting a correct portrayal of the race," Biggers once said.

"I created Charlie Chan as a minor character in a story I was writing and by the time the story, a serial, had ended, readers were writing in for more of Chan."

He sketched out a Honolulu police inspector who spoke in pidgin English and dispensed ancient wisdoms while solving the world's greatest mysteries. When questioning suspects, Chan utters gems such as "The wise elephant does not seek to ape the butterfly" and "When the dinner is ended, who values the spoon?"

For Akron-Canton readers, the 1930 novel *Charlie Chan Carries On* has an extra layer of mystery. The author provides delightful details of local interest.

The plot is about a killer stalking a U.S. tour group on a globe-trotting vacation. The first victim—a Detroit automobile executive—is found strangled in a ritzy London hotel. His hand clutches a key marked "Dietrich Safe and Lock Company, Canton, Ohio," obviously inspired by Diebold Safe & Lock Co.

Two prominent characters are introduced: Akron rubber baron Elmer Benbow and his socialite wife, Nettie, who seem to be an amalgamation of Seiberlings and Firestones.

"He was a plump, genial soul; the naive, unsophisticated sort the British so love to think of as a typical American," Biggers writes. He describes Mrs. Benbow as "a handsome, well-dressed woman who, not being needed at the factory, had evidently had more time for the refinements of life than had her husband."

Throughout the novel, Biggers refers to Benbow as "the man from Akron." The rubber executive mentions the city every chance he gets. "Akron," he says. "You've heard of Akron, haven't you? Akron, Ohio."

Inspecting the mysterious key, a London police officer inquires if Canton is near Akron. "Just a few miles between 'em," Benbow answers. "McKinley came from Canton, you know. Mother of presidents—that's what we call Ohio."

Realizing that the proximity of the cities might make him a suspect, Benbow protests: "We make too many tires in Akron to go round killing off our best customers, the automobile men."

Throughout the tale, Benbow carries a movie camera to film his vacation adventures "for the folks back in Akron." Charlie Chan persuades the rubber baron to show his films to the tour group. After spotting a valuable clue on the screen, the detective urges Benbow to lock up the film. "It would grieve me greatly if you arrived in beloved hometown lacking important reel," Chan says.

Biggers apparently did his homework. One character is named Spicer, the surname of a Summit County pioneer family. Another is Everhard, the surname of a Stark County pioneer family.

Charlie Chan Carries On was such a popular novel that Fox Film Corp. turned it into a 1931 movie starring Swedish-born actor Warner Oland. It was his first appearance as Charlie Chan, a star-making role he would reprise for 15 more movies.

Beacon Journal reviewer Edward E. Gloss wrote: "I like this Chinese detective Charlie Chan, portrayed by the hitherto sinister Warner Oland in *Charlie Chan Carries On*, at the Colonial."

The Akron subplot made the transition to the silver screen. Gloss praised the comedic character of the "big rubber and tire man from Akron, O."

"If they haven't already been planned, we'd suggest more Chan pictures," Gloss wrote.

Mystery novelist Earl Derr Biggers makes frequent mention of Akron and Canton in his 1930 book, *Charlie Chan Carries On*, which Fox Film Corp. turned into a successful 1931 movie starring actor Warner Oland. The author was a native of Warren.

Earl Derr Biggers was 48 when he died of pneumonia in 1933. Charlie Chan's popularity soared on the big screen, but the ethnic stereotypes that the novelist tried to avoid became more prevalent. Oland wasn't Asian. Neither were Sidney Toler and Roland Winters, who later played the role.

Biggers said he got the idea for the detective during a Hawaiian vacation in 1919. Historians credit a newspaper article about veteran Honolulu detective Chang Apana as the character's inspiration.

However, Biggers said he didn't meet Apana until after the third Chan novel. "The character of Charlie Chan is entirely fictitious," he insisted.

Well, the plot thickens. There really was a man named Charlie Chan. He operated a laundry for about 15 years at 40 N. Howard St. in downtown Akron. He was one of only two Asian men living in the city at the time.

In the early 20th century, Chan wasn't a common name in America. U.S. census records reveal only five listings for Charles Chan from 1900 to 1910. Only one man lived in Ohio: the Akron resident.

He was the only one who listed Charlie as his official name. Born in the 1860s in Canton, China, he immigrated to the United States as a teen and opened the Akron laundry in the late 1890s. The business, which was a half-block north of Market Street, doubled as his home. The 1900 census gave his age at 36.

The Beacon Journal interviewed him for a 1900 article about the Boxer Rebellion, an uprising against foreigners in China. The unnamed reporter decided to write in dialect:

"Chan was busy, but he came out from the rear of his laundry long enough to be interviewed. He was told that there is a great war raging in China and he was asked to say something about the Boxers. 'War! War in China! Me no care. Me safe. China bad. Me no go back China.'"

If the quote is accurate, our Charlie Chan wasn't as fluent in English as the fictional detective.

Earl Derr Biggers lived about 40 miles away in Warren. As a young man, he could have hopped the Pittsburgh, Akron & Western Railroad and made it to the "big city" in two hours.

There is no evidence that he met the laundryman. However, Charlie Chan's business was in a prominent location within walking distance of the train station.

If Biggers did come to town, he could have seen the sign. Years later, while trying to think of a good name for a Chinese-American hero, he might have recalled the Akron laundry.

Could "the man from Akron" in *Charlie Chan Carries On* be the title character? Pure speculation. Until we have more evidence, the mystery remains unsolved.

Stars Of Iceland

AKRON HOCKEY TEAM SKATED TO SUCCESS IN 1940S

(Originally published Feb. 27, 2000)

Lightning-quick on gleaming skates, the Akron Stars were one of the hottest teams on ice during the 1940s and 1950s. The semiprofessional hockey team defeated opponent after opponent, capturing league titles and drawing capacity crowds.

Older Akron residents will remember Iceland, the skating rink at 1615 E. Market St. where the Stars reigned supreme.

Klages Coal & Ice Co. opened the facility Dec. 2, 1939, as an outdoor rink next to its plant. Ice was manufactured and cooled by 9 miles of coiled pipes underground.

Within two years, the company built a roof over Iceland. Amenities included a snack bar, dressing rooms, lockers and skate shop. There was seating for 2,500.

Iceland was home to the Akron Skating Club and Akron Hockey Club, and welcomed Holiday on Ice and other touring revues.

Major-league hockey teams, including the Cleveland Barons, Detroit Red Wings, Pittsburgh Hornets and Indianapolis Capitals, held exhibition games there.

The most popular team, though, was formed by amateurs. "I started when I was in high school," said Bob Kallenbach, 71, of Stow. "It was just a bunch of rink rats playing hockey."

Kallenbach, a 1946 East High School graduate, got his start at Iceland by delivering newspapers there. Then he landed a job on the rink's ice crew and quickly sharpened his skating skills. "We'd practice at that arena at 4 in the morning," he said. "We started to get pretty good."

He and childhood pal Herbert "Herky" Brown played hockey with the Cuyahoga Falls Eagles in 1945 before Klages put together a home team for Iceland.

"It started out as just a fun thing for local kids, but when it got—you might say—big time, it got a little more serious," he said. The Stars debuted in November 1946 in the newly formed Ohio State Hockey League.

Joining Kallenbach and Brown in an early lineup were Bill Bowers, Walt Callahan, Bill Downer, Ed Ker-

enan and Dennis Sonners. Canadians Lloyd Storie, a goalie, and Joe Shewchuk, a bruising defender, helped round out the team. "The Canadians made the team better," Kallenbach said.

The Akron Stars' foes included the Cleveland Falcons, Lorain Moose, Toledo Rovers, Dearborn Teamsters and Muncie Chiefs. The team journeyed to Canada to play the Windsor Bulldogs, Westwood Royales, Port Colborne Sailors and St. Catherines Flyers.

"We didn't know anything but winning," Kallenbach said. "There were darn few teams that beat us more than once."

Players didn't earn salaries, but travel expenses—usually a long trip on a cold bus—were paid.

"We had to buy our own skates," Kallenbach said. "They furnished uniforms, padding, hockey sticks. Nobody wore helmets back then. I wish we would've. I got clobbered a few times. It might've saved me a tooth and some stitches."

One of the team's big supporters was former General Tire chairman M.G. "Jerry" O'Neil. "He always saw to it that we got uniforms," Kallenbach said.

Fans filled Iceland to cheer on the hometown heroes. Many were there to see Joe Shewchuk.

"He was a mean sucker," Kallenbach said. "He drew a lot of people in there. . . . He was big. He was lean. He didn't care who he tangled with. He just bounced people around. He got the reputation as a hard-nosed player."

And a broken nose, too, on at least one occasion.

"We would get in fights, but not like they do now," Kallenbach said. "It was not a game of just beating up on people. There was more finesse."

The Stars won the league title in their debut season, the first of many trophies. "We had years where we didn't lose a game, but we didn't have very much opposition either," Kallenbach said.

In fact, the team was too good. The Stars joined the Metropolitan Amateur Hockey League in 1949, but got booted after two games: a 10–3 win over Cleveland Heights and an 11–3 win over Euclid.

The Akron Stars lineup in February 1952: (front row, left to right) Jim Brady, Don Nagel, Bill Hollen, Ray Stout, Jack Davis, Harry Briggs, Bob Warder, (back row) Walt Callahan, Bob Leeson, Al Gallo, Bob Kallenbach, Lou Underwood, Wells Eichmy, Royal Moffatt and Bob Funk.

"It has become increasingly evident that the Akron entry is far superior to other members of the league," league official John Nagy said after asking the team to quit.

The Stars operated as an independent club before joining the Ohio Amateur Athletic Union. Of course, they won that title, too.

After some of the original Stars left, the team continued to pick up talent: Joe Matte, Bernie Parry, Royal Moffatt. Among the popular players were the Crowe brothers—Roger, Wally, Larry and Kingsley—of the Alderville Indian Reserve at Rice Lake, Ontario.

Kallenbach, who joined the Marines in 1950, returned to the team after his military service, leading it to yet another championship.

The Akron Stars suffered their biggest loss in 1952: their home. Ice skaters mourned when wooden floors were installed at Iceland and the rink became the Akron Roller-

cade. The roller rink, which proved to be popular, too, operated until 1990 when it was converted to a bingo hall.

Without a home, the Stars had to play their games after Barons games at Cleveland Arena. "Everybody was losing interest because we didn't have a rink," Kallenbach said. "We weren't in shape because we didn't have a rink to practice. We got back from games at 2 a.m. some nights and most of us had jobs the next day."

In 1957, Kallenbach was hired to work in Chrysler Corp.'s tool-and-die shop. He left the Stars about 1958 and the once-mighty team folded a year or two later.

Kallenbach retired from Chrysler in 1989 after 32 years. Today, he enjoys skating at the Kent State University Ice Arena and sometimes is recognized by former Akron Stars fans.

"It was an exciting time of my life, I'll tell you," Kallenbach said. "I was lucky to be there at the right time."

Outdoors, Au Naturel

AREA NUDIST CAMPS GAINED EXPOSURE IN '30S

(Originally published June 26, 2006)

There was absolutely no truth to the rumor that Akron residents took everything off and ran naked through the woods. Some of them wore shoes.

When looking back on the halcyon days of the 1930s, nude volleyball may be the last image that springs to mind. Well, OK, nude baseball is probably a close second.

In the summer swelter of the Great Depression, however, a merry band of men and women decided to leave everything behind—including undergarments—to frolic in the great outdoors.

A back-to-nature movement that originated in Europe had cartwheeled into the United States, and self-confident Akronites were eager to join. Much to the chagrin of starched society, nudist camps began to pop up on the outskirts of town.

Club members gathered at secluded areas on weekends to exercise and socialize—with minimal concern for sunburns, mosquitoes, thorns and splinters.

Former Akron barber Chester W. Riel, executive of the Natural Friends League, created a flap in June 1934 when he announced the opening of a nudist camp in Portage County.

Happy campers converged in the woods on a 55-acre farm about two miles from Rootstown. (Ahem. If an off-color remark is beginning to form in your mind, please stop it.)

Membership cost $5 to $8, but anyone wishing to join was required to pass a "strict character examination." The official camp roster included 85 men and women ages 21 to 61. Their children were welcome, too. The resort touted itself as a place "where the sun may shine on all equally."

Riel posted a sign to explain the Natural Friends League's principles of nudism: "You may consider yourself on your honor to be ladies and gentlemen, although I hardly believe a true nudist could be anything else," he wrote.

"It is the purpose of this league to inspire within a clean body the fundamentals of health and higher morality. We have been said to be seekers of health through nudism. But I want it made clear to you now that we are not seekers of health but the leaders for others to follow."

Nudists followed a strict regimen every Sunday at the camp. The day began at 5 a.m. with group exercises and a brisk swim. Breakfast was served at 7 a.m. followed by a relaxation hour. From 9 a.m. to 1 p.m., campers enjoyed volleyball, baseball, handball and tennis.

A work session was held from 1 to 3 p.m. Club members were instructed to clear brush, repair roads and perform other chores. The day ended with entertainment from 6 to 8 p.m. "We sit around and sing or talk or tell stories, just like they do in clubs," Riel noted in 1934.

Akron journalists were eager to cover the nudes—so to speak. In the pure interest of journalism, reporters offered to slip off their skivvies to land a big scoop. But Riel would have none of it.

"No, you can't go back there, and you can't take any pictures," he told a Beacon Journal crew. "For some of our members don't care to have their neighbors know they are nudists." Reporters could only stand at the gate and listen to shouts of glee from the woods.

When Akron's newspapers did publish photos of nudist camps, the artistic images were from Europe and other far-away places. The chances of recognizing someone greatly diminished.

The Portage camp's opening was controversial, of course. Some citizens expressed outrage. Some registered amusement. Some wondered how the heck to get there.

Inevitably, the law got involved. "Nudism is a lot of hooey," Portage County Sheriff LeRoy Jones announced. "We're going to take action if these reports are true. What action? Well, we haven't decided. Maybe we could arrest them for indecent exposure."

Jones conducted a raid in July and found a group of naked, middle-aged men clearing brush to set up a picnic table. The sheriff also found a group of women, all wearing dresses, looking after toddlers in the camp office.

He declined to arrest anyone. "Those fellows back there aren't exposing themselves to any women," Jones decided. "I guess there's nothing wrong."

Following a rent dispute, the camp moved in 1935 to Eli Breitenstein's 140-acre farm near Clinton in Summit County. Breitenstein wasn't a member; he just rented the land.

Nudists weren't as happy with the new site. Camp members constantly had to shoo away curious onlookers who trespassed onto the farm.

To make sure there was no hanky-panky at the camp, Summit County Sheriff Jim Flower took a look, too. "From what I've gathered, most nudists look upon nudism as a sort of religion in which the development of the body is the chief aim," he noted. "If that is so, I don't intend to interfere, no more than I would with the members of one of the recognized religious sects."

Jeepers creepers, there were peepers. The Cleveland League of Naturists, which had a camp near Macedonia, got tired of all the gawking and moved to a 50-acre farm near Sharon Center in Medina County.

Naturally, this demanded further scrutiny from officials. "I don't favor nudism," Medina County Prosecutor L. Ashley Pelton announced. "I feel sure it must be against the law."

Dr. Russell Bigelow Abbott, leader of the Sharon Center group, was elected national president during a nudist conference at the farm. Fifty nude delegates from across the nation cast ballots at the gathering.

Abbott explained that going without clothes provided comfort and freedom. "I do it unconsciously," he said in 1934. "I'm so used to it now. And I run around naked in the house. Of course, I have to be careful out in the yard."

Seven nudist organizations were operating in Ohio by the mid-1930s. All professed the highest standards and principals for morality and health. "Our camps are open to any skeptic who harbors the impression that immorality prevails amongst our members," Riel told the Beacon Journal.

After a few years, the uproar subsided. Authorities determined that camp activities on private property were legal as long as they didn't take place within view of the public. Officers left the nudists alone.

Nudist camps may have disappeared from local headlines, but they did not disappear.

Today, the American Association for Nude Recreation cites 50,000 members and more than 270 clubs committed "to fostering wholesome, nurturing environments that promote body acceptance and respect for all persons." Regional resorts can be found in Bath Township, Millersburg and Cleveland.

If the weather is nice, the great-grandchildren of those 1930s rebels might be playing volleyball this weekend.

Kings of the Mountain

FOR NEARLY 40 YEARS, PROFESSIONAL MOTORCYCLISTS RACED TOWARD THE TOP OF PENINSULA HILL

(Originally published July 25, 2005)

To spectators below, the hill seemed impossibly steep. Its rough surface stretched upward toward a nearly vertical summit. Only exceptional men with exceptional machines dared to reach the top. Gravity usually sorted out the rest.

For nearly 40 years, motorcyclists from across the nation competed in a professional hill climb in Peninsula. The Greater Akron Motorcycle Club sponsored the gritty event on a 280-foot bluff north of the village.

Thousands gathered each July to watch daredevils on souped-up cycles try to conquer the hill. Sanctioned by the American Motorcycle Association, the annual competition roared through the Cuyahoga Valley from the late 1920s to the mid-1960s.

"I think that hill was about 10 acres," said Stow resident Bucky Lau, 80, who joined the Akron club in 1957. "We used to have to go down there every year and mow it."

Club member Leon Rumschlag, 76, of Cuyahoga Falls, who worked at the climb from 1953 to 1966, recalls grooming the hill before the event. "Yeah, we spent three or four weeks out there," Rumschlag said. "We had to mow all the grass, fill in all the rain ruts coming down the hill."

Some of the best professional riders in the country competed on that slope, known variously as the Pinnacle, Mount Peninsula and Seikel Hill. They barnstormed across America to race every Sunday, competing for cash prizes, trophies and glory.

Among the big names were Herb Reiber of Milwaukee, Howard Mitzel of York, Pa., Joe Petrali of Sacramento, Calif., Earl Buck of Hazel Park, Mich., Ralph Moore of Indianapolis, Don Farrow of Columbus, Earl Appleby of Canton, Raymond and Duane Nealen of Bedford, Ohio, and Phil and Larry Franz Sr. of Cleveland.

"These were giants to me—like Browns players," said Cleveland resident Larry Franz Jr., 64, a former hill climber whose father won the 1952 national championship in Muskegon, Mich. "Every Sunday, they were the people to look to, you know."

Franz's father was 17 when he built his first motorcycle. The 1926 bike, which the younger Franz now owns, has been appraised at $100,000. It features a Schwinn frame, a Super X engine, a Harley-Davidson gas tank and Indian Motorcycle Co. footboards. "It ran on alcohol and peanut butter oil," Franz said.

Hill climbers often designed their motorcycles. The bikes couldn't be bought at stores. A street bike wouldn't cut it. "A lot of them guys had machine shops where they did their own sketch and made their own parts, did their own engine work," Rumschlag said.

Durability was important. The Peninsula hill could take a toll on man and machine. Many rides ended in a cloud of dust or a splatter of mud. Helmets were put to good use.

Hill climbers competed one at a time, starting from a dead stop at a backboard, and hitting the slope to see who could go the fastest and the farthest. A referee, announcer and scorekeeper kept track of the noisy action in two classes.

Chains on rear tires helped maintain traction. Riders got four climbs in an afternoon. The best ones made it up in 9 or 10 seconds. Others wiped out. "They went up the first hill," Rumschlag said. "Then it kind of leveled a little, then there was a hump, then there was just a little dip, and they shot for the top."

On one wrist, riders wore an 8-inch leather strap attached to the handlebars. If they suddenly let go, the cord shut off the engine, ensuring that the motorcycle wouldn't run wild down the hill if its rider fell off.

THE 'HOOK MAN'

Bucky Lau didn't know what he was getting into when he volunteered in 1957 to work at the top as the "hook man."

As motorcyclists neared the crest, Lau had to determine whether they were going to reach the top or wipe

Pittsburgh motorcyclist Howard Kirk braces for a wipeout as his front wheel lifts off the ground near the top of the Peninsula hill in July 1951. A wrist strap cut the engine when a rider was thrown off the bike.

out. He carried a large hook on a long rope held by a crew of men. "When a bike comes up the hill, if they don't make it, you've got to grab it," Lau said.

"They stick the hook right in the front wheel or hook the frame," Rumschlag said.

"The hell with the guy," Lau said with a chuckle. "He's on his own when he leaves the bike."

The hook man skittered down and snared the bikes while the rope crew took up the slack and held fast. They either pulled the motorcycle over the top or lowered it back down the hill. "They tried to keep the bike from flopping back on top of the rider," said Green resident Richard Robinson, 45, president of the Akron club.

Larry Franz Jr. had a memorable experience in the 1960s during his first hill climb in Peninsula. It was his final try, and he was determined to get to the top. Near the crest, the bike hesitated, and Franz let go. The hook man sprang into action.

"The hooker, that tall, skinny guy, ripped my shirt off," Franz said. "A brand-new Harley shirt. The bike

went over the top, and I went down the other side. It was the first time I ever hill-climbed."

IMPACT ON PENINSULA

A cheer would arise from the crowd when riders conquered the peak. Spectators stood at the top, bottom and sides of the hill. An estimated 5,000 attended some years.

This, of course, brought Peninsula to a standstill on race day. Many residents enjoyed watching the hill climbs. Others weren't as thrilled.

In 1937, a group of citizens circulated a petition urging the Village Council to prohibit hill climbs. Officials turned down the request but agreed to regulate the event, requiring the Akron club to buy a $75 permit.

Rowdy behavior by spectators became a concern over the decades. The hill climbers and motorcycle club were not to blame, officials agreed, but some onlookers were loitering in town and causing problems.

"The village has had a lot of headaches with the misconduct," Peninsula Mayor George Fisher remarked at a 1956 council meeting. "This idea of riding up and down the street on a motorcycle with a bottle of beer in one hand on a Sunday is no good. We're trying to have a decent village here, and we're going to."

The village threatened to revoke the hill-climb permit but gave the event another chance. "There are rowdies who don't belong," club member Harold Haggerty told officials in 1956. "We'll do everything we can to keep everybody in line." The Peninsula hill climb continued to draw big crowds for another 10 years. The competition wasn't quite as steep as it used to be, though, because the middle of the hill had shallowed out from all the use.

In 1966, the club held its final climb. Peninsula declined to issue a permit in 1967, citing "the difficulty of controlling traffic and the huge crowds."

"They didn't want any more," Rumschlag said. "It tied the town up too much. If they had a fire or somebody needed an ambulance, it would be hours before they could get it in there."

A NEW TRADITION

The Akron club, founded in 1919 and incorporated in 1926 with AMA sanctioning, lost its only fund-raiser with the demise of the hill climb. "That's what this club did to support itself," Robinson said. "We now have an event that has taken that over."

In the early 1970s, the club started a new tradition. This will be the 33rd year for the Centurion Poker Run.

"The Centurion supports this club and allows this club to be involved in charitable and community-involved things," Robinson said.

Over the last decade, for instance, the group has raised nearly $100,000 for the Hattie Larlham Center for Children with Disabilities, he said.

Hill climbs are still held in the United States. If you missed out on the action in Peninsula, the Dayton Motorcycle Club sponsors the Devil's Staircase Hill-climb in Oregonia, Ohio, on the second weekend in October.

Franz has happy memories of the childhood heroes he used to see every Sunday. "These guys were before Evel Knievel," he said.

Franz travels to motorcycle shows around the country, displaying his late father's bike, gear, posters and other vintage memorabilia, and he enjoys reminiscing with fans about climbs. "It was like a big family," he said. "I was my father's helper since I was born. I was there every Sunday all my life."

Today, the Peninsula hill is overgrown with large trees. The quiet bluff, now part of Cuyahoga Valley National Park, overlooks the Lock 29 Trailhead of the Ohio & Erie Canal Towpath Trail.

It would be awfully difficult to ride up on a motorcycle, but then again, it always was.

Hatchet Lady

SALOON SMASHER CARRY NATION BROUGHT HER ANTI-LIQUOR CRUSADE TO AKRON IN EARLY 1900S

(Originally published Oct. 24, 2005)

It's tough to say no to an angry woman with a sharp hatchet. God knows, Akron residents learned that lesson. U.S. temperance leader Carry A. Nation, infamous for swinging an ax while smashing saloons, brought her anti-liquor crusade to Ohio in October 1901.

The fiery orator didn't have enough time to cause any permanent damage in Akron, but she did make the most of her brief stop at Union Depot.

Who knew she hated tobacco as much as she despised alcohol? Certainly not the unsuspecting smokers at the train station. The 54-year-old grandmother hopped off the train and began yanking cigars and cigarettes from the mouths of startled travelers. Then she began to chop up the tobacco with her hatchet!

"If there is anything that disgusts me it is to see a man with a whole lot of tobacco in his mouth," she would later explain. "Why, his mouth is just as dirty as a spittoon. Oh, but he is dirty."

Nation was on her way from a speaking engagement in Orrville to another in Cleveland, the birthplace of the Woman's Christian Temperance Union.

A week earlier, she had cooled her heels in a West Virginia jail. For some reason, saloonkeepers didn't always appreciate her patronage. Sometimes they called in the law.

Although she made a name for herself wrecking Kansas taverns in 1900, Nation liked to spread the joy. She was arrested more than 20 times in bars from San Francisco to New York City.

She carried a Bible in one hand and a hatchet in the other. She prayed as she chopped.

Born in Kentucky in 1846, Carry Amelia Moore discovered her life's calling after marrying Dr. Charles Gloyd, a Missouri physician. He was an alcoholic who dropped dead 18 months after their 1867 wedding.

A second marriage to journalist David Nation gave her the unusual name Carry A. Nation (she sometimes spelled it Carrie). As she battered her way across U.S. saloons, he divorced her for desertion in 1901.

Talk about symbolism. The Devil's Auction Company, a troupe of professional actors, was bound for Akron aboard Train 535 on the Cleveland, Akron & Columbus Railroad. Some of the men were playing cards and smoking cigars.

An older female passenger—an imposing figure at nearly 6 feet and 200 pounds—barged into the car and began snatching cigars from the men's mouths. Then she grabbed the cards, too.

The surprised actors weren't as angry as one might expect. They recognized the hatchet-wielding celebrity and introduced her to the rest of the amused troupe. The actors regaled her with the song *Oh, Carrie*, and bought nearly 40 small hatchets, which Nation sold as souvenirs for 25 cents apiece.

When the train stopped at Union Depot off East Market Street, Nation peered through her gold-rimmed glasses and noticed a traveler smoking a stogie. She stalked him, grabbed his cigar and chopped it with her hatchet. She turned her attention to a boy with a cigarette and pounced on him, too. Several travelers danced around, trying to avoid the woman's clutch. The tobacco never had a chance. Chop, chop, chop.

"In the excitement, several people forgot to get their baggage checked," the Summit County Beacon reported Oct. 17, 1901.

Nation sold a few more souvenir hatchets before climbing back on the train for Cleveland. "Ah, how I would like to make a tour of this town," she sighed as she left.

A year later, she got her wish. In 1902, Carry Nation checked into Ferdinand Schumacher's Windsor Hotel, a temperance inn at the northeast corner of South Broadway and Mill Street. She had arranged to speak at the Casino, a vaudeville theater and beer garden at Lakeside Park on Summit Lake.

A beer garden? "Yes, and I am glad of it," she told an Akron reporter. "I am fishing, and I must go where the fish are."

With a hatchet in one hand and a Bible in the other, temperance leader Carry A. Nation smashed many saloons in the early 20th century. She was slightly more controlled during her visits to Akron. Slightly. She yanked cigars and cigarettes from the mouths of travelers and chopped up the tobacco with her hatchet.

Crowds lined up at the Casino to catch a glimpse of "Kansas Carry." It was a strange bill. Her appearance was scheduled between song-and-dance acts.

"I am Carry Nation, the home defender," she told the crowd. "I am the woman that you have heard so much about."

With righteous fervor, Nation began a lengthy dissertation on the evils of alcohol. She proclaimed her complete sanity to the audience, saying she merely was "an old woman" with a "right to destroy."

She condemned saloonkeepers and brewers for getting rich while "they make drunkards and murderers of your boys." She urged all wives to divorce drunkard husbands, saying that would be preferable than raising children from men "diseased in mind and diseased in body."

Nation praised "the hatchet movement," saying a woman with a hatchet is "bound to break down the barriers." Then she likened herself to Moses. "He was a smasher," she said. "All the laws that Moses took down

from Mount Sinai were prohibitions. And I am proud that I can smash saloons."

She had an ax that night, but she kept a promise to the Casino's operators that she wouldn't wreck the joint—even though it wasn't fit for a woman.

"My work is a work of love," she said. "The greatest work I ever did was when I smashed those saloons out in Kansas. The Bible is the greatest hatchet."

Carry A. Nation was 64 years old when she died in Kansas in 1911. She didn't live to see Prohibition take effect in 1920. Government agents happily wielded hatchets in her place until 1933, when the act was repealed. Alcoholics Anonymous was founded two years later in Akron.

Before Carry Nation left town in 1902, she sat for an interview with the Beacon. "I never expect to smash another saloon," she told the newspaper. "I am not going to say I won't but I don't expect to do so. The saloon is but the effect and I am after the cause. "I'm going to smash the cause, understand?"

Striking It Rich

TWO BOYS FIND TREASURE WHILE PLAYING IN WEST AKRON IN 1951

(Originally published May 24, 2010)

Every child knew the chant: Finders keepers, losers weepers. Two Akron boys couldn't believe their eyes when they discovered a small fortune while exploring a field on a lazy Saturday in the spring of 1951.

St. Sebastian students Mike Riegler and Billy Wigley, both 14, were catching garter snakes while exploring a creek off Mull Avenue in West Akron. The scaly reptiles kept wriggling away. "We were out messing around in the creek," recalled Riegler, now 73, who lived on Parkgate Avenue at the time. "We found a couple snakes. I just remember we were looking for a can to put the snakes in."

They noticed a pile of rubbish and old leaves in a lot about 300 yards off South Hawkins Avenue. When Wigley kicked over a tin can, the boys saw something they never, ever expected. Peeking out from the leaves was a dirty, torn $50 bill. The teens quickly forgot about the snakes.

"We started scratching around and found more and more and more," Riegler said. They searched and sifted, collecting dozens of rotting $20 and $50 bills. Some of the currency had fallen apart and was difficult to read.

After 15 minutes of scouring the field, Riegler and Wigley amassed 55 bills totaling $1,400—worth about $12,500 today—and pieces of 15 other bills that were too deteriorated to read. "In them days, it was a lot of money," Riegler said.

There was one major problem. The weather-beaten currency looked fake to the boys. Perhaps it was counterfeit. "We didn't know if it was real or not," Riegler said. "This other kid's dad was a banker at the Dime Bank. So we took it to him to see if it was real."

They hauled the cash to Wigley's home on Pine Grove Drive. E. John Wigley, assistant secretary at Dime Savings Bank Co., inspected the moldy cash and pronounced it legal tender.

Then he said something that the cheerful boys didn't want to hear: "We've got to turn this in."

What? Finders keepers, right? Over the teens' protests, the father called police.

Detectives Andy Royka and Clyde Longacre arrived to confiscate the cash and explained that it would be returned to the boys if the rightful owner didn't come forward in 30 days.

The Beacon Journal reported the unusual find in a front-page story, which sent a ripple of excitement through West Akron.

Police noted that all of the bills were issued in 1934. Had they been in the field for 17 years? Did a bank-fearing neighbor bury it during the Great Depression? Did a gangster rob a store and stash the loot?

Riegler believes the explanation was more innocent. "Well, I think somebody threw some trash out and it was mixed in with the papers," he said. "They probably stashed it in some newspapers."

That also was the theory of Detective Capt. John F. Struzenski, who told the Beacon Journal in 1951: "Somebody is paying a heavy fine. It's against the law to dump rubbish in that lot."

He must have been rooting for the boys. The remark probably made claimants think twice before coming forward.

A McKinley Avenue woman told police that she lost $1,400 in a home burglary in 1950, but Struzenski discounted the claim because she reported a different assortment of bills than those found in the Mull Avenue lot.

In a strange twist, Riegler and Wigley nearly lost some money to police officers. "I had to peddle papers that day and the police department come back and found $200 more in the spot," Riegler said. "The other kid took them back there to it."

The officers wanted to put the money in their pension fund, but a reporter shamed them into putting it in the pile of bills already collected, Riegler said. "The Beacon Journal said they were going to print it if the police took it," he said.

The waiting, of course, was the hardest part. The 30 days seemed to drag. The boys worried that someone might swoop in and claim the money at the last minute, but the original owner never stepped forward.

Akron Police Chief Thomas Lynett meets in 1951 with St. Sebastian students Mike Riegler (left) and Billy Wigley to tell them that they can keep the $1,400 in old bills that they discovered in an empty field on Mull Avenue near South Hawkins.

Akron Police Chief Thomas Lynett called the boys into his office on May 29, 1951, and told them they could keep the prize. Also, they didn't have to worry about spending dirty, torn bills. "They had to send it back to Washington to be replaced," Riegler recalled.

Wigley and Riegler received clean, fresh money and split it even-steven, fulfilling the promise of any child who dreamed of finding buried treasure.

Riegler vividly recalls finding the money, but he doesn't recall ever going on a shopping spree with his newfound wealth. It must have gone into a bank account for later use.

"Mom and Dad took it," he said. "They kept it for us, and I don't know what happened to it."

Billy Wigley grew up to be William E. Wigley, and followed his father's footsteps in business. He retired from Akron National Bank and was 65 years old when he died on May 23, 2002.

Riegler grew up to own Blake Body & Paint Shop on Cuyahoga Falls Avenue in North Akron.

If anyone is tempted to search for old, rotting money in a vacant lot on Mull Avenue, it's probably not worth the effort. Riegler said the boys picked the field clean nearly 60 years ago. "We got it all," he said.

Call of the Wild

AKRON ENTERTAINER PURVES PULLEN WHISTLED WHILE HE WORKED

(Originally published Sept. 17, 2001)

Purves Pullen's act was for the birds. And the bees. And the chimpanzees.

He could bark like a dog, roar like a lion, trumpet like an elephant and grunt like a pig. In short, if Pullen had been around for the Great Flood, Noah could have built a smaller ark.

The Akron entertainer had an incredible gift for birdcalls and animal mimicry. By the end of his 60-year career, he had developed a repertoire of 300 birds and 700 animals and insects, and that is no exaggeration.

"Anybody can be an imitator," Pullen explained during an Akron Times-Press interview in 1937. "All he has to do is get into the right frame of mind. To mimic a certain animal or bird, just listen to it a while . . . I just picture myself as a monkey, parrot, lion, dog or whatever they ask for, and there it is."

You've probably heard his work, but you probably didn't realize it was human. Pullen gave voice to Cheeta the chimp in the 1930s *Tarzan* movies starring Johnny Weissmuller and Maureen O'Sullivan. He played a pet parrot on the *Amos 'n' Andy* radio program in the 1930s.

He performed opposite Ronald Reagan, albeit offscreen, as the voice of the title chimp in *Bedtime for Bonzo* (1951), and returned for the 1952 sequel *Bonzo Goes to College*. If you ever visit Disneyland, you can hear Pullen at The Enchanted Tiki Room. His voice gives life each day to more than 100 birds at the animatronic show in Adventureland.

As the story goes, Pullen developed his talent in the 1920s as a Boy Scout at Camp Manatoc. He would sit under a tree, listen to birds and imitate their calls.

His parents, Almy and Rodney Pullen, who lived at 1386 W. Exchange St., were amused by the chirping, but never dreamed it would lead to a career. At age 21, Pullen landed a job at WADC radio. It was 1930, and for nearly a year thereafter, Akron residents were entertained by the tweets and twitters of Pullen's radio program.

That led to a string of radio jobs across the country: KDKA in Pittsburgh, WLS in Chicago, WJW in Cleveland and the NBC network in New York.

Hollywood soon recruited the young man. His sound effects were in demand as silent movies gave way to talkies in the 1930s. He howled like a coyote for Cecil B. Demille's *The Crusades* (1935). He whistled for actor Buddy Rogers in *Old Man Rhythm* (1935). He squawked for Walt Disney's cartoons.

Pullen's greatest fame, however, was as a featured performer with Spike Jones and His City Slickers in the 1940s. The zany bandleader added Pullen to his flashy, oddball troupe, but first insisted on a new name for him: Dr. Horatio Q. Birdbath.

Doc Birdbath stayed with the group for six years. His vocal effects can be heard on such Spike Jones recordings as *Mother Goose Medley* (1946), *Old MacDonald Had a Farm* (1946), *My Pretty Girl* (1946), *Love in Bloom* (1947) and *Ill Barkio* (1947).

The good doctor, who sometimes performed a ventriloquist act with a dummy named Johnny, toured with Jones across the country, and occasionally played a tuba that squirted water.

Pullen's nephew, H. Craig Pullen, 58, of Wadsworth, remembers going to the Akron Armory as a young boy to see his uncle onstage with Jones. "It was quite a performance," he says. "He did some magic. They would lay him down on a table or a trunk. They would put a sheet over him and, pretty soon, he would rise and rise and go off the stage."

Fifty years later, the show is still vivid to Pullen's nephew. "Spike Jones, what a character that guy was," he says. "This guy would dress in some type of a plaid suit and he had two handguns that he'd shoot up in the air, two chrome-plated handguns, and he had bells and drums. Oh, I would have loved to see him more often."

Pullen and his new bride, the former Frances Bennett, moved to California in the 1940s. He returned to Akron once in a while to visit his widowed mother and brother Harold, Craig's father.

There were so many highlights in Pullen's career that it seems unfair to list only a few. He did birdcalls for Disney's animated classic *Sleeping Beauty* (1959). He per-

Spike Jones (center) is surrounded by his City Slickers (from left) Dick Morgan, Doodles Weaver, Freddy Morgan, Dr. Horatio Q. Birdbath (Purves Pullen) and George Rock.

formed on *The Jack Benny Show*. He appeared in *Ripley's Believe it Or Not!*

He was a guest on Groucho Marx's *You Bet Your Life*, Johnny Carson's *Tonight* show and fellow Akronite Hugh Downs' *Today* show. He even stumped the celebrity panel on *What's My Line?*

Eventually, Pullen settled into a steady job as public relations director for the famous Nut Tree restaurant in Vacaville, Calif., providing puppet shows and toy demonstrations for children.

Scott Corbett, 42, an Ontario, Calif., resident who co-founded the Spike Jones International Fan Club, enjoyed meeting with Pullen in 1989. By then, the entertainer was nearly 80 years old.

"His home was packed with memorabilia, leaving little aisles to walk through," Corbett says. "In one room were scrapbooks he kept from his long career. They stretched over 6 feet."

Pullen was most proud of his 1963 work at Disneyland. "My favorite accomplishment, the one that's gonna last, is that I recorded all the bird sounds you hear in the Tiki Room at Disneyland," he told Corbett.

Pullen was kindhearted and fun to be around, Corbett says. "Doc was like the ideal grandfather," he says. "He loved kids, enjoyed entertaining them anyway possible."

One of Pullen's tricks was taking his dog Roscoe for a walk. The pet wasn't real. It was an empty dog collar on a wire leash. "He would have his 'invisible dog' and walk around public places barking," Corbett says. "He would convince kids that there really was a dog there."

Purves Pullen—aka Dr. Horatio Q. Birdbath—was an entertainer until the end. He died in October 1992 at age 83 in Vacaville, Calif., forever silencing 300 birds and 700 animals and insects.

"He was really a lot of fun, a real positive guy," says nephew H. Craig Pullen. "He had fun with life."

The Killer Flu

DEADLY EPIDEMIC BROUGHT AKRON TO ITS KNEES IN 1918

(Originally published Oct. 14, 2002)

If the gates of hell had creaked open, it couldn't have been much worse. Death roamed the streets of Akron. It was found in a lover's caress, a child's kiss, a stranger's handshake.

There was no place to escape. The Spanish Influenza, a gauze-wrapped nightmare of death and delirium, brought the city to its knees in October 1918. Few families were spared its withering touch.

If you ever visit an old cemetery, you'll notice 1918 engraved on a lot of headstones. The killer flu claimed about 40 million lives worldwide, including an estimated 675,000 Americans.

In less than eight weeks, the epidemic sickened more than 5,000 Akron residents. Of that number, 630 died of influenza and 278 died of pneumonia. In comparison, Akron lost 304 soldiers in World War I. And many of them were flu victims, too.

Akron Health Commissioner Charles T. Nesbitt warned Akron that the plague was coming. He saw the devastation on the East Coast as the sickness spread from city to city. "The epidemic of influenza that is so extensive and so destructive in other sections must in course of time reach Akron," he announced Oct. 3, 1918.

Days later, the flu arrived. It felt like a bad cold at first. People began to sneeze and cough. They suffered chills. A throbbing headache took hold. Bodies convulsed with pain.

Temperatures spiked to improbable highs, producing feverish delirium. Victims struggled to breathe. Their lungs filled with fluid. They coughed blood. And they died.

Or, if they were fortunate, they recovered. Slowly. There was no cure. The only option was to ride out the illness and hope the body's immune system could fend off the virus.

"Upon the appearance of the first symptom of 'bad cold,' go to bed in a well-ventilated room at once and send for a physician," Nesbitt said. "Keep everyone out of the room except a single attendant and the physician."

To avoid contamination, healthy people were urged to wear gauze masks of "six thicknesses of cloth." They were told to wash frequently, avoid crowded places and keep their doors and windows open. Eat well. Sleep well. And, oh yes, don't worry.

That last instruction proved impossible for many.

The first death was reported Oct. 13. Alexander Walker, 18, a motorman for Northern Ohio Traction & Light Co., had been ill for several days. When he began to feel better, he made the mistake of leaving his sickbed too soon. He suffered a relapse, contracted pneumonia and died.

That day, Nesbitt banned all public assemblies in Akron. Schools, theaters, courts and libraries were closed. Church services, sporting events and public funerals were canceled. Akron Superintendent Henry Hotchkiss protested the action. "To close the schools would be the very worst course we could pursue," he said. "It would turn loose 35,000 persons who are now under restraint, and given the best attention of doctors and nurses."

But the health officer's edict became law. Sick people flooded City Hospital, Peoples Hospital and Children's Hospital. The number of flu cases was updated each day in the newspaper, along with names of overnight casualties.

There were so many patients that the new Akron Armory was turned into an emergency ward. Olive Beason led a team of gauze-masked nurses into an abyss of pitiful coughs and moans. Some delirious patients, fleeing imaginary demons, jumped through windows and had to be captured on the streets.

Despite the circumstances, some residents refused to give in to fear. Rubber baron Harvey S. Firestone held a ceremony Oct. 18 to celebrate the streetcar line's extension to Firestone Park.

Among the guests were Akron Mayor Isaac S. Myers, Judge Charles C. Benner, Northern Ohio Traction executive A.C. Blinn, city planner E.E. Workman and dozens of others. Nesbitt was livid when he heard how prominent citizens had defied his ban on assembly. He threatened to arrest the mayor and every VIP at the event. "There must be no letting down of the bars of caution at this time for we cannot assume that we have passed the crest of the epidemic as yet," he said.

Funerals were held in houses. Every day. Everywhere. Only immediate family members were allowed to

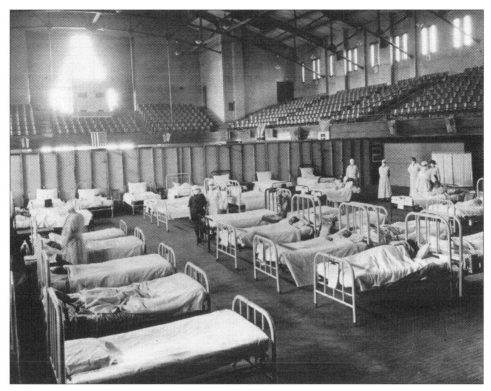

The Akron Armory serves as an emergency hospital for flu patients during the Spanish Influenza epidemic of October 1918. The epidemic sickened more than 5,000 Akron residents. Hundreds of local residents had to be treated at the armory because city hospitals were already filled to capacity with sick people.

attend. "I have notified all undertakers, priests and ministers that these regulations must be strictly enforced," Nesbitt said.

The city remained in lockdown for weeks before immunity grew and flu cases receded. Many residents, especially those who had dodged the illness, began to balk at the restrictions.

On Nov. 11, 1918, the ban was forgotten. An armistice had been signed to end the World War. Thousands of residents rushed onto the streets to celebrate. Nesbitt threw up his hands. A few days later, he lifted the ban. Although the flu would claim more lives that month, the worst was over in Akron.

The exact origin of the 1918 virus remains a mystery today. It may have been a bird flu that mutated or a swine flu that crossed to humans. (In fact, the swine flu scare of 1976 erupted because health experts feared a repeat of the 1918 epidemic.)

The Spanish Influenza's name surely was unfair, though. The virus was detected in America, Europe and Asia about the same time. It wasn't Spain's fault.

The average U.S. life span fell by 12 years in 1918, according to New York Times science reporter Gina Kolata in her book *Virus*. "If such a plague came today,

killing a similar fraction of the U.S. population, 1.5 million Americans would die, which is more than the number felled in a single year by heart disease, cancers, strokes, chronic pulmonary disease, AIDS and Alzheimer's disease combined," she wrote.

Could such a flu strike again? "I can say it's a possibility," said Summit County Health Commissioner Gene Nixon. "However, I think we could respond faster now, understanding the viral kinds of vaccines that we're able to develop. The science in that is fairly far along where we can generally structure a response to that."

Public health departments are always concerned about the potential for influenza outbreaks. "That's why we do a lot of promotion about flu vaccines in the fall," he said.

But a virus isn't the only fear. Bacteria can wreak havoc, too. "I think that our assumption just a decade or two ago that we had beaten bacterial infections through antibiotics is in doubt now with the advent of microbial resistance," Nixon said.

Bacterial infections could be the epidemics of the future. "From a public health perspective, those concern us as much as an influenza outbreak," he said.

Virus or bacteria? It doesn't matter. No one ever wants to go through another year like 1918.

The Hermit

OLD SHACK WASN'T MUCH, BUT IT WAS HOME TO 89-YEAR-OLD GRAVEDIGGER

(Originally published Sept. 10, 2001)

A hermit, a recluse, a loner. Elias Swartout didn't need much in life. He was content to live on the fringe of society, away from the big cities and the noisy crowds.

As long as he had a roof over his head and food in his belly, he really couldn't complain. Besides, if he did complain, who would hear him?

In 1951, the 89-year-old hermit allowed Akron Beacon Journal writer Milt Freudenheim to peek inside his lonely world. Swartout lived in a two-room shack on East Bath Road near state Route 8 in what was then Northampton Township.

He was a scraggly man with a bushy white beard, prominent nose and cataract-clouded eyes. Wild tufts of hair stuck out from beneath his cap. His clothes were rumpled and soiled; his shoes were scuffed and dirty.

He was a man of few words, but he made for an interesting story. All of his earthly possessions were scattered about that cluttered cabin in the woods. In Swartout's world, it made perfect sense to store a push mower next to his lumpy, broken bed. Amid the cobwebs and dust, he kept a fishing pole, flashlight, handsaw and picnic basket.

He had a coal stove to keep him warm. He had a radio to keep him entertained. He had two cats to keep him company. And that was plenty. "I don't want no wife," he insisted.

Swartout was born on March 14, 1862, in Portage County's Brimfield Township, but had lived in Northampton for more than 70 years.

For decades, he worked as a farmhand for landowners Frank Harrington and Art Shellhorn. Later, he served as gravedigger and caretaker at Northampton Cemetery.

A $48 check arrived each month from Ohio Aid for the Aged and that's how Swartout was able to buy supplies. The shack was on property that belonged to the J.K. Rennie family. There weren't many residents in the vicinity, but the closest neighbors looked out for the welfare of the old man.

They built the small cabin for him after his previous shanty collapsed in a storm. They arranged for Cuyahoga Falls to supply him with electricity for $1 a month. For the most part, though, Swartout refused offers of help.

He took a bath once a year—whether he needed it or not. His aversion to soap and hot water was nearly as pronounced as his aversion to women. "I offered him another bath this year," neighbor Lathiel Gaskins told the 1951 reporter. "Elias didn't answer, and after that he kept away from me for a week or more."

As gruff as Swartout was, he did reveal a gentle side during his interview. He picked up a sleeping cat from his bed, placed it in his lap and cuddled the pet while he talked.

Northampton residents had tried to persuade Swartout to move to the Summit County Home for the Aged, but he would have none of that. "I was there once for an operation and I don't want to go back," he said. "I'd lose my pension."

Other residents thought the hermit should be committed to an institution. After all, he had suffered a recent stroke and his arms were partially paralyzed.

The idea was dropped, however, when it was learned that Swartout had no relatives to authorize the action. "Somebody ought to look after him, but it would break his heart if they took him away," an anonymous neighbor told the Beacon Journal reporter.

Dr. Elgie R. Shaffer, Summit County's health commissioner, finally weighed in: "As long as a man is a health menace only to himself, there is nothing we can say."

Elias Swartout just wanted to be left alone, and it appears he got his wish.

The crafty hermit lived to be 93 years old. After years on the fringe, he finally succeeded in disappearing from society in 1954.

He was buried in Lot 104, Grave 2, at Northampton Cemetery, the place where he had toiled for so many years.

Former gravedigger Elias Swartout, 89, rests in his cluttered shack on East Bath Road in 1951. The hermit of Northampton Township and his two pet cats lived on a $48 monthly check from Ohio Aid for the Aged. "I don't want no wife," he insisted.

Swartout's old street has changed dramatically over the last 50 years. You won't find any shacks there today.

Since Northampton merged with Cuyahoga Falls in 1986, the land near East Bath Road has been widely developed. More than 900 homes and condominiums—some costing up to $300,000—have been built in the area. The subdivisions carry such refined names as The Reserve at East Bath, Brookpoint Village, Bath Heights, Camden Knolls, Prescott Green, East Bath Village and Silver Maple Village.

Obviously, Elias Swartout wasn't the only person trying to get away from it all.

Coxey's Army

MASSILLON MAN LED FIRST MARCH ON WASHINGTON

(Originally published April 9, 2001)

America was hurting. A nationwide depression had battered nearly every industry, throwing at least a third of the U.S. work force out of jobs.

Lacking money and hope, many Americans wallowed in misery, unsure of how to fend for themselves or their families.

Massillon industrialist Jacob S. Coxey felt their suffering. He had been forced to lay off dozens of workers from his stone quarry because of the economic plunge.

The government ought to do something, he decided, and someone ought to tell the government what to do.

And, thus, the 40-year-old businessman made history in 1894 by leading the nation's first march on Washington, D.C. Coxey was a scrawny, bespectacled man with big dreams and great gumption. He was talkative and articulate, and always nattily attired in a suit, tie and starched collar.

Coxey proposed a $500 million public works project to build better roads and ease the hardship on America's 4 million unemployed. He said Congress could finance the project by issuing noninterest-bearing bonds.

Coxey envisioned 10,000 jobless workers converging on the nation's capital to demand support for his proposals. He called it "a petition in boots" and "an army of the unemployed."

He drummed up recruits for the protest march, urging unemployed workers to meet him in Massillon for a long journey that would begin on Easter Day. Massillon braced for an influx of thousands, but only 86 marchers turned up on that snowy March 25, 1894. About 40 reporters accompanied them.

Some protesters rode horses and wagons while others pedaled bicycles or walked on the rutted roads. They marched to the cadence of a six-piece band and carried banners with such slogans as "Death to Interest Bearing Bonds."

"Poorly clad, those who had no banners to carry marched along, their hands in their pockets, and many were shivering with cold," the Akron Beacon and Republican reported the next day. "It would have been difficult to find among the lot one man who under ordinary circumstances would not be classed as a tramp."

Thousands of spectators lined the streets that Easter to witness Coxey's Army as it trudged from Massillon to Canton. "Come on! Come on! Join the army!" Coxey urged onlookers. Few heeded the call.

The marchers camped in Canton that night and started toward Pittsburgh at daybreak. Along the way, they attracted handfuls of supporters who agreed to fall in line with them.

The procession continued through rain and mud, over mountains and through valleys. Townspeople offered them food as the marchers plodded onward.

Coxey took advantage of each stop to make a speech in support of his public works proposal. Others joined the ranks.

By the time Coxey's Army crossed from Pennsylvania to Maryland, it numbered in the hundreds. The marchers arrived in Washington, D.C., on April 29—35 days after leaving Massillon—with a force of about 500.

On May 1, Coxey prepared to lead "the army of the unemployed" to the steps of Capitol Hill, where he would give a speech to make the government understand his reasoning. The army marched down Pennsylvania Avenue with an escort of mounted policemen. Thousands of curious onlookers cheered as the group passed.

As the protesters neared the Capitol, though, a massive column of policemen blocked the path. The police escorts kept going, leading the marchers away from the Capitol. Coxey halted his troops. Something was wrong. The police were taking him past his destination. The government wasn't granting him permission to speak at the Capitol.

Coxey's Army doubled back and the police gave chase. Coxey slipped through the waiting crowd and climbed up to the 10th step of the Capitol.

He tipped his hat to the audience and pulled the speech out of his coat pocket. Suddenly, the police were upon him.

"What do you want to do here?" a police captain asked. "I wish to make an address," Coxey replied. "But you cannot do that," the captain said.

Officers grabbed Coxey by the arms and forced him down the steps. Two of his assistants, Carl Browne and Christopher Columbus Jones, protested vociferously and were arrested.

Having traveled a great distance, the marchers were outraged. Heated words were exchanged. Police began swinging their clubs. Chaos. Panic.

What started out as a triumphant day for Coxey's Army ended with an all-out retreat.

Coxey and his two aides were charged with trespassing and sentenced to 20 days in jail. Without its general, Coxey's Army disbanded.

Bitterly disappointed, Coxey returned to Massillon, set his sights on politics and became a perennial candidate. He ran unsuccessful campaigns for U.S. House (1894, 1928 and 1930), Ohio governor (1895 and 1897), U.S. Senate (1916 and 1934) and U.S. president (1932 and 1936).

His party affiliation switched from Greenback to People's to Populist to Independent to Republican to Farmer Labor. The only office he ever won was one term as Massillon mayor in 1931.

Jacob S. Coxey was 97 years old when he died of a stroke on May 18, 1951, at his Massillon home. He lived long enough to witness the New Deal policies of President Franklin D. Roosevelt, including the Works Progress Administration in 1935.

He also lived long enough to settle some unfinished business. On May 1, 1944, the 50th anniversary of his disastrous visit to Washington, Coxey returned to the U.S. Capitol.

He climbed the steps, pulled out the speech that he had written decades earlier and read it proudly to a small but appreciative crowd.

Pictured about the time of his 1894 march, Jacob S. Coxey would become a perennial candidate for office.

Lost in the Woods

CUYAHOGA VALLEY TOWN OF BOTZUM HAS VANISHED ALONG WITH THE CANAL TRAFFIC

(Originally published Aug. 16, 2010)

Botzum Cemetery is easy to overlook. Shrouded by trees on a gentle hill off Yellow Creek Road near West Bath Road in Cuyahoga Falls, the old burial ground is woefully unmarked. Local historians tell us that 150 to 175 people are laid to rest here, yet only five graves have stones after two centuries of erosion and vandalism.

Only one of those faded memorials can be read without much eyestrain: a white obelisk for Charles Augustus Botzum, who died in 1884 at age 17. "Here I lie in this lonely grave, numbered with those called before as ordained by the maker," the epitaph reads. "My work is done. My grave is here. Forget me not."

The inscription could just as easily apply to the boy's hometown, which began life with great expectations but died quietly with few left to mourn.

Down the hill from the cemetery is the intersection of Riverview and Bath roads, a gateway to the Cuyahoga Valley National Park. Bicyclists and hikers exploring the Ohio & Erie Canal Towpath Trail might have trouble imagining a bustling town at the tree-shaded crossroads.

The unincorporated village of Botzum, as it last was known, stood for more than a century in old Northampton Township about six miles north of Akron. Its population crested at 40, but its landmarks included a hotel, general store, tavern, saloon, post office, school, train station, covered bridge, blacksmith shop, sawmill, grist mill, boatyard, two warehouses and a dozen homes.

The town sprouted while the Ohio & Erie Canal was under construction in the late 1820s. Cannons exploded in jubilation July 3, 1827, as Ohio Gov. Allen Trimble rode the first canalboat from Akron to Cleveland.

Massachusetts native Nathaniel Hardy Sr. (1796–1866), a Northampton pioneer who helped build canal locks, opened a hotel where Yellow Creek ran into the Cuyahoga River. He catered to canalboat captains, mule drivers and other laborers as 40 to 50 boats arrived each day.

The town, which became known as Yellow Creek Basin (or Yellow Creek for short), had a tough reputation. Fistfights often erupted when canal workers got drunk at the bars. Meanwhile, horse thieves and counterfeiters lurked in the woods. For various reasons, the village kept changing its name.

Northampton Township surveyor Peter Voris, father of future Gen. Alvin Coe Voris of Akron, had an ambitious plan to develop a town to rival Akron. The Cuyahoga Valley location was ideal because of its endless supply of water power. In 1836, Voris platted 100 acres, which he called Niles.

The name stuck, even if the venture failed. The Panic of 1837, a financial crisis during President Martin Van Buren's administration, scared away investors. Voris sold the Niles property.

One buyer was John George Botzum (1798–1864), a German immigrant who moved to Northampton in 1835 with his wife, Katherine, and eight children.

Local historian Oscar Eugene Olin described the family patriarch as a "sturdy old pioneer" who was "engaged in farming during the remainder of his life and died full of years and in possession of the respect and confidence of the people of the community in which he lived."

Botzum and his heirs raised cattle and sheep and grew grain, fruit and vegetables. They loaded produce onto canalboats for shipment across Ohio.

One son, John A. Botzum Sr., opened a store in Niles in 1858. Historian William Henry Perrin described him as "a good and useful citizen" who had "the respect and confidence of the entire community."

Botzum's younger son, Charlie, who died at 17, was buried at Botzum Cemetery. Older son John Jr. became a famous Akron newsman who lived to be 93. "The town in which I was born seemed a wonderful place years ago," Botzum Jr. told the Akron Sunday Times in 1928.

His earliest recollections were of his father's business. "Upstairs was a great ballroom with a big fireplace at each end," Botzum Jr. recalled. "Up there the dances were held and we often had our home talent shows. On such occasions, people came down from the hills and filled the hall."

He never forgot the stain on the floor that could not be removed. It was blood from an infamous incident on Oct. 27, 1882. Drunk farmhand John Tedrow caused a commotion by accosting guests at a dance in the ballroom. He accidentally tore the jacket of John Brook, who grabbed an ax in rage and hit Tedrow in the head, killing him instantly. Brook was paroled after three years in prison.

Botzum's covered bridge, which spanned the Cuyahoga River for 100 years, was demolished in 1932. It stood on Bath Road near Riverview Road, near where blue herons make their nests today.

Botzum Sr. added the title of postmaster with the opening of the Buckeye post office in his store. The Buckeye name created confusion when people began applying it to the town, too.

The village welcomed a train depot when the Valley Railroad opened in 1880. With Botzum as station agent, the depot was christened Botzum Station, a name the village adopted before settling on the shorter Botzum.

Excursion trains began to visit the valley. The Cleveland Herald's Fresh Air Fund sent 1,483 poor children to Botzum to swim, play and explore the woods. Botzum Sr. handed out 30 bushels of apples to the kids.

Villagers didn't realize it, but the convenience of rail travel would doom the town. The canal was becoming obsolete. By the early 20th century, Botzum's buildings were in decay. The hotel was demolished in 1906, creating an unsolved mystery when human bones were found in the old cellar. Other structures disappeared after the canal closed in 1913.

Conrad Botzum, the older brother of John A. Botzum Sr., preserved the family's 200-acre farm, but neighboring properties were lost. Conrad's five sons—Charles, Harry, Albert, Joseph and Lewis Botzum—turned their attention to business in Akron. They formed Botzum Brothers, a feed and flour store, and later operated the

Dreamland and Orpheum theaters, and started a concrete-mixing business and hardware company.

Much of Botzum disappeared in one fell swoop. In 1922, the family sold 800 acres so Akron could build a $3.7 million sewage disposal plant. The complex opened in 1928, and is still there.

Only 15 residents were left in 1929 when the Baltimore & Ohio Railroad abandoned its Botzum station. No longer would eastbound trains arrive at 7:36 a.m. and westbound trains at 5:19 p.m.

Resident Jack O'Neil told the Beacon Journal at the time: "Fact is, it doesn't matter much whether they stop these trains here anyway. It takes two days to go and come from Cleveland and Peninsula the way it is—it's pretty nigh as quick to walk it."

The 1932 demolition of the 100-year-old Botzum covered bridge over the Cuyahoga River punctuated the town's demise. The Conrad Botzum Farmstead is one of the last reminders of the village. Almost everything else is lost in the woods of the Cuyahoga Valley National Park.

These days, the old business district is a hub of recreation. Hikers and bicyclists enjoy the scenery while the Cuyahoga Valley Scenic Railroad makes stops at a new Botzum depot. Botzum's work is done. Its grave is here. Forget it not.

Letters To Old Santa

CHILDREN KNEW EXACTLY WHAT THEY WANTED IN 1929, AND THEY KNEW JUST WHO TO ASK

(Originally published Dec. 13, 2004)

There was no guarantee that Santa Claus could deliver the goods, but it didn't hurt to ask. Public anxiety was rising in December 1929, the first Christmas of the Great Depression. The daily struggle was getting more difficult, putting a heavy strain on U.S. families. Many children would be lucky to get a single present that Christmas, and the prospects for the next year seemed worse.

In the 1920s, the Akron Beacon Journal published "Letters to Old Santa," a daily feature in which youths could describe the gifts they hoped to receive. Thousands of letters poured into the newsroom each December and hundreds were printed. Many also were read "by Santa himself" on the air at WFJC, the newspaper's sister radio station.

Some letters were amusing and some letters were sad. Some asked for a little and some asked for a lot. Some obviously were written by kids and some obviously were written by parents.

Today, we're reprinting a handful of memorable letters from 1929. They reveal a lot about the era in which they were written and hint at how much has changed over 75 years.

Dear Santa:
I am a little boy 7½ years old. Please bring me an electric train, steam shovel, boxing gloves and a new suit. I will leave you a lunch on the kitchen table. What do you like best to eat?
Bobby Jones, 1818 Adelaide Blvd., Akron

Dear Santa:
I am a good little girl and I want you to bring me a doll, some books and a bag and a little piano. I will look for you.
Norma Walter, 455 Noble Ave., Akron

Dear Santa:
I have been good all this year and I hope you will not forget me. I want a Flexible Flyer sled.
Yours sincerely,
Bobby Phillips, 337 N. Adams St., Akron

Dear Santa:
Will you please bring me a little car for Christmas. I don't care if it is a Ford, but I like a Cadillac pretty good. I want a pair of gloves, too. I hope you are well. I'm fine.
Love to Santa,
Calvin Carlisle, 1212 Georgia Ave., Akron

Dear Santa:
I am a little girl of 4½ years old. My name is Julia Molnar and I been a good little girl and been good to my father and mother. Dear Santa, please bring me a nice dolly. Please, Santa Claus, do that for me.
Julia Molnar, 1812 Main Ave., Kenmore

Dear Santa:
I am a little boy 7 years old and I would like to have a two-wheel bicycle. But yet I don't think there is a Santa Claus, because he didn't visit me last year, and I think Santa Claus is a lot of bunk.
Your little boy,
Sammy Jones, Brittain Road, Akron

Dear Santa:
I am a little boy 8 years old. I want you to please bring me an electric train. Dear Santa that is all I ask you to bring me. Please remember my two sisters, Lovell and Louise.
Your little pal,
Jack Baum, 925 Montana Ave., Akron

Dear Santa:
Please send me a bicycle with red wheels and shining spokes, a football, some books on model airplanes, a sled, and a pair of tubular skates.
With love,
Charles Shook, 212 Second St., Cuyahoga Falls
P.S. Don't forget me.

Dear Santa:
I am going to tell you what my little brothers want for Christmas. The smallest one named Henry wants a small cowboy suit and a small cement mixer. The next is Joe. He wants a cowboy suit, one like Jack Hoxie, and a small truck. The last is Adam. He also wants a cowboy suit like Tom Mix and a two-wheel bicycle. And they all wish you a Merry Christmas.
Yours truly,
William, Adam, Joe and Henry Kaiser, 1189 Seventh Ave., Akron

Dear Santa:
I want to tell you what I want. Here is what I want: a dress, box of candy, set of dishes, rose for my coat, pocketbook and a ring. Dear Santa, fill my stockings full.
Goodbye, Santa Claus.
Juanita Pritchard, 1216 Second Ave., Akron

Dear Santa:
Please bring me some books and games, candy and nuts. I don't want much this year. Please don't forget the poor children. I am 10 years old and I go to Crouse School. Please put this letter in the paper. I will be watching for it. I am pretty good—but sometimes bad. Goodbye, Santa.
Your little friend,
Mildred Zambelle, 695 Fern St., Akron

Dear Santa:
I am afraid I won't be able to go to see you this year as I am sick. When you come to my house, will you please bring me a desk and a coloring set. I will be a good boy. If you have time, will you please read my name over the radio?
Thank you, Santa.
Russell Miles Kline, 365 Eastland Ave., Akron

Dear Santa:
I am 9 years old. Would you please bring me a dolly with long curls and a small trunk with a key. I will look for my letter in the paper every night.
Goodbye,
Aleta Mae Burton, 860 Harvard St., Akron

Dear Santa:
I am trying to be a good boy and for Christmas I would like to have a sidewalk bike and a football and please bring my little brother Milton a sidewalk automobile. I am 8 years old and Milton is 6 and we say our prayers every night.
Dick and Milton Handley, 645 Brown St., Akron

Dear Santa:
Please bring me a desk, Tiddly Winks and Parcheesi game, two books and a scooter bike. I am 9 years old, so you know what kind of books I want. My brother Walter wants an electric train, dump truck and a rocking horse. Don't forget mama and daddy. Bring some candy and nuts.
Your love,
Olga Molohoskey, 14 E. Wilbeth Road, Akron
P.S. And don't forget my Christmas is on Jan. 7. Goodbye.

Dear Santa:
Please bring me a pair of football pants, headgear, a boat that carries airplanes, a Graf Zeppelin, U.S. Army truck, house slippers that are brown, size 3, a moving picture machine, a pair of leather gloves for a boy 9 yearsold, a half-dozen handkerchiefs marked E, slipover sweater, a book and a game for a boy to play. Please bring me all these things because I will be a good boy.
Love,
Elbert Close, 605 Sunset View, Akron

Dear Santa:
I hope you will remember me. I have been very good. Please bring me an airplane set, a sidewalk bike, a pair of snow skates, an Erector set, a few books and games. I am 9. My sister is 3. She wants a doll, cupboard, a mop, a broom, duster, sweeper. My letter is getting long now and I will have to stop.
Your friend,
Kenneth Schlobohm, 76 N. Adams St., Akron

Dear Santa:
We are twin brothers, 6 years old. We are good boys and go to bed early. We would like for you to bring us an airplane and for each of us a nice necktie, a pair of red bedroom slippers, a horn and also please bring us a pair of goats, a goat cart and sleigh bells.
Your little boys,
Wilbur and Wilfred Wood, R.F.D. No. 5, Medina

Dear Santa:
We are two little girls 10 and 5 years old. We would like some games, book, a new slip-over sweater—a red one for me and for Dorothy Faye a tan one—and bring us each a new dress and we would like a doll house with furniture and bring our dolls new wigs of hair and some new dresses. We will try to be real good girls.
Marcella and Dorothy McMullen, 78 Fairview St., Wadsworth

Dear Santa:
I thought I would tell you what I would like for Christmas. I am 9 years old. I would like a doll carriage, about 30 inches high and about 28 inches long. I would like a green buggy, trimmed with tan. If you don't have a buggy, I would like a red scooter bike and a pair of red and blue bedroom slippers.
Elva G. Barnett, 114 Hager Ave., Akron

Dear Santa:
I am a little boy 5½ years old, go to school every day and listen in on the radio every evening to hear you read letters from little boys and girls. I want you to bring me a sheepskin coat and pair of gloves, a big sled because I have to give mine to my little brother and bring some more track for my electric train and nuts and apples, oranges, candy and don't forget my brother Dick. I want you to put this in the Beacon Journal because we take that paper all the time.
Paul Wells, 1062 Packard Drive, Akron

Dear Santa:
My name is Junior Mulvaney. I want a paddle car, a football, an airplane, a dirigible. I am 6 years old. We are poor. I want a pair of shoes too, a number 9 shoe.
With love,
Junior Mulvaney, 606 N. Water St., Kent

Dear Santa:
Please bring me a tool chest, a stamping set and some Lincoln Logs. And anything else you think I should have.
Goodbye, Santa.
Walter J. Chester, 336 12th St., Kenmore

Dear Santa:
Please bring me a sled and a pair of gloves and a box of candy. Don't forget the poor children. I am 10 years old. I have no brothers or sisters.
Your loving friend,
James Holmes, 290 Two Max Drive, Akron

Dear Santa:
I am a little girl 5 years old. My mother is dead and I live with my aunt. I have been a good girl. Please bring me a desk, bicycle and an ironing board.
Marie Pringle, Canton Road, Ellet

Dear Santa:
I want for Christmas a police outfit and a Spirit of St. Louis construction toy, some lead soldiers and a cannon and anything you want to bring me. Don't forget my little sister Rita and my brother Foley. I forgot to tell you I want a motorcycle that goes "put, put, put."
William O. Daniel, 442 Clinton Ave., Akron

Dear Santa:
I have been reading your letters every night. I am 9 years old and go to the cripple school. I have a little brother. He is 3 years of age. I am writing early for I want to see my letter in the Beacon Journal. My brother and I will look for it. I would like to have a new coat, shoes, wristwatch or gold ring and a nice story book. My brother wants an automobile, stockings and new suit, and a picture book. Well, this will be all this year. I wish you a merry Christmas.
Allyne Allen and Jimmie Allen, 623 Cole Ave., Akron

Dear Santa:
My name is Lucille Reynolds. I wish you would send me a doll, writing paper, doll buggy, pencil box, box of crayons and candy. I am 5 years old. Am good girl. Help sister Bessie with dishes.
Yours truly,
Lucille Reynolds, 769 Iota Ave., Cuyahoga Falls
P.S. Want comb and brush.

Dear Santa:
I like you very much. I saw you downtown. My name is Mary Cecilia Maurer and I am 5 years old. I wash the dishes and once I washed them and dried them and put them away. I care for the baby and hold her bottle. Please bring me a table, chairs, dishes and one doll. I guess this is all I can say today. I wish you a merry Christmas.
Your little friend,
Mary Cecilia Maurer, 70 Jewett St., Akron

Dear Santa:
I broke my leg on Armistice Day. I read your letters every day so I am writing to tell you what I want. I want a train, a loop de loop toy, a pair of shoes, a dark gray suit. I will have my stocking hanging up. Please fill it with candy, nuts and oranges. I am 8 years old and in the third grade.
Melvin Lee House, R.F.D. No. 4, Kent
P.S. Please put this in the Beacon Journal as we have no radio.

Statue Reflects Lasting Sorrow

GLENDALE CEMETERY MONUMENT DEDICATED TO
ETERNAL GRATITUDE FOR UNKNOWN SOLDIERS

(Originally published Nov. 10, 2008)

She mourns for men whose names will never be known, the brave soldiers who marched off to battle and disappeared in a haze of smoke.

A long-haired woman in a flowing robe has maintained a 100-year vigil in front of the Civil War Memorial Chapel at Glendale Cemetery in Akron. Her sad eyes gaze toward the ground as she dangles a rose in her right hand and clutches a floral wreath with the left.

A respectful crowd of 10,000 attended the Memorial Day 1909 dedication of the marble statue known as Grief. The monument, which honors the unknown dead of the Civil War, was a gift from a secret donor in the Buckley Post of the Grand Army of the Republic, a Union veterans group.

The benefactor didn't want any public recognition, but a speaker at the May 30 unveiling ceremony surprised everyone by pointing into the audience and revealing the man's identity.

Aging veterans rose early that morning, assembled on Main Street and marched to the cemetery. They decorated the graves of their comrades and then gathered at the Gothic chapel that they had dedicated in May 1876.

The new monument was hidden beneath giant cloths in front of the shrine. Throngs of people gathered to watch the ceremony. "The perfect weather combined with the beauties of the landscape to make the scene memorable," the Beacon Journal reported on June 1, 1909. "The lawns, the hillsides and the buildings near the chapel were crowded with men, women and children. Many of them were relatives and friends who had gathered with the Grand Army men to visit the graves of soldiers."

The patriotic program featured many highlights. Judge Newell D. Tibbals read Abraham Lincoln's Gettysburg Address. Buchtel College music professor Gustave Sigel led the German societies Liedertafel and Saengerbund in *The Day of the Lord*. Gertrude Seiberling, wife of Goodyear co-founder F.A. Seiberling, sang

The Star-Spangled Banner. Navy veteran Jules Michelson unfurled a new U.S. flag.

While the Eighth Regiment band performed *America*, the Women's Relief Corps tugged on ropes at 11 a.m. and the draperies pulled back from the 10-foot monument. The audience cheered and waved handkerchiefs as the bright-white statue came into view. Akron citizens beheld a life-size granite figure standing inside a four-column temple. Inscriptions on the base read "To Our Unknown Dead 1861–1865" and "Erected by Buckley Post No. 12, G.A.R."

Maj. E.F. Taggart, past commander of the post, made the unveiling official: "I dedicate this monument to those who fell in defense of their flag and who are sleeping in unmarked graves."

Publishing magnate Paul E. Werner, operator of the Werner Printing & Lithograph Co., delivered a prophetic speech on the tragic reality of war. "This talk of universal peace is a well-meant vision, but war will never cease," he said. "It must be. This country has had war and will have war again. You must do everything to train and prepare your youth to be ready when the time comes."

When his address was nearly finished, Werner looked into the audience and spotted a familiar face. Straying from the program, he told the crowd that the grand monument originally was intended as a modest tablet, but a good-hearted fellow at the Buckley Post had volunteered to pay for a more elaborate tribute.

The anonymous donor commissioned Alex Guthrie and Francis Rogers to carve the Grief statue at Akron Monumental Works, 18–20 N. High St. "I know it will displease him for me to mention him here, but I know, too, that it will please all of you and therefore I feel that it is my duty to do it."

He motioned to Col. George T. Perkins, 73, chairman of the B.F. Goodrich Co., and urged the crowd to give three cheers. Perkins was the son of Col. Simon and Grace Perkins, and grandson of Akron's founder, Gen.

A granite statue of Grief gazes toward the ground as she dangles a rose in her right hand and clutches a floral wreath with the left. Dedicated 100 years ago at Akron's Glendale Cemetery, the monument honors the unknown dead of the Civil War.

Simon Perkins. He had not delivered a public address in years, but audience members called out: "Speech! Speech!"

The Civil War vet hemmed and hawed before reluctantly standing to address the group. "I am a member of Buckley Post, of which I am very proud," Perkins said. "As such, I of course assisted in securing this monument, but it belongs to the post and is due to its efforts.

"What prompted me especially was my personal interest in my regiment. I had 20-odd men who were left hurled in the battlefields of the South. They are lying there today rotting in their graves, but we have no record of them. It is to those men particularly that this monument is directed."

The ceremony concluded with a rifle volley, bugle call, flag-raising and a reprise of the national anthem.

A year later, Perkins joined his lost comrades of battle. He died of a blood disorder at 74. His casket rolled past the grieving monument on its way to the Perkins family plot at Glendale Cemetery.

The Civil War chapel and its monument to unknown dead served as the center of Memorial Day commemorations throughout the 20th century. Holiday observers placed wreaths at the foot of the monument while color guards stood at attention.

The robed woman stared down sadly as holiday crowds fell from tens of thousands in the early 1900s to mere dozens by the late 1980s. She maintains her quiet vigil today, one century later, mourning our unknown dead while many others have forgotten.

Old Man Eloquent

PRESIDENT JOHN QUINCY ADAMS LEFT A GOOD IMPRESSION ON AKRON

(Originally published Feb. 18, 2001)

With all due respect to George Washington and Abraham Lincoln, we're going to talk about someone else today. This Presidents' Day, it seems appropriate to honor John Quincy Adams, the sixth president of the United States and the first man to follow his father's footsteps to the nation's highest office. (Who was the second man? Hint: His middle initial is W.)

Adams wasn't "The Father of His Country" or "The Great Emancipator," but he did play a role in Summit County history. He helped legitimize Akron as the county seat.

Adams, the son of second president John Adams, was the first candidate to win the White House without winning the popular vote. In the 1824 election, Andrew Jackson had more votes than Adams, but neither man had an Electoral College majority because of a four-way split.

The election was thrown into the House of Representatives, which elevated Adams to office. Jackson got revenge in 1828 by defeating Adams after one term.

It can be argued that Adams was a more effective leader after his presidency. In 1831, he was elected to the U.S. House from his home state of Massachusetts and served 17 years in Congress as a leading foe of slavery. One of his great achievements was helping to establish the Smithsonian Institution.

Adams didn't intend to visit Akron on Nov. 2, 1843. He was traveling on the Ohio & Erie Canal from Cleveland to Cincinnati, where he was to lay the cornerstone of the city's new observatory. Akron officials learned of the statesman's journey and sent a committee to meet his boat at Lock 21, somewhere north of present-day Memorial Parkway.

The delegation persuaded the former president to come to Akron for breakfast and give a 20-minute speech while his boat slowly worked its way through the canal's locks. The former president agreed to the proposal and a carriage rushed him into town.

Church bells rang and messengers went door to door with news of the important guest. With only an hour's notice, most of the city's population—about 2,000—crammed into the Summit County Courthouse, which was still under construction.

Adams arrived at 8:30 a.m. and was met with hearty cheers and applause. Mayor Harvey H. Johnson welcomed him, saying: "We not only recognize in you one who has spent a long, active and useful life in public service, but we are at once reminded of the time of the foundation of this great republic.

"We behold in you, sir, a link between us and one of its mighty pillars. The same hand that guided you in youth affixed the signature of John Adams to the Declaration of Independence."

Akron residents quickly learned why Adams had been nicknamed "Old Man Eloquent." Although visibly tired from his journey, the 76-year-old politician, pleased with the spontaneous gathering, whipped up a delicate cloud of oratory.

"I have lived long and been much engaged in public affairs, and these greetings may partake, somewhat at least, of a curiosity to see an old man worn out by the cares of state—an ante-revolutioner—an old oak stripped of its foliage, dying downwards from the top," he told the crowd.

Only decades earlier, he said, Akron couldn't have mustered such an enthusiastic welcome. The land was just a dense forest lined with Indian trails, he said. "It seems as though a person in this Western world was witnessing a new creation—a new world rising from disorder and chaos to order, happiness and virtue. What will this country be in half a century from this time? Its career has scarcely begun.

"Cherish that spirit of improvement which has made it what it is. Apply your mighty energies to the work, call on your country for assistance and may God speed you." After his speech, the consummate politician shook hands with every man and "kissed every one of the ladies and all the babies," The Summit Beacon reported.

He then was escorted by carriage back to his canalboat, now south of town, where he continued on his way to Cincinnati.

The first Summit County Courthouse, pictured as it looked in 1890, was dedicated in 1843 in the presence of most distinguished guest. Now occupying this site on High Street is the current courthouse, completed in 1908. (INSET) John Quincy Adams, the sixth president of the United States, won the White House without a popular or Electoral College majority.

Adams' impromptu appearance was a coup for Akron, which only a year earlier had been elected the county seat—2,978 votes to 1,384—despite fierce competition from Cuyahoga Falls. A rivalry had raged since February 1840 when Summit was carved from Portage, Stark and Medina counties.

The statesman's visit in 1843 cemented Akron's reputation as the center of Summit. It also served as the dedication of the county's new courthouse, which stood more than 60 years on High Street before being demolished to make room for the 1908 courthouse that exists today.

John Quincy Adams served his country another four years before suffering a massive stroke in the House of Representatives. That sad, inevitable day was fore-shadowed in 1843 by The Summit Beacon's account of Adams' visit to Akron:

"Many were the fervent wishes that the old man's life might be lengthened—that the years that are rushing upon him and bearing him down to the grave might press lightly upon that aged brow and those feeble limbs—that he might be long spared to stand up in the halls of legislation and battle for right, for liberty, for the oppressed, and never grow weary."

"Old Man Eloquent" died at age 80 on Feb. 23, 1848, in the Speaker's Room of the House. His final words, reportedly, were: "This is the last of earth, but I am composed."

Godspeed, John Quincy Adams. Happy Presidents' Day.

The Great Raymond

FAMOUS AKRON MAGICIAN DAZZLED THE WORLD WITH HIS WONDERFUL BAG OF TRICKS

(Originally published Oct. 23, 2006)

Akron magician Maurice Raymond lived a charmed life. He circled the globe seven times, mesmerized audiences from Europe to Asia and earned royal decorations from 14 monarchs. The world knew him as The Great Raymond, and he certainly lived up to that title.

On any given night, he pulled rabbits out of hats, sawed lovely assistants in half, made inanimate objects disappear and performed daring feats of escape.

Raymond billed himself as "The King of Mystery," "The Miracle Man of Magic" and "The Man Who Laughs at Locks." His contemporaries included Harry Houdini, Howard Thurston and Harry Blackstone.

At an early age, he knew exactly what he wanted to do. Maurice Raymond Saunders, the son of Martha and William W. Saunders, was born in 1877 at the family's home on Fir Hill in Akron. The father was an artist and photographer who worked with his brothers Addison and George at Saunders Portrait Co.

Addison Tresize Saunders (1856–1939), a doting uncle who dabbled in magic tricks, introduced his nephew to the world of prestidigitation. "I can recall standing spellbound as a child and watching my uncle toss coins into the air and make them disappear," Raymond recalled years later. "He would do tricks with oranges, which fascinated me when I was 4. From then on, I resolved to be a magician."

Uncle Addison allowed his 9-year-old nephew to join him on a summer magic tour. Young Raymond began to learn the tricks of the trade, and the rest, as they say, is mystery. At age 10, Raymond joined the Adam Forepaugh Circus as an animal wrangler. By 15, he had a spotlight act as "The World's Youngest Magician."

He performed before Queen Victoria at Buckingham Palace in 1894 and formed his own troupe in his early 20s. Raymond's first wife, Luella, served as his assistant.

The magician had a regal presence in a long black suit with starched shirt and white bow tie. His trademark tricks included cracking an egg in a skillet and transforming it into a live duck, and escaping from a sealed crate in which he had been bound and handcuffed.

Appearing in circuses, vaudeville acts and headlining shows, Raymond toured North America, South America, Central America, Europe, Asia and Australia. He learned to speak at least six languages fluently.

Raymond's wild adventures became part of his mystique. He hunted tigers in India, rode elephants in Siam, explored jungles in Borneo, purchased shrunken heads in Ecuador and survived the 1906 San Francisco quake.

He boasted of owning a ruby ring that once belonged to World War I spy Mata Hari. Raymond said a chief inspector in Paris had given him the ring, which supposedly had been wrestled away from the spy after she attempted to raise it to her lips.

"It has a sinister history and use," an Akron journalist noted. "A flick of the fingernail and the stone flies back to reveal a hidden cache for a poison pellet. The two bands of ornamental filigree work open and reveal two more hiding places for the concealment of secret messages."

The Great Raymond traveled from continent to continent, selling out theaters and halls. Somewhere along the way, Luella vanished. It wasn't part of the show. After three years apart, the couple finally divorced.

Raymond's second wife, Pearl Gonser, became an even bigger part of the act. A concert harpist, she had studied at the Royal Conservatory of Music in Brussels and was a former member of the Boston Symphony.

Using the stage name Madame Litzka, she served as Raymond's assistant and performed selections during intermission on "her $10,000 harp."

The couple settled in England in the 1930s while continuing to tour. When World War II erupted, they fled for America, a fortuitous decision that may have saved their lives. A German bomb destroyed their old home.

Raymond hadn't visited the United States since 1920, but he knew where he wanted to live. He and Litzka moved to Akron in 1940 and bought a home at 121 N. Arlington St.

"Now I'm going to stay home and perform before my own people again," Raymond said. The white-haired magician scheduled four shows that October at Good-

Akron magician Maurice Raymond, known worldwide as The Great Raymond, hand-
cuffs his wife, Madame Litzka, before sealing her in a sack and locking her in a trunk
at Goodyear Theater in October 1940. The escape act was the grand finale of his show.

year Hall with tickets ranging from 50 cents to 99 cents.
Without his old company, Raymond hired girls from
the Adeline Ott Lahrmer Studio to serve in the chorus
line and help with illusions. "Girls! Magic! Thrills! Sen-
sational! Startling!" the ads teased.

The homecoming shows were a big success, with
boisterous crowds turning out to see Akron's famous
illusionist. The tricks that delighted the world were a
thrill for Akron, too.

Raymond, 63, rolled up his shirt sleeves to demonstrate that he had nothing hidden in his jacket. Audiences couldn't figure out how he produced an endless
supply of eggs from a top hat or pulled live pigeons
from silk handkerchiefs.

The highlight of every performance was Raymond's
grand finale, an act that he titled "Metempsychosis." He
described it as "the illusion that mystified Edison and
Einstein."

"Madame Litzka, one of his assistants, was handcuffed, tied in a cloth sack and locked in a trunk which
was then securely bound with rope," the Beacon Journal
explained. "The assistant suddenly reappeared and the
trunk was opened by a delegation from the audience
who found the Great Raymond in the trunk, also tied
in a sack and handcuffed. And this transformation took
place within the space of a few seconds."

Over the next few years, Maurice and Litzka Raymond were treated as local celebrities. They performed
multiple engagements at the Akron Armory, Summit
Beach Park and Barberton High School, including afternoon matinees for children and midnight shows for war
workers. Sponsors included the Akron Police Benevolent
Association, the Bowlers Victory Legion, the Barberton
Service League and Infantile Paralysis Fund.

The Great Raymond and Madame Litzka also put
on shows for young fans at Akron Children's Hospital,
St. Thomas Hospital, Edwin Shaw Sanitarium and the
Summit County Children's Home.

In March 1944, Raymond held four farewell per-
formances at the Armory. He and his wife planned to
embark on a U.S. tour before moving to New York. He
bid farewell to his hometown and hit the road again.

Raymond was 70 years old in 1948 when he died in
Manhattan. He had hoped to tour Europe after the war,
but failing health prevented him from going back.

His widow buried him in the Ohio town where he
learned to perform magic as a child. A modest marble
slab rests over the plot in Section O, Lot 5 at Akron's
Glendale Cemetery. It bears the name of Maurice Raymond Saunders, better known as "The Great Raymond."

He dazzled the world for more than 50 years. When
the final curtain closed, he took his secrets to the grave.

A Double Life

AKRON PHILANTHROPIST'S SECRET SHOCKED MANY WHO THOUGHT THEY KNEW HIM

(Originally published Feb. 12, 2001)

If it hadn't been for the funeral, philanthropist George Stevens would have taken his secret to the grave. The 80-year-old executive was greatly admired for his business acumen, his kindness, his generosity. He had guided a major company to prosperity while donating a fortune to charity.

He was regarded as "a prince among men" in his hometown of Akron and his adopted home of Hartford City, Ind. Yet, one community knew something the other did not. George Stevens was a black man.

Old photos reveal a distinguished-looking gentleman with gentle eyes, a prominent mustache and a neatly trimmed beard. Although Stevens lived in Hartford City for 30 years, no one ever guessed that the town's wealthiest resident was the son of former slaves.

Minerva and William Stevens had followed the Underground Railroad to Akron after escaping from Virginia in 1857. They settled on land near the present site of Akron City Hospital, and William found work as a barber.

George was born in 1860, followed by brother Grant and sister Mary. George and Mary inherited their father's light skin, while middle child Grant had brown skin like their mother.

Stevens' childhood essentially was colorblind. His best friends were two white boys: C.W. Seiberling, the future co-founder of Goodyear, and J. Edward Good, the future hardware magnate for whom Good Park is named.

The three boys enjoyed playing along the banks of the Ohio & Erie Canal, getting into mischief and having sleepovers at each other's homes. They would remain friends for life.

Stevens attended public schools and graduated from Akron High. He completed a year at Buchtel College, but dropped out when he ran out of money.

He worked as a stove repairman until his mechanical skills caught the eye of Barberton founder Ohio C. Barber, who hired him as chief engineer at Portage Strawboard Co.

When the Barberton Fire Department formed in 1895, the 35-year-old Stevens became the city's first fire chief and wrote the squad's regulations.

Stevens met a German immigrant named Eva and fell in love. The two were married about 1904, but tragedy was ahead: Eva drowned in a 1909 accident. The couple never had children.

A heartbroken Stevens decided to make a new life for himself in Indiana after being hired in 1911 as a consultant for the Fort Wayne Corrugated Paper Co. He became a chief engineer and later moved to the company's mill in Hartford City, eventually working his way up to director.

In the predominantly white town of about 7,000, Stevens never told anyone of his family roots. He lived alone in the Hotel Hartford and was driven to work by a chauffeur. Co-workers talked him into joining the Rotary, Elks and Masons, but he otherwise kept to himself.

Stevens compounded his wealth through wise investments. He donated more than $50,000 to charities in town. Everyone in Hartford City thought they knew him.

The entire town mourned on April 8, 1940, when George Stevens died of heart disease. The paper mill closed for the day.

"He possessed a broad view of life and spread his doctrines among his friends through his pleasant mannerisms and pleasing disposition," the Hartford City Evening News eulogized.

A delegation of city officials traveled 300 miles to attend Stevens' funeral at Billow's Chapel in Akron and burial at Glendale Cemetery. The funeral was packed with many prominent Summit County residents, including C.W. Seiberling, J. Edward Good and Barberton planner William A. Johnston.

The Indiana visitors noticed many black mourners at the funeral and assumed they were the philanthropist's former servants.

That's when a tearful Grant Stevens introduced himself as the brother of the deceased. "Hartford City had

Akron native George Stevens donated thousands of dollars to charity after working his way up the corporate ladder at Fort Wayne Corrugated Paper Co. in Indiana.

the shock of its existence in April 1940," the Blackford County Historical Society recalled in its 1986 history book. Residents were "numb and in shock" when they learned the truth that had been hidden from them for 30 years.

No one could believe it.

"Stevens' color wouldn't have mattered much, after everybody met him," Hartford City newspaper editor Ralph Monfort later would say in a 1958 article in Ebony magazine.

Yet, looking back, it's impossible to believe Stevens would have been given the opportunity to succeed in the 1920s and 1930s if his secret had been revealed.

He kept silent and prospered beyond his dreams, but it came at the expense of his identity.

Today, George Stevens' benevolence is still felt in Akron. In 1930, he set up a trust fund to benefit his surviving relatives. The money was divided among 10 relatives as long as they lived. After that, the money would be used for Akron's betterment.

In 1991, the assets of the George Stevens Fund were transferred to the Akron Community Foundation. Since then, the fund has contributed $165,753 in grants to 16 local groups, including the YMCA, Boys and Girls Clubs of Summit County, the Volunteer Center, Cuyahoga Valley Youth Ballet, Mobile Meals and Ohio & Erie Canal Corridor Coalition.

According to the most recent quarterly statement, the Stevens fund's balance is $1.2 million. It's George Stevens' lasting tribute to Akron, the place he always called home.

The Reading Room

WEST AKRON SIBLINGS OPERATED BIG LITTLE BOOK
LIBRARY IN 1934, AND THE KIDS LOVED IT

(Originally published April 5, 2004)

Sure, the building may have seemed small from the outside, but it was packed to the rafters with great adventures. Inside, Dick Tracy battled gangsters, Tarzan wrestled lions and Buck Rogers zapped aliens.

Popeye lived there. So did Betty Boop, Little Orphan Annie and many other characters. All were waiting to whisk some brave child on a fantastic trip to a distant land. It only cost a penny or two.

Seventy years ago, the smallest library in Akron made its public debut. West Hill resident Edward Naher Jr., 12, an imaginative boy with a good mind for business, converted his backyard playhouse into the Big Little Book Library at 52 Grand Ave.

While many youngsters were content to open small lemonade stands in 1934, Naher preferred to think big—in a manner of speaking.

He loved reading Big Little Books, a series of novels adapted from comic strips, and he knew other kids did, too. "They were very popular," recalls Naher, a Medina resident who will turn 82 this month. "The kids were just clamoring to get their hands on Big Little Books."

Whitman Publishing Co. introduced the stubby, hardcover books in 1932, and other companies soon jumped on the bandwagon. The books were about 300 pages long—4½ inches high by 3¾ inches wide—and fit perfectly in small hands.

The illustrated novels cost 10 cents, a pretty steep price for a kid growing up in the Depression. Many youngsters couldn't afford them, but Naher was among the fortunate. His father, Edward Naher Sr., co-owned a prosperous business, Naher and DeHaven Meats at 838 W. Exchange St., and was happy to buy the books for his children.

The Naher boy wondered if he might be able to turn his 50-volume collection into a small business while providing a service for neighborhood children who might not otherwise get to read many titles.

"So I thought that would be a good idea if we worked up some kind of a small company so they could come in and rent them for a while," Naher said.

He and his 10-year-old sister, Phyllis Jean Naher, already had a good location. Their backyard playhouse, which had started out as an open-air sandbox with a roof, took on a more businesslike atmosphere with the addition of cream-colored walls, a floor, windows and door.

Brightly colored books lined the walls. "My dad put shelving around inside this playhouse," Naher said. The inside decor consisted of a rug, a desk, two benches, two chairs, a mini cash register and a large sign touting the National Recovery Administration, a U.S. agency that promoted fair trade.

A padlock on the front door guarded against anyone attempting an illegal checkout.

The Naher children posted signs on the playhouse and advertised the new library by tying typewritten cards to poles in the neighborhood. Business hours were 2 to 6 p.m., but curious customers wandered by all day. "If anyone came along, I was usually home and I would go up and unlock the door," Naher reminisced.

The young librarian had a rather complex system, which he explained to an Akron Times-Press reporter for a 1934 article: "I charge one cent for a card, then one cent for keeping either one or three books for three days, and one cent a day for each book after that."

Naher and his sister were the only two library members who didn't have to pay, but they definitely earned their keep. "My brother put me in charge when he had something else to do," recalls Phyllis Naher Hayes, 79, who now lives in Honea Path, S.C. "I would just hang around and wait for customers to come."

There wasn't a lot of space in the one-room facility. If the books had been any bigger or the patrons any taller, this operation might not have run as smoothly as it did.

About 30 youngsters joined that first month. Most customers were Portage Path Elementary pupils who lived near Grand Avenue, although some traveled from as far as Mayfair Road in Merriman Hills.

"As I recall I'd get their name and address and telephone number—if they had a telephone," Naher said.

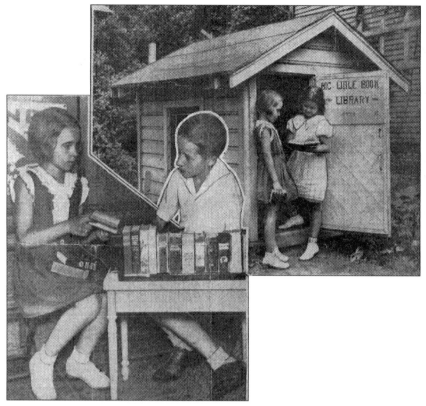

Phyllis Naher, 10, and her brother Edward, 12, work at the Big Little Book Library in
these 1934 images from the Akron Times-Press. Phyllis greets customer Nancy Ellis
at the entrance of the former playhouse in the back yard at 52 Grand Ave. in Akron.

The young librarians maintained a list of titles to keep track of inventory. Inevitably, some borrower would forget to return a book in the allotted time. "If their books were overdue, they would owe like a couple pennies, you know," Hayes said. "So I would collect the change."

Within a month of operation, the library collected about $2 in dues and fees. "That was a big time when we'd collect the money, even if it was pennies," Naher said.

One customer did have to pay an 11-cent late fee, but that's about as tough as the penalties ever got. If the librarians lost a book, it was rare. "We just waited until they came back," Hayes said. "Eventually, they did."

The Big Little Book Library opened in the spring and continued to operate throughout the summer. The siblings believe they closed up shop when classes resumed that fall. "It wasn't in existence for a long period of time," Naher said.

The Nahers returned to Portage Path and gave up their library jobs. From there, they would go to West High School.

Ultimately, Edward Naher traded in his pennies for dimes. He landed a position at the Dime Savings Bank, the forerunner of today's National City Bank, and worked there for 45 years, retiring in 1984 as a vice president.

"I did just about anything," he said. "I was a messenger when I first started."

Today, it's sad to say, neither Naher nor Hayes owns a single Big Little Book. They don't remember what became of their large collection. "That was a long time ago," Hayes said.

The novels they rented for a penny a book are highly prized among 21st century collectors. Many 1930s titles are valued anywhere from $25 to $100 or higher. One 1934 Buck Rogers book recently sold for nearly $800 in an Internet auction.

Nobody got rich from the Big Little Book Library, but the small business was still a big success for one important reason. "The kids liked it," Naher said.

Political Vision

BLIND MAYOR, REPRESENTATIVE BEAT OBSTACLES WITH WIFE'S HELP

(Originally published May 21, 2001)

George J. Harter's blindness was a disability, but it wasn't a political handicap. Voters elected him six times as state representative and once as Akron mayor—proving that a person doesn't need eyesight to have political vision.

Harter and his wife, Sophia, were a remarkable couple who broke societal barriers in the 1930s and 1940s. She served as her husband's "eyes" and was a trusted adviser, ultimately succeeding him in political office.

George Harter was elected to the Ohio legislature during the Democratic Party's sweep of 1932, a year in which Franklin D. Roosevelt, a man who also had a disability, won the White House.

The road to public office took a few twists and turns. Harter was born in Mulberry, Ind., on March 16, 1883, and moved with his family to Akron at age 14. After finishing the eighth grade, he went to work in the composing room of the Akron Daily Democrat, a newspaper that evolved into the Akron Times.

Journalism ran in the family. Harter and his three brothers were destined for newspaper careers. In fact, his older brother, Edward, co-owned the Times.

Capitalizing on the family talent for the written word, George Harter transferred to the newsroom and eventually worked his way up to managing editor. Later, he opened his own printing shop and ventured into advertising and public relations.

Life changed forever in 1926 when a 43-year-old Harter noticed that his vision was beginning to dim. A visit to the doctor brought grim news: Harter had retinitis pigmentosa, a disease that destroys the retina and optic nerve. He would be blind within a few years.

Harter and his wife, Sophia, whom he had married in 1909, made the transition together. As his vision disappeared, she became his guide, always at his side, helping him overcome daily obstacles. She read the newspaper to him each day, and escorted him to appointments.

"Of course, it was a blow when his blindness first came," Mrs. Harter would recall two decades later. "At first, after the specialists told us that there was no hope of his seeing again, it seemed like we were up against insurmountable odds. Then we got into a routine and we found it wasn't so hard after all."

Refusing to succumb to his disability, Harter decided to run for the state legislature in 1932. He campaigned on a pro-labor platform of lowering taxes and repealing Prohibition, and won nearly 60,000 votes in Summit County, the most of the 10 local candidates for the Ohio House.

He would remain in the state legislature for the rest of the decade, winning re-election every two years. Colleagues from both parties praised him for his integrity and wisdom.

His main causes were worker pensions, welfare relief and helping the elderly and disabled. His wife remained at his side, reading every piece of legislation to him, while his photographic memory retained the details.

Harter was quite content in the House, but the Summit County Democratic Party persuaded him to run for mayor in November 1941 against Republican incumbent Lee D. Schroy. To the surprise of many, Harter defeated the three-time mayor by more than 7,000 votes.

"I am grateful to the people of Akron for their expression of confidence," Harter said during his acceptance speech. "A great responsibility has been placed upon me."

A month before Japan bombed Pearl Harbor, Akron's mayor-elect touched upon an issue that would dominate his administration.

"In America's defense effort, which may mean the destruction or the continued progress of our form of government, our city is a vital link in this great chain of democracy," he said. "I believe that a well-prepared Akron will contribute to our national unity."

After the United States entered World War II, Harter made Akron's war effort his primary concern. He promoted scrap metal drives and rationing, urging city residents to forego "all unnecessary expenditures and conserve every resource."

During the national emergency, "politics stands adjourned," he proclaimed. That philosophy may explain why Harter lasted only one term as mayor—politics never stands adjourned in Akron.

Akron Mayor George J. Harter and his wife, Sophia, cast ballots in 1943 at their West Hill precinct. Harter, a Democrat, faced Republican Councilman Charles Slusser in the mayoral election.

Republicans turned out in full force for the November 1943 election. Harter was defeated by the GOP's Charles Slusser, a Ward 9 councilman, by a vote of 32,484 to 22,665. Yet, Harter's interest in public service was not done. In 1944, he ran for his old seat in the Ohio House, and easily won election.

It would be his final victory. Harter was hospitalized in February 1945 because of a liver ailment. He battled the illness for three months before slipping into a coma and dying at age 62 on May 19, 1945.

His wife was at his bedside. "George passed on very easily," Sophia Harter told reporters. "He just slept away."

Harter's widow proved to be an adept politician as well. She ran for the state legislature in 1947 and was elected.

During her one term in office, Mrs. Harter promoted public housing, urban renewal and a revision of Ohio's tax laws. She described herself as "a liberal and an advanced thinker in public affairs."

Sophia Harter was 67 when she died on May 13, 1954, after a short illness. She was buried next to her husband at Rose Hill cemetery. In death, just as in life, she remains faithfully at his side.

All The Marbles

KENMORE BOY CAPTURED NATIONAL TITLE 75 YEARS AGO

(Originally published June 30, 2003)

Alfred J. Huey was the boy who would be king. He rose from the dust of Kenmore, vanquished an army of opponents and captured the national crown.

His gleaming empire was built of glass and clay. His loyal subjects were taws, aggies, commies and moonies.

Alfred J. Huey, 11 years old, was the king of the marbles. The Summit County boy catapulted to fame 75 years ago at the 1928 National Marbles Tournament in Atlantic City, N.J.

He was pitted against the country's greatest players—46 boys and one girl—at the sixth annual competition. More than a half-million children had played in local and regional tournaments for the chance to compete in the national event.

"Atlantic City! Gee, I'm the first Kenmore boy to go," Huey told an Akron reporter before the event. "Won't it be swell? Guess I'll have to do a lot of practicing now."

Huey, a seventh-grader at Smith School in Kenmore, earned passage as Akron Times-Press suburban champion. He was joined by John Collier, 13, the newspaper's Akron champion. It would be another year before the two entities merged.

Marble tournaments were big news in those days. The Scripps-Howard Co., owner of the Times-Press, sponsored the national competition.

The wide-eyed Ohio boys stayed at the Knickerbocker Hotel on Atlantic City's Boardwalk along with their chaperones, Times-Press marble writer Paul Van Camp and his wife, Doris.

Thousands of spectators gathered around 10-foot rings set up on the beach June 28. The game was called Ringer: 13 marbles were placed in the center, and the object was to knuckle down and shoot them out of the ring. The player who knocked out the most marbles was the winner.

Huey, the son of Jacob and Maria Huey, had practiced like crazy before Atlantic City. He built a ring in his back yard on Norway Avenue and took shot after shot. If it rained, he moved indoors and played on the rug.

"I could just feel I was getting better every day," he later said. The practice paid off. He thumbed his way past the marble champions of Covington, Ky., Toledo and Lancaster, Ohio.

This was tense stuff. A hush fell over each ring as players duked it out. Collier, the Akron champ, fell short of the semifinals. But Huey, showing remarkable poise, continued to advance.

Before one match, would-be intimidator William Wojcik of Wheeling, W.Va., bragged that he could play left-handed and still beat Huey. The Kenmore boy crouched on the ground and silenced his rival in three games.

The only time that Huey appeared to get rattled was during a semifinal match with crowd favorite Gladys Coleman, 13, of Harrisburg, Pa. The girl knew how to play!

She took the first game 12–1 and was ahead 6–0 in the second game before Huey came back to win.

Marble slingers fell left and right. Huey beat John Melone, the pride of Hoboken, N.J., and Hyman Craven, the pride of Baltimore. When the dust cleared, only one other player was left standing: Dominic "Nick" Cartelli of New Britain, Conn.

Huey and Cartelli squared off in the finals July 3, 1928. The audience cheered as the two boys entered the ring. "Come on, Ohio!" some shouted. The momentum went back and forth as the players took their shots. Cartelli won the first game 7–6, but Huey took the next two, 12–1 and 9–4.

Cartelli tied it up with a 9–4 win in the fourth game, but the fifth game was the turning point. Huey, sober-faced and calm, came back with a vengeance. "Never once did he falter," Van Camp wrote. "It was just—bing, bing, bing—with a big cheer every time Al's shooter connected with a mib. He won 11–2 and it took the heart out of Nick."

Huey captured the sixth game 9–4 and roared into the seventh. Inevitably, it came to a final shot. Huey put chalk on his hands, rubbed sand on his shooter, took aim and fired.

Marble champion Alfred J. Huey, 11, of Kenmore, displays his winning technique in 1928. He holds his hand still while knuckling down, just moving his thumb and forefinger while letting the shooter go.

"Bing," Van Camp wrote.

Alfred J. Huey was the national marble champion. The boy, so cool and collected, melted down before the crowd. He sobbed and sobbed. Tears of joy. Tears of relief.

"Gee, I couldn't help crying," he later said. "I was the happiest kid in the world, but I couldn't help crying."

Akron history buff Michael Cohill, a marble enthusiast, said Huey was like someone straight out of central casting. "You couldn't have picked a more perfect little boy," Cohill said. "The quintessential American boy. He was cute and he was charming and he was friendly. And he could speak to adults. He just did everything right."

A delegation of Kenmore officials welcomed Huey back to town July 5. Mayor Paul Hollinger and Fire Chief Fred Kelly hoisted the boy onto their shoulders for the cameras. "This here stuff is all mighty fine, but I believe I'd like to see my mother," Huey confessed.

On July 6, Kenmore and Akron held a big parade for the marble king. Wearing a crown of gold, Huey rode down Main Street in an open automobile with his mother. Motorcycle police led the way and bands played as crowds lined the sidewalks all the way to Kenmore.

"What a great way to honor a child," Cohill said.

Huey received a treasure trove of prizes for his national victory. His winnings included trophies, plaques, a tomahawk and an autographed 10-gallon hat from cowboy star Tom Mix. He appeared in a national newsreel and got to meet President Herbert Hoover at the White House.

Huey's aim was always true. He grew up to be the quarterback for Kenmore High School and the Akron Red Peppers. He excelled in golf and bowling, too. He served in World War II.

"Al Huey stayed here his whole life," Cohill said. "He worked at Goodrich, raised his children here and had a wonderful life."

Huey's daughter, Candace Egert, who lives in Green, says her father was an easygoing man with a good sense of humor and a great love of sports. "He was a very considerate person," she said. "I'd say quiet, but not shy."

She has a scrapbook of 1920s articles about her father and owns a handful of mementos. She remembers playing marbles with her brother, Alfred, when they were kids. "We had a dirt floor in the garage, and we would play," she said.

But the funny thing is, she doesn't recall her father ever talking about the national title.

"No, mostly my grandmother did," Egert said. "She's the one that gave me the scrapbook, the plaque and the trophy."

Alfred J. Huey died Jan. 17, 1992—more than 60 years after his big moment in the national spotlight. His obituary briefly noted the marble title.

Marbles just aren't as popular as they used to be. "Kids need more of that in this day and age," Egert said.

North by Northwest

TALLMADGE AVENUE BRIDGE LINKED NORTH HILL TO WEST HILL IN 1931

(Originally published Sept. 4, 2006)

The shortest distance between two points was not a straight line. After the 1913 flood washed out the small iron bridge over the Little Cuyahoga River, there was no easy way to travel between North Hill and West Hill.

Akron motorists were forced to take "the long way" through downtown to reach a destination on the other side of the valley. For nearly 20 years, travelers grumbled about the inconvenience to commuting. A man could stand on North Hill and wave to another man on West Hill, but the two couldn't shake hands unless one of them hopped into an automobile and drove around for 20 minutes.

"North Hill folk want their direct connection westward open again," the Akron Times-Press reported in September 1931. "Highway engineers would save thru east and west motorists much profanity, and expedite thru travel.

"Many road maps show West Tallmadge Avenue, extending thru to Merriman Road on the west, and Cuyahoga Street, on the north. Tourists westbound from Youngstown try to drive straight west from Main Street on this route, run into road closed signs, and inch their way downtown and onto West Market Street."

Public officials agreed that a "crosstown highway" would be of great benefit to the community, and pledged to extend Tallmadge Avenue to Merriman. It wouldn't be easy, though. In addition to building a state-of-the-art bridge, construction crews would need to pave the crumbling dirt paths that served as roads before the 1913 flood. Plus, the Baltimore & Ohio railroad track would require a trestle on the west side of the valley.

Funding was difficult to obtain for such a costly project during the Great Depression. Ultimately, the city, county and state would have to work together to get the job done.

In March 1931, Summit County commissioners awarded a contract to the Clemmer-Noah Construction Co. to build a $60,000 bridge. County surveyor Hal Sours noted that the reinforced-concrete bridge—to be built in four sections—would be 207 feet long and 60 feet wide with 8-foot walkways on either side. Clemmer-Noah promised to hire 75 local laborers and use Akron materials for the job.

The Ohio Highway Department provided $150,000 in gas tax funds to pave the road. The Akron City Council chipped in $25,000 for grading and sewer work. Unfortunately, there were unforeseen delays. The valley terrain was softer and soggier than engineers had anticipated.

Crews expected to encounter a rock foundation at 40 feet while sinking the pilings for the Little Cuyahoga bridge. Instead, they found clay subsoil and had to dig 60 feet.

Workers slogged their way through the project and completed the bridge Sept. 30, 1931, but a paved road would not reach it for another year. A tremendous amount of fill dirt—more than 25 feet deep—was needed "to lift the roadway out of the bottomlands." Plus, a sanitary sewer would need to be installed.

Akron Service Director E.A. Kemmler advised the city against opening the street until at least the following spring. "It is absolutely necessary that the fills and the sewer be permitted to settle through the winter to insure a satisfactory job when it is completed," the Beacon Journal reported.

In 1927, the city had replaced a trunk sewer about 3 feet in diameter nearly 40 feet underground. The tile structure ran down the hill to the river.

Instead of redoing the entire line during the 1931 construction, the city moved only a segment of it—near the new railroad overpass—and buried the rest under tons of fill dirt.

That was a tragic mistake. The original sewer wasn't designed to hold all that weight. The line was installed before anyone knew a paved road would cover it. The sewer was prone to rupture.

Contractors began pouring concrete for the "northwest approach" in August 1932. The project was completed within three months.

After nearly 20 years of detours, motorists were allowed to take the bypass Nov. 5, 1932. "The West Tallmadge Avenue improvement, providing direct through highway from the east to the west without necessity of

Construction workers build a West Tallmadge Avenue bridge over the Little Cuyahoga River to link North Hill with West Hill in September 1931. This view was taken from the North Hill side of the valley looking west on what is now Memorial Parkway.

traveling downtown streets, was completed Friday," the Beacon Journal reported. "The state highway department did the paving, the city did the grading and sewering and the county built the bridge over Little Cuyahoga river."

A beautiful drive through wooded hills, the heavily traveled route became known as Tallmadge Parkway. The first hint of trouble arrived in August 1948 when a 30-foot section of road collapsed beneath the back wheels of a truck loaded with steel drums. The driver escaped injury, but the cave-in created a pit nearly 25 feet deep on the west slope.

Over the years, a sewer leak had undermined the road. City workers discovered a second break in September. They patched the sewer, filled in the holes and repaved the road in a $15,000 project.

The disaster that broke Akron's heart occurred July 21, 1964, when a fierce storm dumped 3 inches of rain. A 47-year-old mother was driving her 10-year-old daughter and a neighbor girl on the parkway when the road

collapsed. The car plunged into a 40-foot hole created by a sewer break.

A crowd of strangers stopped to save the cave-in victims. Akron Patrolman Ronald Rotruck, 28, and volunteer Hugh O'Neil, 19, descended into the pit and rescued the mother and 13-year-old neighbor. When they went back to save 10-year-old Claudia Shidler, the muddy hole caved in on them, killing the two rescuers and the girl.

The parkway was closed for 100 days after the tragedy. The city spent more than $370,000 to repair the damage and build another sewer line. Once again, drivers had to find a new route.

The Akron City Council voted in January 1965 to rename the road Memorial Parkway in honor of the cave-in victims. Today, the commute from West Hill to North Hill has never been easier, and drivers take it for granted.

A four-lane bridge was constructed in 1996 to replace the 65-year-old span. It was built with $3.6 million in county, state and federal funds. The human toll of Memorial Parkway cannot be calculated.

Inka Dinka Duo

AKRON NIGHTCLUB ENTERTAINER EDDIE JACKSON WAS COMEDIAN JIMMY DURANTE'S SIDEKICK

(Originally published Aug. 14, 2006)

Vaudeville star Eddie Jackson felt all washed up in Akron. The old act had fallen apart. The circuit had shut down. Paying the bills wasn't exactly a cakewalk for a song-and-dance man in the Depression.

Sure, Jackson was thankful to have a job in show business, but he missed the bright lights of New York. When he used to tread the boards as Jimmy Durante's sidekick, the world was full of laughter and applause.

Hot-cha-cha-cha-cha!

Durante, the big-nosed, gravel-voiced comedian, was in Hollywood making movies. Jackson, the high-strutting, tuxedo-clad crooner, was in Akron marking time.

He wandered into town in the 1930s because he had friends here. He didn't really have any better place to go. So he stayed for nearly a decade.

Nightclub owner Joe Levin hired Jackson to serve as entertainment manager of the Wagon Wheel, a popular hangout at 121 S. Main St. in Akron. Jackson performed his top-hat-and-cane routine and booked acts at the downtown club as well as the Wagon Wheel clubs at 10 S. Case Ave. and 1179 Grant St.

The South Main establishment was a block south of the Akron Palace Theater, where Jackson and Durante had performed nearly 30 times with dancer Lou Clayton in the vaudeville team of Clayton, Jackson & Durante.

Jackson looked back fondly on the act's early years in New York City. "Back in 1916, Jimmy and I were playing the Alamo Club in Harlem," he once told a reporter. "He was no entertainer in them days—just a piano player with a five-piece band. I was singin' and struttin' and doin' all right for myself. Then in 1924 we joined with Lou Clayton and started the old Club Durante. It was a speakeasy. They were happy days. We was a team. Lou did the dancing, Jimmy played piano and told jokes. I sang and strutted."

In 1928, the trio got a big break as a ragtime act on the Keith-Albee vaudeville circuit, which had hundreds of theaters, including Akron's Palace. The boys enter-

tained audiences across the country and appeared in the Broadway musicals *Show Girl* and *The New Yorkers*.

Within a couple of years, though, vaudeville was dying. Durante folded the act in 1931 to try his luck in Hollywood. He invited Jackson and Clayton to join him as business associates, and they did for a time.

The happy-go-lucky comedian catapulted to fame in movies and radio. Audiences loved "The Schnozzola." Every other sentence out of Durante's mouth seemed to spawn a national catchphrase.

Hot-cha-cha-cha-cha. I gotta million of 'em. Everybody's gettin' in on de act. I'm mortified. Good night, Mrs. Calabash, wherever you are.

Durante's theme song, *Inka Dinka Doo*, became a big hit. Meanwhile, Jackson was beginning to feel restless.

"Mostly I did benefits without pay," he later recalled. "I just didn't want to hang around Jimmy. I wanted something to do. I went back on the road. Things got bad. I didn't want Jimmy to know where I was, so I up and left. I didn't want no money from Jimmy or nothing."

So he came to Akron. Washed up in his 40s.

Among his friends here were Palace Theater Manager Sid Holland, Colonial Theater Manager Bob Rhodes and Strand Theater Manager Millard Ochs.

Jackson lived at the Hotel Akron, set up shop at the Wagon Wheel and did his best to entertain local audiences. With Holland's permission, he posted a note backstage at the Palace: "Call on your old friend, Eddie Jackson, at the Wagon Wheel on South Main Street."

Many stars took him up on the offer. After performing at the Palace, they went to the club to see Jackson strut his stuff. Among the entertainers who visited were Bert Lahr, Ted Lewis, Martha Raye, the Andrews Sisters, Tommy and Jimmy Dorsey and a young Frank Sinatra.

Around 1942, the Ritz Brothers—Al, Harry and Jimmy—stopped at the Wagon Wheel, too. They chatted with Jackson about old times and learned that he hadn't talked to Durante in years. By then, the comedian had a

Hot-cha-cha-cha-cha! Popular comic Jimmy Durante (left) and song-and-dance man Eddie Jackson performed together for more than 50 years.

big radio show in New York. "He needs you," one brother told Jackson. "And we're going to tell him where you are."

Jackson begged them not to do it, but they didn't listen. Less than a month later, Durante made a surprise visit to Akron. Jaws must have dropped when The Schnozzola walked into the Wagon Wheel.

Two old pals from New York had a happy reunion. Durante told Jackson it was time to put the act back together. Did the singer care to join him on the radio? Yes, he inka dinka did.

Jackson maintained his Akron address for two more years, but his heart belonged to New York. He was Jimmy Durante's sidekick, after all.

In addition to radio and movies, the act performed to sold-out crowds at the Copacabana. "If it ain't the top, it's a long way from the bottom," Jackson told the Beacon Journal in 1944. The comeback was a success, and the timing was perfect. Durante easily made the leap to television, and Jackson joined him on *The Colgate Comedy Hour*, *The Ed Sullivan Show* and *The Jimmy Durante Show*.

"Everybody says I'm bigger than I've ever been," Jackson told a reporter in 1953. "Why, I had to send out a thousand pictures to fans today. I've never sent out pictures before. I've never been so happy in my life."

Durante chimed in: "Before, they thought his stuff was old-fashioned. Now everybody wants to hire him."

Despite shifting trends in music, the singer never changed his tune. He preferred to strut on stage rather than swivel his hips. "I like the beat of rock 'n' roll, but I can't catch the lyrics," Jackson explained in the late 1950s. "If you put a gun to my head and asked me to name three words in any rock 'n' roll tune, I couldn't do it—not even to save my life."

Durante and Jackson had a much-publicized split in 1958 but patched up their differences the following year. They remained together until health problems forced Jackson to retire in the early 1970s.

"I believe in doing the other fellow good; I never hurt anybody in my life," Jackson once told an interviewer. "I don't mind how big the other fellow's yacht is, or how green his yard is—just so there's a little green in my own yard." Even when a vaudeville star felt all washed up in Akron, there was always a little green.

Jimmy Durante died in 1980 at age 86. His sidekick Eddie Jackson joined him six months later at age 84.

Together again. Good night, Mr. Durante and Mr. Jackson. Wherever you are.

Please Tell Me

AKRON NEWSPAPER COLUMNIST GAVE SAGE ADVICE ABOUT
LIFE AND LOVE IN EARLY 20TH CENTURY

(Originally published Feb. 14, 2005)

Hopeless romantics poured out their hearts to Jane Ellis. She always knew what to say or do in every situation. Lovesick girls, infatuated boys, secret admirers and star-crossed lovers were among the multitudes who sought her counsel. Each day's mail brought a new batch of yearning, pining and longing.

Someone needed to talk some sense into these young fools. From 1910 to 1915, Ellis dispensed advice in Please Tell Me, a daily column for the Akron Press newspaper. It can best be described as an early 20th century version of Dear Abby, Miss Manners and Heloise—all rolled into one feature—but locally produced at the Akron newspaper's office at 71 S. High St.

Ellis served as the women's page editor for five years, but evidently wrote under a pen name. There is no listing for a journalist named Jane Ellis in 1910 census data or Akron directories.

Whoever she was, the lady could write. Ellis displayed a dry sense of humor in her wise, succinct replies to written pleas. She kept Akron on the straight and narrow until 1915, when her feature was abruptly discontinued. After that, the city was beyond her help.

In honor of Valentine's Day, we've decided to reprint some of the queries that graced Ellis' column during its five-year run. It's interesting to see how much of her advice still holds true. It's even more interesting to see how much has changed in 95 years. Enjoy!

Q: I am a blond with large brown eyes, and am just 16 years of age. Do you think I am old enough to marry a handsome man of 21 with raven black hair and beautiful blue eyes?
A: You are too young to marry anyone—ugly or handsome, blue eyes or black. You have several years yet before you need trouble your head about such matters.

Q: Should a girl speak to a young man friend when passing him on the street if he fails to tip his hat?
A: Yes. His rudeness would not justify her in an act of discourtesy.

Q: Does the man or the woman enter a streetcar first? Which leaves the car first? Which does first when descending stairs; when ascending them?
A: A woman always enters a car first. Upon leaving it, the man goes first. In each case, he is better able to assist the woman he is escorting. A man precedes a woman in ascending steps and follows her when descending them.

Q: All the fellows that come to see me want to hug and kiss me. I refuse to be treated in such a manner, but they don't pay any attention to what I say. What can I do?
A: If you don't know that it cheapens a girl to let every fellow that comes along hug and kiss her, then it's time you heard it. You can stop such insulting treatment if you care to.

Q: My girlfriend is visiting in New York and doesn't answer my letters. Do you think she will ever come back?
A: I don't know, sonny. New York chaps are awfully stunning creatures.

Q: I am a girl of 18, and "they say" I am pretty. I have a number of admirers, who often ask me to go to places of amusement, but I refuse, for I do not care for boys' society. My friends tell me I'll be an "old maid." Do you think I should go out with young men when I don't care to do so?
A: No, but do not mope around home all the time just because you do not like the boys. Get out with the girls and have a good time in a natural, wholesome way, and I prophesy that before long the right man will find you and that your ideas will change amazingly.

Q: When a boy walks to school with a girl and does not offer to carry her books, should she hint for him to carry them? Should a girl allow a boy to wear her jewelry?
A: The answer to both these questions is certainly not!

Q: My hips are small as compared to my shoulders. Can you tell me an exercise whereby they will become larger?

A: Walking, running, tennis or any outdoor game in which the muscles of the leg are brought into play, frequently, will increase the size of the hips. However, I do not think you need feel bad because your shoulders are a little larger than your hips. It is much prettier than to have hips a great deal larger than your shoulders.

Q: I am a young girl, 18 years of age, and desperately in love with two young men who are very good friends. They both seem to think a good deal of me, and I do not know which of them I love best. Every time I go out with one, the other seems to be angry at me. So please give me your advice.

A: You are not very much in love with either of them, or you would be able to choose one as "the man." You should, in fairness to these men and yourself, choose one or the other, and not encourage them both. You can't marry them both, and you are only causing hard feelings between friends by keeping both of them on your string.

Q: A young man who has paid me attentions for three months has asked me to marry him. Do you think our acquaintance too short for me to make such a promise?

A: Wait till you know him better.

Q: I am 13 years old, 5 feet 3 inches tall and weigh 108 pounds. Am I too young to go with a boy to places of amusement?

A: Several years too young.

Q: I was asked to call on a young lady at 8 o'clock. I arrived late in the afternoon and stayed to supper. She went out at 7:30, promising to return in a few minutes. At a quarter past 9 she hadn't come back, and I have not heard from her since. What shall I do?

A: Nothing. The young lady was rude. But you shouldn't have come before the time set.

Q: A young man has a few pictures of me which I have begged him to return. He refuses to do this. How can I get them back?

A: I'm sure I don't know. Let this be a lesson to give away photos less promiscuously.

Q: How can I know if a girl really cares for me or is not just amusing herself with my attentions?

A: You can find out by asking her to marry you.

Q: A strange man sitting beside me in a picture show gave me his name and talked to me. Would it have been wrong to give him my name?

A: He should not have spoken to you and it would have been worse for you to give him your name. There are many men who make a practice of going to picture shows to become acquainted with girls. The best way is to squelch them or change your seat. If this is not convenient, call the usher and complain to him that you are being annoyed.

Q: I am 16 years old and living at home. My mother is very strict and insists that I come in every evening at 10 o'clock, although most of my friends stay out as late as they please. What shall I do?

A: Mind your mother, like a good girl. She is wiser than the mothers of your friends.

Q: I am 25 and in love with a girl of 25. But her mother won't consent to the marriage unless she lives with us and tries to manage our love life. What shall I do?

A: You two are old enough to take care of your own hearts. Ask your sweetheart to choose between her mother and you.

Q: The other night a young man friend brought me home from a dance and, against my will, kissed me good night. For this I slapped him, and he, losing his balance, fell down the steps and hurt his arm. I feel that I owe him an apology, and still it makes me angry to think he would kiss me against my will.

A: You are the one entitled to the apology. He did something he should not have done; therefore, he should suffer.

Q: I am 44 years old, though I could pass for about 30. I want to pay regular attention to some lady, but I seem not to be attracted to anyone near my own age. Do you think a girl of 17 or 18 is too young for me?

A: I think you would find a more lasting companionship with a lady 30.

Q: I am engaged to a young man, but I have found out that he has a bad temper and is selfish and conceited. What shall I do? If I broke the engagement, would it be right for me to keep the ring he gave me?

A: I advise you to break the engagement if you feel that your fiancé has such a disposition that you cannot be happy with him. But you must return the ring.

Q: I am 23 and am terribly in love with my employer. He is 45. He is the most wonderful man I have ever seen. He does not make love to me exactly, but he is so kind that I am sure only his strong will keeps him from confessing the truth to me. What shall I do?

A: Imitate the goodness of the wife. Get another position. Evidently you are in the wrong place. It is highly probable that the man actually loves his wife.

Q: I have been paying attention to a young lady and I am fond of her. But she is of a quiet disposition and I am very lively. Do you think it would be advisable for us to marry?

A: I think marriage is always a risk between two persons devoid of congenial tastes.

Q: I am in love with a young man who is a sailor. But my friends tell me not to waste any affection on a person in that profession. What do you advise?

A: There are good men in every profession. If you have found one, keep on loving him.

Q: How can one cultivate love?

A: In the rich productive soil of a pure, unselfish heart, with gentleness, thoughtfulness and perseverance as implements. Always you must watch for and cut down the weeds of self-seeking and sensuality, or they will kill this rare plant.

Q: What is the luckiest day of the year on which to be married?

A: Any day is lucky if you find the right partner.

Ride of the Future

FIRST MONORAIL WAS THE LAST ATTRACTION AT SUMMIT BEACH

(Originally published Aug. 4, 2008)

The future arrived in a bright flash of silver. Sunlight glinted on steel and aluminum as Summit Beach Park unveiled its shiny new attraction in August 1957.

A sleek monorail train glided 9 feet off the ground on a ¾-mile track along the eastern edge of Summit Lake. "This isn't a thrill ride," Summit Beach Manager Ed Palmer told the Beacon Journal. "It's something new, something different—a ride of the future."

The 25-cent excursion was a first and a last. It was the first commercial monorail to operate in the United States. It was also the last ride built at the Akron park.

Akron businessmen William F. Burse and John Braziel, co-founders of Ohio Mechanical Handling Co., designed and built the monorail in their shop at 1856 S. Main St. The company was founded in 1945, and its primary business was building and installing overhead cranes, conveyors and other equipment at rubber factories.

The company had high hopes for the future of monorails. "You could run these things right down Main Street or from city to city," Burse noted in 1957. "This is just a sample of what we have in mind."

The monorail system featured 11-foot aluminum cars with tubular steel frames, Plexiglas roofs and foam-rubber seats. The cab, which pulled four passenger cars, had a 4-cylinder, gas-powered engine, a Ford automatic transmission and hydraulic brakes. A framework of steel beams supported the track.

"It was a nice, enjoyable ride. Very smooth," recalled William "Bud" Burse, 70, president of the company and son of the co-founder. "It had pneumatic tires that ran on top of the rail."

He helped set up the monorail in 1957 before its Aug. 17 debut. The new ride, which had seating for 32 adults or 48 children, instantly became the park's star attraction—more popular than the roller coaster, fun house, carousel, bumper cars and other amusements. In those days, parkgoers bought tickets for individual rides instead of paying a single fee at the gate.

Although the monorail was capable of traveling 60 mph, operators kept it below 20 mph. "It wasn't really a fast ride. It was a slow ride," recalled Bud's brother,

Robert "Bob" Burse, 60, the vice president, secretary and treasurer of Ohio Mechanical Handling. "You went up and around the trees."

Barberton historian Bernie Gnap, 59, who grew up on 17th Street in Kenmore, recalls packing picnic lunches with a childhood chum and hiking up the hill to a scenic spot off Sixth Street. "It was a wonderful vantage point," Gnap said. "We called it 'The View.' You could look down and see Summit Beach Park. You could see the whole configuration of the monorail."

Fifty years later, he can still picture the metallic gleam of the monorail as it traveled along the shoreline and looped back. "There was a lot of sunshine reflected off the lake," he said. "I remember the silver band of the track and the cars. It was all very bright silver in the sunshine."

Akron native Gary Morrison, 61, who could see the lake from his childhood home on Caroline Court, has fond memories of the monorail. One of his favorite stories about Summit Beach Park involves that ride.

A rubber company was having its annual picnic at the park when a group of monorail passengers became unruly, Morrison said. The guests demanded a discounted fare and refused to leave their seats when the ride operator declined to cut a deal.

"He couldn't reason with them," Morrison said. "So he took them up on the monorail to a high point . . . He put the keys in his pocket, slid down the supports that kept the monorail up and went over to Cannova's and had him a couple of brews."

Morrison said park personnel tied ropes to horses to pull the cars to a spot where the chastened passengers could exit. "Oh, my goodness," Bud Burse said with a chuckle upon hearing the story. "It might be."

The ride of the future soon had a baby brother. Ohio Mechanical Handling also built a kiddie monorail for Playland Park in Springfield Township. That smaller ride, which had a seating capacity for 32 children, traveled along a 300-foot loop about 3½ feet off the ground.

Gnap recalls his mother, Annie, pointing out the contraption on South Main Street when it was being

Businessmen John Braziel (left) and William F. Burse, co-founders of Ohio Mechanical Handling Co., look over their monorail at Summit Beach Park on Aug. 12, 1957.

assembled in the company's parking lot. "Of course, I got very excited," he said.

The Summit Beach monorail returned the following summer and continued to sell a lot of tickets, but it was one of the few bright spots at the park in 1958. The resort, which traced its roots to 1887 as Lakeside Park, had fallen into disrepair. Paint peeled off buildings and weeds sprouted from cracks on the midway.

When the season ended 50 years ago, nobody knew the ride was over forever. It wasn't until Summit Beach failed to open in 1959 that the truth was revealed. The park was closed.

Kenmore native Earl Gessman, 77, of Coventry Township, who enjoyed going to Summit Beach from the 1930s to 1950s and kept a scrapbook of park memories, didn't want to believe the place was gone.

He went to the old park, found an opening in the fence and roamed the midway. Vandals had ripped doors off hinges, smashed holes in walls and tossed trash around the midway. "I spent so much time in there, and it just made me sick to see something like that," he said.

While the skeletons of rides littered the park, the monorail had been spared. It found new life at a new location. Ohio Mechanical Handling workers dismantled the ride, hauled it by truck to Sandusky and reassembled the parts at Cedar Point. They reconfigured the track, built a loading station, added a second train and painted the cars white and blue. The installation cost $125,000.

"Cedar Point wasn't much when we went up there," Bud Burse said. "It was all dirt roads and it was pretty run down. They brought it back."

The monorail became the most popular ride at Cedar Point in 1959. On a single day that summer, it carried 13,000 riders. "We were the concessionaire up there," Bob Burse said. "We had two other rides: Satellite Jets and the Flying Coaster."

That same year, Disneyland opened a monorail at Tomorrowland. The California park had the gall to advertise its system as "the first in America."

Cedar Point's monorail operated through the 1960s. Park owners asked the Akron company to expand the ride. "We didn't have any money to pursue it farther than that," Bud Burse said. "Cedar Point wanted us to put one all the way down through the park, but they didn't want to finance it. They wanted us to do it."

It was a changing era. Cedar Point was planning to institute one-price admission fees and end contracts for operators. "We only had an eight-year contract up there, and then they didn't want any more concessionaires," Bob Burse said.

By the early 1970s, the Akron monorail hit the end of the line. "They took it out and scrapped it," he said. "It's all gone."

Today, Ohio Mechanical Handling Co. specializes in cranes, conveyors, hoists and custom fabrications. Akron's shrinking tire industry has curtailed the demand for overhead cranes, but the company is doing a lot of structural work, including stairs and mezzanines.

There's always a chance that a customer might want to try the ride of the future. If anyone asked the company to build another monorail train 50 years later, would it take the job? "Yes, I think I would," Bud Burse said. "I'd say yes."